MANIFEST AND OTHER DESTINIES

MANIFEST
and
OTHER DESTINIES

Territorial Fictions
of the
Nineteenth-Century United States

Stephanie LeMenager

UNIVERSITY OF NEBRASKA PRESS · LINCOLN AND LONDON

Chapter 2 originally appeared as
"Trading Stories: Washington Irving and the Global West,"
American Literary History 15 (Winter 2003): 683–708.
Reprinted by permission of Oxford University Press.
Chapter 5 originally appeared as
"Floating Capital: The Trouble with Whiteness in Mark Twain's Mississippi"
ELH (Summer 2004): 405–32.

Library of Congress Cataloging-in-Publication Data
LeMenager, Stephanie
Manifest and other destinies: territorial fictions of the
nineteenth-century United States / Stephanie LeMenager.
p.   cm.—(Postwestern horizons)
Includes bibliographical references (p.   ) and index.
ISBN 0-8032-2949-6 (cloth: alk. paper)
1. American fiction—19th century—History and criticism.   2. West (U.S.)—
In literature.   3. United States—Territorial expansion—History—19th century.
4. Literature and history—West (U.S.)—History—19th century.   5. American
fiction—West (U.S.)—History and criticism.   6. Western stories—History and
criticism.   7. Frontier and pioneer life in literature.   I. Title.   II. Series.
PS374.W4L45   2004
813'.3093278—dc22
2004015269

Set in Quadraat by Bob Reitz.
Designed by R. W. Boeche.
Printed by Thomson-Shore, Inc.

CONTENTS

ACKNOWLEDGMENTS

Thanks are due to the many people, some known to me and others distantly admired, whose intellectual courage and generosity have made the writing of this book possible. This project began as a dissertation at Harvard University, where I was fortunate to find a challenging and fiercely dedicated advisor in Philip Fisher, whose mentoring has both enabled my research career and given me very high standards to emulate in my own advising and teaching. Lawrence Buell, a member of my dissertation committee, played a significant role as catalyst, introducing me to developments in the New Western History, New Regionalism, and Environmental Studies which have proven crucial to my emergence, post-graduate school, as an independent scholar. Sacvan Bercovitch prodded me to confront material history, stern advice for which I am grateful. John Stauffer generously read my dissertation after its completion and offered useful suggestions toward revision. The University of California at Santa Barbara, where I have taught since 2000, has provided an exciting scholarly environment and entry into the innovative intellectual culture of the UC system—a "western" academic culture that has shaken up some of my old assumptions and forced me to consider how my longtime interests in local places and politics might be re-imagined in international or transnational contexts. I would like to thank all of my colleagues in the English Department at UCSB for providing an environment that not only encourages, but actually nurtures, Junior Faculty research. Those colleagues who have read my work or have drawn me into productive conversation about it deserve special thanks. Giles Gunn, Carl Gutiérrez-Jones, and Richard Helgerson offered the very best sort of mentoring as the book neared publication, and Candace Waid and Kay Young gave me powerful readings of the manuscript in its final stages. E. Cook and Christopher Newfield provided sharp commentary on earlier drafts. Thanks also to Patricia Cohen, Benjamin Cohen, John Majewksi, James F. Brooks, Virginia Scharff, José Aranda, Anne Lounsbery, Rebecca Kneale Gould and Bethany Schneider for reading and commenting upon portions of the book. The Southern California Americanist Group provided a supportive environment in which to air a chapter. Kudos to my students at both Harvard and UCSB for not being afraid to ask questions, or to argue with me, or to demand the best that I can give them. Finally, I want to express my gratitude to the University of Nebraska Press and the series editors of *Postwestern Horizons* for treating this project, and its writer, with the greatest care and respect.

Without family and friends, writing wouldn't be the everything that it sometimes feels like it is, and it might not happen at all. During the final stages of revision of this manuscript, my apartment building burned down, and all of my belongings had to be relocated. If it hadn't been for a handful of very good people, this manuscript might never have made it to the press. Most of those who were there are those who have been there for a long time, and who have made it possible for me to rebuild again and again. To Barbara, Sally, Bill, Spencer, Kathy, Geoff, Mort, Denise, Janice, Nancy, Chloe, and Boz. Without whom, nothing.

MANIFEST AND OTHER DESTINIES

INTRODUCTION
Manifest and Other Destinies

When the Louisiana humorist Thomas Bangs Thorpe set out to illustrate the cosmopolitanism of the Mississippi Valley in an 1855 article for *Harper's New Monthly Magazine*, he chose to describe the baggage area of a steamboat. "Upon the examination of the baggage you meet with strange incongruities," Thorpe began,

> —a large box of playing-cards supports a very small package of Bibles; a bowie-knife is tied to a life-preserver; and a package of garden seeds rejoices in the same address as a neighboring keg of powder. There is an old black trunk, soiled with the mud of the lower Nile, and a new carpet-bag direct from Upper California; a collapsed valise of new shirts and antique sermons is jostled by another plethoric with bilious pills and cholera medicines; an elaborate dress, direct from Paris, is in contact with a trapper's Rocky Mountain costume; a gun-case reposes upon a bandbox; and a well-preserved rifle is half-concealed by the folds of an umbrella.[1]

Thorpe's list, almost a poem, describes a nation uncomfortably settling into the continental possession achieved by the U.S.-Mexican War. One year before Thorpe published his reminiscence the Kansas-Nebraska Act had dramatically underlined the problem that the West, as a possible extension of the slave territory, had always posed for the national project. Thorpe's bowie knives, gun powder and Bibles might have been ordered by John Brown for his abolitionist guerrillas in Kansas.[2] The "garden seeds" that suggest the prairie homesteads of pioneer authors like Eliza Farnham and Caroline Kirkland compete with "playing cards," "cholera medicine," a Parisian dress and a trapper's costume, all indices of an international commerce that circulated disease, slave cargoes, environmental devastation, and the false economies of gambling and speculation from the Mississippi Valley to the California mining camps. The Mississippi River was, and had long been, an image of the United States' Manifest Destiny, but it is one that now seems troubling because it denatures the West, tying western lands to the circulation of commodities through domestic and world markets. The river was to be the western farmer's market road, or, more bombastically, the western farmer's passage to India. The Mississippi River suggests both a local and global world, a settler nation's internal opening to difference and to

I

a maritime commercial empire that is difficult to conceive as nature's work. Like the seas that bordered North America and the seemingly uninhabitable deserts that divided it, the Mississippi complicated the dominant symbolism of continental settlement in the nineteenth century. In the rhetoric of U.S. expansion, places that resemble passageways rather than lands to be farmed—places like deserts, oceans, and rivers—figure as eruptions of the foreign on the projected map of U.S. nationhood. In fact, what such fluid sites reveal are complex regional histories.

In *Manifest and Other Destinies*, I read the United States' emergence as a continental nation in the nineteenth century through U.S. authors who elaborate a cultural nationalism both older—because more British—and newer—because more global—than Jeffersonian and Jacksonian visions of sturdy yeomen subduing the West. The authors I address, from canonical figures like Mark Twain, Herman Melville, Washington Irving, and James Fenimore Cooper to a variety of lesser-known political and popular writers, find themselves challenged by environments that resist the agrarian symbolism of the sacred plow and the necessary accouterments of republican virtue.[3] The counter-narratives of Manifest Destiny generated by apparently landless places like deserts, oceans, and rivers suggest theories of U.S. nationhood that Henry Nash Smith labeled "mercantilist" or "maritime" in his classic study of the North American West, *Virgin Land*. Smith did not take these versions of Manifest Destiny seriously because they seemed to him to be too "literary" and too "southern," and at any rate they apparently went underground when the railroad entered the West and the myth of the garden was underwritten by a new industrial technology.[4] Yet, as Smith himself demonstrated so many years ago, the promise of a commercial West networked to the world through great western rivers has had a prolonged and significant life in U.S. literature. It could be said that the most famous evocations of the frontier, the early national wests of James Fenimore Cooper and the more contemporary wests of Mark Twain, were deeply informed by the sociopolitical possibilities of water and theories of commercial, ocean empire derived from both Cooper and Twain's personal experiences of sea trade. Before Cooper became a writer, he was a sailor, in the U.S. Navy and the merchant marine; Twain, of course, began his adulthood as a river pilot on the Mississippi.

Nineteenth-century theories of commercial empire that took the oceans rather than the agricultural homestead as the originary site of national character defamiliarize the continental West by situating it within the emergent system of international capitalism; these commercial versions of Manifest Destiny foretell contemporary transnational or global articulations of the nation-form. Paradoxically, nineteenth-century theories of commercial empire also produced narratives that acknowledge the uniquely embedded histories of regional locales. Western places that for European Americans most resembled the oceans in their resistance to settlement or governance by a single state defied the abstraction of expansionist discourse, with its characteristic collapse of continental space into providential temporality. As many scholars have noted, the rhetoric of U.S. expansion turned the varied cultures and climates of the North American West into "destiny," a simple temporal marker of the nation's future settlement.[5] The locus classicus of this rhetorical obliteration of western historical particularity is John L. O'Sullivan's 1845 essay on the annexation of Texas in the United States Magazine and Democratic Review, where O'Sullivan coined the phrase "manifest destiny" by pronouncing Texas a symbol of "the fulfillment of our manifest destiny to overspread the continent allotted by Providence for the free development of our yearly multiplying millions."[6] In 1845, when this infamous article was published, Texas would achieve statehood and become what Herman Melville called a "Fast-Fish," tied unquestionably to the United States. But Melville also predicted in Moby-Dick that the United States would never achieve its ultimate ambition of yoking "the great globe itself" to its providential imperatives.[7] In the nineteenth-century United States, the difference between the West and "the great globe" at times seemed negligible, because until even trouble spots like the desert West were settled by U.S. pioneers, the West could appear as both potentially domestic and perpetually international.[8] Western regions known for their extreme aridity repelled emigrants from the United States, as Brigham Young recognized when in the 1850s he mapped the Mormon Empire of Deseret across the Great Basin. Western river valleys promised to bind the nation by a network of watery roads, and yet such regions also invited the influx of "foreign" persons and goods that the western physician and write Daniel Drake warned "dilute and vitiate [patriotism]" in his 1834 Discourse on the History, Character, and Prospects of the West.[9] Unbuildable, unfenceable western places generated troubled U.S. nationalisms aware of the resilient international contexts that compromised the settler-nation's expansionist project.

The phrase Manifest Destiny often shouts to us from the typewritten page in capital letters, made vertical in its orientation, a monument to the expansive idealism and equally expansive violence that have sponsored the

3

United States' imperial claims on the North American continent and the world. As a rhetorical marker of dominant ideology, Manifest Destiny is always in danger of achieving transcendence, even where it is reviled. In recent years the New Western History and cultural studies of U.S. imperialism have worked to complicate the monolithic Manifest Destiny by demonstrating its varied articulations over time, through twentieth-century assertions of imperial desire internationally and, on the home front, against immigrants, ethnic and religious minorities, and even local environments.[10] Border studies introduced a more rigorously theorized spatial dimension to Manifest Destiny, and analyses of the U.S.-Mexican border have been particularly helpful in exposing the multi-directional crossings and changing national affiliations that haunted the nineteenth-century United States' continental claims.[11] But borders that we now recognize as international are not the only theaters in which Manifest Destiny has revealed its instability through contradictory representations and practices. As Gerald Vizenor's useful elaboration of Manifest Destiny as "manifest manners" suggests, Manifest Destiny gradually became a set of spatial and representational conventions that normalized the United States' expansionist project. Yet there have been times and places where the ideology of Manifest Destiny failed to achieve the terminal normalcy of manners, where even those who promoted it did not know how to make it look easy and natural.[12] *Manifest and Other Destinies* gravitates toward the inconsistencies, reversals and doubts that open nineteenth-century rhetorics of expansion to genuine, if unwanted, engagement with historical environments that resist the collapse of international or ecologically "foreign" spaces into the United States' domestic embrace. The categories of space that I examine—deserts, oceans, and rivers, share characteristics in common with Michel Foucault's concept of heterotopia, the species of counter-site that Foucault theorized as "simultaneously mythic and real contestations of the space in which we live"— in brief, sites that challenge hegemonic spatial representations and praxes like Manifest Destiny and, in so doing, inspire revisionist historiography.[13] But my aim is not to use contemporary theoretical concepts simply to expose the limitations of nineteenth-century thinking about space. Rather, I want to suggest that a diverse collection of nineteenth-century U.S. writers, including some who overtly endorsed the United States' march across the continent, elaborated their own mythic and real counter-sites to contest the space in which they lived, a space which was continentalist in its geographical reach and nationalist in its political emphases.

4

I address nineteenth-century writers who examine the production of the space "America" with a self-consciousness that reveals that critical movements which seem contemporary, like border studies or the New Western History, in fact have been previewed in nineteenth-century U.S. literature. Clearly relevant to this study is Richard White's generative concept of "the middle ground," the place "in between cultures, peoples, and empires," in which we see "an odd imperialism and a complicated world system."[14] Although White's historical "middle ground" effectively disappears with the rise of Euro-American hegemony at the start of the nineteenth century, the writers I address remember "the middle ground" in the continent's deserts and rivers, thereby reopening the nineteenth century to counter-narratives that are now more readily associated with colonial and early national contexts. Moreover, I argue that Washington Irving, Herman Melville, Mark Twain, and even James Fenimore Cooper were dimly aware of Patricia Nelson Limerick's revisionist assertion that "the events of Western history represent, not a simple process of territorial expansion, but an array of efforts to wrap the concept of property around unwieldy objects."[15] Animal skins, valuable minerals, ocean megafauna, liquor, and captive or enslaved persons circulate through the literatures I explore as the unwieldy objects of regional economies that almost mock concurrent nineteenth-century images of the yeoman's fee-simple empire. Troubling commodities, like slaves or silver or bison, that refuse the simplified Lockean definition of property as land intermixed with labor arise in U.S. literatures of expansion and exploration as images of what is too foreign, or again too local, to be incorporated into the nation's "providential" future. Sometimes such unwieldy properties produce prescient self-critique, and dismay at what now seems a proto-globalist desire to departicularize everything, even social life, by commodifying it. Fears of the regression of human civilization to a deracinated consumerism and even fears of the loss of human sentience haunt U.S. literatures that confront the turbulent cultures of the West's commercial contact zones.

Although I am interested in the peculiarities of literary genres such as the historical romance, romantic history, travel narrative, humor, and the popular form that came to be known as "the western," my archive of texts is not organized by generic concerns but, again, by a set of sociopolitical problems that have been expressed through historically distinct regional locales. I use the loose terms "literatures," "narratives," and "rhetorics" throughout this study to characterize an archive that includes canonical literature as well as

5

newspapers, dime novels, exploration journals, and political tracts. In my choice of primary texts I do not adhere to Wallace Stegner's famous criteria for authentic western writing, as many of the literatures I address do not "take place West of the 100th meridian" nor are they written by authors who would be considered authentic westerners by contemporary standards.[16] But then the nineteenth-century West that I explore was not yet a symbolically coherent or geopolitically recognizable region of the United States, and it is part of my project to construct a prehistory of "the West" and "the westerner" as seen from the perspective of U.S. writers and readers. Some of the narratives I address, including a sampling of works by canonical U.S. writers and well-known early western writers like Timothy Flint, were notorious critical and popular failures precisely because they failed to point the way toward a legible concept of westernness. James Fenimore Cooper's *The Prairie* was judged a failure by both eastern and western critics, who dismissed the novel's representations of western landscapes as indicative of Cooper's lack of imagination or simple ignorance of the West. Yet *The Prairie* culled the diaries of western explorers to describe the arid Plains—a forbidding scene neither eastern writers nor the early western writes of the Ohio Valley had yet dared to describe. Timothy Flint's *Life* of the explorer James Ohio Pattie was a popular failure, perhaps because it ends with a warning to would-be pioneers to stay away from dangerous and foreign western territories. We might well expect works that refused to naturalize the westward course of empire to meet with tepid public response in the nineteenth-century United States and to be summarily forgotten after continental "destiny" was achieved. Yet I think that these failed works are well worth rereading because their authors have been credited with shaping the dominant symbolism of Manifest Destiny and U.S. nationalism—so their slip-ups, as it were, reveal the fissures in that symbolism, the fact that even its makers found it at times unusable. Some of the narratives I examine, like Washington Irving's romantic histories of the Far West and the humor and criminal biographies of early southwestern writers, were popular and even esteemed by their contemporary audiences. The popularity of these works, all of which essentially challenge expansionist designs, is inexplicable if we conceive of Manifest Destiny operating in the nineteenth century as it has been seen to operate from the hindsight of the twentieth—as depoliticized, naturalized *myth*, in the Barthesian sense.[17]

Manifest and Other Destinies questions the persistence in U.S. literature and public debate of certain peculiar images of resistance to the advancing settler nation, such as the Great American Desert, a geographical fantasy of the Great Plains inaugurated in 1810 by Zebulon Pike which has made multiple reappearances throughout the nineteenth and twentieth centuries. Imagined or real counter-sites like the Great American Desert provide the foundation of my archive, as I draw upon authors who share a common interest in representing regional environments that operated as heterotopias, interrupting accepted national histories and forcing a reevaluation of what kind of future might develop from the nation's past. As Krista Comer has suggested, landscape serves as a "wild card" in literary representation, "a vehicle for commentary on the link between the local and the global" and, in a broader sense, a key to what matters most in a culture—what is most defended, desired, conflicted, or vulnerable. [18] Although great rivers like the Mississippi drew settlers to their fertile banks, the culture of such river highways was cosmopolitan, even urban, and so tied to international imperial mechanisms like the slave trade that even the celebrated Mississippi produced no easy images of nationhood. Yet the river generated many literatures that, through their legacy in the work of Twain, came to be recognized as quintessentially "American." Invariably, writers that address spaces that consist of water rather than land, or uncultivable land, offer a complex expansionist rhetoric that both shares in and exceeds the agrarian, racial, and Christian emphases associated with the ideology of Manifest Destiny.

Although in this book I allude to the most well-known nineteenth-century articulations of Manifest Destiny, such as the Indian Removal debates of the 1820s and 1830s, John L. O'Sullivan's editorials in the *Democratic Review* of the 1840s, and the mobilization of anti-Catholicism and the anti-Spanish *leyenda negra* (Black Legend) in U.S. popular literature, these blunt expansionist tools are not my primary interest. Since I have sought out U.S. writers for whom continental settlement has been virtually unimaginable, "pioneer" literature plays only a minor role in this study. As a result, I have pushed to the margins the writings of the women pioneers who, as Annette Kolodny has shown, provided significant early correctives to the masculinist rhetoric of settlement. [19] Few nineteenth-century women wrote of the United States' *commercial* expansion, although some, like the Santa Fé trader's wife Susan Shelby Magoffin, eloquently chronicle the rigorous international trading cultures of the North American West. [20] Moreover, women abolitionists like Harriet Beecher Stowe recognized the commercial space of the Mississippi as a scene of the breakdown of cherished national values because of the visibility of the domestic slave trade on the Mississippi and its tributaries. The critique of Manifest Destiny offered here is necessarily a critique of patriarchal assumption, just as it is necessarily a critique of the assumed normalcy and inevitability of Euro-American dominance in North America. I pursue the question of the degree to which self-critical counter-narratives can be generated at the very sites of hegemonic dominance, and my returns to the extravagant, troubled, and *published* dreams of Euro-American men intend to expose Manifest Destiny as a hegemonic process unsettled from within by "pressures not at all its own," in Raymond Williams's phrase. [21] That these pressures from within took imaginative form as desired and resistant places is of particular interest. My desire to defamiliarize the United States' claims to continental nationhood has kept the bulk of my study inside what is now the United States, continually refocusing within the nation's current domestic territories in order to stress the unnaturalness of nineteenth-century continental claims and the internationalism of nineteenth-century North American regional cultures. This project does not address every America or every American West, but I hope that it invites a fruitful conversation among what may have seemed rather closed U.S. literatures, ideologies, and spaces and diverse, non-European or non-Anglo articulations of "our America."

I think it important to recognize that the United States was not only an ambitious and imperial nation, but also, as Immanuel Wallerstein argues, a semi-peripheral nation on the world stage for much of the nineteenth century. [22] As Mark Twain quipped after the United States' attempt to annex the Philippines at the turn of the twentieth century, U.S. imperialism abroad represented an attempt to achieve a belated world centrality, to "get a back seat in the Family of Nations." [23] In part the relative weakness of the U.S. state, especially prior to the Civil War, generated rhetorics of an infinitely expandable empire. In the *Democratic Review*, John L. O'Sullivan asserted that "the representative system as practically enjoyed in this country, will admit of an indefinite expansion of territory." This indefinite expansion might be achieved "in establishing commercial and other business relations with and in the territories of our neighbors, [that] beget a community of interest between us. . . ." [24] This rhetoric of reciprocal commercial interest and borderless empire coming from a visionary Democrat in the 1840s sounds almost postmodern, a far cry from the same John O'Sullivan who proclaimed just a few months earlier that "the Anglo-Saxon foot is on [California's] borders . . . armed with the plough and the rifle." [25] It

8

was difficult for even O'Sullivan to choose which version of expansionist discourse best represented U.S. character, though he finally settled on a Southern, circum-Caribbean model when he sided with the Confederacy during the Civil War.[26] Though it might now seem obvious where the centers of U.S. power were in the nineteenth century, and which were the directions of imperial movement, a significant number of nineteenth-century expansionists did not seem sure. The networks of economic activity extending from the Great Plains into Upper Canada and from the Mississippi River through New Orleans into the Gulf of Mexico and the Atlantic world suggest that O'Sullivan's "indefinite" expandibility might have been a euphemism for decenteredness. Antonio Negri and Michael Hardt's concept of late twentieth-century global Empire as a "decentered and deterritorializing apparatus of rule that progressively incorporates the entire global realm within its open, expanding frontiers" would not be entirely out of place in the *Democratic Review* of the 1840s.[27] Amy Kaplan has argued convincingly that Hardt and Negri make unnecessarily fine historical distinctions among nineteenth-century U.S. imperialisms and late-twentieth century global Empire.[28] Yet the "openness" recognized by nineteenth-century expansionists connotes the weakness of U.S. borders as much as a desired global dominance. My point is simply that it is important not to reify the centrality of the United States as a world power by reading the nineteenth century through a twentieth-century conventional wisdom that itself seems outdated as we now recognize significant realignments and new networks of influence on the world stage.

In the interest of keeping local histories alive in this analysis, I prefer to speak of empires and imperialisms in the plural, and of the surprising attraction of nineteenth-century expansionist rhetoric to regional networks of power that were irreducible to the nation's larger imperial vision.[29] While my work has been informed by theories of global empire and dynamic postmodern conceptions of place as, to borrow Doreen Massey's phrase, "the location of the intersection of particular activity spaces,"[30] the questions I pursue are very much embedded in historical times and places. For instance, I ask why the Great Plains were repeatedly referred to by antebellum U.S. writers as, when they were not deserts, another Asia. Should this rhetoric be dismissed as an archaism, too "literary" to bother with, or does it in fact suggest some interesting thinking about the nodes, and styles, of continental power? Similarly, repeated nineteenth-century references to the Mississippi River as a metropolitan space rivaling the Atlantic coast and as the West's link to the world reveal the Mississippi as a possible seat of global dominance. The West of the Mississippi Valley, which by the heyday of U.S. regionalist literature in the 1880s would have been considered the South, was once imagined as a miniaturized world system, as was the desert, "Asiatic" West of the Great Plains, where hides were produced in the hinterlands for metropolitan distribution centers at Montreal, St. Louis, Santa Fé, Chihuahua, and the Northwest coast. The relevance of the Pacific Ocean to an emergent global capitalism is obvious, but literatures that treat ocean industry reveal the western seas, islands, and coasts as irreducibly distinct regions that both enable and disrupt the circuits of U.S. capital. The seas can be, and have been, conceived as material regions just as the varied continental wests can be, and have been, conceived theoretically as commercial networks.

As Henry Nash Smith suggested so many years ago, in the nineteenth century southerners were more likely to view western places as fatally articulated with international markets; however, the fact that this vision of the West was predominantly southern is not a good reason to dismiss it. The Mississippi Valley and its links to the Caribbean and Atlantic world still tend to drop out of western regional studies, and the antebellum Mississippi is often recognized as somewhere other than "the West" by Americanists. Yet as Timothy Flint, Daniel Drake, and other early western writers knew, the Mississippi Valley had been no less the West than the more conventionally western valley of the Ohio. The later nineteenth-century writings of Mark Twain, and Twain's own multi-regional persona, figure in this book as historical models of how the regional imagination of South and West can be conceptually joined—to each other and to global concerns like international imperialism and slavery.

Mark Twain's interest in the mining regions of California and Nevada and in the possibility of U.S. commercial dominance of Hawaii can be traced to his youth as a commercial river pilot on the Mississippi, a position that allowed Twain to cultivate a water-based theory of empire that privileged mobility and trade. Twain's piloting career began with a trip down the Mississippi that could be characterized as a "southern" imperial fantasy—he was planning to travel to the Amazon basin to make a fortune in the coca trade.[31] As a person whose youth and writing vacillated between South and West, Twain is well placed to figure as perhaps the first self-conscious New Western historian, a cultural critic who ably rewrites the United States' sentimentalized regions as distinctive nodes in an expanding capitalist market.

Twain's much discussed rants against imperialism, particularly the abuse and domination of indigenous peoples in the Philippines and the Congo, complement a more ambivalent interest in another form of imperialism that was commercial and not colonial. Twain's anti-imperialist rage interacts quite curiously with his lifelong obsession with U.S. business culture to create a conflicted insider's critique of market capitalism as it was expressed in the domestic slave trade on the Mississippi River and in the market for precious metals in the Far West. I think it important to delineate the roots of Twain's late-century cultural critique in the earlier economic praxis with which he was familiar. [32] Twain theorizes continuity among colonial elaborations of maritime empire, including the international slave trade, antebellum U.S. expansion into the West, and later nineteenth-century imperial ventures outside the borders of the United States. Finally, Twain teaches us the importance of recognizing that what now seem separate regions, the West and South, could once be seen as a single physiographic region, as John C. Calhoun suggested, which itself was articulated to international interests. [33] Twain's western history is never one in which slavery figures as merely incidental to western development, as it did in Frederick Jackson Turner's influential late-nineteenth-century essay, "The Significance of the Frontier in American History."

The sketchy autobiographical writings from Twain's late career continually return to a joke form reminiscent of the "bits" that peppered his stage performances of the 1860s, to jokes about selling something that does not belong to you. [34] In the autobiographical fragments Twain published in the *North American Review*, he jokes about selling a stranger's dog to the celebrated "Indian fighter" Nelson A. Miles; in expurgated pages from Albert Bigelow Paine's autobiography of Twain what is stolen and resold is Twain's own writings, with his erstwhile publishers playing the part of thieves. We come closest to the tragic heart of the joke in the *Adventures of Huckleberry Finn*, where it is the man known as "Huck's nigger, Jim" who is sold and resold all along the Mississippi River by people who do not own him, including the well-meaning hero. This bit about selling what does not belong to you is one of Twain's fundamental plots, and it concisely indicates the moral and economic drift that haunts a series of antebellum writings about commercial expansion by James Fenimore Cooper, Timothy Flint, and Washington Irving; by Martin Delany, Herman Melville, and Richard Henry Dana, Jr.; by western explorers, criminal biographers and humorists like the Alabama Johnson Jones Hooper; by abolitionist writers such as Lydia Maria Child;

and by pro-slavery apologists. All of these authors invoke historically distinctive Wests which are rocked by an exploding market culture that might accidentally produce consequences other than a happy division of labor and the "softening of barbarous manners" that Montesquieu famously associates with commercial intercourse in L'Esprit des lois. Just as "America" functioned for John Locke and Adam Smith in the early modern era as a testing ground or enabler of classical liberalism, in the nineteenth century the desert West, the western seas, and the old southwestern territories around the Mississippi River functioned as theaters in which the ancient contest of commerce and virtue had to be played out.

The contest of commerce and virtue in western deserts, rivers, and oceans was of particular interest to the United States' emergent middle-class, a class anxious to prove its social value by valorizing the sites of market culture. The U.S. middle class that began to define itself in the late eighteenth and early nineteenth centuries as a "distributing" class recognized itself in spaces that resisted what J. G. A. Pocock has called the land-based concept of patriotism. European agrarian theories contributed to U.S. conceptions of republican virtue the notion that only land ownership enables moral personality by preventing the development of specialized interests. [35] Hence Thomas Jefferson recognized "the small land holders" as most fit for the franchise, "the most precious part of a state." Western deserts, oceans, and rivers could all be conceived as spaces ill suited to this agrarian moralism, and these virtually landless spaces helped give shape to the vague structures of feeling that bound the emergent business sector as a class. I suggest that the city was not the only imaginary or practical home of commercial character and that urban clerks, like Herman Melville's infamous Bartleby, were not the only literary representatives of the human costs of commercial culture to the middle class itself.

In the United States' premier business journal of the 1840s, Hunt's Merchants' Magazine, both sailors and far western trappers are identified as "active agents" of the distributing class, and both figures are by turns sentimentalized and reviled. The influential Hunt's might be productively contrasted to the Democratic Review as an organ of expansionist rhetoric, one that offers an internationalist, commercial interpretation of western and national interests. Hunt's describes western trappers as "demi-sauvage" but also recognizes them as the key to commercial dominance of Britain in the greater West, which the magazine perceives as the United States' most proximate world stage. When the Boston publisher James T. Fields collected samples of clerks' poetry for *Hunt's*, he included a poem by a young man who projects himself into the role of a weary sailor:

> "Unmask, bold Traffic! Thou art weaving now
> Thy golden fancies round the seaman's brow;
> Thou hast at will the magic power to guide
> His heart from home, and child, and cherished bride."[36]

Sailors and trappers did the intimate dirty work of commerce, which, to the young clerk who imagined their adventures, made them appear as patriotic avatars of himself. Agents of commerce who performed manual work lent a visibility and urgency to the often "invisible goods" produced by the more entrenched members of the commercial class.[37] Fringe members of the commercial class, like sailors and western trappers, also enabled the articulation of a self-critical liberalism. Nineteenth-century reform literature abounds with references to sailors' malnutrition and sexual diseases, problems of sentience that reveal the unequal distribution of goods in a supposedly just market society. The relationship of western traders and trappers to various American Indian nations, whom they engaged in injudicious barter, was also a topic of temperance literature; the ravages of the hide and liquor trade make their way, in muted form, into Washington Irving's western histories. Perhaps the slave trader, moving his human cargoes through the extensive river systems of the old Southwest, inspired the most blunt articulations of middle-class self-hatred and denial; slave traders figure in the Alabama lawyer David Hundley's *Social Relations in Our Southern States* as at once "detestable" and the most "productive" of citizens.[38]

To the literary imagination, the virtually landless West that could not be farmed offered both assurances of commercial theories of value and profound critiques of the apparently natural justice of the market. The commercial imperialisms that I contrast to more familiar continentalist rhetorics might be understood, in narrow political terms, as Whig retorts to the Democratic emphases of Manifest Destiny, given the American Whig Party's linkage to business interests, Whig and earlier Federalist distrust of westward expansion, Whig emphases on market regulations and the political implementation of moral imperatives, including, for some Whigs, abolitionism. Much of the literature I address includes direct responses to the Panic of 1837 and the embarrassments caused by what Whigs viewed as Andrew Jackson's perilous expansion of a credit economy that favored dishonest parvenus. The western humorists who wrote in the highly priced national sporting journal *Spirit of the Times* were primarily concerned with the crisis of value that they believed Jackson had generated in his home region, the Mississippi Valley.[39] Some abolitionist and pro-slavery writers in the 1830s recognized Andrew Jackson's economic policies as enabling the domestic slave trade by allowing the proliferation of southwestern wildcat banks, and thus contributing to the profound devaluation of "the human" imaged by the domestic traffic in African-American "chattel."[40] Even Mark Twain, with his acknowledged literary debt to southwestern humor, the vague Know-Nothingism present in his letters of the 1850s, his belated abolitionism and his conflicted Republicanism after the Civil War, could be recognized as an inheritor of Whig sensibility. Yet the literatures I examine are written by Whigs, notorious Democrats like James Fenimore Cooper, and radical abolitionists. At any rate, no literary artifact can be reduced to party ideology or assumed to have elicited only partisan interpretation.

My analysis of the territorial fictions of the nineteenth-century United States proceeds as a series of case studies of literary efforts by U.S. writers to capture the form and affect of distinct western places which they recognized as defined neither by the sovereignty of the U.S. state, nor by the *Volkish* spirit that some American Romantics associated with incipient nationhood, but rather by the rivalrous and sometimes devastating negotiations characteristic of open markets. The affective economies recognizable in literatures treating international, commercial regions are themselves organized by the emotional states of greed, wonder, and fear. Stephen Greenblatt has discussed wonder as a primary, pre-moral emotion in the context of an analysis of Renaissance exploration literature which reveals the paucity of frameworks Europeans had available to them for seeing, let alone understanding, indigenous Americans. [41] But of course in the nineteenth-century United States, "Indians" and "black" Americans were copiously if erroneously narrated, and international trade and contact were well enough established that wonder at other people, if it was felt at all, had a brief career. The emigrant in Missouri might experience a flicker of it when she first sighted a slave coffle, disguised as a pageant, being driven to market on a local road; likewise the federal agent might briefly experience it when he found himself lost in the southern Plains, unable and even unwilling to produce an accurate rendering of the regions he and his colleagues explored. In both of these cases, taken from narratives I discuss, wonder cedes to analysis in which ethical consternation or aesthetic shock struggles with self-interest. Exactly who gains from this commerce in slaves? What can a region that will never be farmed contribute to the national project?

While specific geographical settings frame my analyses, what interests me is how, in local instances, these spaces were seen and felt, from both the relative distance of authors who attempted to endorse national expansion, and from the relative nearness assumed by travelers, abolitionists, and popular authors who for various personal and professional reasons found themselves living in the West or writing passionately about it. A variety of U.S. writers who addressed western places that they believed could only be subjected to commercial dominance recognized, if regretfully, the groundlessness of agrarian, racist, and Christian arguments for national progress. For writers who assumed that commerce underwrote national destiny, the nature of the nation was groundless, like the market itself and the apparently landless or uncultivable environments that supported it. Such writers found themselves questioning the ethnocentric concept of the frontier and the westward orientation of civilization; rhetorics of commercial expansion recognize, if regretfully, a variety of centers. *Manifest and Other Destinies* is a chronicle of North American space as it was imagined by anxious profit-seekers, and I discover in their writings predictions of an unhappy transnationalism. This is not a study of practical alternatives to Manifest Destiny but of self-contradictory versions of it that either knowingly or unwittingly include counter-narratives, manifestations of the latent self-criticisms and doubts that were generated alongside expansionist fervor. I consider western regions which were vital to the national project, some of which already were or were about to become U.S. territory in the nineteenth century and all of which are now inextricably linked to national character. Yet none of the regions I explore were particularly amenable to nationalist sentiment or even the "bipolar unities" and uneasy incorporation of dissidence that Sacvan Bercovitch has argued constitute "the symbol of America."[42] I am attempting to disassemble the continental territory of the United States into the loose collection of local and international economies that it was imagined to be by some of the United States' most celebrated writers in the era of the most self-conscious fashioning of the nation-state. My critique of Manifest Destiny begins in nineteenth-century literatures whose complicated articulations of expansionist desire reveal the internationalism, incomplete nationalization, and even de-nationalization that actually defined western places. In approximately the same period that the *western* congealed into a popular literary genre in the United States, and the West congealed into the imagined locus of national character, U.S. writers began to articulate a postwestern and postcontinental cultural criticism.

This book is structured by the imagined geography that it explores, dividing into three sections that treat: desert, ocean, and riverine western landscapes. The first section begins in the Great American Desert, the arid region at the approximate center of North America, which was described as a space of radical instability and economic negotiation. Chapter one, which opens the section, treats the first American historical romance to be set on the Great Plains, James Fenimore Cooper's *The Prairie* (1827), a novel that I suggest offers an intimate account of a more widespread representational problem. The Great Plains by their arid and treeless nature undermined rhetorics of Manifest Destiny and unique "racial gifts," raising the possibility that what looked like inevitable national progress across the continent might, in fact, end nowhere, in a landscape that resisted both agrarian settlement and white bodies. Cooper's desert setting disabled his preferred genre, the historical romance, forcing him to find alternate means of expressing nationalist sentiment. A reading of Cooper against the geologist and botanist Edwin James's account of Stephen H. Long's expedition to the central Plains (1819–20), the earlier exploration narrative of Zebulon Pike (1810), and several contemporary captivity narratives reveals a vision of North America's "inland deserts" as resiliently international scenes that might be shared indefinitely amongst American Indian nations and "unnaturalized" Euro-Americans.

Chapter two offers a comprehensive analysis of literatures of western commerce that builds on Cooper's discovery of the desert West's precocious transnationalism to theorize a relationship between the western desert and world. Here I suggest how romantic historiography was undermined by commercial rhetorics which offered an anachronistically postmodern account of the North American West as a space of racial and ethnic mixing, dislocation, even de-nationalization. As Washington Irving discovered in *Astoria*, by far the most famous romantic history of western commerce, U.S. commercial imperialism in the Far West was generating a new and sophisticated form of savagery that threatened to reverse the course of empire and effectively "un-civilize" the United States. The western trade in animal skins and whiskey suggested the creation of passions, the very agents of irrationality that commerce, in the early modern period, had been hoped to restrain. The racial outcomes of western trade were equally uncertain, as this commerce seemed to favor hybrids, people whose passions were thought to be tempered by divided race loyalties. In the desert West the rationality of purportedly rational economics, and the rationality of democratic/capitalist imperialism, broke down, for Irving and a host of lesser-known writers, from the trapper Zenas Leonard to the famous biracial trader and Crow "chief," James Beckwourth.

The second section addresses the oceans, which I see represented as postwestern space by several influential nineteenth-century authors. This section offers the oceans as a paradigmatic heterotopia against which the various troubling sites of the landed West might be measured and reconceived. In the single chapter that comprises this section, I look at how the peculiar sociopolitical and environmental qualities attributed to the sea in the nineteenth century contested, represented, and inverted rhetorics of Manifest Destiny focused on western lands and the future promise of agrarian empire. The sea and West exist in charged, dialectical tension in nineteenth-century U.S. literatures, and in the tension between these two coveted domains we can recognize the evolution of a postwestern, postfrontier theory of U.S. empire and nationhood. It is worth seriously revisiting questions such as why Edgar Allan Poe's Arthur Gordon Pym favors the *Journals of Lewis and Clark* above all other books stowed in the hold of the *Grampus*, or why Herman Melville and James Fenimore Cooper proclaimed the West "over" and the sea the new landscape of the nation's future, or why Richard Henry Dana, Jr., recognized both the oceans and the western coasts of California as grave threats to the United States' national character. The character of the nation seemed, to several prominent writers, to hang in the balance between West and sea, both of which were heterotopic spaces in the nineteenth century, given how little many U.S. writers actually knew about the Far West. Because this chapter treats a topic—the oceans—that has served as the focus of a great deal of productive work in cultural and literary studies in recent years, I believe that it needs no special introduction; I use the oceans as yet another conceptual window into the difficulty of conceiving the nineteenth-century West as national property.

The third and final section treats the Mississippi River and the riverine region that surrounds it—a region now referred to as the "old" Southwest. This section presumes that the Mississippi has been a paradox in U.S. cultural representations, at once a sentimentalized conduit for the West's produce and a highway that hosted the domestic slave trade, which was both the nation's most lucrative and most morally devastating antebellum commercial enterprise. Chapter four begins in the decades prior to the Civil War, when the Mississippi engendered in its varied chroniclers—humorists, dime novelists, abolitionists and anti-abolitionists—narratives that imaged a variety of alternatives to and exaggerations of the claims of Manifest Destiny. From the 1830s through the 1850s the old Southwest produced imaginary nations within nations, fantastic empires, and mutant semi-national confederations. Literary and political rhetoric disseminated images of the river pirate John Murrell's regional confederacy of slave thieves, John Brown's fluid abolitionist "state," and the pan-African empire of Martin Delany. The same broad region that produced what the South Carolina novelist William Gilmore Simms called the United States' "native speech," the same region that played a fundamental role in the development of a uniquely national crime literature and a unique form of retributive justice—the region of lynching, laughing, and the excessive, popular body—was also the region where the nation was imagined to mutate into other nations, or indeed into an entity altogether hostile to the nation-form. I argue that the slave market conducted on and along the Mississippi contributed more than any other factor to the drift in national and racial identities visible in popular humor and crime fictions that trace their origins to the old Southwest.

The final chapter incorporates the Mississippi River fictions of Mark Twain into a broader portrait of Twain as a cultural critic and historian who denatured the claims of Manifest Destiny in the same era that the ideology of "the frontier" worked to naturalize an earlier period of continental expansion. I read Twain's late writings against his classic river novels, his unpublished novella *Tom Sawyer's Conspiracy*, and his youthful letters from the Nevada Territory to suggest how the market cultures of the antebellum Southwest and the miner's desert set the course for his development as a critic of the United States' claims on the world stage. Finally, in Twain's early twentieth-century short story, "Extract from Captain Stormfield's Visit to Heaven," I recognize a wry attempt to imagine the real Manifest Destiny in what might be called simply "destiny"—death. This short story presents a surprisingly contemporary image of the "post-mortem" United States, and especially California, as multicultural dystopias in which the historical temporality so often obliterated in the language of Manifest Destiny returns with a vengeance.

I wish to conclude this introduction with a few words about terminology. Although one of the goals of this project is to defamiliarize continental nationhood, stressing the fact that "America" neither is nor ever has been a synonym for "the United States," I do sometimes use the terms "America" and "American" in this book, for specific reasons. First, I may use "America" to allude to a historical idea of nationhood that has included self-aggrandizing, imperial assumptions. Secondly, I often address portions of North America, or ocean spaces, that were not entirely colonized or claimed by any one nation at the time they were written about; the geopolitical blurriness of such regions requires a flexible usage of "U.S.," "American," "U.S./American," and "North American."

I. DESERT

INVENTING THE AMERICAN DESERT

Where and how did we gain the idea that the desert was merely a sea of sand? Did it come from the geography of our youth with the illustration of the sand-storm, the flying camel, and the over-excited Bedouin? Or have we been reading strange tales told by travelers of perfervid imagination—the Marco Polos of today? There is, to be sure, some modicum of truth in the statement that misleads. There are "seas" or lakes or ponds of sand in every desert; but they are not so vast, not so oceanic, that you ever lose sight of the land.

JOHN C. VAN DYKE,
The Desert: Further Studies in Natural Appearances (1901)

When John Van Dyke and Mary Austin wrote about western deserts in the early twentieth century, it had become possible to recognize that "desert" and "land" were not mutually exclusive categories. The transvaluation of the North American desert that Van Dyke and Austin helped bring about rescued deserts from an essentially moral condemnation. In the Bible, the desert was a godless place or a place where faith would be severely tested. In the nineteenth-century United States, a nation deeply inflected by Biblical paradigms as well as Jeffersonian associations of farming with virtue, deserts were places that could not be turned into productive farmland and therefore inherently uncivilized or threatening. As Donald Worster has shown, the late nineteenth-century discourse of desert reclamation that led to the National Reclamation Act of 1902 reveals both newly sophisticated, scientific definitions of desert ecosystems and the persistence of moralism in the rhetoric of continental geography.

John Wesley Powell's influential survey of 1878, *Report on the Lands of the Arid Regions*, employs the words "redeem" and "redemption" so often that it begins to sound like a bizarre captivity narrative, with western lands hostage to their own aridity and the United States betting its legitimacy upon its ability to deliver the West from unfortunate weather.[1] Late-century promoters of a federally sponsored irrigation empire imagined the deserts of the United States as testing grounds for a new technocratic rationality, while primitivists like Mary Austin celebrated the mystical pull of a "long brown land" that resisted human logics and bodies. Neither group recognized deserts as appropriately national space. Not until Wallace Stegner's famous mid-twentieth century definition of the West as "aridity above all else," a region whose fragile ecosystems suggested the fragility of national ideals, did "the

23

desert" appear as a possible synonym for "the United States."[2] Yet Stegner's was a regionalist project, and his arid West symbolized a partial America explicitly antagonistic to the decadent, unnatural East. The weird particularity of the United States' western deserts meant that they would never be amenable to the idealized abstractions that advocates of Manifest Destiny had employed to envision the vast North American continent as a culturally unified nation.

Decades before John Wesley Powell carefully divided the United States' arid lands into the "sub-humid" region of the Great Plains and the truer deserts of what Powell called the Rocky Mountain region, images of the continent's "inland deserts" served U.S. writers as a geopolitical euphemism for western landscapes that inspired crises of imagination. When I speak of "inland deserts" in the following chapters, I refer to a series of real and fictive physiographic regions, beginning with the Great American Desert, an area roughly contiguous with the Great Plains, and moving across the Rocky Mountains into the Great Basin, the Colorado Plateau, and southern California. I focus most sharply upon the Great American Desert because this region no longer exists under the name of "desert," so it is a nineteenth-century fiction that nonetheless prophesied some of the United States' unique failures of settlement and colonization. The Great American Desert was born in Zebulon Pike's 1810 memoirs of his expeditions across the Great Plains. Pike identified an ecological and sociopolitical dilemma that he variously called "the inland deserts," "the Great Sandy Desert," and "the prairie problem." Pike's idea was that a significant portion of the recently purchased Louisiana Territory in fact could not be cultivated and, as a result, this land was by its very nature resistant to Euro-American bodies. Pike described a prairie landscape that had a distinct if implicit racial character: it was not white; in fact, it was off-white, brownish, and bald. Pike's prairie deserts looked a little bit like stereotypical Indians. These deserts were geographic images that contested nationalist ideology: such "landless" lands predicted that U.S. civilization, which was undergirded by theories of the relationship of agriculture to republican virtue, would prove unsustainable at the approximate center of North America. Before the more optimistic journals of Lewis and Clark were published in 1814, Zebulon Pike offered readers in the United States a geopolitical future limited by "inland deserts" that could be one of two things: barriers to U.S. expansion or ideal habitats for other nations, particularly American Indians. In brief, early in the nineteenth century Pike imagined the United States' future heartland as the navel of a decidedly foreign "world" that, through his catchy geo-graphical metaphors, began to circulate in the nation's geography books, emigrants' guides, and political rhetoric.

Ten years after the publication of Pike's travels, Stephen H. Long's expe-dition to the central Plains confirmed and elaborated "the prairie problem." It was Long who named the Great Plains "the Great American Desert." As late as the 1840s and 1850s, when the Oregon Trail had entered national symbology and U.S. settlers regularly passed through the Plains, influential business journals like New York City's *Hunt's Merchants' Magazine* and New Orleans's *DeBow's Review* still predicted that the Plains would remain "Asi-atic" wastelands, meaning that they would host fiercely competitive trading and raiding cultures inimical to incorporation by the United States.[3] Josiah Gregg, a Santa Fé trader whose 1844 memoir offers one of the first encour-agements that the high prairies might be cultivated and settled, nevertheless represented himself as a white "nomad" whose racial character had been deranged by prairie life. "I have striven in vain to reconcile myself to the even tenor of civilized life in the United States," Gregg lamented, "and have sought in its amusements and its society a substitute for those high excite-ments which have attached me so strongly to prairie life."[4] Gregg's nostal-gia for a pleasure and risk-seeking, wandering life casts him as a prototype of the celluloid cowboy, but in 1844 Native Americans had not sufficiently "vanished" to make this self-proclaimed white nomadism wholly attractive. It could still be disturbing to imagine North American nature challenging and dissolving the racial and cultural truisms that sponsored the United States' imperial march to the Pacific.

The West's "inland deserts" offered the United States' first writers of international reputation, Washington Irving and James Fenimore Cooper, a passage into the unstable core of national consciousness in the 1820s and 1830s. Irving's two romantic histories of the Far West and Cooper's histori-cal romance, *The Prairie* (1827), all treat arid, unbuildable scenes. The prairie desert of Irving's first western history, *Astoria* (1836), appears as a space of immense, almost unimaginable scale, disorder, and movement that seems wholly resistant to incorporation. "[I]t is to be feared that a great part of [the Far West] will form a lawless interval between the abodes of civilized man, like the wastes of the ocean or the deserts of Arabia. . . . Here may spring up mongrel races, like new formations in geology, the amalgamation of the 'debris' and 'abrasions' of former races, civilized and savage . . . the descendants of wandering hunters and trappers. . . ."[5] As if compelled to repeat a story that could never be resolved, Irving returned in his second western history, the *Adventures of Captain Bonneville* (1837), to the topic of another failed imperial venture in another "desert" West, the trading company that the hapless Louis de Bonneville attempted to create in the vicinity of the Rocky Mountains. Once again Irving envisions an uncultivable landscape supporting a regional culture that is ethnically diverse and essentially international:

> An immense belt of rocky mountains and volcanic plains, several hundred miles in width, must ever remain an irreclaimable wilderness, intervening between the abodes of civilization, and affording a last refuge to the Indian. Here, roving tribes of hunters, living in tents and lodges, and following the migrations of the game, may lead a life of savage independence, where there is nothing to tempt the cupidity of the white man. The amalgamation of various tribes, and of white men of every nation, will in time produce hybrid races like the mountain Tartars of the Caucasus.[6]

Irving's status as one of the United States' most respected writers meant that his evocations of North America's inland deserts, however discouraging, would survive beyond any political usefulness they might have had in the early national period as reminders of the perceived necessity of Euro-American or "white" consolidation east of the Mississippi River.

In the years that saw the publication of Washington Irving's Miltonic panoramas, it would seem there was little reason for European Americans to fear amalgamation with American Indians or the fatal dissolution of the United States' continental ambitions in an international interval dominated by nomadic traders. The skepticism evident in Stephen H. Long, Cooper, and Irving about their nation's geographical and political destiny could be seen as a conceit. The 1835 Treaty of New Echota marked a crucial success of Indian Removal and the division of the powerful Cherokee nation. In 1836 Narcissa Whitman crossed the Rocky Mountains with her husband to establish Methodist missions along the Columbia River, an event that has long been imagined as the beginning of the Great Migration of U.S. settlers to Oregon in 1842.[7] The creation of a northern continental boundary with Britain at the 49th parallel would not occur until 1846, but it was the year 1836 that gave birth to the battle cry "54° 40′or fight," a slogan signaling the United States' resolve to claim the vast Oregon Territory.[8] If continental destiny was not yet manifest in the 1830s, it was rapidly becoming so.

Still, the dry lands of the West and plains presented a dilemma that, as Irving suggests, was socio-political because representational. The whole idea of the West, including the highly desirable coastlands and river valleys of Oregon and California, was tainted by contiguity to apparently forbidding, arid landscapes. The prairie problem was a little bit like a virus that could not be contained. In fact, large tracts of what is now Kansas, Nebraska, Oklahoma, Arkansas, and Texas would not be used for agricultural purposes until the 1860s, when Texas cattlemen pushed northward with their herds and boosters began to tout the Plains as "the All Year Grazing Country." By the 1870s, dry farming techniques and new irrigation technologies promised to redeem the sub-humid Plains, if not the more arid country west of the Rockies; it seemed that only the Mormon Empire could survive in the Great Basin. [9] Earlier concerns about the Great American Desert would never entirely be put to rest, as waves of drought throughout the late-nineteenth and early-twentieth centuries kept pushing settlers out of the mid-continent, eastward toward the Mississippi Valley or further west to California. On the eve of the Dust Bowl, one of the federal government's hopeful irrigation men declared that through technology "the nation is now one country, not two strips of country, with a desert between"—as Pike, Long, Irving, and even Cooper had predicted it would be. [10] The Dust Bowl soon said no to this twentieth-century optimist and reasserted the "two strips of country with a desert between" hypothesis.

The environmental peculiarities of the Plains states which once comprised the heart of the imaginary Great American Desert continue to generate narratives of "middle America's" cultural peculiarity and resistance to national ideals. Approximately the same areas imagined by nineteenth-century expansionists as only suitable for Indian settlement—areas claimed by dissident religious and political communities, including radical abolitionists, black freedmen, and Mormons—appear in contemporary media as sub-national zones of unimaginable rural poverty and peculiar crime. [11] Gothic midwesterns like Truman Capote's *In Cold Blood*, the 1999 film *Boys Don't Cry*, and the Nebraskan director Alexander Payne's *Election* (1999) and *About Schmidt* (2002) renominate Kansas and Nebraska as sites of national irrationality and anomie. Recently the western writer and journalist Timothy Egan has written a series of articles in *The New York Times* that treat the mushrooming of poverty and crime in Plains states like Nebraska and Kansas, and in Mountain states like Utah, where failing farms and dependence upon government subsidies have produced a new economy based in the produc-

27

tion of methamphetamine. [12] The "lawless interval" of the mid-continent that Washington Irving predicted would be sustained by trade in liquors and animal skins is now imagined as a regional culture dependent upon the marketing of synthetic speed. Of course historical continuities should not be overstated, but it seems that the representational crisis known as the Great American Desert has been succeeded by the imagined geo-cultural aporia of "the heartland."

The barrier to national fulfillment that various writers, beginning with Zebulon Pike, recognized in the prairie deserts of the mid-continent cannot be reduced to the model of a binaristic, east-to-west moving "frontier." In fact, what we see in some early narratives of these desert wests is a surprising willingness to recognize cultural influence flowing against Euro-American traffic, from the West's inland deserts to the North and East. In The Prairie, James Fenimore Cooper recognizes Plains Indians like the Pawnee creating a prairie lifestyle in which national identities are continually reinscribed through commercial activity, namely the traffic in skins, horses, and women. This "Indian" commerce—really commerce co-created by Native American and Euro-American agents—becomes Cooper's model for how the United States might occupy and identify itself with the continent's uncultivable regions. A variety of narratives that address the Great American Desert elaborate a version of commercial empire where multidirectional traffic and reciprocal influence among distinct national communities is the norm. Irving's Astoria and The Adventures of Captain Bonneville, Edwin James's chronicle of the Stephen H. Long Expedition of 1819–20, James Fenimore Cooper's The Prairie, Zenas Leonard's Adventures (1839), Josiah Gregg's Commerce of the Prairies (1844), and Susan Shelby Magoffin's Santa Fé diaries, which are some of the primary narratives I address, posit a U.S. national culture divided against itself by its trade routes, both multi-ethnic and international, consisting of various classes forced together without the cement of common interest or the unifying cause of war. The atypical "westerns" I read in the next two chapters are narratives of a western desert appropriately conceived by U.S. writers as an alternate America or even a perpetually a-national space. It was thought that the Great American Desert might brutally limit the United States' national ambitions, breaking the nation into two coastal republics. Oppositely, the Great American Desert might become the key to the nation's dynamism, a valuable internal opening to the world. Mary Austin's late Romantic concept of California's deserts as "lands of lost borders" figures forth in antebellum representations of the inland deserts as a political economic idea of lost borders, a preview of postmodern concepts of borderless empire. Yet the uniqueness and even hostility of the various environments and cultures that existed within the broad geographical range covered by the phrase "the inland deserts" insured that these imagined territories could not be seen too abstractly. Nineteenth-century narratives of the West's arid lands offer significant alternatives to versions of Manifest Destiny that depend on ideas of assimilable or easily expendable western peoples and open, arable country.

1. THE AMERICAN DESERT, EMPIRE ANXIETY, AND HISTORICAL ROMANCE

Much was said and written at the time concerning the policy of adding the vast regions of Louisiana to the already immense and but half-tenanted territories of the United States. As the warmth of controversy, however, subsided and party considerations gave place to more liberal views, the wisdom of the measure began to be generally conceded. It soon became apparent to the meanest capacity that while nature had placed a barrier of desert to the extension of our population to the West, the measure had made us the masters of a belt of fertile country which, in the revolutions of the day, might have become the property of a rival nation . . . If ever time or necessity shall require a peaceful division of this vast empire, it [the Purchase] assures us of a neighbor that will possess our language, our religion, our institutions, and it is also to be hoped, our sense of political justice.

> JAMES FENIMORE COOPER, *The Prairie* (1827)

. . . From these immense prairies may arise one great advantage to the United States, viz.: The restriction of our population to some certain limits, and thereby a continuation of the Union. Our citizens being so prone to rambling and extending themselves on the frontiers will, through necessity, be constrained to limit their extent on the west to the borders of the Missouri and the Mississippi, while they leave the prairies incapable of cultivation to the wandering and uncivilized aborigines of the country.

> ZEBULON PIKE, *The Expeditions of Zebulon Montgomery Pike* (1810)

. . . Scarcely a day passes without my experiencing a pang of regret that I am not now roving at large upon those western plains.

> JOSIAH GREGG, *Commerce of the Prairies* (1844)

Opening *The Prairie* in the uncertain moment just after the Louisiana Purchase, James Fenimore Cooper eliminated the possibility of setting the novel in a familiar, already settled locale that could inform its outcomes. Cooper's refusal or inability in *The Prairie* to give the "vast regions of Louisiana" the kind of legendary history easily associated with his other historical romances suggests the challenge that those dry western lands vaguely categorized as "the Great American Desert" posed to the project of U.S. nationalism. *The Prairie* is the first historical romance about the United States to be set on the supposedly desert-like Great Plains. The Great American Desert enforced an eruption of material history into the historical romance that undermined Cooper's authorial license, forcing him to a relatively faithful mimesis of the United States' imperial anxieties. As Nathaniel Hawthorne warned in his famous theorization of historical romance in the preface to *The House of the Seven Gables*, the Romancer exposes himself to "an inflexible and exceedingly dangerous species of criticism" by assigning his "fancy-pictures" to an "actual locality."[1]

Insofar as the Great American Desert could be considered an actual locality, it disrupted Cooper's attempts to smoothly connect a "by-gone time with the very present that is flitting before us," in Hawthorne's words.[2] Yet the tensions that undermine the anti-referential privilege of the Romancer in *The Prairie* are also problems of imagination, and insofar as the inland deserts were projections of nationalist doubt they spelled out a world that *was* Romantic because it engaged the possible rather than reifying a probable, already hegemonic understanding of North American space. Yet the possible worlds of the inland deserts were worlds no one in the United States wanted. As a literary setting, the inland deserts infringed on no one's property in actuality because they could not be seen as property at all.[3] In the Jeffersonian political theory that energized expansionist fervor in the antebellum period, wealth, natural rights, and disinterested participation in government all relied upon land that was not too dry to be farmed.

The fact that the Great American Desert could not be seen as farmland or real estate made it, in fact, always on the verge of becoming too real. Its fantastic or Romantic elements (extreme aridity, a hostile nomad population, disorienting mirages, monstrous bison) made the western desert a scene of the impossible—neither real in any reassuring sense nor possible in a way that enabled the fashioning of a "subjunctive world of fiction," in Terence Martin's words, which might produce desirable images of nationhood.[4] Deserts or lands suspected of being deserts made for recurrent crises in nationalist symbol making. For decades they remained uncategorizable and intractable fictional territories: at best a useful barrier to the extension of Anglo-American population, or perhaps the border of a sister republic, as Cooper imagined, or home to the peripatetic and international trading culture which the Santa Fé trader Josiah Gregg recalled fondly in the 1840s.[5]

While white nomads like Josiah Gregg may have been the advance guard of the United States' empire, as Eric Sundquist has argued, their stories, like the prairie deserts of the mid-continent, were not easily incorporated into ideologies of national progress.[6] Gregg sounds like an imitation Daniel Boone, reluctant harbinger of democratic civilization, when he remarks that "the wild, unsettled, and independent life of the prairie trader makes perfect freedom from nearly every kind of social dependence an absolute necessity of his being."[7] But Gregg's ode to freedom rings out on the plains of New Mexico, a "region of asperities" whose appeal is altogether distinct from that of Boone's Kentucky and whose vitality, Gregg recognizes, depends upon the commerce and actual interdependence of several nations. The prairie trader is not simply a type of the Kentucky hunter because, quite simply, his prairie is not Kentucky.

"I can hardly be called a settler," Natty Bumppo explains in The Prairie, "seeing that I have no regular abode . . ." And "you are mistaken, friend, in calling me a hunter; I am nothing better than a trapper."[8] Never an apt representative of Jeffersonian agrarianism, on the Plains the Leatherstocking is also dissociated from the mythology of the white hunter that, as Richard Slotkin has shown, naturalized the United States' conquest of American Indian territories and nations.[9] "Nothing better than a trapper," Bumppo, in The Prairie, has become, like many of his adopted Pawnee brethren, a laborer in an exploitative and international economy, following the "one business that can be followed here with profit"[10] (emphasis mine). Without recognizable game, arable land, or even a forest cover that allows for tracking and hiding, the high prairies offer no home for the narrative of woodcraft and Indian fighting, the appropriated "savage" skills that typically justify Bumppo's presence on Indian land. The equally savage skills of trapping and trading are associated with a fetishized profit and deny the white culture hero any deep claim to the landscape, so that Cooper can effect no fictional inheritance, from the Indian through Natty, of a prairie estate. As the first U.S. historical romance to be set in the Great American Desert, in what is now Nebraska, The Prairie offers a deep account of a more widespread representational problem. The prairie deserts by their very nature, as that nature was conceived, problematized rhetorics of Manifest Destiny and unique racial gifts, raising the possibility that what looked like national progress across the continent might end in a landscape which opened the United States to an inescapably international, disorienting world.

Precarious Possessions

The possession of the Far West by the United States proved precarious not only because the boundaries of the territory Thomas Jefferson purchased from France in 1803 were always, as Napoléon had conceded, happily uncertain. The abstract problem of mapping the boundaries of the Louisiana Purchase was complemented by the problem of filling in the map with an appropriate image of U.S. national experience. The contest between the absolutely contradictory images of garden and desert which attached to the Great Plains made a unitary concept of the Louisiana Territory unthinkable; the imaginative construct "the Plains" was fragmentary, really self-contradictory, even for Jefferson, who is typically represented as creating the region as a grassland Eden to be settled by republican farmers. True, Jefferson's 1803 *Official Account of Louisiana* introduces the idea that the entirety of his newly bought West is an "almost spontaneously" yielding garden, an idea that would be trumpeted by generations of advocates of Manifest Destiny.[11] James Fenimore Cooper's 1848 paean to Manifest Destiny, *The Oak Openings*, performs the bombastic reinvention of Jeffersonian continental thinking that justified Andrew Jackson's displacement of Native American nations and the United States' invasion of Mexico in 1846. For Cooper, in 1848, the whole North American continent figures as "a glorious gift from God, which it is devoutly to be wished may be accepted with due gratitude . . . by those who have been selected to enjoy it."[12] The elect were of course those mythic Anglo-Saxon farmers who came to justify the inaugural violence of the settler-nation.

For Thomas Jefferson, as for the younger Cooper of the 1820s and 1830s, the equation was not so simple. In an amendment to the U.S. Constitution which Jefferson drafted (and never proposed) in order to justify the legality of the Louisiana Purchase, Jefferson suggested that some portion of the new territory "north of the 31st parallel" might become a permanent Indian colony.[13] The idea of an interval of unpatriated peoples in the Far West was born simultaneously with the idea of a continental United States. Moreover, after 1810 when Zebulon Pike had suggested that large sections of the Louisiana Territory were "deserts" unfit for cultivation, Jefferson endorsed the notion of a sister confederacy in the environs of the Columbia River Basin as an alternative to continental settlement.[14]

As is evident in the correspondence between Thomas Jefferson and John Jacob Astor that is published in Washington Irving's 1836 history *Astoria*, Jefferson's hope that some "enterprising mercantile Americans" would settle the Columbia Valley complemented Astor's own self-interested dream of commercial empire. "I considered as a great public acquisition the commencement of a settlement on that point of the Western Coast of America," Jefferson writes to Astor, "and looked forward with gratification to the time when its descendants should have spread themselves thro' the whole length of the coast, covering it with free and independent Americans, *unconnected with us* but by ties of blood and interest, and enjoying like us the rights of self government"[15] (emphasis mine). Jefferson speculated that the continent might be divided between an "Atlantic" and a "Mississippi" confederacy, each organized around a vital water trade.

In a series of editorials for the St. *Louis Enquirer* written between 1818 and 1819, Thomas Hart Benton, who as a senator from Missouri became a vocal booster of western development, also argued that "this republic should have limits" and predicted the division of the continent into separate but friendly nations. Setting the natural boundary of the United States at the ridge of the Rocky Mountains, Benton prophesied that "in planting the seed of a new power on the coast of the Pacific ocean, it should be well understood, that, when strong enough to take care of itself, the new government should separate from the mother empire, as the child separates from the parent. . . ."[16] Henry Nash Smith has emphasized just how stubbornly Benton cleaved to his notions of the West as a coastal section organized around sea trade, resisting even the popular idea of a transcontinental railroad well into the 1850s. James Fenimore Cooper looks at the continent with similar double vision when in the opening paragraph of The *Prairie* he celebrates the Louisiana Purchase as the promise of a western coastal republic separated from the United States by the Plains and the Rocky Mountains. Again, "if ever time or necessity shall require a peaceful division of this vast empire, it [the Louisiana Purchase] assures us of a neighbor that will possess our language, our religion, our institutions, and it is also to be hoped, our sense of political justice."[17]

Cooper's indecision about continental futures in The *Prairie* is particularly significant given that he originally saw the novel as a conclusion to the Leatherstocking series, sequel to The *Pioneers* (1823) and The *Last of the Mohicans* (1826). It is fitting that Natty Bumppo dies in The *Prairie* in a landscape that was, in 1827, just a little farther west than the farthest West that U.S. pioneers had attempted to settle. Yet for this very reason Cooper's setting, in what would be approximately present-day Nebraska, was at the time of its writing too messy to support an image of the expanding United States. The *Prairie* is a particularly anomalous and unstable narrative for Cooper, since the imaginative projection of the nation was the object that drove all of his work. Cooper's *The American Democrat* (1838), whose celebration of representative government is undermined by an at times piquant nostalgia for the leadership of a natural aristocracy, represents only his most practical attempt to write the nation, as he wished it, into being. Cooper originally had hoped that *American Democrat* would be used as a textbook for the study of U.S. government in the public school system of New York, but, ironically, it was displaced by the more critically nuanced vision of a European—the New York schools chose Alexis de Tocqueville's *Democracy in America*.[18] Although Cooper denigrated the power of the press to form public opinion and governmental policy in *American Democrat*, throughout his life he seized upon literature, and the press, to inform national and civic ideals. The Leatherstocking series, which Cooper correctly thought would be his lasting work, dealt with a number of national themes at what critics since D. H. Lawrence have identified as "the mythic level." The attribution of "mythic" qualities to the Leatherstocking series implies that the series worked to resolve the nation's cultural and historical conflicts through carefully crafted, slant re-iterations of those conflicts. As Roland Barthes suggests, myth is ideology made to seem natural, and history, inevitable. But again, in *The Prairie* the Nebraskan "desert" is a spatial concept suggestive of an impossible future; it disarranges any literary attempt to naturalize present ideology by connecting it to a flexible and distantly legendary place of origin.

Even in its own day *The Prairie* failed to be embraced as a significant contribution to the United States' national mythos. *The Prairie* was well received in Europe, a favorite of Cooper's Parisian friends, but it received mixed reviews in the United States and did not sell as well as the two earlier Leatherstocking novels. *The Prairie* was remarked by some of its most famous readers, like William Cullen Bryant, to succeed or fail on the basis of its setting. In the context of my discussion, this becomes a suggestive fact. From Belgium, Cooper wrote to an American friend that he had been "followed twelve posts by a first-rate artist," the landscape painter Verboek-Hoven, who was enamored of *The Prairie* because he felt that it realistically depicted Western flora and fauna.[19] In contrast, William Cullen Bryant believed that *The Prairie* failed precisely because its setting was too particular and strange. Bryant saw in Cooper's choice of location for his romance a failure of authorial purpose. Writing of *The Prairie* in the *United States Review and Literary Gazette*, Bryant laments that Cooper "has not allowed himself a very large abundance of materials out of which to construct his narrative. The action of the piece is religiously confined to the prairie, from which it is named, a vast open country, with an undulating surface, with here and there a few bushes in the hollows, a single heap of rocks, and a river." [20] Bryant's frustration with Cooper's choice of a prairie setting where "the store of images and situations . . . is soon exhausted" suggests that U.S. authors should keep out of the continent's less promising landscapes. Cooper, a "man of genius," as Bryant concedes, falters in this novel because he addresses the wrong West.

Five years later, following his own visit to Illinois, Bryant could imagine a future prairie nation, writing in his poem "The Prairies" of a dream in which "the low of herds" and the "rustling of the heavy grain" fill the wild lands that were once fitted only to buffalo. [21] Of course by the 1830s Illinois had proven to be prime farmland. Bryant was not alone in regarding Cooper's attempt to write a novel about (what would become) Nebraska as an essentially stupid and "bold experiment." [22] The western physician and writer Daniel Drake adds a unique regional tinge to Bryant's critique, noting that Cooper's "failure" in The Prairie could be chalked up to his lack of real experience in the West. [23] Yet when Drake speaks of writing the West, he refers to the already well-known wests of Ohio and Kentucky. Similarly, Robert Baird, a writer of emigrants' guides who was eager to characterize himself as—unlike Cooper—a real "western man," acknowledged that "respecting the character of these districts [west of Missouri and Arkansas], . . . it is impossible to speak with much accuracy." [24]

The undirectedness or, in Bryant's terms, the "exhaustion" of Cooper's plot in The Prairie underlines the uncertain social and political value of the region he describes. The Prairie appears at first glance to be a novel about settlement; it features a clan of squatters—aptly named the Bushes—moving west to stake a claim, and two displaced young couples, the genteel Duncan Middleton and his bride Inez de Certavallos, and the recognizably middle-class Paul Hover and Nelly Wade. Setting what is essentially a double-marriage plot—for Middleton will recover Inez from captivity amongst the squatters and Hover will marry Nelly Wade—in a landscape devoid of cultural value, Cooper seems to argue, against uncertainty, for the growth of the United States' population across the continent. But by the end of the novel all of his major actors have turned back east, save Natty Bumppo, who dies at a Pawnee village on the Plains. In the end no one remains.

The novel's plot extends beyond its primary stage of action, the prairies, by means of a frame narrative set on the eastern shores of the Mississippi. There we find Middleton and Hover established as proprietors of tidy estates much like Marmaduke Temple's New York digs in *The Pioneers*. What happens to the Bush family at the end of the novel is radically uncertain. This would suggest the truth of Bryant's exasperated remark that "it should seem very difficult to make much of such a race of people in a romance." [25] *The Prairie* violently sets at odds Cooper's already contradictory commitments to verisimilitude and novelistic propriety. He defines novelistic propriety in his preface to *The Pioneers* as the insistence of "[r]eviewers, readers of magazines, and young ladies" that a novel be "in keeping," sneering that it is difficult to discern which aesthetic or social criteria the vague "in keeping" recommends. [26] While European, even feudal, hierarchies could be imagined in the military society of colonial New York or among the Federalist aristocracy of post-Revolutionary New York (the social settings of *The Last of the Mohicans* and *The Pioneers*) it would be fair to say that the collection of motley actors that Cooper projected into the Far West defied keeping to the representational limits of those English novelists who influenced Cooper and who enjoyed popular approval in the early nineteenth-century United States.

The novelist of manners—and Jane Austen's *Persuasion* inspired Cooper's first novel, *Precaution*—or the romantic social novelist most readily compared to Cooper, Sir Walter Scott, would be hard pressed to represent the deserts of North America through the narrative movements and themes typically associated with their sub-genres. In his attempts to represent the Highlands, Scott faced a somewhat similar challenge to Cooper's, but he did not offer solutions that could be transposed easily to the Great Plains, particularly given their still uncertain history in the 1820s. The Great American Desert called for a new chronotope, in Mikhail Bakhtin's terms, a new time-space, and while Cooper recognized the uniqueness of the region he rather passively responded to it, allowing it to get the best of his craft. It was on the basis of his failure to adequately invent a more successful means of depicting the inland deserts that Cooper criticized *The Prairie* when he reflected on it at the peak of his career in the 1840s. Specifically, Cooper regretted that he had "not confined the characters to those naturally connected with the ground, to the rude backwoodsman and his family group [the Bushes], with the Pawnees and the Dacotahs, all moving about Natty. . . ." [27]

The absurdity of the plot that links together *The Prairie*'s genteel actors, Middleton and Inez de Certavallos, suggests that they really are imaginatively disconnected from the novel's scene of action. Middleton, a military officer at New Orleans, pursues his young bride Inez, a Creole, onto the plains because she has been inexplicably kidnapped by the squatters. By this crude means Cooper incorporates genteel, Europeanized characters into a story of the Far West and awkwardly alludes to the difficult amalgamation of Spanish (or, as of 1821, Mexican) and U.S. interests in the vast Louisiana Territory. By the 1840s it may have been easier for Cooper to see the Great Plains as a tableau most fitted to characters "naturally connected to the ground," also a scene that need not include European colonials, because by this time the Oregon Trail was wide open and continental settlement by the United States had been assured. But in 1826 when Cooper sat down to write *The Prairie* in New York and Paris, it was more difficult to imagine a U.S. population "naturally connected" to this contested locale. He could not use any prior model of United States' citizenship or settlement.

Territorial Fictions

When Cooper represented, in *The Prairie*, a clan of squatters traipsing across the "bleak and solitary" country between the Rocky Mountains and the banks of the Platte, he realized that he was anticipating. Neither of the two primary sources he used to construct the historical context of the narrative— the *Journals of Lewis and Clark* and the account of the 1819–21 expeditions of Stephen H. Long—claimed the Great Plains for U.S. pioneers. Although Daniel Boone had established a homestead on the upper Missouri in 1799, a fact noted in *The Prairie*,[28] agricultural settlers did not cross the plains until the 1830s, and even then most of them kept going, through the South Pass in the Rockies of southern Wyoming, to reach the more fertile valleys of the Columbia and Sacramento rivers. Cooper wrote *The Prairie* in 1826, but he set it in October 1805, roughly a month before Lewis and Clark arrived at the mouth of the Columbia. Cooper's choice of historical time in this novel does not reflect the typical desire of historical romance to displace contemporary acts of conquest into a deep past.[29] *The Prairie* reveals just how shallow the United States' past in the West had been and how little government policy or public opinion about the desert West had changed from the era of Lewis and Clark to his own time of writing. Although Meriwether Lewis generally con- firmed Jefferson's hopes for the fertility of the vast Louisiana territory, he anticipated Pike's assessment of the region as desert in a letter to his mother where he wrote that "there can exist no other objection to it [the prairie country, beginning approximately at what is now Omaha] except that of the want of timber, which is truly a very serious one."[30] Anyway, the primary— if not chiefly expressed—goal of the Lewis and Clark expedition had to do with settlement in only the most indirect manner; the primary goal of the expedition was to strengthen the United States' stake in the international fur trade and to seek a viable Northwest river passage for U.S. trappers. [31] The Lewis and Clark expedition might have foretold U.S. expansion across the continent, but its ideas of expansion were informed by the old British model of maritime commerce.

Lewis and Clark encountered several trappers' boats when they ascended the Missouri in 1804. In 1807, the year after the expedition, traders and trappers from the United States descended upon Saint Louis, hoping to stake their claim in the lucrative trade, and as soon as the ice broke on the Missouri it was filled with trappers' barges, pirogues, and canoes. [32] By the 1820s, the "Missouri Trapper" had become the type of United States' presence in the little-known western territories beyond the Mississippi. The influential Ohio Valley writer James Hall was among many writers to memorialize this type in one of his early "Letters from the West," published in the Philadelphia magazine The Port Folio. Hall wrote these letters while riding down the Ohio River to Illinois. In "The Missouri Trapper," Hall recounts the legendary history of Hugh Glass, a trapper who supposedly saved himself from devastating wounds inflicted by a bear by crawling some 350 miles across the Plains from Grand River, South Dakota, to a trading post on the Missouri. Deprivation marked the life of trappers, who in Hall's "The Missouri Trapper" are pictured as often starving and forced to "devour [their] pelfry," a practice that certainly indicated the unprofitability of U.S. business in the Far West. [33] Like Hugh Glass, Natty Bumppo in The Prairie represents the United States' somewhat desperate attempts to keep moving into the continent—hence the octogenarian Leatherstocking's determination to traipse across the Great Plains even though he has no horse. Bumppo's weak excuse for traveling on foot with an exhausted hunting dog reveals the unfittedness of this kind of character for this kind of West. Somewhat irrelevantly, the Leatherstocking explains: "Horses I have never craved, nor even used, though few have journeyed over more of the wide lands of America than myself, old and feeble as I seem. But little use is there for a horse among the hills and woods of York—that is, as York was, but as I greatly fear York is no longer. . . ." [34] The ineffectuality of Bumppo's anachronistic technologies in this novel, such as his stealthy walking and the rifle that he can no longer use, suggest, as does the character Hugh Glass's crawling, the diminishment of the white hunter in western landscapes that could not be made to mimic eastern forests and farmlands.

When Daniel Boone (or the more successful Natty Bumppo of other Leatherstocking novels) walked, it was understood that his walking was a means of mastering the wilderness, of attaining a necessary intimacy with yet-to-be-settled places while leaving the fewest possible traces in them. Walking makes the hunter less conspicuous to hostile Indians and leads him to unexpected vistas predictive of future settlement—in Boone's case, the future settlement of Kentucky. The early western writer Timothy Flint's best-selling Biographical Memoir of Daniel Boone (1833), is particularly invested in following the imperial footsteps of the white hunter: "From this point the descent into the great western valley began. What a scene opened before them. . . .'Glorious Country!' they exclaimed. Little did Boone dream that in fifty years, immense portions of it would pass from the domain of the hunter—that it would contain four millions of freemen. . . ."[35] In contrast, in the Great American Desert a view into the distance only fetches a mirage. In The Prairie what appears on the horizon as a buffalo in full charge turns out to be the explorer's "own ass," in Cooper's terms—a pack-mule. The mirage, a physical peculiarity of the Great Plains anxiously explained by its early narrators, becomes yet another manifestation of the uncertain political future of the inland deserts.

The account of the Stephen H. Long Expedition, which was compiled by the expedition's botanist and geologist, Edwin James, and published in 1823, likens travel in the Great American Desert to the near extinction of the human body. The dreary prognoses of the Long chronicle are worth considering, given that it was probably the only source material about the Great Plains that Cooper took with him to Paris when he was finishing The Prairie.[36] When the novel was ready for publication, Cooper gave his copy of Edwin James's account to his friend the Duchess de Broglie, whom he felt would appreciate the realistic depictions of Plains Indians to be found in the volumes. The expedition's scientists did accurately predict the future demise of the buffalo and the near starvation of the Plains nations. But the realism of the Long Expedition's Account consisted not only, as Cooper implied, in its relatively careful anthropology. The conflictedness of its tone quite realistically reflects the crossed purposes of federal policy in "Indian Territory," which included both the protection of American Indians and the regulation or homogenization of Plains tribes under the banner of a nationalized trade in animal skins and hides. James's focus on the explorers' problems of movement in the Account points to larger doubts about the United States' claims to the continent. "We had travelled [a] great part of the day enveloped in a burning atmosphere," James recounts in one typical journal-entry from the last leg of the trip, "sometimes letting fall upon us the scorching particles of sand, which had been raised by the wind, sometimes almost suffocating by its entire stagnation, when we had the good fortune to meet with a pool of stagnant water. . . ." [37] This pool of stagnant water was, in James's phrase, the day's "treat." The Long account is unique in the genre of expedition narrative for its consistently sheepish tone and its frequent admissions of failure. In fact, Long's party did not accomplish most of the goals outlined for them by then–Secretary of War John C. Calhoun, who imagined the expedition as a sequel to the Lewis and Clark expedition of fifteen years before.

Calhoun advised Long to take "the instructions of Mr. Jefferson to Captain Lewis" [38] as a guide for his own movements, a suggestion which betrays, again, just how little new thinking about the fabled "American desert" had been done since the start of the nineteenth century. The War of 1812 and the immediate postwar reconstruction had turned the country's attention away from these western territories, and popular interest in all aspects of the Far West only completely revived in the years immediately prior to Long's assignment. It was the negotiation and final enactment of the Transcontinental (Adams-Onís) Treaty of 1819 that made another federal expedition into the Great Plains imperative. Without any clear notion of the territories under consideration, John Quincy Adams had persuaded the Spanish minister Luis de Onís to allow him to draw the United States' territorial boundary clear to the Pacific. By drawing this transcontinental line, Adams reenacted and exaggerated the Louisiana Purchase; he would remember the Transcontinental Treaty as his greatest act as Secretary of State under James Monroe. [39] Yet when Long's men moved through what is now Kansas, Oklahoma, Colorado, and Texas in 1819 and 1820 the wonder which had accompanied the Lewis and Clark party was gone, giving way to a tired cynicism reflected in James's narrative.

What had happened to the Far West in the interval between Lewis and Clark and Long is that it had solidified into a complex regional economy, but not a national place. Plains nations like the Pawnee, who appear relatively removed from the fur trade in Lewis and Clark, had been drawn almost to the center of it by the time James wrote. It was the Pawnee's desperate struggle to get a living in the newly fierce trading culture of the Plains that made them appear particularly degraded to travelers like Washington Irving, who traversed the Plains in 1832, just one year after a smallpox epidemic on the central Plains had devastated several Indian nations. [40] Moreover, the ancient struggles for the Far West's resources—among Britain, France, Spain, Russia, and the United States—had not so much disappeared by the early 1820s as they had become petty and personal; they were reenacted through small-scale, bitter rivalries among individual traders. The famous Missouri Fur Company chief Manuel Lisa, a Creole with few ties to any national government, appears as a trickster figure in both Zebulon Pike's exploration narrative and in *Astoria*, Washington Irving's history of the Pacific Fur Company: in both narratives Lisa attempts to extort money from U.S. explorers by seizing their interpreter for debt. Pierre Chouteau, another Creole trader virtually without a country, surfaces in several contemporary narratives as a slippery friend to typically naïve, half-lost explorers.

As a result of long uncertainty about the value of continental claims, the Stephen H. Long Expedition differed from the expedition of Lewis and Clark in tone if not in purpose. This second expedition was designed, as Lewis and Clark's had been, primarily to establish military posts on the upper Missouri to protect the fur trade, to strengthen relations with and among Indian tribes, and to diminish the influence British trading companies were still feared to exert upon the tribes. The Harvard professor and influential editor of the *North American Review*, Edward Everett, contributed an essay about the Long journals to the *Review* in 1823 that betrays great anxiety about British, Russian, and Spanish influence in the mid-continent. Among the cultural elite of Massachusetts, at least, doubts about the United States' ability to hold Louisiana were very much alive even twenty years after the Purchase. Lamenting that the Long party was, in its second year, underfunded, Everett sarcastically remarks, "[I]f we are poor, let us put off these proud airs; truckle to the British, court the Russians, beg pardon of the Spaniards, and shake hands with the pirates. . . . Get the British East India Company to charter our extravagant frigates and seventy-fours; and see, in the last resort, if the emperor of Russia cannot be prevailed on to farm the valley of the Missouri at the halves." [41] Everett's outrage at federal stinginess may be displaced, in part, from the disgrace that hovered about the Long party, whose many small but significant problems included: their failure to locate the sources of either the Platte or Red rivers, their failure to introduce smallpox vaccination amongst the Pawnee, the theft of invaluable notes by three deserters, and errors in the calculation of latitude and longitude that compromised the geographical value of the party's findings.

In fact, Long was underfunded in the second year of his expedition because of the paltry successes of his first year. Moreover, the failure of the expedition to locate the source of the Platte River in its second year, and the party's mistaking the Canadian River for the Red River, put off still flickering hopes for the discovery of a river passage northwest to the Columbia. The expedition's choice not to seek the location of the source of the Canadian River, which they were essentially the first party to survey in any detail, was criticized by later geographers. Reuben Gold Thwaites characterizes Long's lassitude in this instance as a symptom of the "carelessness" and apparent "indifference" that marred much of the party's findings. [42] The enthusiasm of Edward Everett, who attributes to the expedition the project of "taking possession of the empires, which Providence has called it [the United States] to govern," [43] is nowhere shared by Long's men, whose despair permeates James's account. It is hard to believe that Everett's jingoistic praise of the Long expedition is in any sense a "reading" of the Long journals. Even the official map of Long's expedition, which cursorily labels the region between the Alleghenies and the Rockies "the Great American Desert" functions as a negation of the continentalist dream that spawned the expedition. [44]

What James's account of the Long expedition offers is a detailed description of a "dreary and disgusting" landscape which induces "terror," a landscape of scarce game and scarcer water where infectious ticks create swollen tumors in the legs, swarms of flies lay their eggs in "white blankets" upon a night's repast, wild berries induce devastating headaches, and soup must be made using water red with buffalo dung. This landscape worthy of Edgar Allan Poe or Hieronymus Bosch defies exploration and makes a mockery of the explorer's map. When compared to the Long journals, Poe's fake and supposedly sensational exploration diary, The Journal of Julius Rodman, seems almost tame. Finding themselves in lesser-known regions southwest of the Arkansas River, Long's men make note of the ridiculous generality of their geographical renderings: "Were we to designate the locality of a mineral, or any other interesting object, as found twenty or thirty days' journey from the Rocky Mountains, we should do nearly all in our power." [45] In fact, as the party soon discovers, they have been quite lost.

The Geographical Limits of Whiteness

The almost willful refusal of the Long party to adequately map the region they explore—to the extent that they compile what amounts to an anti-exploration narrative—indicates not just the uncertain cultural-political status of the region they describe. The explorers' sheepishness also indicates the single strategic value that had been attributed to the arid West by the federal government since the 1810 explorations of Zebulon Pike. I refer to Pike's assertion that the Great American Desert would be an invaluable *barrier* to the extension of white U.S. settlement. Of course such an idea, that white settlement had to be contained, was wholly antithetical to the aims of those preaching Manifest Destiny in the 1840s, when hero-explorers like John C. Frémont (who really discovered almost nothing that had not been previously discovered) offered geographies of the continent meant to encourage U.S. pioneers.

Once Oregon Territory emigration got heavily under way, the "prairie problem" began to be corrected, but inconsistently. The Santa Fé trader Josiah Gregg's 1844 memoir equivocates about whether the southern Plains are "sterile" or really desirable for U.S. settlement, although Gregg attempts to convert some of the very features of the region once imagined as freakish into positives. The prairie mirage, according to Gregg, is "yet another exemplification of its [the region's] purity." The "constant alarms" offered by hostile Indians "serve to keep one constantly on the alert and to sharpen those faculties of observation which would otherwise become blunted . . . ." The air itself is so "sanative" that even the most brutal surgery (an amputation Gregg describes with sensationalistic relish) has an immediately successful result. [46] As Gregg attests, he himself was one of many invalids who in the 1830s were sent down the Santa Fé trail in a last-ditch attempt at recovery—and Gregg's personal recovery, like the later recovery narratives of the famously robust invalids Owen Wister and Theodore Roosevelt, confirms the broader image of the desert West as a space of regeneration. In the 1840s such fantasies of the almost literal extension of the national body into the Great Plains were more common. Stephen H. Long had little access to this more optimistic nationalist cant in 1820, and he echoed almost to the letter Pike's assertion of ten years earlier when he recommended to John C. Calhoun that the Plains be recognized only as "a frontier . . . of infinite importance to the United States, inasmuch as it is calculated to serve as a barrier to prevent too great an extension of our population westward." [47] Paradoxically, the same era that produced John Quincy Adams's transcontinental line to the Pacific imagined "too great an extension" of the United States' population as potentially destructive to the Union.

Calhoun was one of several political figures in the mid-1820s who recognized in Thomas Jefferson's idea of the creation of the Great Plains as an "Indian Territory" a means by which the United States could possess the continent without settling it. The recommendation that the prairie deserts best served "nomadic" Native American populations had been reiterated to Calhoun by Long, but Indian Territory, along with the related project of the removal of all American Indians to a supposedly permanent colony in the mid-continent, had long been a desirable solution to perceived problems of white American consolidation. Far from unmarked norms, whiteness and an idealized U.S./Americanness seem to function as besieged territory in the debates around Indian Removal. In a never-published Constitutional amendment treating the Louisiana Purchase, Thomas Jefferson had given the legislature power to trade white settlers' claims west of the Mississippi for comparable claims on the river's eastern shore;[48] Jefferson was willing to force the consolidation of white settlements east of the Mississippi to insure stronger national boundaries. But the rhetorics of white containment and its complements, Indian Removal and resettlement, were always undermined by expansionist ambitions driven by land hunger and disregard for Native American interests. The very year, 1825, that John C. Calhoun submitted his bill to Congress advocating the creation of a "permanent" Indian territory "for themselves and their posterity," he also sent a team of surveyors to mark the Santa Fé Trail, which he hoped might be linked to the old Cumberland road from the Atlantic coast to create a great national highway.[49] These dreams in the 1820s of elaborate roads uniting the Atlantic seaboard with the Mexican territories of the Far West were enacted, on the ground, by white traders and later settlers who moved into Indian Territory, making that geopolitical concept, in its purest form, a dull embarrassment as early as the 1840s.

Movements to formally define an Indian Territory and promote a pan-Indian territorial government were repeatedly struck down by politicians, many of them Southerners, who, as Reginald Horsman has noted, feared that the incorporation of one non-white state into the Union would lead to the incorporation of others, such as Haiti or the free-black settlements of Canada.[50] The Civil War provided Northern politicians with an opportunity to renegotiate and diminish Indian Territory, as the Five Civilized Tribes (the Cherokees, Chickasaws, Choctaws, Creeks, and Seminoles) had reluctantly sided with the Confederacy. In the 1890s, the allotment program presided over by the Dawes Commission dissolved tribal ownership of lands and erased the very small "Indian Territory" that remained, in what is now Oklahoma. When in 1905 leaders of the Five Civilized Tribes drew up a constitution and asked to be admitted to the Union as the state of Sequoyah, their last-bid attempt at corporate government within the United States was summarily refused, and the idea of an Indian state formally killed. In fact, officially Indian Territory had always been defined negatively and in contradictory terms, just as American Indians themselves are defined by the Constitution of the United States as both foreign nations and a domestic, intracontinental "problem." [51] Indian Territory was destined to remain a (shrinking) territory within the central United States that was neither a sovereign foreign nation nor a legitimate domestic polity. [52]

The development of the idea of Indian Territory and the familiar rhetoric of arguments for Indian Removal in the 1820s and 1830s are worth reconsidering, if only to elaborate how the presence of an imagined Great Desert in the middle of North America helped to create "Indians" and European Americans as distinct nations and races. The idea of precarious or imperfect possession that informs James Fenimore Cooper's representations of his protagonists' failed settlement of Nebraska in The Prairie was similarly expressed, in the 1820s and 1830s, by advocates of Indian Removal to describe American Indians' precarious hold on territories *east* of the Mississippi. These advocates of removal suggested that the Indians, as they referred to all Native American nations, were naturally suited to arid lands they did not yet occupy—the desert West fortuitously presented itself as the Indians' proper territorial state.

Senator John Elliot of Georgia, advocating John C. Calhoun's 1825 Indian Territory bill on the Senate floor, argued that the "tract of country lying between the Arkansas and Missouri rivers" swarmed with game and was a paradise for Indian hunters: "Nature could hardly have formed a country more fitted to such a purpose [colonization by the Indians]." [53] Moreover, Elliot concedes, "it is a part of the country which will not answer to our [white America's] purposes of social intercourse and compact settlement." [54] William Cooper, James Fenimore Cooper's father and one of the first settlers of the colonial "west" of New York, founded John Elliot's assumptions about the environmental needs of white pioneers in his classic blueprint for Euro-American settlement, A Guide in the Wilderness (1808). Like Senator Elliot, William Cooper had asserted that European Americans thrive only in very specific social and spatial conditions; they require "condensation," so town-builders should limit settlers' lot sizes whether the settlers like it or not. [55] Senator Elliot appears quite troubled to find William Cooper's model of Euro-American "compact settlement," itself a variation on the plan of the seventeenth-century theocratic communities of New England, in the Indian reservations of his native Georgia—and nowhere else in that rather haphazardly settled state. It is the nature of these reservations as compact, Euro-American-style settlements with all the amenities of "civilization" that piques Elliot. Elliot comments on the unsuitedness of well-ordered reservations to the southeastern tribes; he refers particularly to the Cherokee. The Senator is sure that, living so much like their white neighbors should be living—and aren't—the Cherokee must be terribly unhappy, "surrounded, as they are at this time, by a white population, and improved by roads, and other facilities of intercourse with the adjacent country." [56] Cherokee advocates of assimilation, like Elias Boudinot, editor of the tribal newspaper the *Cherokee Phoenix*, noted the heavy irony in this kind of paternalistic critique. In an 1831 editorial for the *Phoenix*, Boudinot wrote: "The policy of the United States on Indian affairs has taken a different direction, for no other reason than that the Cherokees have so far become civilized as to appreciate a regular form of government." [57]

Many politicians pushing Indian Removal followed John Elliot in identifying the deterioration of Indian character with the condition of being "surrounded" by white Americans and compactly settled like white Americans were supposed to be. "So true is this position," Senator Elliot argued, "that, while you can scarcely point to a nation of Indians wasting away . . . in their native wilderness, I know of no tribes within the states, surrounded by a white population, who have not declined." [58] Elliot's analysis uses the spatial metaphor of proximity between Indians and whites to express the more familiar claim that American Indians have very little *time* left as unassimilated, living cultures. "I am brought to the conclusion, that two independent communities of people, differing in color, language, habits, and interest, cannot long subsist together—but that the more intelligent and powerful will always destroy the other." [59] Similarly, Lewis Cass, governor of Michigan Territory and secretary of war under Andrew Jackson, compared the effect of an adjacent white population upon Indian tribes to that of an "incubus" sucking their lives away. [60] In his Second Annual Message to Congress, Andrew Jackson argued that Removal would free Indians from the metaphorical toxicity of willful state governments: "It will separate them from immediate contact with settlements of whites; free them from the power of the States; enable them to pursue happiness in their own way. . . ." [61] In

Notions of the Americans (1828), James Fenimore Cooper uses metaphors of proximity and contagion to describe the incorporation of the Five Civilized Tribes within the United States ("some of the southern tribes have already endured collision with the white man," "there is just ground to hope that the dangerous point of communication has been passed," and so on). [62] Here whiteness figures as disease, moving across space and destroying healthy distances between national populations.

Perhaps less surprisingly, Plains Indian accounts of the history of white-Indian contact also image Euro-Americans as disease, specifically the small-pox, measles, whooping cough, and cholera that were introduced to Plains Indians with Euro-American contact and trade. As Colin Calloway notes in his analysis of the Yanktonai Sioux Lone Dog's pictographic historical chronicle or "winter count," Euro-Americans play a minor role in Yanktonai historical reckoning of the period from 1800 to 1871, where whites appear only in seven references to trade and four references to disease. Pictographic symbols of smallpox, whooping cough, measles, and horseshoes commemorate the major period of white invasion. [63] The Yanktonai seem to have had a more pragmatic response to the "incubus" that Cooper and Cass can describe only metaphorically, without making reference to the European pathogens introduced to Native America. Kiowa legend also includes a figure of Euro-America called Smallpox—a pocked white man riding a black horse. [64]

For a time, the Great American Desert appeared as a solution to all crises of racial health. Like other advocates of Indian Removal, James Fenimore Cooper imagined racial health in geographical terms, arguing, for instance, that Indians *craved openness*, so where better to place them than in the seemingly unbounded prairies of the Great American Desert? "As you recede from the Mississippi," Cooper argues in *Notions of the Americans*, "the finer traits of savage life become visible and, although most of the natives of the Prairies, even there, are far from being the interesting and romantic heroes that poets love to paint, there are specimens of loftiness of spirit . . . to be found among the chiefs. . . ." [65] Cooper, Lewis Cass, and John Elliot all posit the inland deserts as a site of perennial recuperation for Indians, a retreat from white contagion. These arguments in favor of Indian Removal conveniently de-historicize the Great Plains, sidestepping the fact that the supposedly pure culture of the Plains nations of the seventeenth and eighteenth centuries developed in conjunction with Spanish, French, and British trading concerns in that region. The apparently natural and healthy "nomadism" of many Plains nations had been encouraged by European commercial interest in animal skins, captives, and precious metals that might circulate, through the Indians, from Spanish or Mexican territories toward the European settlements of the North.

The popular image of American Indians as nomads made it easier to argue that they should be confined to arid lands that could not be farmed, but the "nomad" idea proved problematic insofar as it equated a prized trait of Euro-American culture, mobility, with a presumed weakness of Indian racial character. In an influential article for the *North American Review*, "Removal of the Indians" (1830), Lewis Cass offers nomadism as the great paradox of American Indian existence; in Cass's view, Indian cultural paralysis is reinforced by a paralyzed native economy based in constant physical movement, the pursuit of game. Always moving, literally, the Indians never stood still long enough to "grow up." Advocates of Removal overlooked the potentially destructive energy of the nomad paradox (excessive physical movement equals cultural stasis), the fact that it might be used to describe white nomadism, too, as not "progressive." But some U.S. politicians recognized the problem. James Barbour, secretary of war under John Quincy Adams and one of the few politicians who took a genuine interest in Indian affairs, defined indigenous "nomadism" as white land hunger. In his remarkably cynical and self-accusatory "Bill for the Preservation and Civilization of the Indian Tribes," written in 1826, Barbour argues, "some of them [the Indians] have reclaimed the forest, planted their orchards, and erected houses, not only for their abode, but for the administration of justice and for religious worship; and when they have so done, you send your agent to tell them they must surrender their country to the white man, and recommit themselves to some new desert, and substitute, as the means of their subsistence, the precarious chase for the certainties of cultivation." Barbour's policy for allotment of property to individual American Indians rather than to tribes appears to be a reflection of his profound distrust of white "barbarians." "The individual appropriation of land gives a sanctity to the title which inspires respect in *nations the most barbarous*. It would repress, *with us*, any thought of disturbing it" (emphasis mine). [66]

Barbour's enthusiasm for allotment marks him as a proponent of Indian improvability and individual progress rather than the more rigid racialist thought that began to dominate the U.S. scene after the 1820s. The anxious necessity of reimagining American Indians as a single race, alike in capability and need, is evident in Lewis Cass's influential ethnological speculations of the 1830s, which accompany his arguments for Removal and implicitly support the policy. Arguing from current knowledge of the origin of American Indian languages east of the Mississippi from four linguistic stocks, Cass concludes that all Native peoples are "in all the essential characteristics of mind, manners, and appearance . . . one people."[67] This essentially linguistic definition of "a people" suggests Romantic concepts of national *geist* in which a nation's character is said to derive from its language and climate; the Romantic notion of the *Volk*, underpinned by older theories of the relation between climate and racial character, helped U.S. politicians justify the removal of American Indians from lands over which they were supposed to have "a very imperfect possession"[68] to lands environmentally "fitted" to them. Even Zebulon Pike had remarked, in an albeit half-hearted attempt at anthropological speculation: "We know that the manners and morals of the erratic nations are such (the reasons I leave to be given by the ontologists) as never to give them a numerous population; and I believe there are buffalo, elk, and deer sufficient on the banks of the Arkansas alone, if used without waste, to feed all the savages in the United States one century."[69] As in early modern climate theory, here the idea of the homeland and the idea of the *Volk* mutually create one another. "In this situation," John Elliot concludes as he imagines the southeastern tribes pushed out of their stifling, compact towns and onto the Great Plains, "all the wants of such a people will be provided for."[70]

Even non-traditionalist American Indians like Elias Boudinot did not cherish the Great American Desert for its essential fittedness to American Indian lifestyles. Boudinot's promotion of the Cherokee language and literacy (an unsurprising stance, given his editorship of the bilingual *Phoenix*) suggests the Romantic association of language with national character, yet his nationalism was not really racialized (it did not include, as some whites fantasized, "all Indians"), nor was it specifically linked to any landscape. After Andrew Jackson's obstruction of Supreme Court decisions in favor of Cherokee interests (particularly the 1832 *Worcester v. Georgia* case), Boudinot merely realized that, in order to survive as a corporate body, his people had to move. Perhaps his enthusiasm for the Cherokee syllabary allowed him to conceive of nationhood as potentially portable, even to a place as unappealing as the desert West. At any rate, Boudinot's major mistake was to trust the promise of Native American sovereignty implied in the 1835 Treaty of New Echota, which he signed and was later murdered for signing since it violated an 1829 Cherokee law prohibiting the cession of tribal lands. Boudinot's rival for leadership among the Cherokee, the traditionalist John Ross, was less naïve, but also less effective in his negotiations with the United States.[71] Ross asked the federal government to pay for Cherokee lands with either full citizenship for the Cherokee or enough money to move them far beyond the continental ambitions of the United States, perhaps into Mexico.

Largely unconcerned with real American Indian interests, white advocates of Indian Removal created "the Indians" as a nation at a sub-governmental, emotional level; they created "one people" of the Indians at a time when it was beginning to be feared that the scattered populations of whites in the United States would not coalesce. Indian Removal responded to Euro-American perceptions of whiteness as lacking a bounded territory—of whiteness as a racial marker of self-interested, de-centering mobility. The state of Georgia had presented the federal government with the possibility of secession in 1827 over the issue of the removal of the Cherokee, which the federal government had promised to expedite as early as 1802.[72] The 1821 Missouri Compromise and the debates leading up to it indicated the growing disparity between slave-owning and non-slave-owning interests in the United States and the possibility of Southern secession.[73] The problem of "local interest," as James Fenimore Cooper identified it in 1828, already presented a serious threat to the Union in the 1820s. "It is plain that the people of a country in which there is so great a diversity of soil and climate must pursue different employments," Cooper remarked, adding hopefully, "[I]s not this fact rather a motive of harmony than of dissension?"

Really, Cooper argued, in 1828 "the ordeal of the durability of the union" had "passed."[74] He was willing to suggest to the European, primarily British audience he addressed in *Notions of the Americans* that: "The spirit of greatness is in this nation: its means are within its grasp. . . ." Still, and here *Notions* flirts with ambivalence, national greatness depended, apparently, upon a condensation of "industry, art, capital" which had not fully occurred. "Until now the Americans have been tracing the outline of their great national picture," Cooper writes elsewhere in *Notions*. "The work of filling up has just seriously commenced. The Gulph [sic] of Mexico, the Lakes of Canada, the Prairies, the Atlantic, form the setting. They are now, in substance, a vast island, and the tide of emigration, which has so long been flowing westward, must have its reflux."[75] The return of Cooper's settler-protagonists to the eastern shores of the Mississippi in *The Prairie* enacts the white reflux that he hoped would guarantee a robust national future.

What was an imaginable destiny for the Great American Desert in the 1820s—a permanent Indian Territory and, potentially, an Indian State to complement and reinforce the confederated States of white America—perversely resurfaces in Cooper's later historical romance, The Oak Openings (1848), as the pathological fantasy of an American Indian villain named Scalping Peter. Peter is "an Indian without a tribe" who moves through the narrative brandishing a ceremonial scalping pole that supports seven white scalps that flutter like living flags. Exemplary of the one-race notion that justified federal attempts to relocate Indians to an appropriate "desert" homeland, Peter's familiarity with and honorary membership in a variety of tribes between the Great Lakes and the Arkansas River allows him to begin, Tecumseh-like, a pan-Indian confederation. Peter's Indian nation threatens to annihilate, rather than consolidate, white American settlements. Only his unlikely conversion to evangelical Protestantism—an ungainly plot device that surfaces halfway through the novel—prevents him from achieving his aims with the help of British forces on hand for the War of 1812, the novel's historical setting. In a novel that forcefully and simplistically defends Manifest Destiny, Cooper naturally recognizes the danger of racialized nationalism in the wrong hands. But given the historical period that this later novel treats, the years immediately preceding the War of 1812, Cooper might have stifled Scalping Peter's anti-white confederation by more realistic means than a snap conversion. In this period, and for many years after it, the thriving trading cultures in the mid-continent encouraged the competition rather than consolidation of Native American communities. This local but internationally driven economy was another dimension of the Great Desert that assured its continual resistance to both U.S. nationalism and a sovereign pan-Indian state.

Precarious Possessions (II)

The deep topic of Cooper's The Prairie is precisely the relationship between the resistant landscape of the Great American Desert and the resiliently international economy it has fostered, namely the fur trade and its satellites, the traffic in horses and women. What is surprising about The Prairie is that its unlikely plot resolutions do not easily support the national mythos and are realistically in keeping with the suspended destiny of its setting. In this sense The Prairie is a highly unusual historical romance, given that historical romances of the 1830s through the 1850s typically resolve contemporary political problems by displacing them onto a deep past in which

53

similar problems have already been conclusively worked out. As I have implied throughout this chapter, this historical romance actually entertains the possibility that a geopolitical entity other than the United States, or *any* single nation, will thrive at the approximate center of the North American continent. Richard Slotkin recognizes *The Prairie*'s importance as a "post-frontier" novel reflecting an historical moment, from approximately 1819 to 1840, when territorial acquisition was temporarily stalled and the frontier was, erroneously, believed to be closing.[76] For me, Slotkin's qualifier "post-frontier" suggests not only a time-bound and mistaken knowledge about when and where U.S. expansion would end, but also a way of thinking that moves beyond binaristic "frontierism" to consider other directions of cultural movement and alternate notions of progress. Cooper's post-frontier perspective in *The Prairie* temporarily forces him out of continentalism and allows him to imagine the lively socioeconomic scene of the Great Plains in a manner that seems to anticipate contemporary theories of transnational networks of sovereignty and economic desire.

The pragmatic, functional culture of *The Prairie* defies the progressive emphases of the historical romance as Cooper typically employed the genre, following Sir Walter Scott. For Cooper, the Plains are not readily allied to a distant and therefore microcosmic past but to a persistent present where the war is still on—a present which perpetually fails to engender a *national* future. Cooper's treatment of Plains Natives in *The Prairie* lacks the directed nostalgia (their "doom" is not yet sealed) associated with, for example, Francis Parkman's romantic histories or with Cooper's own representations of American Indians in the earlier Leatherstocking novels, *The Pioneers* and *The Last of the Mohicans*. The novel is proto-anthropological in its insistence that apparently irrational and personal behaviors are socially and economically functional, if "primitive." The purportedly Indian passion for vengeance is de-emphasized here. Cooper's recognition of his setting as both a local world and the representative scene of international economic contention makes *The Prairie* kin to narratives which feature mercantile or piratical ships, like Richard Henry Dana, Jr.'s *Two Years before the Mast*, Daniel Defoe's *Robinson Crusoe*, and Cooper's own classic sea novel *The Red-Rover*. The ship-worlds of those narratives represent temporary and highly contingent social orders adrift in the palpably international and legally indeterminate space of the sea. To Cooper, as to Melville in *Moby-Dick*, the Great Plains resemble the ocean, and not merely in the simplistic visual sense that both appear as vast, undulating landscapes. In The Prairie Cooper suggests the similar sociopolitical meaning and feel of the Great Desert and the sea, each a field of economic endeavor and risk, each a region of international contention that falls outside the jurisdiction of any single state, and each an instigator of the non-judgmental, premoral sense of wonder.

Cooper begins The Prairie by signaling the inappropriateness of his setting as a U.S./American place. While The Pioneers and The Last of the Mohicans immediately present a traditional landscape or scene, The Prairie begins with an allusion to a scene, the Plains, through a reflection of the political goals of the Louisiana Purchase. Immediately Cooper suggests that the social import of the Purchase is unresolved, and he is liberal in his rendering of the many things that it could represent: "a barrier of desert," "the property of a rival," or, "if ever time or necessity shall require" it, a "peaceful division of this vast empire." [77] The Louisiana Purchase is the metaexchange that frames the novel's plot, which proceeds through a series of smaller exchanges. Every exchange, Cooper suggests, is a species of risk whose value will remain suspended. The principle of exchange suggests an iterative rather than progressive temporality; it resists evolutionary schema or "endings." The incompatibility between the structural principle of exchange and nationalist rhetorics is suggested in the novel by Hard Heart, the young chief of the Pawnee Loups. "And where were the Pawnee Loups when this bargain [the Louisiana Purchase] was made?" Hard Heart asks Natty Bumppo. "Is a nation to be sold like the skin of a beaver?" [78] Hard Heart's double allusion to the Louisiana Purchase and the fur trade suggests both the exploitation of Plains Natives and the more general problem of how any idea of the nation can survive in a landscape defined by casual, often injudicious barter. We might reconsider that what really makes the Great Plains, in William Cullen Bryant's terms, a "meager" setting is that here nothing remains in its place. Skins, lands, persons all can be traded, with the value of each changing, repeatedly, over time.

The great symptom in the romance of this problem of indiscriminate exchange versus the consolidation of a nation or social world involves the idea of inheritance. Cooper makes it clear that he sees inheritance as untenable on the Plains. Despite his acid critique of primogeniture in The American Democrat, Cooper, as can be readily observed in the two Leatherstocking novels prior to The Prairie, favored the inheritance plot as an engine of novelistic action. Bess, in The Pioneers, is unequivocally an heiress, and is even called "the heiress," while Oliver Edwards is a displaced heir; their marriage and the restitution of Edwards's (né Effingham's) claim is the novel's broadest story. In The Last of the Mohicans, Uncas's return to the Turtle Clan of the Delaware and his reinstitution to the inherited role of clan chief involves essentially a re-working of the Effingham plot. It is only much later, in The Oak Openings, that Cooper begins to associate Indians with a different kind of plot, when he imagines a tribal council of Scalping Peter's anti-white coalition as an example of the kind of Jacksonian public he came to despise, a public swayed by the wheedling of demagogues rather than the reason of gentlemen. Cooper's earlier association of American Indians with gentlemen had allowed him to argue comfortably for Indian rights on the premise that Indian land was an aristocratic inheritance usurped by class-climbing settlers.

The formative role allowed the inheritance plot in Cooper's earlier Leatherstocking novels leaves him at a loss in The Prairie, given that he imagines the region he describes in this novel as what he calls an "empty empire" productive of no real property, nothing to inherit. William Cullen Bryant's remark that the novel's setting is insufficient ("here and there a few bushes in the hollows, a single heap of rocks, and a river") includes the idea that without arable land, liberal civilization and, presumably, the historical romance, cannot develop. "If you have come in search of land," Natty warns the Bushes, "you have journeyed hundreds of miles too far, or as many leagues too little."[79] But the Bush family's perverse disinterest in settlement is one of the novel's many peculiar surprises. Run out of Tennessee for shooting a sheriff who prosecuted him for an illegal land claim, Ishmael Bush is a composite, contradictory figure: the speculator, absentee landlord, and struggling peasant.

Bush's primitive communism, expressed in his oracular pronouncement that "the air, the water, the ground are free gifts of man, and no one has the power to portion them out in parcels," suggests an idea of legacy now associated with the romanticized "Ecological Indian," in Shepherd Krech's current term.[80] In fact, the Sauk leader Black Hawk makes an almost identical remark in J. B. Patterson's 1834 Autobiography of Black Hawk.[81] But when Bush chides his eldest son with the reminder that "few fathers portion their children better than Ishmael Bush," he is not initiating a discussion of usufruct; rather, the settler argues that he can write his son a deed for any land because, while he is interested in property, he is not interested in the restrictions placed upon it by his social betters. Bush's invention of a unique idea of negative property or *unlettered* property that resists the mechanisms of law—and inadvertently resists the social privilege of inheritance—places him in the ranks of those "climbing" settlers whom Cooper despised, men like the irate tenants of the infamous Rent Wars that divided New York in the 1840s. But in the context of the Plains, Cooper, usually a spokesman for the landed classes, actually approaches Bush's position. After all, "the surrounding country offered so little that was tempting to the cupidity of speculation, and if possible, still less that was flattering to the hopes of an ordinary settler of new lands." [82] Without lands that can be worked up into real property, the Plains obscure the difference between ownership and usurpation or theft.

The absence of the retrospective-projective mechanism of inheritance on the Plains means that all alliances in this region will be apparently nonproductive, or at least they will not produce what was to be the United States' fundamentally agrarian narrative of origin. In a "landless" context, purchase or exchange and theft emerge as equally valid means for establishing social ties. The equalization of the terms "trade" and "theft" in *The Prairie* betrays its debt to its primary source, Edwin James's account of the Stephen H. Long Expedition, insofar as that narrative depicts the experience of Plains Natives as have many anthropological monographs since, in terms of a controlling metaphor of exchange which includes both positive and negative reciprocity as socially functional behaviors. *The Prairie's* play with the scarcely perceptible distinction between "trade" and "theft" in the American Desert constitutes one of its particularly prescient additions to the expansionist rhetoric of its own era; in this socioeconomic problem we can see a dim forecast of Patricia Limerick's recasting of westward expansion as the struggle "to wrap the concept of property around unwieldy objects" and the equally difficult struggle to differentiate between the rights of squatters and thieves. [83] Later century narratives like John Rollin Ridge's *Life of Joaquin Murieta* (1854) or María Amparo Ruiz de Burton's *The Squatter and the Don* (1885) deliver more politically informed critiques of the misuse of the default "right of prior claim" exercised by Anglo settlers in California, where the United States' frustration of Mexican land titles made questions of property ownership a particularly tortured subject. But Cooper tentatively raises the problem of what a "squatter" is, and how squatters betray the apparent sanctity of the United States' settlement culture. When Ishmael Bush and his family are robbed of their cattle and horses by the Dacotah, Natty explains to Bush, "I do not call them robbers, for it is the usage of their people, and what may be called prairie law." Bush's reply, "I have come five hundred miles to find a place where no man can ding the words of the law in my ears," proves him to be more with the Sioux than against them.[84] It is only robbery's status as a regulative principle that disturbs the settler. Bush's use of the word "plunder" to denote his personal effects suggests that theft is normative for these white nomads. Cooper focuses the reader's attention on this figure of speech by nervously explaining it as merely a quaint regional usage—he actually discovered the phrase in James Hall's "Letters from the West."

The Prairie presents the dissolution of the difference between the terms theft and trade as a product of the vigorous commercial culture of the Plains. Although Cooper may not have known exactly how much the international market for animal skins drove this regional culture, he does choose to restyle the Leatherstocking in this novel as "a miserable trapper," in Natty Bumppo's own terms. "The art of taking the creatur's of God in traps and nets is one that needs more cunning than manhood," Natty laments, "and yet am I brought to practice it in my age."[85] Although the necessity of trapping appears to arise from Bumppo's infirmity, he also admits that, again, "I know of but one business that can be followed here [on the Plains] with profit."[86] Recall that it was the association of trapping with profit that encouraged the Leatherstocking to travel to the Great Lakes at the end of The Pioneers, when, for the first time in his life, he needed money—to clear the two-hundred-dollar fine which Judge Temple had imposed upon him and then paid in his stead. Being a trapper is both "miserable" and necessary, even "profitable," on the Plains because these prairie deserts cannot support the kind of narrative of skill which previously defined the Leatherstocking's relationship to his landscape. On yet another level, the Plains thwart inheritance and its ideological implications for white America: Natty cannot inherit the Plains through virtuoso performances of "savage" skills like hunting, sighting, and tracking. If trapping beaver and even the trading of skins that implicitly occurs outside of the novel's scene of action are skills associated with Plains Natives, these skills, because they describe a process of commodification, do not readily connect either American Indian or white characters to the ground; they do not imply the resistance and conquering of matter that, according to Slotkin, typically links the conventional "hunter's story" to agrarian ideology.

Nor is The Prairie a novel based in the self-justifying Anglo-American accounts of Indian fighting which bolstered the self-confidence of the early republic. Cooper realizes that a Sioux raid on the settlers' horses and cattle that occurs early in the novel cannot be described in the hot, racially-charged terms of vengeance, because it is so clearly a symptom of economic self-interest if not, precisely, prairie law. Whether or not Cooper knew that horse-raiding represented a satellite to the fur-trading economy of the Plains, nevertheless his inclusion of such a raid as a primary symptom of the region's functional "law" is telling. On the Plains in the period Cooper describes, horses were a kind of universal commodity or money, both because everyone could use one—especially when buffalo hunting for the robe trade became a crucial economic activity—and because horses could be gotten, or stolen, anywhere. By the late eighteenth century the horse raid had become the primary form of warfare amongst Plains Natives. Such warfare was conducted amongst Native American nations and also practiced upon whites, and it was smaller in scale and more geared toward individual profit than traditional Plains wars. Status for the horse-raider consisted in the number of horses he could take. Persons who obtained many horses could and typically did make them available for trade, which was regulated by tribal chiefs. Raids facilitated the circulation of horses from centers of supply in the Spanish or Mexican Southwest to centers of demand across the Plains all the way to Upper Canada. The horse raider's stolen capital ultimately benefited international markets as well as his particular tribe. [87] As Cooper seems to have known or at least intuited from the sources he used for The Prairie, Native Americans on the Plains were not, in this period, simply at war, but rather enmeshed in a powerful economy. This economy was, again, both local and international, as it began and ended in European and Asian markets where beaver and later buffalo hides were extremely desirable commodities.

National Anti-Bodies

Cooper explores the tension among regional, national, and international interests on the North American Plains through the highly unusual captivity narrative that is embedded within The Prairie, the peculiar story of how the Spanish Creole, Inez de Certavallos, is kidnapped by the squatters. Three other well-known captivity narratives from the years that precede the first great wave of U.S. migration to Oregon, including the pamphlet novelist E. House's A Narrative of the Captivity of Mrs. Sarah Ann Horn (1839), Timothy Flint's Personal Narrative of James O. Pattie (1831), and Zebulon Pike's exploration diaries, also use captivity as a device to test the feasibility of U.S.

settlement of the continent's inland deserts. These narratives treat distinct locales and distinct geo-political issues. Inez de Certavallos's captivity begins in New Orleans and ends in what is now Nebraska, Horn is taken in the Republic of Texas and winds up in Saint Louis, Pattie, a Kentuckian, is imprisoned in San Diego after years of trapping and trading across the Rockies and Plains, and Pike is captured by Mexican officials after illegally crossing into Spanish territory on the upper Rio Grande River. Each of these narratives takes an unconventional approach to the captivity genre that belies radical doubt about the limits and sanctity of the United States' national body in the Far West. In fact, the captives in these narratives could be said to represent anti-(national) bodies that repulse expansionist designs and prove the absolute incompatibility of the United States with arid, resiliently international western territories. Here we find not only unredeemed captives, but captives made to signify the impossibility of their redemption and restoration to a recognizable national or racial polity. The relatively broad geographical range represented in these narratives is useful because it reveals the extent to which the "prairie problem," as Zebulon Pike called the resistant scene he imagined on the Great Plains, contributed to the imaging of other western deserts, like southern California.

The cultural work of captivity narrative is typically imagined in the terms Roy Harvey Pearce established over a half-century ago.[88] The narratives are, rightly enough, seen as justifications for hostility against Native Americans and for the larger project of imperial expansion because they portray the vulnerability of frontier families to "savages" whose inhumanity renders them expendable. Christopher Castiglia's recent feminist rereading of the captivity genre highlights the importance of the white female body in particular as a means of defining a national symbolic and the potential threat of female captives who, in his terms, "articulate a 'hybrid' subjectivity," adopting attributes of their captors.[89] Not surprisingly, the problem of the imperfectly national captive is particularly evident in narratives set in places that had long been subject to conflicting geopolitical claims.

One of the largest symptoms of Cooper's indecisiveness about the meaning of the "vast tracts" of the Louisiana Territory is his choice to tell a story of a Spanish American, or Creole, held hostage by U.S. citizens. This most obvious racial-national reversal, which indicates that the reader's sympathies are to be directed toward the Creole, Inez de Certavallos, and away from the squatters, is complicated by the fact that Inez is either literally or virtually invisible throughout the narrative. Inez cannot be seen by anyone save her captors, the Bushes and their kin, when she is hidden in their tent for the first quarter of the novel. She is absurdly described by her captors as a "decoy" of an exotic species of animal that has been brought onto the dry prairies to attract others of its kind. When Inez finally emerges from the confining and deliberately eroticized "folds" of the squatters' tent, she remains even more visually improbable than Cooper's typically lifeless heroines. He writes:

> Her person was of the smallest size that is believed to comport with beauty, and which poets and artists have chosen as the *beau ideal* of female loveliness. Her dress was of a dark and glossy silk and fluttered like gossamer around her form. Long, flowing, and curling tresses of hair, still blacker and more shining than her robe, fell at times about her shoulders, completely enveloping the whole of her delicate bust in their ringlets, or at others, streaming in the wind. The elevation at which she stood prevented a close examination of the lineaments of a countenance. . . ."[90]

And fortunately so, I might add, because it is almost painful to imagine Cooper attempting to render the woman's face with the same emphases on visual indeterminacy—excessive miniaturization, movement, and shimmer—that inform his description of her dress and hair.

Of course Inez's virtual invisibility hinders our sympathy, transforming her body into a mystery which may seem consonant with Cooper's conventional portrayals of racially indeterminate heroines like Cora in *Last of the Mohicans*. But although Inez, like Cora, attracts the attentions of American Indian men intuitively drawn to her racial charge, the difficulty of visualizing her also makes her the most ethereal, or least sexualized, woman in *The Prairie*. The robust Nelly Wade and Paul Hover, Anglos both, are more clearly a physical couple than Inez and the dour Middleton, who, again, appear as unlikely representatives of gentility adrift in a climate inhospitable to class. Yet Cooper does not treat Inez with the respect conventionally due his saccharine "females."[91] He does not limit the reader's perspective to that of her chivalrous husband. Natty Bumppo pokes into the folds of Inez's tent. Obed Bat, the scientist who has accompanied the squatters onto the Plains, speculates about whether the "beast" in the tent is of the two- or four-legged variety. The squatter's jealous wife even voices a suspicion of Inez's sexual availability: "the man is in that tent ag'in! more than half his time is spent about the worthless, good-for-nothing!"[92] Inez is at once the most genteel female in the novel and its surrogate slave, vulnerable to both the Jezebel myth and pseudoscientific speculations about polygenesis or distinct racial species. Given that Inez is actually kidnapped by a slave trader in the squatter's family, it is likely that Cooper intended her captivity as, among other things, a test case for the idea of the extension of slavery into far western territories.

Inez's almost ridiculous multiplicity, as a figuratively black/white, Spanish/American, lady, slave, wife, and (possibly) whore, makes it clear that Cooper was not yet willing to limit his imagination about what kind of Euro-American culture would be brought into lands west of the Mississippi. Inez's body delimits nothing in particular and suggests both how easily imperial anxieties were sexualized and how open was the image of the putatively "white" woman in the Far West. We can easily see the equation of female pioneers with a belated nationalization of western territories in twentieth-century histories that seize upon the 1836 journey of Narcissa Whitman across the Plains as (at last!) "the coming of the white women" and the domestication of the continent. Josiah Gregg eagerly contended, as have more reputable chroniclers since, that white women traveled across the Plains before Mrs. Whitman. Gregg mentions the "extraordinary" presence of "a Spanish family" including women and "two respectable French ladies" among the caravan that carried him from St. Louis to Santa Fé in 1831.[93] The fact that these women are Creoles does not diminish, for him, the implicit (white) racial claim that their early presence establishes in the region. With less fanfare, Edwin James remarked Manuel Lisa's Creole wife, whom he met during the Long Expedition's 1819–20 travels on the Plains, as possibly the first white woman in the Far West. Susan Shelby Magoffin, who traveled the Santa Fé Trail with her trader husband in 1846, recognized that the novelty of white womanhood actually offered local New Mexicans a pleasure akin to that of a freak exhibition: "a 'monkey show' in the States never did a better business than he [my husband] could have done, if he had set me up at even dos or tres reals."[94]

The semi-autobiographical captivity narrative of Mrs. Sarah Ann Horn, an Englishwoman who accompanied her husband to settle in the Republic of Texas in the 1830s, suggests just how radically detached from static racial or national meanings "white womanhood" was while Mrs. Horn remained in the southern Plains, from roughly 1833 to 1838. The Horn narrative was published in St. Louis as a pamphlet novel by a hack writer, E. House, who claims to have taken dictation from Mrs. Horn. The narrative's correspondence to what is historically known of the Horn captivity suggests that House either really knew Mrs. Horn or knew what sorts of details to expect from such history. In the narrative, Mrs. Horn recalls being mistaken for a Texan by General Santa Anna's army and called "American" by both the Comanche and Spanish settlers; House suggests that she was almost as indistinct and contradictorily meaningful to her various captors as the character Inez is to Cooper. Mrs. Horn's ability to speak Spanish humanizes her, somewhat, to the Comanche who are fluent in this language, but Mexican fellow captives look upon her with suspicion. Yet a Mexican gentleman buys her from the Comanche and generously welcomes her into his home, while a wealthy U.S. citizen virtually kidnaps her and sets her to work as his menial servant.

As Castiglia aptly remarks, Mrs. Horn's captivity is a prime illustration of how female captives remained virtual captives, even after they had been released from Indian bondage, to men intent upon controlling their actions and self-representations.[95] But Mrs. Horn's narrative should be more carefully historicized, given that the trading of female captives had become a significant economic activity within the larger trading culture of the Plains by the 1830s. Comanche raids on women of the Spanish settlements date back to at least the eighteenth century, but many other Plains nations entered into this international trade in captives as the market for buffalo hides grew hotter. The preparation of hides was time-consuming, and it was culturally designated as women's work, so as the pressure to produce hides increased, the need for female laborers increased with it. Female captives, many of whom would be ultimately incorporated into polygynous households, performed this newly necessary labor.[96] Mrs. Horn, like Rachel Plummer, another woman taken captive by the Comanche in this period, reports being forced to dress hides. The perversity, or perhaps the overriding regional identity, of the U.S. citizen who "rescues" Mrs. Horn from Comanche bondage is evident in his choice to put her to work making up linen shirts, an activity roughly analogous to the preparation of hides.

Mrs. Horn's narrative represents the southern Plains as an economy that disrupts expected national allegiances and exceeds the powers of any existing state. When she is finally released from her Anglo-American captor, Mr. Hill, she turns to Washington DC, asking for federal assistance in retrieving her two young sons from the Comanche. "In answer, we were informed that they [the Comanche captives] were without the jurisdiction of that government, and that it was impossible for them to act with reference to the subject"—she must seek redress with the Republic of Texas, itself fighting border incursions and petitioning to be incorporated into the United States.[97] Not surprisingly, Mrs. Horn's greatest wish, at the end of the narrative, is to return to England. By its very remoteness and commensurateness with its island territory, England appears as the one viable state in a narrative where all else, really the entire middle section of North America, is fractured. Perhaps only an Englishwoman of this period could represent so pointedly the weakness or irrelevance of the United States as an imperial power. Although the novelist, House, attempts to mobilize some of the typical rationales that could be used to explain the United States' failures to redeem its citizens and impress foreign nations with its power, none of these rationales makes sense in the context of Mrs. Horn's narrative. Mrs. Horn's supposed explanation for leaving Texas without her elder son (she learns that the younger has died) includes an anti-Catholic sentiment which seems perfunctory by the end of this unusual biography. "In all that land there is little short of a famine of the 'bread of life;' gross moral darkness reigns,"[98] Mrs. Horn concludes, but the remainder of her narrative is less concerned with a "dark" Mexican Catholicism than it is with the simple fact that her only status among all the men of this contested region is that of a slave. Since her elder son has been adopted, apparently happily, into a Comanche band, there is certainly no reason for Mrs. Horn to remain.

All of the captivity narratives I discuss augment, in some small or quite conspicuous way, the Black Legend of Spanish decadence, incompetence, and immorality which Roberto Fernández Retamar has succinctly labeled "a handy ideological weapon in the inter-imperial struggle."[99] One of the most clear-cut effects that Cooper's captivity narrative has in *The Prairie* is the displacement of the patriarchal privilege of Inez's Creole father, Don Augustín, whose "superstitions" prevent him from rescuing her—that job, of course, falls to her husband Middleton, the U.S. pragmatist who supplants the Creole patriarch. Cooper unself-consciously recognizes the trafficking in women, or, euphemistically, intercultural marriage, as the easiest means of joining Mexican and U.S. interests. "Catholic and the Protestant, the active and the indolent, some little time was necessary to blend the discrepant elements of society. In attaining so desirable an end, woman was made to perform her accustomed and grateful office."[100] But the strength of the local priest's hold on Inez problematizes the desired amalgamation; Inez begs Middleton to be like her father "in *everything*," meaning that she wishes him to convert. Her kidnapping efficiently interrupts this tension and gives Middleton the moral upper hand because he believes Inez can be found and succeeds in redeeming her; in contrast, the Creoles imagine she has been translated to Heaven to save her from marriage to a Protestant "heretic," and they give up the search. Upon the return of Middleton and Inez to New Orleans, "the joy of Don Augustín and the embarrassment of the worthy Father Ignatius may be imagined," Cooper gloats.[101] Certainly Inez's rescue confirms that a Spanish woman is safest in the arms of a U.S. soldier, although this resolution does not erase the troubling fact that it was a pioneer from Tennessee who abducted her in the first place.

The apparently familiar legend of the rescue of a Creole woman by a U.S. citizen whose superior courage proves the "rightness" of U.S. possession of Spanish or Mexican territories is also complicated in James O. Pattie's *Personal Narrative*, which debuted in 1831 in Cincinnati, an antebellum center of western publishing. In this narrative of multiple captivities, Pattie rescues the daughter of a former governor of New Mexico from the Comanche to earn her undying loyalty ("the gratitude of such captives, so delivered, may be imagined").[102] But Pattie proves squeamish about the sort of amalgamation Cooper recommends, and he repeatedly spurns Jacova, a woman so in love with him that she refuses to leave his side even when Spanish troops attempt to escort her to her father. This rescue is one of the many incidents in Pattie's *Narrative* "borrowed" from other sources, and it in fact resembles a similar scenario in the early western novel *Francis Berrian* (1826), written by Pattie's editor and probable ghost writer, Timothy Flint, who was the well-known biographer of Daniel Boone and editor of Cincinnati's *Western Monthly Review*. There can be no doubt of Flint's early and strenuous faith in U.S., Anglo-Saxon "destiny" in the West, a continentalist ambition so idealized that it seems to have been imported, undamaged by local conditions, from Flint's Puritan ancestors in Massachusetts. Flint's notorious chauvinism reveals itself in the Pattie narrative through the literary trick of interpolation, wherein various persons (Indians, Mexicans, and French) who come into contact with Pattie's gang of soldier-trappers improbably express their gratitude for the United States' presence in the West. An Iotan warrior inexplicably defends Pattie's men from a Comanche war party and voices his hope to have earned "the love of a good and brave people by defending them." Later a French captain who has unwisely befriended the Comanche "observed in a tone apparently of deep compunction, that if he had had the good sense and good temper to have listened to my apprehensions and cautions, both he and his people might have been now gaily riding over the prairies."[103] Clearly the French deserved to lose Louisiana.

Despite its bombast, the Pattie narrative falls short of claiming the southern Plains, or California, where Pattie ends his travels, for the United States. Pattie's—or Flint's—resistance to the idea of amalgamation with the women of the nations now occupying these regions is, as I've suggested, one major hindrance to imperial vision. In her monumental study of the popular literature of the U.S.-Mexican War, Shelley Streeby has found that U.S.-Mexican War romances typically suggest a variety of outcomes, not all of them favorable to the interests of U.S. expansionists.[104] Just as many U.S. imperialists balked at taking "all Mexico" after the successes of the U.S.-Mexican War because of racist fears about the incorporation into the United States of a nation of "Indians," here, too, what is otherwise a clear-cut endorsement of U.S. occupation of all the West founders in racial phobia. Each time James Pattie is approached by the grateful former captive Jacova, he summarily flees from her to enjoy a more satisfying reunion with his father. This metaphorically incestuous father-son romance suggests a wishful return to an easier era of expansionist fervor, when "the West" consisted of Ohio and Kentucky rather than regions powerfully claimed by Mexico. It also suggests the fatal sterility of a racially purist continental agenda. Pattie's father, the aging Kentucky hunter Sylvester Pattie, has accompanied his son to New Mexico and taken a job there directing a copper mine. James Pattie reiterates his choice of his father over his Creole lover: "I had the pleasure once more of receiving the affectionate greeting of Jacova, who gave me the most earnest counsels to quit this dangerous and rambling way of life and settle myself down. . . . I thanked her for her kindness and good counsel, and promised to follow it, after rambling another year in the wilderness—Thence I went to the mines, where I had the inexpressible satisfaction again to embrace my dear father." Months, perhaps even a year and later, Pattie again spurns Jacova to rush to the mines, where "I had the high satisfaction once more to hold the hand of my father."[105] Physically vulnerable and never quite at home in New Mexico, Sylvester Pattie becomes a substitute wife, displacing the Creole woman whose captivity and deliverance fail to produce the lifetime protectorship and amalgamation of national interests that such romances promise. Jacova's submission to Pattie in marriage is, symbolically, his due, but he fails to accept it, regardless of its happy implications for U.S. expansion.

In fact, the only striking instance of erotic conversation between Pattie's men and the people who inhabit the southern Plains involves a performance that suggests that white skin privilege is so natural and evident that even

American Indian women contemplate improving their lot through a sex trade in Anglo men. Somewhere along the Gila River, a group of American Indian women beg a fair-skinned, blond man (whom Pattie's biographer Richard Batman believes must have been Pattie himself, since he was depicted as fair and blond in contemporary engravings) "to strip himself naked that they might explore him thoroughly, for they seemed to be doubtful of his being alike white in every part of his body." Choosing to omit a full account of this encounter, Pattie simply concludes, "They certainly seemed to prefer our complexion to theirs. . . ."[106] Later in the narrative the writer-editor Timothy Flint further naturalizes whiteness, comparing European American traders amidst a crowd of "swarthy savages" to "no more than a little patch of snow on the side of one of the black mountains." [107] This metaphor's expression of the (albeit lovely) diminutiveness of "whiteness" suggests the nervous combination of strident racial nationalism with a sense of the Far West's overwhelming numbers of a non-white or at least non-U.S. population. Whiteness figures in the Pattie narrative as a luxury item and hothouse flower, capable of producing pleasure in its potential consumers, but not hardy.

Pattie's racism is a clear symptom, in the narrative, of his strategic weakness, and this weakness is confirmed by his inability to save his father from death in a San Diego prison where both Patties are held captive on suspicion of being spies for the old Spanish colonial regime by the second Mexican governor of California, José María Echeandía. James Pattie's guilt about this incident is compounded by the fact that he inadvertently caused his father to push into California; when James refused to purchase a new trapping outfit for his father in Santa Fé, Sylvester paid a "traitorous" Creole to do it for him; the Creole instead stole all of his money, forcing the elder Pattie to try to make up his lost fortunes on the Pacific coast. James Pattie's hearty invocations of the Black Legend in San Diego ("What nameless tortures and miseries do not Americans suffer in foreign climes from those miserable despots!") fail to erase the fact that the unnatural death of Sylvester Pattie, one of the original Kentucky hunters, augurs badly for a post-Revolutionary generation intent on imitating and besting their fathers' and grandfathers' western claims.

A similar intergenerational anxiety and despair at the bewitching landscape of the "inland deserts"—which are decidedly not Kentucky—is evident in the expedition narratives of Zebulon Pike, whose tour of the Plains in 1806 and 1807 included a brief captivity by Spanish forces. Limerick has quipped that Pike is a prototype of the illegal alien who betrays that the original direction of border transgression was north-to-south. [108] Whether or not Pike intended, as is now widely believed, to be taken captive in order to spy in Spanish territories, he still suffered a variety of unintentional embarrassments that reminded him of the smallness of his force and the precariousness of U.S. claims in the Louisiana Territory. When Pike informs a grand council of Pawnee that they must replace the Spanish flags hanging in their village with U.S. flags, the Pawnee's unenthusiastic response prompts him to suggest that instead both flags might be represented. "This [my initial request to replace the Spanish flag with the American flag] probably was carrying the pride of nations a little too far," Pike reflected, "as there had so lately been a large force of Spanish cavalry at the village, which had made a great impression on the young men, as to their power, their consequence, etc., which my appearance with 20 [sic] infantry was by no means calculated to remove." [109] Pike still fantasizes the deliverance of Mexico from Napoléon by a grand "army of Americans," but his local experience does not complement this extravagant projection of his nation as a world power. Anxious neither to overplay nor underplay his part in continental destiny, Pike concedes that "all the evil I wished the Pawnees was that I might be the instrument, in the hands of our government, to open their ears and eyes with a strong hand, to convince them of our power." [110]

By the time Timothy Flint and James Pattie collaborated on Pattie's personal narrative, in 1831, it was safe to assume that at least a majority of American Indians had been awakened by "a strong hand" to the power of the United States. Still, Mexico resisted. Pattie, unlike Zebulon Pike, does not acknowledge Mexico as a legitimate political or military entity. Pattie depicts the Mexicans as simply frustrating him and holding desperately to their territory with a flurry of bureaucratic instruments. The passport Mexican officials demand of him, Pattie notes, offered them a means of stalling for time and insulting him by casting him as either a soldier or a slave, the two primary classes of person who carried passports in the antebellum United States. Since Pattie's memoir makes clear that he has not followed in the footsteps of his father or grandfather and proved a successful soldier on the frontier, the option "slave" is more fitting. This son of a Kentucky hunter and grandson of an Indian fighter finds himself literally in the position of a slave in the last leg of his journey home when, dead broke, he attempts to stow away on a Mississippi steamboat bound for the North. A family friend finally pays his passage home to Kentucky, although—and this is a fact from Pattie's biography not included in Timothy Flint's narrative—when Pattie arrived in Kentucky he was disinherited by his grandfather. The Indian fighter may have disapproved of the failed expedition. "If there is a lesson from my wanderings," Pattie's narrative concludes, "it is one, that inculcates upon children, remaining at the paternal home in peace and privacy; one that counsels the young against wandering far away, to see the habitations, and endure the inhospitality of strangers."[111]

Whether James O. Pattie and his intrusive editor Timothy Flint repeat James Fenimore Cooper's call for a restorative reflux of U.S. settlers from the Far West, or whether this apparent message to just stay home actually could be read as a call to arms might be judged from the immediate reception of the *Personal Narrative of James O. Pattie*. Unlike Timothy Flint's other books, many of which were reviewed in both his adopted hometown of Cincinnati and in the national press, the Pattie narrative received only a small notice in the Cincinnati newspaper that sponsored its publisher. Later, in 1835, a French naturalist praised the narrative because, unlike so many exploration narratives of its kind, it gave a thorough accounting of local landscapes.[112] This obscure praise, the only praise the narrative received in its own day, once again points to the imaginative problem of an environmentally and culturally inhospitable desert West. About such a place, too much could be said. When it was, the popular mind, anxious about its resistant western empire, chose not to listen.

2. DESERT AND WORLD

A demi sauvages, et souvent en guerre avec les naturels à qui ils [trafiquans et trapeurs] enlèvent le gibier et les fourrures par leur rivalité, étant aussi experts qu'eux à la chasse, ils ne sont guère en état de publier leurs voyages et leurs découvertes, quand ils survivent aux dangers de ce genre de vie.

Half savage, and often at war with the natives, whose game and furs they [traders and trappers] take in their rivalry, being as expert as they at the hunt, they are hardly in a position to publish their voyages and discoveries, even if they survive the dangers of this kind of life.

CONSTANTINE RAFINESQUE,
"Abrégé des voyages de Pattie, Willard et Wyeth" (1835)

In an 1835 article for the Bulletin de la Société de Géographie, the French naturalist Constantine Rafinesque lamented that although fur trappers and traders had wandered the Far West for years, they only rarely offered their memoirs—and when they did, they made few observations of geography or indigenous culture. In other words, the landscapes of western commerce were insufficiently narrated. [1] Yet it could also be argued that through the 1830s it was trade more than any other activity that gave imaginative definition to the North American West. An 1834 Act of Congress "to regulate trade and intercourse with the Indian tribes" offered the Jacksonian era's simplest official division of national and extra-national lands. The Indian Intercourse Act dictated that "all that part of the United States west of the Mississippi, and not within the states of Missouri and Louisiana, or the territory of Arkansas" would be an un-nationalized West which would go by the euphemistic name of "Indian Territory," [2] at least provisionally. The negative terms through which this Act gives shape to the western country ("not within . . .") suggest traders' necessary emphasis upon negotiable and shifting contact zones rather than localized settlements. Trading literatures offer an alternate version of the United States' Manifest Destiny that can be described as imperialist, but in a sense that now seems anachronistically postnational. [3] Although the Far West was literally pre-national territory in the first decades of the nineteenth century, its ultimate incorporation into the United States was of only secondary concern in trading narratives, since these texts emphasized international efforts toward profit. The primitive version of international, regional economy that undermined the privilege of romance in James Fenimore Cooper's The Prairie blossoms into more self-

conscious theories of a regional "world system" in literatures that specifically address commerce on the inland desert.

To borrow the terms of sociologist Michel de Certeau, the Far West,
for the trader, was a "place" rather than a "space," a shifting theater of
action rather than an abstract template for nationalist prophecy. [4] Traders
and trappers represent the Far West as both local and international, and
this makes it a difficult literary setting in an era of strident nation-building.
What we now recognize as postmodern theories of "place" (as, in Doreen
Massey's phrase, "the location of the intersections of particular bundles of
activity spaces, of connections and interrelations, of influences and movements") did not seem liberating to nineteenth-century U.S. writers who
began, grudgingly, to perceive place in approximately such terms. Their theories of place, such as they were, emerged from experiment, from the con-
crete, embodied intersections, connections, and interrelations among nations and races that they observed. Traders and trappers who went west for
commercial gain saw inland deserts filled with peoples who were not U.S.
citizens and in relation to whom the smattering of U.S. citizens in the region
appeared dependent and relatively incompetent. Presciently postmodern
theories of place and commercial theories of empire did not produce images
of either the virtuous settler-nation of Manifest Destiny or the civil, cosmopolitan societies that were supposed to result from international commerce, according to the early modern British and Continental discourse of
mercantilism. The hard facts of international competition for resources in
the Far West interrupt nineteenth-century forays into proto-global utopianism, such that the local, in the geographic image of western deserts,
figures as the return of the repressed. Essentially the Great American Desert
offered an object lesson in the excesses of globalist thinking and the limits
of productive abstraction. It is no wonder that U.S. traders and trappers
often tried to forego detailed depictions of the arid western landscapes they
traversed, as the naturalist Rafinesque complained.

Traders and Tourists

In one of the rare trading narratives that indulges in significant geographical description, the Narrative of the Adventures of Zenas Leonard (1839), the
Far Western landscape appears immediate and unstable, contingent upon
human activity and equally unpredictable changes of climate. For Leonard,
who went all the way to the Pacific (in his words, to "the end of the Far West")
with a company of trappers in 1831, "taking a view of the country" was as

important as profit. Leonard's earnest attempt to narrate the Far West and even to contemplate its future annexation to the United States accounts for the marketability of his narrative, which was originally published as a series of articles in a small Pennsylvania newspaper and then brought out in a book edition. But Leonard's pictures of the West do not express an uncomplicated Manifest Destiny. Rather, they inspire contemplation of the mutability of Nature in contrast to the limiting fixedness of Art and, implicitly, of imperial design. In the Rocky Mountains, Leonard reflects: "If Dante had designed to picture in one of his circles, the Hell of Stones, he might have taken this scene for his moddle [sic]—This is one scenery in the vicinity of the Rocky Mountains; and perhaps an hour's travel would present another of a very different character—one that the artist who designed to depict a beautiful and enchanting landscape would select for a moddle." [5] Leonard's West finally exceeds all models, presenting itself as a series of living, variable wonders and risks, including sinkholes, interior icebergs, bears and rival traders who deliberately withhold local knowledge and steal the furs and traps of competitors.

Not surprisingly, the prophecy of the United States' destiny that Leonard finally wrings from the Far West is uncertain. In answer to the question of whether the United States will finally dominate the continent, Leonard delivers a brave "yes," then qualifies his assertion. "But this [work of incorporation] is left undone by the government, and will only be seen when too late to apply the remedy. The Spaniards are making in-roads on the South—the Russians are encroaching with impunity along the sea shore to the North, and further North-east the British are pushing their stations into the very heart of our territory, which, even at this day, more resemble military forts to resist invasion, than trading stations." [6] A rivalrous international commerce complicates imperial desire, making the trading zones of the Far West resistant to clear-cut narratives of progress. Again, the trading culture of the inland deserts challenged the U.S. literary imagination because it could neither be nationalized nor entirely rationalized. It appeared as a spreading commercial culture that did not automatically implement loyalties to the U.S. nation-state. Nor did this trading culture cultivate in Euro-Americans or American Indians the willingness to engage in the kind of exchange that J. G. A. Pocock has defined as the "sociability" considered by eighteenth-century Britons (and colonial Americans, according to T. H. Breen) to be a happy by-product of commercial relationships.

In trading narratives, the authority of the U.S. state is not necessarily "manifest" in the sense of being readable to U.S. trappers or traders and their American Indian and European counterparts; however, state authority is expressed through the objects of commerce that the United States, like Britain before it, hoped would bring "civilization," through emulation and dependency, to rival cultures and would-be colonists. But unlike the artifacts of gentility, such as the piano, that Richard Bushman recognizes as gentrifying the U.S. hinterlands, the primary articles of trade in the deserts of the Far West, animals skins and liquor, could not be conceived as productive of manners. Narratives that depict Far Western trade indicate that it was not at all a given that this trade would pave the way for an advancing civilized nation. If anything, the hide and liquor trade suggested the creation of passions, the very agents of irrationality that commerce, in the early modern period, had been hoped to restrain. It was in the Great American Desert, a landscape that because of its aridity seemed capable only of supporting commercial dominion, that the irrationality of purportedly rational, classical economics, and the irrationality of democratic/capitalist imperialism, became most conspicuous. Even after racial and agrarian arguments for the United States' Manifest Destiny on the continent had achieved hegemony, the alternate possible worlds conceived by agents and historians of Far Western commerce continued to undermine the blunt assumptions of these more familiar imperial designs.

The problem of depicting an environment produced by economic irrationality is significant. The intractability of the Great American Desert haunts even major literary efforts that have been recognized as deploying rhetorics of commercial empire to annex the Far West to U.S. imagination. Washington Irving's attempt to represent the Far West in *Astoria*, his history of John Jacob Astor's Pacific Fur Company, is exemplary of the problem of reconciling national purpose to the lived experience of international trade. Irving composed *Astoria* from the diaries and letters of traders and trappers involved in Astor's attempt to found a trading company at the mouth of the Columbia River, and he consulted a variety of other traders' and explorers' accounts to deepen the context of his history. Finally, the trading culture of the Far West resists Irving's apparent intentions, just as it resisted many of his contemporaries when they were likewise engaged in romantic historiography and the complementary effort of nation-building. Because Irving was, arguably, the first U.S. author with a truly international reputation, the representational problems he confronts in *Astoria* are significant, even if these problems went largely unnoticed by his contemporary audience. *Astoria* was, like most of Irving's histories, a popular book. It was supposed to be romantic history, a celebration of the progress of U.S. national culture across the continent and the representative man, the culture-hero John Astor, who had made continental possession imaginable. These are the terms Irving used to describe the aims of the book to his nephew Pierre Irving, who served as his research assistant on the project: it was to be "something that might take with the reading world, and secure to him the reputation of having originated the enterprise and founded the colony that are likely to have such important results in the history of commerce and colonization."[7] The word "colony," at least, indicates future U.S. settlement. But the bulk of the history suggests more mobile and impermanent versions of conquest.[8]

But, then, Washington Irving was notoriously mobile, a perpetually "homeless" mind, as Jeffrey Rubin-Dorsky has called him; he was an expatriate even at Sunnyside, the Hudson Valley home where, legend has it, he planted ivy that he had clipped from Sir Walter Scott's estate at Abbotsford. Critical reclamations of Irving always return to the question, really the problem, of his nationality. His obeisance to foreign models must be awkwardly accounted for now, and he, too, had to account for it.[9] By the early 1830s, Irving was still drawing on the success of the *Sketch-Book* (1819–21), whose enduring popularity in the United States had some uncomfortable relation to its assurance that culture was a British property. He had been living abroad for seventeen years, was badgered by friends claiming to be eager for more "American" material, provoked by the chest beating of younger Democrats, fearing disloyalty, "dammed up with the necessity of producing a work upon American subjects," in his words.[10] Back in the United States, Irving's chance encounter aboard a Lake Erie steamboat with the Indian Commissioner Henry Ellsworth resulted in his 1832 trip to the southern Plains, a trip that he translated into the gentle farce *A Tour on the Prairies*, which was published in 1835. With the immensely popular *Tour* Irving proved that the Pawnee hunting grounds could be transformed by the genial voice of Sir Geoffrey Crayon into a series of picturesque genre scenes. Philip Hone, the mayor of New York, credited Irving with turning the West into "the very best kind of light reading."[11] Edward Everett went so far as to argue that "the American father, who can afford it, and does not buy a copy of Mr. Irving's book, does not deserve that his sons should prefer his fireside to the bar-room;—the pure and chaste pleasures of a cultivated taste, to the gross indulgences of sense."[12] Irving's well-traveled pen performed wonders; in his western diaries he even renders a dull prairie hillock as a French pâté.[13] To his fans, Irving had won the "prairie deserts" by making them legible to Euro-American armchair tourists.

This reading of Irving's repatriation via the device of the western tour is well known. But it remains a curiously under-explained fact that as early as the 1830s, decades before the popularity of the virtual tours of forgotten America offered by literary regionalism or the virtual foreign tours offered in the cosmopolitan fictions of Henry James, Washington Irving was able to recognize that fashioning himself as a tourist complemented and even trumped the more conspicuous nationalist self-fashioning that character-ized his own era—the dialogues around Indian Removal being a key exam-ple. Irving leapt past what we might call "the old imperialism" of Indian Removal and the larger project that came to be known as Manifest Destiny to embrace what has been called "the new imperialism" of tourism. To con-temporary eyes, the tourist, wryly characterized by anthropologist Sylvia Ro-driguez as a species of "amenity migrant," hardly seems like a figure of na-tional character more promising than, say, the yeoman farmer. Yet Irving's *A Tour on the Prairies* suggests just this unlikely possibility. The argument that Irving, writing in 1834, was simply innocent of the malign connotations of tourism in our postmodern era cannot be made in his defense. As several critics have noted, *A Tour on the Prairies* anticipates contemporary critiques of tourists as insensitive plunderers and addicts of pseudo-event. In fact, the comedy of *A Tour on the Prairies* has multiple agendas and, finally, a rather unsettling effect. Pleasant genre scenes like Irving's tale of a bee hunt, al-ready a stock feature of pioneer memoir by 1835, are challenged by a self-conscious recognition of the essential worthlessness, even destructiveness, of the "pacifying" mission that makes Irving's tour possible. The leader of the Irving party, Henry Ellsworth, was one of three Indian commissioners sent west by Andrew Jackson to clean up the boundary disputes and general strife created by the Indian Removal Act of 1830. Ellsworth appointed Irving the expedition's "Secretary protem" when the real secretary failed to appear. Irving knew that his first tour of North America after years of self-imposed exile was also a thankless and morally questionable military duty, and, again, curiously, he chose to represent his doubts.

Bravado and guilt seem to compel Irving to describe himself and the Rangers who escort the party as like "bands of buccaneers penetrating the wilds of South America, on their plundering expeditions. . . ."[14] Irving al-lows conspicuous overhunting and gluttony to mar the "charm" of western sport, portraying his men killing buffalo only for their tongues, which were considered trophy. Plains Indians, whom Irving at the start of the trip imagined as "remnants," prove disturbingly present throughout the *Tour*, "entertaining themselves excessively at the expense of the whites" with mimicry and derisive song. [15] Irving describes an Osage chant delivered around his campfire one evening as "related to ourselves, our appearance, our treatment of them, and all they knew of our plans." He continues: "This mode of improvising is common throughout the savage tribes; and in this way, with a few simple inflections of voice, they chant all their exploits in war and hunting, and occasionally indulge in a vein of humor or dry satire, to which the Indians appear to me much more prone than is generally imagined." In his western diaries, Irving records still more Osage "satire," a sharp response to the Jacksonian argument that Indians must practice agriculture: "well father—you go to our great father . . . tell him to find me one two three negros to cut wood & plough for me and Ill be willing to be happy like white man but for a man 50 years old to have to plough &c—Im too old. . . ." [16] Irving's incorporation of biting American Indian humor into his memoir is typically read as evidence that he was a more accurate limner of American Indian cultures than some of his famous contemporaries and successors— Cooper, for instance, or the director John Ford.

While I think that Irving well deserves such relatively faint praise, what strikes me as most interesting about these glimpses of the tourist as seen by the toured upon in his work is the implication that in his early western travel narrative—the first tourist memoir to be set in the "desert" west of what are now Kansas and Oklahoma—being seen critically or negatively might actually enable certain kinds of nationalist claims. The phrase "seeing and being seen" that has been used to characterize the tourist experience by Patricia Limerick and others not only images the psychodynamics of tourism, but it also describes the reciprocal visibility that is a necessary precondition of shame. To be a tourist is literally to enter into the space of shame, where one conspicuously looks and is looked at in return; visibility and exposure to ridicule are factors of touristic experience as formative as more appropriative acts of vision. Not only did Washington Irving realize this, which in itself is somewhat surprising, but he also realized that the shame attached to being a tourist from the United States in the as-yet "international" Plains of the 1830s was not *really* a bad thing. Through the vehicle of shame, Irving managed to claim, quite perversely, that the United States was an identifiable and dominant power in the Far West as of 1835. [17]

In *A Tour on the Prairies*, Irving replaced the threat of international or interracial war on the "Pawnee hunting grounds" with the pseudo-threat of shame or ridicule at the hands of the satiric Osage. In his memoir the shame of the U.S. tourist in the Great American Desert figures as a gentle, intellectualized version of cultural bravado, a means of signifying dominance without making strenuous and necessarily warlike predictions of future settlement. To be laughed at by American Indians whom one is paying for "authentic" experience might not be as romantic as the exploits of the Leatherstocking or Daniel Boone, but Irving's self-characterization as a sheepish tourist suggests (quite prematurely) that the war, as it were, has been won, that travelers from the United States were not only essentially safe in the Far West as of 1835 but also already occupying center stage, a position of extreme visibility in the complicated world-system that defined the North American continent. Always a critic of U.S. national culture, Irving found a way of turning what he perceived as its coarseness or foolishness to the service of Manifest Destiny, essentially discovering in the plundering and bumbling tourist a figure through which a culture's self-hatred might be made perversely complicit with its most ambitious designs.

Irving implied in *A Tour on the Prairies* that the worst that the United States would *ever* encounter in the Far West was an unflattering mirror. This apparently "critical" message could achieve popular success at a time of strident nation-building, the 1830s, because it wisely superseded the knottier problems and rationales of "the old imperialism" which was really at work: namely, the problems of war and ethnic cleansing that had begun as Indian Removal got underway and U.S. filibusters and explorers in Mexico's western territories made warlike noises. Seizing tourism as his central narrative problem in the Far West, Irving managed to gloss over the most difficult political questions confronting the United States in the decade leading up to the U.S.-Mexican War. *A Tour on the Prairies* not only inaugurates the genre of western tourist memoir but it also initiates a relatively risk-free cultural criticism that reiterates the fortunate shame which is a marker of the tourist's *and* the culture critic's already-achieved privilege. Perhaps Washington Irving invented himself as a self-critical tourist as a means of avoiding the diminishment and sheer invisibility that affected other contemporary travelers in the Far West. When the trials of captivity in the Great American Desert endured by the likes of James O. Pattie, Sarah Ann Horn, and Zebulon Pike failed to regenerate the ambitious and expanding United States, the pseudo-

trials of tourism had to be created. Again, the self-critical tourist's shame at least implied recognition.

As the first self-consciously touristic treatment of the Far West, *A Tour on the Prairies* suggests that tourism stepped in where a more romantic nationalism feared to tread. Western tourism began not so much as a new imperialism but as a complement to the old imperialism, offering imaginative coverage of areas which were resisting more traditional and real forms of appropriation. In the literary history of the United States, the Great American Desert was a place that seems to have destroyed explorers and settlers like Pike and Pattie, and generated tourists. This problem could be interpreted as a symptom of this early West's authentic authenticity, the genuine insult it offered to the cultural and racial chauvinism of the expanding United States. The pseudo-safety of Washington Irving's touristic shame and all the ideas of U.S. mobility and excess that attached to it was an evasive simulation, injecting U.S. imagination into the Far West in a complex and enduring way. What Irving made readable on the western deserts, namely the U.S. tourist's shamefaced, consumeristic plundering, quickly replaced less readable narratives of cultural or racial bewilderment. In 1835 *A Tour on the Prairies* sprung up in the desert West like a literary Las Vegas, making the Great American Desert for the first time a repository of national meanings that, if they were not all flattering, were at least memorable, even conspicuous. It could be argued that tourism is one of the first variants of commercial imperialism to suture "the desert" to the United States' national imagination, a version of conquest preceding rather than following the more certain outcomes of international and interracial war.

Irving's Interval: The Time-Space of Commerce

The complex but successful agenda of *A Tour on the Prairies* breaks into high drama in Irving's later and darker western histories, *Astoria* (1836) and the *Adventures of Captain Bonneville* (1837). In *Astoria*, Irving introduces "the lawless interval," which seems very much like what Bakhtin has called a chronotope, the paradigmatic time-space that James Fenimore Cooper felt he had failed to construct for his desert setting in *The Prairie*. Irving's interval roughly corresponds to the Great Plains, though it does not precisely refer to any known geographical region. Rather, "the interval" stands in for all those wests that Irving and other authors recognized as intractable and resistant to nationalization. In Irving's Miltonic panorama, the interval appears as a space of radical mobility, aggressive self-interest, and ethnic amalgamation.

[I]t is to be feared that a great part of [the Far West] will form a lawless interval between the abodes of civilized man, like the wastes of the ocean or the deserts of Arabia. . . . Here may spring up mongrel races, like new formations in geology, the amalgamation of the "debris" and "abrasions" of former races, civilized and savage . . . the descendants of wandering hunters and trappers. .`.. We are contributing incessantly to swell this singular and heterogeneous cloud of wild population . . . by the transfer of whole tribes of savages from the east of the Mississippi to the great wastes of the Far West. . . . Here they may resemble the great hordes of the north, "Gog and Magog and their bands." . . . "A great company and a mighty host," all riding upon horses, and warring upon those nations which were at rest, and dwelt peaceably, and had gotten cattle and goods.[18]

In part Irving, like Cooper, participates here in what Richard Slotkin identifies as the premature "postfrontier" phenomenon that seized the U.S. imagination in the years between the War of 1812 and the 1840s, a period when few significant territorial acquisitions were made and belief in the Great American Desert confirmed (wrongly) the end of westerly progress. But Irving's desert suggests alternate empires rather than despair at the apparently stalled progress of the United States. The interval is heavily populated, a unique and thriving economy. Here the frenetic, self-interested movements of metaphorically "Asian" and "Arab" subjects, Indians and trappers, challenge the peaceable development of citizen-agrarians, those who "had gotten cattle and goods."

Irving describes the diverse, propertyless peoples of this Far West through geological and meteorological metaphors ("the amalgamation of the 'debris' and 'abrasions' of former races," "this singular and heterogeneous cloud") that lend to their diversity the fatality, or finality, of weather. The interval population does not exist on a clean timeline where the next step is obviously extinction or civilization, the terms that, as Lucy Maddox has shown, neatly frame almost every major U.S. author's account of Indian "nomads."[19] Some of the nomads in Irving's landscape are European. Irving's interval has an uncertain temporality. It suggests the possibility of real failure—that Thomas Jefferson may have been wrong, that Louisiana may have been too big for the infant republic, that Andrew Jackson may have been wrong, that Indian Removal only made the West less amenable to the national project, and that John Astor may have been wrong, too, that trade in the Far West could lead to foreign invasion and race suicide. When Henry Schoolcraft, James Fenimore Cooper and others criticized Irving for allowing Astor to buy his literary services, they failed to take into account that, in *Astoria*, the visionary merchant is challenged by a landscape which resists his designs in part because it is already too caught up in the manic capitalism he represents.[20]

Perceptive critics such as Peter Antelyes do not stray far from the conclusion of Irving's principal biographer, Stanley T. Williams, that the book "presented no tough problems of American politics."[21] Yet *Astoria* entertained the "tough" possibility that the Far West might never, in fact, be incorporated into the United States. Moreover, it implicitly recognized John Astor, or at least his brand of commercial imperialism, as responsible for this (literally) unsettling possibility. One of *Astoria*'s earliest reviewers, Everett Emerson, elaborates the crucial connection later readers have found less telling, the connection between an imperialism based in trade and the failure to establish—or preserve—national cultures. Emerson begins his critique of *Astoria*, in the *North American Review*, with a rant against the ravaging of West Africa by the slave trade ("this entire quarter of the globe has been subjugated by nations, that never set foot upon it"); the relevance of this barbaric "traffic" to the Astorian venture can only be surmised.[22] With a touch of sour grapes, Emerson lays the burden of Far Western underdevelopment on the British, into whose "hands" the Oregon "country is rapidly passing, in reality. . . ."[23] Since the takeover of Astoria by the British North-West Company during the War of 1812, the British have opened the Far West to a disturbing diversity: "Of the restless spirits, who swarm in every part of the country, or flock to it from Europe, a few are already trying their fortunes in this *ultima Thule*. What natural advantages it may offer as the residence of civilized man, cannot perhaps be fully determined."[24]

Emerson's sense of an "ultima Thule," like Irving's "lawless interval," is a site of commerce that resists nationalization. In a polemical review in an 1840 issue of the *Knickerbocker* Irving himself warned, "A little more delay on our part and wily Commerce will have woven its web over the whole [Western] country, and it will cost thousands of lives, and millions of treasure, to break the meshes."[25] Had "Commerce" become a euphemism for Britain? Both Irving and Everett Emerson evince a distaste for commercial imperialism and an implicit endorsement of colonialism which goes against what John Carlos Rowe has convincingly shown to be the "anti-colonial imperialist" rhetoric of much U.S. literature.[26] Emerson was willing to say what

Irving could not: that Astor, too, had contributed to the unsettling of the West by failing to establish "a chain of posts from the Pacific to St. Louis." This would have been a first step toward real colonization or annexation. Astor's scheme ignored the interior and was too purely commercial: "The furs were to be taken up by Mr. Astor's vessels at the mouth of the [Columbia] river, and carried to market."[27] Really, without government funding or support, Astor's design could not include continental settlement, even in the provisional form of a chain of hunting posts. Naturally enough, Irving deemphasized the limitations of Astor's project, following the "genius" of his biographical subject to imagine the Far West as "various expeditions and adventures by land and sea," a scene of movement and trade that was "necessarily of a rambling and somewhat disjointed nature." Still, Irving hoped to at least *represent* Astor's efforts as conclusive: "the facts, however, will prove to be linked and banded together by one grand scheme, devised and conducted by a master spirit."[28] Everett Emerson recognized in *Astoria* the compositional unity Irving sought ("a great variety of somewhat discordant materials is brought into a consistent whole"). But Emerson's failure to find a consistent purpose, or a Manifest Destiny, in the text is belied by his own peculiar juxtapositions. Emerson's review is a fragmentary mélange of anti-imperialist rant, Anglophobic rant, gentle critique of Astor's commercial monomania and even gentler, in fact *faint*, praise of Irving's good "humor" and "taste." Emerson's responses point to the significant ghosts within *Astoria*'s ideological machine. It was not really a history of national progress.

Irving may have been particularly conditioned to see the Far West as an international trading mart, the scene of lawless exchanges rather than future agrarian settlement, because of his early experience among merchants and his general skepticism about the value of U.S. national culture. Brought up in the New York City of John Astor, Irving had intimate trading connections. His older brother and brother-in-law were both fur traders near Albany, and as a young man Irving clerked for the New York lawyer Josiah Ogden Hoffman, who brought him, on a business trip, to the North-West Company of Montreal. Irving's dislike of the United States' "commonplace civilization" is well known, but more interesting is his proximity, in space and time, to several secessionist conspiracies. Irving's nephew Pierre suggests that he was a casual admirer of Aaron Burr, a family friend; by Irving's own admission he disapproved of, but was largely untroubled by, Burr's two almost burlesque secessionist schemes. Irving admitted to being impressed by the rhetoric, if not the arguments, of the South Carolina nulli-

fiers, who led him to doubt, still without significant alarm, the "long existence of General union" through the 1830s.[29] During Jefferson's Embargo
of 1807, Irving smuggled thousands of dollars into Montreal, a common
enough activity among northeastern merchants that yet betrayed stronger
loyalties to British Canada, a natural trading partner, than to Washington.
Fur trade connections made Irving sympathetic to the smuggling, and when
he wrote about Astor's western ventures he retained his youthful images of
the "heroic" and multi-ethnic Northwest Company as his ideal, even though
John Astor's Pacific Fur Company had been bought out or "taken" by this
same British concern. Perceptively, British critics embraced *Astoria*, even
though in it Irving questions Britain's claim to the Oregon country.[30]

Irving's depictions of western trading cultures in *Astoria* suggest a nig-
gling fear that a certain portion of the continent, the Plains, or the Rockies,
or perhaps the Pacific Coast, would never belong to the United States, *not
really*. Perhaps this "fear," which is present in many U.S. narratives of the
Far West prior to the 1840s, was really a means of excusing commercial
ambitions that might not result in annexation. Louis de Bonneville, the soldier and trader who is the subject of Irving's second history of the Far West,
argued from his own somewhat deflating experience that "the Indians of the
prairies are almost innumerable" and "their mode and principles of warfare
will always protect them from final and irretrievable defeat"—best, then,
that "we remain satisfied with maintaining peace upon our own immediate borders" and profit where we can.[31] The Swiss Count de Pourtales, a
tourist who accompanied Irving's party onto the Plains in 1832 and bartered
with local Indians, predicted the demise of the Indians but simultaneously
imagined the Plains as an exotic trading empire crisscrossed by camels in
which he might live, surrounded by "a double rampart of Osages to protect
me against the Americans, those commercial Thebans."[32] Perhaps such extravagant visions of the inland deserts as resistant or "Oriental" economies
were finally put to rest by unquestionably national events like the great migration to Oregon in 1842, the U.S.-Mexican War or the California Gold
Rush. In 1851, the Treaty of Fort Laramie, which drew colonial boundaries
around the Indian nations of the West and sanctioned U.S. roads through
Indian Territory, made it clear that the Far West was, in fact, undergoing
nationalization, being made safe for the white mobility that had become
synonymous with national character.

Yet the fantasy that the Far West should remain in some sense open, international and even gloriously irrational had been compelling to European

Americans—and it has remained so, as is evidenced by the enduring popularity of commercial adventure narratives like Richard Henry Dana, Jr.'s *Two Years before the Mast* (1840), which essentially founds the Anglo myth of California as the continent's open door to economic, cultural, and psychosexual regeneration. As Mark Twain beamed in a letter he wrote from Hawaii to the *Sacramento Union* in 1866, "what state in the Union has so splendid a future as California? Not one, perhaps. She should awake and be ready to join her home prosperity to these tides of commerce that are so soon to sweep toward her from the east and the west."[33] Richard Henry Dana, Jr.'s California of the 1830s was an exploitative commercial culture, and also a scarcely nationalized, scarcely Mexican coast, an open enough continental border that naturally appealed to later generations facing the closing of the frontier and "the risk of isolation," in the terms Brooks Adams used in the 1890s to justify imperial designs on the *farther* West of Asia.[34] Both historical and contemporary laments about the disappearance of the frontier betray nostalgia for a period in which manifest destiny had not solidified into "manifest manners," for a period when continental outcomes were still theoretical.[35] As many scholars have noted, the twentieth century has proved remarkably interested in keeping "the frontier" alive as a rhetorical term, and it has served imperial rhetorics as well as the gentler interests of environmentalists and eco-tourists. In a recent front-page article in *The New York Times*, the western journalist Timothy Egan announces, happily if somewhat too hopefully, that a Native American "frontier" is coming back to the Great Plains: "as the nearly all-white counties of the Great Plains empty out, American Indians are coming home. . . ." Rutgers University professors Frank and Deborah Popper suggest that the experiment of white U.S. settlement on the Plains has been "the largest, longest running agricultural and environmental miscalculation in American history."[36] With record droughts and unemployment plaguing the Great Plains since the 1990s, what might have once seemed an eco-nostalgic fantasy of revamping the Plains as a "Buffalo Commons," an open range populated with the bison hunted to virtual extinction by 1883, now seems almost viable.

Re-imagining the Great Plains as extra-national space again reopens the continent to cultural and ecological renewal and, less happily, reassigns American Indians to the liminal position (neither "within" the U.S. nor fully self-governing) that they were made to occupy in the shrinking Indian Territory which finally "closed" with federal refusal to recognize the state of Sequoyah and the creation of the state of Oklahoma in 1907. Echoes from the paternalistic nineteenth-century "friends of the Indian" pursue the otherwise rich prospect of a returning Native American "world" at the approximate center of North America. George Catlin, the itinerant painter and proto-ethnographer who in the 1830s first imagined a buffalo commons and national park in the Great Plains would no doubt be pleased by the prospect of a Native American bison range that might be sealed off from the potential dangers of international or interracial exchange.[37]

Hybridity as Self-Interest

George Catlin, like Washington Irving, portrayed the Far West as a place of self-interested movement as well as dangerous intermixture in his comprehensive *Letters and Notes on the Manners, Customs, and Conditions of North American Indians* (1844). Catlin's famous reverie of the region's future includes an immense buffalo kill, "men mixed (red and white) with the countless herds that wheeled and eddied about, that all below seemed one vast extended field of battle . . . in other parts, regiments, battalions, wings, platoons, rank and file, and 'Indian-file'—all were in motion." The instigator of this deadly pageant is a passionate trade, originating in the centers of white settlement: "I cast my eyes into the towns and cities of the East, and there I beheld buffalo robes hanging at almost every door for traffic; and I also saw the curling smokes of a thousand Stills—and I said, 'Oh insatiable man, is thy avarice such!' "[38] Catlin's linkage of avarice to ethnic mixing ("red and white") and, finally, to scenes of carnage and death suggests Washington Irving's unique economic analysis of racial mixing or hybridity as enabling and enabled by international commerce. For Catlin, the simple mingling of Euro-American and Native American men engaged in a buffalo hunt is symptomatic of the passions (avarice, desire) that inspire commerce but that are also potentially destructive to the individuality, and survival, of species. Catlin's prediction of the overhunting of the American bison includes the suggestion that avarice blurs and disarranges racial character. In the discourse of eighteenth-century commerce, the passions were imagined as both "interior and exterior" forces of disorder.[39]

George Catlin's willingness to portray Indians as merely "victims and dupes of white man's cupidity" in trade is balanced by a real but muffled fear of what else white commercial passions might create. His too-ready answer to the legacy of the whiskey and buffalo trade is his vision of a National Park, a largely aesthetic solution; it will support in perpetuity a "beautiful and thrilling specimen," the bison and Indian hunter "in his classic attire, galloping his wild horse." Catlin saw Indians' "classic attire" as the primary symptom of their culture (savages, he reasoned, are naked) and he meticulously painted and collected and showed Indian clothing in his Gallery. Clothing was a stay against chaos; it was also bound to appreciate once the Indians met their "righteous" doom. It is tempting to speculate that Catlin might have hastened this doom by stimulating the robe trade as he lovingly enumerated the uses and beauties of Indian costume. Beneath the robes, and the ambitions of the showman, the naked savages were gathering. In darker moments, Catlin foresaw the fur trade producing a predator nation bound to overflow the Plains once the region had become a "gameless" waste filled with "300,000 starving savages; and in their trains, 1,500,000 wolves." "Who is to resist [their] ravages?" he worried. [40] In Washington Irving's second western history, The Adventures of Captain Bonneville (1837), Irving expressed a similar fear that once the "essentially evanescent" fur trade had utterly consumed its resources, "some new system of things . . . will succeed among the roving people of this vast wilderness . . . just as opposite to the habitudes of civilization." [41]

While Catlin saw trade with the Indians as a precursor to annihilation, Irving viewed it as a precursor to something even more disturbing: the commercial interval that does not necessarily pass away, the uncivilized culture of unscrupulous exchange, identity trading, and most shockingly, interbreeding. "The amalgamation of various tribes, and of white men of every nation," Irving imagines, will produce "hybrid races" in the Far West "like the mountain Tartars of the Caucasus." [42] Irving had glimpsed such amalgamation firsthand at the home of the Creole trader Auguste Pierre Chouteau, Jr., whose family had founded Saint Louis and become deeply interlinked, through trading activities, with the Osage nation. Supping at Chouteau's home on the Neosho River, Irving noted in his journal that he was "waited on by [a] half breed—sister of Mr. Chouteau's concubine. . . . Half breeds loitering about the house. Dogs and cats of all kinds strolling about the Hall. . . . In These establishments the world is turned upside down[:] the Slave the master—the master the slave." [43] Robert Young reminds us that hybridity is not only a postmodern catchphrase but also the nineteenth century's word, expressive of the tension between imperial desire and anxious boundary maintenance that characterized British efforts at empire-building in Africa and Asia. [44] Yet Irving uses the word "hybrid" (nine years before Young notes the first instance of its use, by the fanatic Alabama physician Josiah Nott, to indicate "human mixing") to describe the result of the imperial ambitions of a fairly weak state, as the United States was when Astor's men went west in 1810. The imperialist imagination that Amy Kaplan has identified as present in U.S. literature long before the "episode in American foreign policy" that ends the nineteenth century had a significantly different scope in the 1830s than it would in the era of the Spanish-American War. [45]

After all, Fort Astoria was easily taken by the British during the War of 1812, only one year after its founding. Until the 1830s, as Irving and Everett Emerson attest, Oregon was more settled by the British than by the United States. Somewhere in the vicinity of the Rocky Mountains in the early 1830s, Zenas Leonard met a group of twenty-five trappers from the British North-West Company who claimed that the Astorian settlement had "revived," "and was now increasing rapidly, under the supervision of the British, and contained 150 families, the major part of which are English, Canadian, French, and Indians, and but few Americans." [46] In his textbook of the New Western History, It's Your Misfortune and None of My Own, Richard White emphasizes the instability and changeableness of U.S. continental claims. As late as the 1830s and 1840s, the U.S. federal government could not help its private citizens, traders, and filibusters to claim continental territory. Texas was repeatedly denied entry to the Union until 1845 because the Union could not weather the sectional debates it provoked. Moreover, throughout the 1850s Southerners imagined themselves leaving the Union to join a more profitable Caribbean Empire. John L. O'Sullivan, the same visionary Democrat and self-styled Young American who coined the phrase "manifest destiny," finally supported the Confederacy and imagined a beneficial secession. The pre–Civil War insecurity of the Union and the fact that, in the world, the United States was still a semi-peripheral nation, made the prospect of hybridity both more of a threat and actually more appealing to antebellum writers. George Catlin nervously suggested that "the manufacture of woolen robes" would be a much wiser venture "of national importance" than the fur trade, hinting at the value of an interregional protectionism. [47] But Irving expresses a guilty attraction to unregulated and hybridized western economies.

The ethnically mixed coureurs des bois, voyageurs, and freemen who populate Astoria are, in Irving's words, "certain classes which have derived their peculiar characteristics from the fur trade," babes of the market. [48] These are, ironically or perhaps deliberately, the most vividly described persons in his narrative. They displace the European American settlers and colonists for whom, supposedly, the Astorian venture has been performed. As morning breaks on the first New Year's Day at Fort Astoria, it is the "French holyday spirit of the Canadian voyageurs" that guarantees a celebration in the depressed and squalid camp. [49] An ingenious ruse of the Scotch-Canadian factor McDougall, who pretends to hold the smallpox virus in a glass bottle, assures that the traders will retain the loyalty of the local Chinook. [50] McDougall's marriage to a Chinook woman—an "absurd marriage" in Everett Emerson's phrase—further strengthens the intercultural trade. French-Canadians who race their canoes on the Hudson River at the start of Astor's enterprise signal Astor's commercial muscle to a crowd of astonished, no doubt pallid, New Yorkers. Irving credits the multi-ethnic Canadians in the company with a "constitutional vitality" [51] notably absent from Anglo-American principals like Wilson Price Hunt, the Saint Louis merchant who rather incompetently leads Astor's overland party.

The great white villain of *Astoria* is Jonathan Thorn, a priggish naval lieutenant whom Astor made captain of the first ship he sent around the Horn to the Pacific Coast. Thorn, whom Irving had apparently met in New York, provoked the massacre of his crew by refusing to bargain with the chief of the Neweetie, a Nootka community of the Northwest coast. So insulted was Thorn by the prices the chief asked for sea otter skins that he threw him overboard, an insult that begged for retaliation. Thorn's economic literalism, which Irving marks by repeatedly referring to Thorn as "the honest man," suggests a fetish for identity. The play and bravado of bargaining, its suspense, irks Thorn; his failure to play kills. The chapters leading up to Thorn's murder read as darkening comedy, with Thorn furiously writing Astor about the improprieties of his Canadian passengers and crew. Even their ceremonial donning of kilts to impress the King of Hawaii (and Kamehameha is impressed) reads to Thorn as "a frantic gambol." [52] When Thorn hears Gaelic spoken aboard ship, he envisions mutiny. Of course this cautionary tale of bad trade and interethnic warfare produces the question of why the savvy Astor would hire a callow Navy man to carry a group of Scotch-Canadians to the Indians. Irving attributes Thorn's failure to disobedience, because he refused to take seriously Astor's warning not to allow Indians aboard ship—but disobedience cannot adequately account for his treatment of the creative Scots-Canadian factors. Although Irving doesn't label Astor's nationalist pretensions, literally embodied in Thorn, as his *folly*, that reading is certainly available in his history.

What Irving doesn't emphasize in *Astoria* is that the Pacific Fur Company which founded Astoria was a partnership that included significant Canadian investment. During the War of 1812 the Canadian factor (McDougall) whom John Astor had put in charge of fort Astoria merely sold it back to the British. Astor had hoped that this international venture would stimulate investment in his American Fur Company—which *was* a U.S. corporation in which only American citizens could hold stock, but he also had hoped it would be a model for international business cooperation that might draw more British or even Russian capital his way. [53] War intervened and, years later, the famous Washington Irving was asked to frame the venture as a national project. This wasn't a cover-up, but it did require an exceptional definition of nationalism. Irving chose to imply that the strength of a democratic nation lies exclusively in its private citizens, whose economic energy necessarily exceeds the powers of the democratic state. Perhaps Irving's perspective is most aptly described as Tocquevillian. Touring the United States roughly a year before Irving toured the southern Plains, Alexis de Tocqueville noted that the federated states were in the process of uniting, but only through their "commercial ties"; the federal government itself "is visibly losing strength" despite Whig fears of King Andrew Jackson. [54] Today Tocqueville's prescriptions for democratic nationalism (commerce, roads, newspapers) suggest Benedict Anderson's concept of a synchronic, deracinated nationhood. After Tocqueville it has been well nigh impossible to imagine the United States as anything other than a nation without culture, in either the Romantic, anthropological sense of *Gemeinschaft* or the Arnoldian sense of "civilization." Unlike today's market populists or even eighteenth-century market popularizers, Tocqueville recognized the market as an uncertain peace-keeper, producer of competitive, perpetually anxious society. Washington Irving saw the deracinated, economic American as a type—often identified, as I've suggested, as a hybrid. There were good and bad hybrids in Irving's lexicon. The German-American John Astor suggests the productive energy of the immigrant committed to making his way in a New World. Other hybrids, like the "roving" bands of "mongrels" Irving foresees plundering the agrarian settlements of the Far West, figure as decadents addicted to risk and greed.

The salient feature of the stereotypical hybrid is his or her infertility; for years it was argued, by Josiah Nott and other advocates of the racialist and virulently racist theory of polygenesis, that "mulattoes" could not reproduce. [55] Metaphorically, I suggest, the problem here is one of interest without sufficient passion. The hybrid is supposedly infertile (not producing), scheming, self-interested, alienated, disloyal. Approximately the same terms are applied positively to describe the ideal mercantile capitalist of Albert O. Hirschman's early modern Europe, where interest, the euphemism coined to describe the ever-consistent passion of avarice, was imagined as a check to more unruly passions. Commerce had a "*douceur,*" a gentleness similar to the harmless flirtation that the French also called "commerce." It overrode provincial loyalties and the love of fame. [56] The North American fur trade was initially imagined as a means of cultivating American Indian "interest" and deferring intercultural war—as John C. Calhoun observed, "the Indians themselves are not proper judges of their own interests." Louis de Bonneville saw the establishment of trading posts on the southern Plains as the only means of pacifying the Comanches, and the trader James Beckwourth noted the pacifying effect of trade on the "simple Crows" who "supposed that the posts, with their contents, were the property of the nation, and that the whites who were in charge there were their own agents."[57]

But the degree to which the interest of U.S. traders was bound up with Indian interest and the creation of hybrid culture was harder for white Americans to acknowledge. The sexual commerce between white traders and Indian women, a practice which often cemented trading relationships, had no gentleness, according to most writers who addressed that subject; here was a monstrous perversion of commercial sociability. In *Astoria*, the apparent cleverness of Astor's Canadian factor McDougall, who marries a Chinook woman, quickly reveals itself as treachery when McDougall sells Fort Astoria to the British. Irving depicts the sexual transgression as symptomatic of disloyalty to "the company" and the state. Intermarriage between white traders and American Indian women called for the disrobing of the euphemistic "interest." When faced with such sexual mixing Euro-American writers invoked what Pocock has summed up as "the patriot ideal," an anticommercial agrarian discourse which links civic virtue with territorial settlement, the possession of real property, and the cultivation of domestic, patriarchal economies. The moralistic and racialized agrarianism that finally solidified into the dominant rhetoric of Manifest Destiny in the later 1840s and 1850s offered a uniquely clichéd version of this postfeudal ideology of virtue.

Sentimental stories of Native American women abandoned by heartless traders abound in the literatures of the commercial West, and while these anecdotes no doubt reflect a real disregard for American Indian women on the part of many Euro-American men, the stories are based in the unlikely assumption that American Indian women could excite no other passion than greed. Edwin James, chronicler of Stephen H. Long's expedition into the central Plains, describes a trader's decision to marry an Omaha woman as a ruse to gain an edge over his competitors; after enjoying the success of this effort for several years, the trader takes his profits, including his two half-Indian children, back to Saint Louis and a second "white or civilized," "amiable" wife. The Omaha woman he leaves behind returns to him as a beggar: "I can find some hole or corner into which I may creep, in order to be near [my baby] and sometimes to see him. If you will not give me food, I will, nevertheless, remain with you until I starve before your eyes."[58] Whether James represents this Omaha woman's behavior as aggression or self-abasement is an open question, but regardless it proves ineffectual until the U.S. government, who sponsored James's expedition, intervenes. The trader is reprimanded and the Omaha woman given back one of her babies by the government, whose role as regulator of trade in Indian Territory included imposing penalties on whites who entered Indian Territory without trading licenses or passports, who settled amongst the Indians, and who—while living amongst the Indians—initiated "correspondence, by letter or otherwise, with any foreign nation or power." These rules—ostensibly made to protect American Indians from white incursion—also served, of course, to discourage an undesirable mixing of racial and national populations.

In the rhetorics of western commerce, the amalgamation of ethnic and national populations does not figure as "amalgamation" in quite the same sense that nineteenth-century racial theorists use that word to indicate "scientific" arguments for racial distinctiveness; rather, such ethnic/national mixing figures as illegal or simply bad commerce, an abrogation of civic responsibility. In the two major Acts of Congress treating trade with the Indians (of 1802 and 1834), U.S. citizens without traders' permits were not only prevented from living in Indian Territory, but licensed traders were also forbidden from "barter" with Indians, which included the exchange of useful items as well as the horse-swapping that was an almost continual necessity and recreation on the Plains. The exchange of women, though not explicitly mentioned, could easily fall under the category of illegal and potentially destructive "barter." One and only one kind of exchange between U.S. traders and American Indians was sanctioned, and that was the purchase of animal furs and skins. Congressional lawmakers attempted to repress the inevitable complications of a total, lived economy.[59]

The distinction between official policy toward barter and barter in practice is vividly illustrated through the antagonistic relationship of the Swiss tourist Count de Pourtales and Henry Ellsworth, the Indian commissioner who ostensibly led the Irving Party through portions of what is now Kansas and Oklahoma in 1832. Ellsworth felt that his expedition was disgraced by Pourtales's frequent advances to Native American women. "Stimulated by the example of [the Creole trader] Colonel Chouteau," Ellsworth fumed, Pourtales embarrassed the party by trying to seduce an Indian woman at a mission school; always his pack was "loaded with trinkets for the squaws."[60] Pourtales, in his *Journal*, equivocates: "[E]xperts assure me that there are few Lucretias among [the Creeks] who resist advances accompanied by little gifts or who even resist the attack against their modesty waged by the chance of owning a bottle of whiskey. How would I know?"[61] When Pourtales was temporarily separated from the Irving party, lost on the prairie, Ellsworth took the opportunity to comment on his moral location. Ellsworth wrote, "and here let me ask if [?] it is so dreadful to be lost for a time! What is it to be lost for eternity!"[62]

The trader and trapper James Beckwourth offers a tortured description of intermarriage in his notoriously fictive and collaborative memoir, where he, or his ghost writer Thomas D. Bonner, recounts his years as a trader and adopted "chief" among the Crows. The mixed white and African-American heritage that Beckwourth suppresses in the *Life and Adventures of James P. Beckwourth* (1854) may contribute to his unusual self-consciousness and candor about his marriages (or purported marriages) to Crow women. "It is a universal adage, 'When you are among Romans, do as the Romans do,'" Beckwourth rationalizes. "I conformed to the custom of a people really pagan, but who regarded themselves both enlightened and powerful. I was risking my life for gold, that I might return one day with plenty, to share with her I tenderly loved. My body was among the Indians, but my mind was far away. . . . Experience has revealed to me that civilized man can accustom himself to any mode of life when pelf is the governing principle. . . ." Portraying himself as a repentant prostitute, Beckwourth attempts to soften the pointed interest of the trader-husband. A few paragraphs later he goes farther—too far—translating his self-interest into altruism. "Self-interest . . . while it gratifies . . . individual desires, at the same time enriches and advances society, by adding its acquisitions to the mart of commerce."[63] Edgar Allan Poe parodies this sort of strained valorization of the problem of self-interest in the Far West in his spurious and fragmentary *Journal of*

Julius Rodman, an un-acclaimed magazine series that drew heavily on Irving's *Astoria* and *Captain Bonneville*. Poe's trapper-narrator trumps James Beckwourth's rationalizations by simply denying that economic imperatives can hold sway against the purifying influence of western nature. "Interests, which, in the settlements, would have been looked upon as of the highest importance, were here treated as matters unworthy of a serious word, and neglected, or totally discarded upon the most frivolous pretext." Poe's trapper-narrator concludes: "Men who had traveled thousands of miles through a howling wilderness, beset by horrible dangers, and enduring the most heart-rending privations for the ostensible purpose of obtaining peltries, would seldom take the trouble to secure them when obtained, and would leave [them] behind . . . rather than forego the pleasure of pushing up some romantic-looking river. . . ." [64] Poe's parody forces the question of why narratives of economic adventure, like Irving's *Astoria*, were popular, since in fact it could not be said that they offer the "romantic" or pastoral pleasures of nature writing. Certainly James Beckwourth and his ghost writer can only awkwardly account for the compromised pleasures of life on the commercial frontier.

Beckwourth's self-portrait as *economic man* is somewhat of a disguise, but it also plays into stereotypes of the self-interested and traitorous "mulatto" which were eagerly drawn from the memoir by those who knew Beckwourth was biracial. Most famously, Francis Parkman describes Beckwourth, whom he never actually met, as "a mongrel of French, American, and Negro blood . . . a ruffian of the worst stamp, bloody and treacherous, without honor or honesty. . . ." [65] At times, Beckwourth's judgments of himself— or Bonner's judgments of Beckwourth—complement Parkman's, as when Beckwourth confesses that, despite his advocacy for Indian temperance when living among the Crow, he enthusiastically participated in the whiskey trade. Describing, essentially, the tragedy of the commons, Beckwourth demurs: "If I had refused to sell it to the Indians, plenty more traders would have furnished it to them . . . and [I] would deprive my embarrassed employer of a very considerable source of profit." [66] Beckwourth's narrative ends with the juxtaposition of a poem, purportedly written by him, to a heartbroken Indian maiden ("And when I left the heroine / A tear stood in her eye") with a plan for Indian extermination that he openly offers to the U.S. government. Beckwourth's prescient strategy: "send an army of hunters" to make war on the buffalo and starve the Indians. With disappointing consistency—or consistent inconsistency—Beckwourth later ap-

pears in at least some historical accounts as the guide who is forced to
lead Colonel John Chivington's army to a sleeping Cheyenne village at Sand
Creek, Colorado Territory, enabling the shockingly brutal Sand Creek Massacre of 1864, where two hundred or more American Indians were killed
and brutally mutilated.[67]

Place and Accountability

While the hybrid may have been specifically associated with the transfor-
mative/destructive potential of trade, all traders were imagined as couri-
ers between producers and consumers possessed of a dangerous power to
stimulate desire. Temperance literature addressing Indians and merchants
pointedly suggests that traders, who in reformer Horace Mann's succinct
phrase "create nothing," are characters of limited visibility, without an enduring workplace (if you create "nothing" you can work anywhere), nearly
as mobile as the commodities they bartered and sold. In fact, the itinerant
lives of many traders in the Far West did make them less accountable for
moral transgressions than they might otherwise have been. Their lives, and
their memoirs, tend to trace series of dislocations: trading narratives are different from other kinds of travel narrative in that they have no geographical
or moral center, no "home," and so they are rarely didactic.

The story of the liquor trade and its growing presence in the Far West
is, perhaps, the classic history of commercial imperialism on the North
American continent: in this history it is easy to imagine liquor as the invisible agent of state power, creating appetite, restructuring economies, and
remaining fluid and virtually unaccountable. Yet liquor flowed in many directions and sometimes backfired on the same state agents who attempted
to use it to promote dependence and (euphemistically) "sociability" among
American Indians. Corn whiskey was a product of the United States: it could
be stored and transported easily, and thousands of gallons of it were carried
down the Missouri River as rations for boatmen and soldiers stationed at
the new forts built to *regulate* trade in Indian Territory. When Washington
Irving was returning from the prairies on a Mississippi steamboat, he saw
evidence of government attempts to keep whiskey out of Indian Territory, "a
red boat bearing U.S. troops on an expedition to destroy whiskey stills";[68]
of course the fact that the liquor patrol boats were red—easily distinguish-
able from a long distance by smugglers—suggests some ambivalence in the
government's liquor policy. The 1820s have been described by historians
as a prolonged binge in the United States; this decade still marks the high

94

point of U.S. liquor consumption. American Indians, as early as the 1820s, were targeted as a drinking people, as if such a phenomenon were unique in this wet era. Secretary of War Lewis Cass wrote in 1827 of "the inordinate indulgence of the Indians in spirituous liquors," adding that "among other nations, civilized and barbarous, excessive ebriety is an individual characteristic."[69] But with Indians, it was national. The same was said about white Americans—by British travelers, by Temperance Reformers, by medical professionals.

The 1830s mark the backlash, the radicalization of the Temperance movement; by the early 1840s it had become associated with the sensational tactics of the working-class men's club the Washingtonians, who commissioned Walt Whitman's temperance novel *Franklin Evans*. One of the first "lessons" presented in *Franklin Evans* is the destruction of the Indian nations by liquor, a vision of the United States' possible future. "I can conceive of no more awful and horrible, and at the same time more effective lesson" (than the destruction of the Indians by rum), one of Whitman's temperate speakers intones with the grim relish typical of the temperance novel's "immoral didacticism," in David Reynolds's terms.[70] By the 1860s, the lesson of Indian alcoholism had become shtick: Randolph Marcy, a United States Army officer and explorer whose accomplishments include tracing the Red River to its source, writes a "border comedy" for *Harper's* about impersonating an Indian, in which the centerpiece of the performance is his portrayal of a drunken Sioux and the reflex-like response of a mealy-mouthed reformer: "What a melancholy fact it is, gentlemen, to see these magnificent specimens of the human race thus bent upon their own destruction. . . ."[71] As Marcy's respondent suggests, white Americans all too easily imagined Indian appetite as distinct from the commercial passions that in fact created white, middle-class comfort and its complementary ethos of self-restraint.

Lewis Cass made the premise that American Indians valued liquor over all other commodities the primary *raison d'être* for Removal, citing as proof the complaint of a Potawatomie chief after a dry treaty negotiation in Chicago: "Father, we care not for the money, nor the land, nor the goods. We want the whiskey."[72] The Cherokee editor Elias Boudinot made a similar argument for Removal as an antidote to American Indian alcoholism when he debated Removal with the principal Cherokee chief John Ross. There are many instances on record of Native Americans denouncing the liquor trade, as in the famous speech of Little Turtle of the Miamis to Thomas Jefferson: "Your children are not wanting in industry; but it is this fatal poison which keeps them poor." In Black Hawk's Autobiography, Black Hawk recognizes whiskey and patent medicine as "bad" plunder, tossing these items into the Mississippi River. James Beckwourth's adopted Crow relatives shun whiskey, and Beckwourth's memoir reads as, in part, an odd sort of temperance novel in which the most "productive" (warlike) Indians are those who refuse drink. For his part, Beckwourth recognizes the introduction of whiskey to American Indians as simply what it was—the development of underdevelopment, or "the connivance of government agents" hoping to weaken the tribes.[73]

Reformers writing to merchants who sold liquor to white customers described the liquor trade as an example of the market mechanism working too well, so well it was criminal. One "prize-winning" author for American Quarterly Temperance Magazine complained that liquor sellers sinned because they created mere consumers of their customers. "The mere consumer does nothing to benefit the producer. Like the horse leach, he cries give give. . . . No government has ever acted on the principle that a class of mere consumers is necessary or useful, and such a class has never existed but as objects of compassion or dread."[74] Whether or not this reformer would label American Indians as "a class of mere consumers," his definition suggests that to buy liquor is to be nonproductive, therefore not fully a citizen but (as the Indian was already imagined) a "domestic dependent," ward of the state. Horace Mann, in a temperance address to grocers and retailers, acknowledged the economic advantage of "turning [customers] into drunkards" but stressed that this strategy would produce diminishing returns over time. Mann hoped that merchants living in a community for more than two years would see the value of making their customers more productive and withhold liquor.[75] After two years, Mann reasoned, morality became economical. Even this distinguished educator could not wed economic logic to the rhetoric of civic virtue.

In Indian Territory traders' licenses expired after three years, while such licenses were issued for a two-year term east of the Mississippi. The shifting allegiances among traders and tribes makes it unlikely that Mann's simplistic formula (morality = economy + time) could apply. Jim Beckwourth's multiple and changing identifications with European Americans, Crows, and Cheyennes is perhaps an extreme example of the switching of affiliations that characterized Plains life once the fur trade entirely framed the region. In Black Hawk's Autobiography, Black Hawk acknowledges a readiness to court "two Fathers" or European trading partners instead of one in the era of the War of 1812, because the British promised less than the United States did but offered more—and anyway the Sauks realized that their interests were not identical with those of either Britain or the United States. When John Astor wrote to Thomas Hart Benton complaining of search and seizure laws designed to curb liquor sales to Indians (a letter that tellingly does not make it into Irving's *Astoria*) he was acting against British competition rather than in the long-term welfare of Native American trading partners. As Beckwourth sarcastically noted in regard to the Crows, only the "simple" could imagine that traders belonged to the Indians they served or regarded the trading post as a seed of community.[76]

Contrary to Beckwourth, a yearning for trading post "culture" is evident in Sallie Wagner's *Wide Ruins*, a memoir of her tenure as a trader on the Navajo reservation in the 1930s. Wagner's real investment in her Navajo customers reflects the progressive orientation of the Bureau of Indian Affairs in this later period. In the 1930s the paternalistic activism of the BIA under John Collier produced both valuable and problematic results (the stock reduction program on the Navajo reservation, which wounded tribal identity but sustained grazing lands, being a prime example). Sallie Wagner's many small acts of kindness to the Navajo are balanced by a wider development plan designed to put the Wide Ruins Navajo at the center of a growing international market in Indian craft. Here the "interest" of the Indian and the trader merge, but as Wagner and her husband engage in almost Pavlovian exercises to persuade Navajos to use "more traditional" weaving techniques and more marketable patterns, the warm vision of *Gemeinschaft*, the organic community grown up around the trading post, fades. The tribe's pine nut harvest will end up in New York's Little Italy, and their rugs in New York, Los Angeles, and London. The trader's memoir enacts "the local" as a node in broad and often international networks of economic desire. Such networked localism makes even the shaky moral arc of ethnographic memoir ("we came, we lived among them, we were utterly changed") difficult for the trader to claim.[77]

The complex localism of trading culture also problematizes the dramatization of conflict, as is noticeable in Susan Shelby Magoffin's diary of her year as a trader's wife in New Mexico, from 1846 through 1847, at the start of U.S. aggressions in the so-called "Mexican War." Magoffin's wartime diary is remarkably free of nationalist cant, and the claims that she makes upon the New Mexican landscape are gentle. In fact, her observations of local environments are almost as dedicated to the elaboration of overlooked minutiae (for example, her encomiastic rendering of a piñon tree ends with a hyper-focus on tiny "balls of resin" at its base) as are Mary Austin's later desert renderings; like Austin, Magoffin's observations of "indigenous" culture are generally sensitive, romantic at worst. Daily excursions to the market at Santa Fé allow her to develop a working fluency in Spanish and unexpected intimacies. On 17 September 1846 Magoffin writes: "And today I have been engaged with market people in the first place, here is my little protégé, with her nice napkin of * y totos [tortas—little cakes]; how the little thing excites my sympathies and I can almost say affections . . . she is the possessor of some extraordinary qualities."[78]

Market days, the casual exchange of recipes, confidences and modas with local women bring Magoffin to accept this "other country," as she initially describes New Mexico, as a provisional home. The U.S.-Mexican war, which brought Stephen Watts Kearney into Santa Fé only a few weeks ahead of the Magoffins, offers a narrative framework to the diary that imposes a wider meaning scarcely relevant to the events Magoffin chooses to record.[79] Moments of productive exchange jar against news from the various fronts: "She presented me with some tortillas. I warrant if I should see her ten years hence she would recollect her 'Comadre' and the black bottle [given in trade]. We hear that Calafornia [sic] has been taken by Com. Stockton."[80] The oddness of this sort of juxtaposition reflects the unique status of the Magoffin family as long-time Santa Fé traders whose actions during the War reflected a vested interest in protecting "the trade," which meant, among other things, not offering undue offense to Mexicans. James Wiley Magoffin, the brother of Susan's husband, paved the way for Kearney's relatively "peaceful occupation" of New Mexico through negotiations with Governor Manuel Armijo, who was the cousin of his own New Mexican wife. The New Mexicans wanted "the trade," apparently, more than the Sonorans, who threw Magoffin in jail for acting as a spy.

As Susan Shelby Magoffin's diary progresses and the war heats up, she becomes more conscious of the possibility that the trading culture her husband inhabits may provide merely a pretense of getting along, that the international exchanges she enjoys may be expressions of fear as well as international sympathies. Toward the end of this short diary, Magoffin describes herself and her husband (now rather nervously attempting to leave Mexico) encamped on a battlefield littered with bones; an old Mexican woman brings eggs and bread down to the Magoffin camp to sell. Magoffin's description of her encounter with this woman neatly encapsulates the anti-climactic and morally nebulous "conclusion" of the diary: "she stoped [sic] at our tent door, she looked up at me, and said, 'take me with you to your country,' 'why,' said I. 'le guerro V. los Americanos?' [the war with the Americans?] She neither answered yes or no, but gave me a sharp pinch on my cheek, I suppose to see if the flesh and colour were natural—and said 'na guerro este' [there is no war]. The pinch did not feel very comfortable, but I could but laugh at her cunning reply."[81] This old woman's pinch figures as the sting of a history that cannot be suppressed and comments ironically (as does Magoffin's responsive "laugh") on Magoffin's own attempts throughout the diary to imply that "there is no war." Magoffin's characteristic mingling of anxious denial and cosmopolitan disinterest cannot be supported in a battlefield littered with bones. Again, the materiality and specificity of place interrupts a proto-global utopianism.

The literatures of western commerce rarely include a consistent moral tone or satisfying commitment to conflict, and this lack of legibility seems to be related to their unique enactments of place or setting. One key reason for what Washington Irving identified as the "disjointedness" of his Astoria is that this romantic history, sharing so many of the nationalist tendencies of its genre, nonetheless makes no convincing territorial claims. Where a coherent, conventional understanding of narrative landscapes as real property is not operative, it is difficult to represent patriotism, affiliation in wartime, or even the projected virtue of a future state.[82] Denied the assurances of turf, the literatures of western commerce offer conflicts in which opposition itself can only be guessed at, because the players are so many, so changeable, and, in some cases, so far away.

New York, London, Hamburg, and Canton were the key nineteenth-century markets for North American furs, the places in some sense most responsible for these trading stories of the Far West. Numerous references to beaver hats and buffalo robes in fashionable magazines like Harper's and Godey's Lady's Book attest to the wide U.S. appetite for the West's natural resources. Beaver hats, which became less fashionable in the 1840s when the silk hat was the rage in Paris, nevertheless continued to signify a gentleman's virility at the turn of the century, when Harvard freshmen who dared to wear beaver were "rushed" or swept across Harvard yard by upperclassmen anxious to protect their status. The rakish hero of a saccharine romance in Harper's, circa 1868, wears a "hideous beaver hat, hideous in spite of its being fashionable, and sleek, and shiny"—the phallic imagery here too easily recalling Freud's discussion of the (fur) fetish as displaced castration anxiety. Female readers of *Godey's* are consoled that though they may think "they have little claim to an invitation to an opening at 'Oakford's' so long celebrated for black beavers," nevertheless "they will see their claim is quite as good as any gentleman can put forth." Subversively, but all in fun, the beaver offers virility to women: "Here, on this pure marble slab, are boxes of gauntlets, the neatest and prettiest that ever reined in a horse; graceful riding-whips, crossed in stars; and, above all, the crowning novelty of the season, the BRIDAL RIDING HAT!"[83]

Buffalo robes, which were fashionable additions to the equipage of winter carriages or sleighs as early as the 1830s, were clearly associated with the western hunt and a peculiar western virility that few northeasterners could claim, save metonymically. In story after story from *Harper's* and *Godey's*, protective male suitors, many "recently returned from the West," enwrap their sweethearts in buffalo robes to save them from the New England blast. A poem from *Harper's*, January 1873, describes the buffalo robe's unique role in winter courtship:

> What if our hands, by chance, you know,
> Under the buffalo-robe should meet?
> I wonder who would the wiser be,
> As we went dashing along the street![84]

The buffalo robe offered a complex response to the simple human desire to be sheltered. The robes betray the warmth of middle-class commercial passions. More specifically, they index a primitivism exotic and familiar, imaginatively "located" in the Far West but easily traced back to northeastern cities.

Coda: Imaginative Underdevelopment

The degree to which the Great Plains were crisscrossed by fierce economic strategies, all of which were generated or reinforced by international markets, becomes clear in Edwin James's treatment of individual relationships among Euro-American and Native American traders in his account of the 1819–20 expedition of Stephen H. Long. James is always surprisingly critical of the institutions—particularly the U.S. trading concerns—that the Long Expedition intended to strengthen in the Far West. James's *Account*, which was James Fenimore Cooper's primary historical reference for the *The Prairie*, was also one of the many sources that Washington Irving used in order to reconstruct his "lawless interval" in *Astoria*.[85] In contrast to Irving's almost unwitting moments of critical insight in Astoria, James clearly delineates how Native American interests and competitive strategies were manipulated to reinforce a context that would, in fact, bring about the socioeconomic underdevelopment of the Great Plains.

One of Edwin James's anecdotes in his chronicle of the Long Expedition treats the Saint Louis trader Pierre Chouteau's displacement of a band of Osage from their traditional territory. Chouteau convinced the band, called the Osage of the Oaks, to relocate from the banks of the Missouri to a tributary of the Arkansas River so that he might claim them in his unofficial trading zone, in the process stealing them away from the well-defended trading field of a rival, the Missouri Fur Company chief Manuel Lisa.[86] The superimposition of traders' zones or fields of business upon more traditional, though perhaps equally economically determined, Native American territories points again to the flexibility of the concept of place in this era, a flexibility apparently enforced by some American Indians as well as by white Americans and Europeans. If we are to believe Edwin James, a striking interrelation of Native and Euro-American interests is apparent in that the Osage can be convinced to change their geopolitical orientation in order to work as producers for the distributing "company" headed by Chouteau. Another of James's anecdotes, in which an Omaha man kills a tribe member in order to defend the trading interests of his Creole employer, reiterates the predominance of a company loyalty, on the Plains, which in some cases supplanted more traditional or national obligations.[87]

New corporate structures developed on the Great American Desert as European and Euro-American traders aligned themselves with Native American producers, changing the organization and sometimes the location of tribes in the process of incorporating them into a system in which Indians were both the primary producers of hides or fur and key consumers of the European-manufactured goods imported by trading houses as payment for hides and fur. Well known are the inequities of these hierarchical economic units. The Pawnee chief Sharitarish put it succinctly to President James Monroe: "There was a time when we did not know the whites. Our wants were then fewer than they are now. They were always within our control. We had then seen nothing which we could not get. But since our intercourse with the whites, who have caused such destruction of our game, our situation is changed."[88] Most shockingly, perhaps, traders used exorbitantly priced, adulterated whiskey (often adulterated with substances like tobacco and cayenne pepper) to gain the "loyalty" of the tribes and to encourage them to overhunt. The fur trade also devastated tribal social structures through the common practice of traders promoting American Indian men to become chiefs in their tribes. Traders supplied their designated chiefs with the arms and trade goods necessary to maintain that role, then used them as factor-informants to set prices favorable to the traders' interests. The archetypal example of this corruption of tribal social structure involves the Omaha chief Blackbird, who was given a supply of arsenic to be administered to dissenters in his tribe by a trader interested in securing Blackbird's power over the Omaha. Both Edwin James and Washington Irving, in *Astoria*, use Blackbird's treachery to promote an image of Indian innocence tainted by Euro-American opportunism, an image that comprises, in a nutshell, the conventional wisdom about the effects of trading upon American Indians. [89] Even Lewis and Clark separated "good" from "bad" Indians on the basis of their relative nearness to white traders and trading centers, with the Lacotah, the Missouri River branch of the *Oceti Sakowin* or Sioux, figuring as pirates on account of their position as exacting middlemen in the trade. [90]

The apparently philanthropic interest of authors who condemn trading as harmful to Indians is undermined by the fact that, typically, Euro-American accounts of this commercial West most condemn those American Indian nations who most profit from the trade, usually those who situated themselves at the crossroads of Euro-American trade networks. For example, the Crow, who are roundly scorned in Irving's *Astoria*, became, along with the Cheyenne, crucial middlemen in the regional economy of the Plains by intercepting the flow of horses from the Spanish settlements of the southwestern Plains against the flow of guns from the Canadian-American Northeast. [91] In an 1869 article in *Harper's New Monthly Magazine* called "Winter on the Plains," the Cheyenne are depicted as introducing liquor to a more innocent "producing" tribe, the Kiowa, in order to obtain buffalo robes for trade with whites. [92] Irving's critique in *Astoria* of Wishram, an "aboriginal trading mart" between the Columbia Valley and the Blue Mountains, represents perhaps the most famous Anglo literary portrait of an American Indian urban center. Quoting from the journal of "an honest [U.S.] trader," Irving describes Wish-ram as "like our great cities . . . the head-quarters of vitiated principles." [93] The double rhetorical move of, here, locating the corrupt metropole in the American Indian village and, as I describe earlier, recognizing the corruption of the American Indian as a kind of contagion from Euro-American economic systems, oversimplifies the actual mechanisms of empire which brought Native Americans into what was not only a national but a world market.

While pro-business journals from the era of the writing of *Astoria* such as *Hunt's Merchants' Magazine* characterized the business enterprise or traffic as a type of productive war,[94] Irving's Euro-American traders collapse traffic and war together under the rubric "Indian behavior," a rubric which carries with it connotations of volatility and dishonesty. Plains Indians, in *Astoria*, are characterized most generally as "restless roving beings, continually intent on enterprises of war, traffic, and hunting."[95] On the Plains what passes for "traffic" between Indians and whites is, Irving suggests, fierce competition for small prizes. The "Indian mode of recovering [a] horse" believed stolen, according to one Astorian whose own horse has been "recovered" from him by a Snake, is to sneak away with the horse in the night.[96] In *Bonneville*, several Blackfoot disguised as elk plunder the traders' camp of small items while the traders sleep and while their mystified watchman looks on.[97] Perhaps the paradigmatic instance of Native American trickery or false-friendship which Irving describes occurs in *Bonneville* when a party of Crow encamp with Bonneville's men and succeed in picking their pockets and removing the buttons from their coats while pretending to give them "brotherly" caresses. The Crows' petty thefts in this instance will be matched, later in *Bonneville*, by the cruel salesmanship of a white trader who convinces a naked and starving mountain tribe to trade food for buttons.[98]

Because Native American trade relationships had a deep social dimension and white traders were often called "brother" or "father" by Native American counterparts to signify a relation of reciprocity in trade, the particular violation of trading protocol signified in the Crows' brotherly caress suggested to the white traders that what they had hoped were static cultural norms amongst American Indian groups are, in fact, open to dissembling and play. The Crows' disruption of the familial metaphors so often seized upon by white traders and government agents to assure their own gain piques the traders, shattering their conception of commercial manners. "Captain Bonneville and his men . . . were by no means disposed to renew their confiding intimacy with these crafty savages, and above all, took care to avoid their pilfering caresses."[99] The pilfering caresses of the Crows are reiterated, in *Bonneville*, in the self-interested generosity of a Nez Percé chief who gives Bonneville a horse as a gift, only to demand that Bonneville in turn gift his family, with an implied threat against non-reciprocation.[100] I see Irving's fundamental limitation as an historian of the volatile regional economies of the inland deserts in his willingness to pile up just these sorts of examples of false friends. His point seems to be that Plains actors of every ethnic affiliation are, essentially, members of what he calls "insinuating families." This patronizing familial metaphor neatly elides the question of whether Native Americans really represent foreign nations, as the commerce clause of the United States' Constitution suggested that they did. Irving's reduction of the commercial, "desert" West to a small-scale domestic economy invites an anthropological analysis of it and represents it as traditional economic praxis that is not merely Native American but pre-capitalist.

It was the anthropologist Marshall Sahlins who first noted that, for all of Marcel Mauss's emphases upon the "primitive" economy as a total system of giving, Mauss actually assumes that the basic experience of social life in the absence of a sovereign or state power will be war. Locating the essence of communal feeling in the *hau* or spirit of the gift, Mauss really argues for the tenuousness of community amongst "primitives," a tenuousness made obvious by the fact that the memory of fellow-feeling must be continually circulated in manifest forms. [101] Pierre Bourdieu has argued that there really isn't much difference, finally, between Mauss's "total system of giving" and a modern market economy; mainly, the amount of time allowed to pass before reciprocation takes place distinguishes the gift from a blatantly "economic" exchange. Mauss's "primitives" are proto-capitalists, and vice versa. But Irving falls back upon the more comfortable idea that the Plains nations are innocent of any and all market mechanisms, and he seizes upon the term "feudal"—a term that had become familiar and dear to him through his European historical studies—in order to designate a peculiarly archaic quality of life in the inland deserts. Savage life "is in fact a caricature of the boasted romance of feudal times; chivalry in its native and uncultured state, and knight errantry run wild." [102] It was passion unhindered by interest, fierce loyalty, love of tribe (or nation or race), and fame. Here is an anticapitalist West that was simply unprepared for John Jacob Astor's sweeping commercial "development."

Certainly this argument, which appears at the very end of *Astoria*, is meant to be more comforting than the possibility, raised again and again throughout the narrative, that the wildness of the Great American Desert could be equated with an excess of economic interest, the sort of interest John Astor himself wanted to capitalize on and which had nothing to do with the paternalistic and "filial" commitments associated with feudalism. Wavering again in his final chapter of *Astoria*, Irving suggests that if, after all, the Far West were an untamable and resolutely international market, the British should be held responsible for that travesty. "In *our* hands, besides the roving bands of trappers and traders, the country would have been explored and settled by industrious husbandmen"[103] (emphasis mine). Here of course Irving echoes, again, Everett Emerson's suggestion that British commercial ambition has turned the Far West into a magnet for ragtag opportunists.

This provisionally nationalistic conclusion ignores the fact that the British set a standard for empire-building which is introduced at the start of *Astoria* and which Astor is measured against, to his detriment, throughout. The British did what Astor in fact could not do; they created "dependents" of the Indians, they created a mimic feudalism. In the old North-West Company of Montreal, the same company that "villainously" steals Astoria, Irving as a young man noted how "the aristocratical character of the Briton shone forth magnificently, or rather the feudal spirit of the Highlander. Every partner who had charge of an interior post, and a score of retainers at his command, felt like a chieftain of a Highland clan, and was almost as important in the eyes of his dependents as of himself." [104] At company dinners, these retainers, "a mongrel legion," "half-breeds, Indian hunters," "feasted sumptuously without [the company halls] on the crumbs that fell from their [the chiefs'] tables. . . ."[105] These mongrels, unlike those loosed in the Rockies and on the Plains, knew their place.

Facing the Far West, Irving had to come to terms with the fact that the United States had, at least for the time being, missed the glory days of mercantilism, when companies had the powers of nations and merchants were truly kings. The United States simply was not able to sponsor a great western trading company. As usual, British precedents beckoned to Irving, and he yearned for the controlled internationalism of the old British companies, the Hudson Bay Company and the North-West, with their lengthy apprentice systems and stable hierarchies and "castle-like" forts and banquet rooms ringing with "bursts of loyalty and old Scottish songs" seconded by (weaker) strains of "old French ditties" and "Indian yelps." [106] These were the sort of companies that suggested a commercial civilization might be made of even the least promising scraps.

In contrast, John Astor's Pacific Fur Company had failed—a fact that, to his credit, Irving never entirely avoids. What did this failure foretell? In terms of continental destiny, not much; Irving himself would help negotiate the settlement of the northwest boundary dispute with Britain at the 49th parallel in 1846.[107] By the early 1880s the buffalo would be virtually extinct, as George Catlin and Edwin James had predicted. As James Beckwourth imagined, the Plains Indians would, finally, be starved out. But John Astor's failure in the Far West, or the difficulty of valorizing his adventure, allowed Washington Irving, one of the first U.S. authors of international reputation, to express a more conflicted and a more real "Americanness" than he might otherwise have done. Finally, it was in the Far West, source of totemic buffalo robes and beaver hats, imaginary site of national character long before Frederick Jackson Turner's speech at the 1893 World's Fair— it was in that West that Irving discovered a national character equivalent to hybridity, avarice, and doubt. His popular history of Far Western trading culture is only the most conspicuous example of U.S. imperial rhetoric that, because commerce rather than land was its primary object, envisioned a dangerously permeable and de-centered empire. Like the open ocean, the inland deserts of the West inspired a postwestern theory of nationhood in which the nation-form was conceived as improvisatory and always in danger of collapsing into recalcitrant regional particularities.

II. Ocean

3. THE POSTWESTERN SPACE OF THE SEA

Though so short a period ago—not a good life-time—the census of the buffalo in Illinois exceeded the census of men now in London, and though at the present day not one horn or hoof of them remains in all that region; and though the cause of this wondrous extermination was the spear of man; yet the far different nature of the whale-hunt peremptorily forbids so inglorious an end to the Leviathan. Forty men in one ship hunting the Sperm Whale for forty-eight months think they have done extremely well, and thank God, if at last they carry home the oil of forty fish. Whereas, in the days of the old Canadian and Indian hunters and trappers of the West, when the far west (in whose sunset suns still rise) was a wilderness and a virgin, the same number of moccasined men, for the same number of months, mounted on horse instead of sailing in ships, would have slain not forty, but forty thousand and more buffaloes . . .

HERMAN MELVILLE, Moby-Dick (1851)

Herman Melville's Moby-Dick declares the West essentially "over" in 1851, when the American bison still had roughly thirty years to await their near extinction and American Indians of the Great Plains still represented a very palpable threat to U.S. pioneers. Melville's postwest is a fictional world in which the continental territories that recently had been taken in the U.S.-Mexican War are already wholly domestic and Manifest Destiny, if it is to have any continuing significance, must be considered in global terms. "What to the apostolic lancer, Brother Jonathan, is Texas but a Fast-Fish?" Ishmael asks, with some irony directed at the archetypal Jonathan, "[I]s not Possession the whole of the law?"[1] Later Ishmael turns his fast-fish, loose-fish jurisprudence to Mexico and "the great globe itself," declaring both of these to be yet Loose-Fish.[2] Moby-Dick locates its hope, insomuch as the book has hope, in the assumption that some territories, perhaps Mexico or the more nebulous "world," will remain elusive of U.S. dominance and elusive of representation, fulfilling the promise that the Far West, with its seemingly impenetrable deserts and hostile nomads, apparently failed to deliver. The novel's many metaphorical comparisons of western deserts and prairies to the oceans use these arid and resistant western landscapes as vehicles of comparison. In other words the West's prairie deserts play the role of that which can be imagined and described, the metaphorical term, while the oceans and its creatures are the less familiar subjects of metaphor or "tenors," in I. A. Richards' vocabulary. "The great Kentucky mammoth

109

cave of [the whale's] stomach," the "snow-covered prairie" that is his brow, the old bull whale who is "like a venerable, moss-bearded Daniel Boone," the monomaniac Captain who is a leader of "prairie wolves . . . in the trail of the bison"[3]—what is interesting about all of these metaphors is that they assume that only the oceans can be new. This is a perverse assumption, considering that in 1851 the golden age of U.S. shipping was over, and in 1859—although of course Melville could not know this, petroleum would be discovered and the whaling industry rendered obsolete. Meanwhile, North America's western territories would continue to provoke anxiety and desire. The "western" turned out to be an enduring literary and filmic genre, while sea fiction, as Cesare Casarino notes, was replaced by science fiction, sea ships with space ships.[4] Melville's argument that the West is no longer an interesting topic as of 1851 does not reflect history as it developed so much as it reflects a call for a change in geopolitical orientation in the period of the United States' emergence as a continental nation. Moby-Dick is a premature postwestern, offering a pastiche of the western genres that were available to Melville in order to naturalize a theory of commercial empire that could not adequately be imagined in either national or continental terms.

In the first chapter of Moby-Dick, Ishmael offers the reader an easy way out of the West's infamous Great American Desert, the vaguely defined arid region once thought to be a warning that the United States could never fully incorporate western territories into its national domain. Ishmael's solution to the dilemma of a desert West that resists the nationalist symbolism of the sacred plow is simple: just head toward water. "Let the most absent-minded of men be plunged in his deepest reveries—stand that man on his legs, set his feet a-going, and he will infallibly lead you to water, if water there be in all that region. Should you ever be athirst in the great American desert, try this experiment, if your caravan happen to be supplied with a metaphysical professor."[5] Perhaps this thirsty caravan would end up in Ishmael's own "insular" city of Manhattan, where they might try their luck again, as western emigrants, by traveling around Cape Horn on the next ship bound for the Northwest coast. Of course Ishmael's proposed experiment is a joke, but its humor pointedly dismisses what was conceived in the nineteenth-century United States as the productive problem of resilient western landscapes.

Even the stubborn Henry David Thoreau followed the direction of the national gaze when he declared that his inborn compass needle "always settles between west and south-southwest. The Future lies that way to me."[6] Ishmael's still more perverse compass takes him to a mid-Atlantic port that "commerce . . . surrounds with her surf."[7] Yet Melville knows that Manhattan signifies a passage into western territories just as marvelous, and just as prospectively "American," as the landed West: the prime whaling grounds of the Pacific Ocean were cruised by the United States more than any other nation by the 1840s, when ships from the United States represented three-quarters of the world's whale fleet. Western water and the huge payoffs in international commerce that it represents render the promise of agrarian empire in the landed West, and all possible threats to that promise, relatively quaint. The aridity of some western regions is a problem only if you are so limited as to imagine land, agricultural land, as the only form of national property. "Go visit the Prairies in June," Ishmael continues, "when for scores on scores of miles you wade knee-deep among Tiger-lilies—what is the one charm wanting?—Water." [8] Solution: don't go there. Ishmael's disregard for the charms of the prairie suggests, in part, merely a sailor's competitive bid for his chosen element, yet his insistence that whales, un-like buffalo, cannot be driven to extinction betrays a larger claim. "We account the whale immortal in his species, however perishable in his individuality," Ishmael concludes, after listing a series of reasons why whales, unlike buffalo, will never be killed off. [9] Melville's poetic accounts of the oceans in the late series *John Marr and Other Poems* depict the "hungry seas" as the repository of all lost things. "Who takes the census under the sea?" Melville asks in "Bridegroom Dick," implying that if such a census were attempted the body count would be innumerable. In "Pebbles," the sea declares itself thus: "Implacable I, the old Implacable Sea: / Implacable most when I smile serene— / Pleased, not appeased, by myriad wrecks in me." [10] As Lawrence Buell has noted, Melville's recognition of the oceans as a fragile global commons is incomplete. In fact Melville believed that "under the paleotechnic constraints of 1840s whaling, whales posed a greater threat to their human pursuers than their pursuers did to them." [11]

Melville recognizes the oceans as a truly foreign element that, unlike the continental West, proves impervious to the human body techniques that, when too successful, make extractive industry synonymous with the extermination of "valuable" species. The oceans would save industry from entropy. Further, the oceans were not an arena in which human sentience could lose sight of itself, projecting and reconstituting itself as capital; Melville suggests that sailors constantly feel and live their labor, in the whale's unctuous "casings" and "bible leaves" of blubber that they press for oil, in the vertiginous height of the masthead, in the chafing rigging, in the wind-filled sails, in the ocean that buffets and sprays and ingests them, a palpable "grave already dug," as Ishmael suggests when suffering from his characteristic "blue hypos." The ocean, for Melville, is where capitalism, in the peculiar hybrid of mercantile and industrial modes that whaling represents, appears at its most natural, as a *feeling* "hunt" which—because it takes place upon the seas and not in a fragile western wilderness—never really has to end. The whale's survival at the conclusion of *Moby-Dick* makes it an antitype of the "great bears" of the West who, as in Thomas Bangs Thorpe's famous 1834 story "The Great Bear of Arkansas," inevitably surrender to undeserving emigrant-hunters who have invaded their lands. Moby-Dick's persistence insures that there will be other Ahabs, Starbucks, Flasks, and Stubbs. Ishmael's actual survival at the end of the narrative is almost incidental. As I will argue, Melville makes the ocean the site of the naturalization of a global capitalism that, like an idealized Nature with a capital "N," seems eternal. Taken as a natural mode of production, whaling allows the rapprochement of commercial rhetorics and an earlier, pre-commercial discourse of passion.[12] By locating a passionate and undying capitalism in the oceans, Melville proposes the oceans as a bigger, better sequel to the tired Far West, "in whose sunset suns still rise." What this old, landed West offers the postwestern *Moby-Dick* is a storehouse of compelling images, primarily images of sentience that render the necessarily abstract ideas of global commerce and global commons more local and immediate.

In recent years, some of the most productive work in cultural studies has taken the image of the ship as its *point d'appui*. Paul Gilroy names the ship as a new chronotope "less intimidated and respectful of the boundaries and integrity of modern nation states" in his sweeping study of the diasporic cultures of the Black Atlantic. James Clifford offers a cultural anthropology grounded in "routes" rather than "roots"—riffing on Gilles Deleuze and Félix Guattari's concept of a routed or *rhizomatic* modernity—and declares spaces like ships as the icons of this new "traveling," rather than situated, anthropology.[13] Cesare Casarino proposes the modernist sea narrative "a laboratory for the conceptualization of a world system that was increasingly arduous to visualize, the more multiple, global, and interconnected it became."[14] Donald Pease compares C. L. R. James's Ellis Island, where James was held as a political prisoner under the McCarran Internal Security Act of 1950, to Melville's *Pequod*, which James recognized as a staging ground for a struggle between hegemonic liberalism and an international working class.[15] The proliferation of the ship as an icon of modernity and global or proto-global capitalism owes a debt to Michel Foucault's declaration, in the 1967 lecture "Of Other Spaces," that the ship above all other modern sites represents his concept of "heterotopia," a space which is a "simultaneously mythic and real contestation of the space in which we live" and that at once represents, contests, and inverts all other sites in a culture. Brothels might be heterotopias, or theaters, or cemeteries, but as a fragment of "the world" that literally touches "the world" from point to point and carries pieces of "the world" with it and yet is at the same time a self-contained, self-referential unit, the ship offers a peculiar challenge to representation.[16] The paradox of the ship/world generates anti-representational thinking, theories of space. Curiously, even nationalists in the nineteenth-century United States used the ship/world paradox, in a crude sense, to theorize ways out of then current spatial models. It is my intention in this chapter to look at how the peculiar sociopolitical and environmental qualities attributed to the sea in the nineteenth-century contested, represented, and inverted rhetorics of manifest destiny focused on western lands and the future promise of agrarian empire.

The sea and West exist in charged, dialectical tension in nineteenth-century U.S. literature, and in the tension between these two coveted domains we can recognize the evolution of a postwestern, postfrontier theory of U.S. empire and nationhood. Although for years critics have made cursory note of equations of "the West" and "the sea" in U.S. literature, the West/sea analogy should not be seen as merely "aesthetic" and politically neutral nor as indicative of a monolithic frontier ideology that incorporates a variety of environments. It is worth seriously revisiting the questions of why, for instance, Poe's Arthur Gordon Pym favors the exploration journals of Lewis and Clark above all other books stowed in the hold of the *Grampus*, or why Melville and James Fenimore Cooper continually use the prairies as metaphors meant to realize the oceans, or why Richard Henry Dana, Jr.'s analysis of admiralty law repeatedly slips into reveries about what he thought was the "lawless" western country of California. The character of the United States as a nation seemed to hang in the balance between West and sea, both of which were heterotopic spaces in the nineteenth century, given how little many U.S. writers actually knew of the Far West. What West and sea forced, in part, was an exploration of which modes of production most readily lent themselves to virtue. Was virtue allied to commerce, as the early moderns had argued, or was it a quality reserved for farmers, men politically disinterested due to their self-sufficiency, as Jeffersonian agriculturalists proposed? What might happen if it turned out that the West was like the sea, after all, and more suited to commercial enterprise than to farming? In turn, what if the sea could be farmed? In short, the oceans supported theories of commercial imperialism that, when applied to the West, threatened to denature it, while the West generated images of embodiment that threatened to expose the nature of global commerce on the oceans as a war of attrition.

The Oceans and National Imagining

Speaking in 1839 at the Mercantile Library Company of Philadelphia before an audience of clerks and patrons, the New York congressman and merchant John Sergeant described what he saw as the role of commerce in the developing United States. "It pervades all society," he gushed, "it is the overpowering employment; it meets you every where—on the land and on the water."[17] Very quickly Sergeant sketched a theory of the nation's commercial culture, which he implies is its national culture, that moves the location of culture outside of Philadelphia and into the oceans. Sergeant defines a nationalism based in water and movement. He continues: "The lofty spar and the white sail, soliciting the impulsive power of the wind, the slow-moving boat, the rapid steamer, with its column of dark smoke spangled with stars of fire, the lumbering wagon and the flying car—these, and thousands besides, are the implements of commerce, perpetually in motion, and making the civilized world vocal with their mighty din."[18] Wagons, trains, and above all merchant ships give voice to the ambitions of the United States in this thumbnail sketch which has deep roots in Enlightenment, universalist histories where commerce appears as the agent that moves societies from barbarism to civilization. What Sergeant expresses is a businessman's version of U.S. empire that is less uniquely American because of its commercial focus.

It was not only simplistic self-flattery that compelled John Sergeant to speak to an audience of the converted in Philadelphia about the great commercial noise the United States was making on the world's oceans. His commercial theory of nationhood reflects a desire to assert the United States' prominence in the world-system at a time when the United States was still, in Immanuel Wallerstein's terms, ambitious but "semi-peripheral."[19] A persistent envy of British dominance of world shipping surfaces throughout the influential Hunt's Merchants' Magazine in the 1840s, where it appears that the business sector in the United States was still attempting to model the relatively new nation after Britain's island empire. Merchants located in cities on the Atlantic coast recognized themselves on a virtual island, like Ishmael's insular "city of the Manhattoes," that was surrounded by two oceans; the Atlantic to the east and, to the west, the continental ocean of the prairies. Commercial dominance had to be accomplished in both realms, because, according to the business community, commercial dominance was what the United States had been created to achieve.

In *Notions of the Americans* (1828), the fake travelogue that James Fenimore Cooper wrote for a British and European audience, Cooper asserted that the democratic institutions of the United States favored a commercial empire that originated in the oceans, since a nation is bound to "become more commercial, and consequently more maritime, precisely as her institutions become more free." [20] The Massachusetts Whig Edward Everett went so far as to argue that the American Revolution was solely inspired by a desire to compete with Britain for shipping privileges. "The American navigators could find no walls nor barriers on the face of the deep, and they were determined that paper and parchment should not shut up what God had thrown open," Everett writes in *Hunt's Merchants' Magazine*. [21] Cooper elaborates his theory of commercial dominion by suggesting that the very geography of the United States opens it to the oceans rather than to western prairies. "[The nation] possesses such an extent of coast, such rivers, such bays, and such a number of spacious and commodious havens, as are the property of no other people." Moreover, Cooper contends that advocates of agricultural settlement in the West must confront the "obstinate, glaring, and long-continued fact, that the American has and does neglect the tillage of his virgin forests, in order to seek more congenial sources of wealth on the ocean." [22] Ultimately, Cooper argued, the prairies would repel would-be colonists who would then scramble back in a "restorative reflux" to the riverine coasts. [23] As Thomas Philbrick has noted, at the same time that Cooper was writing his first Leatherstocking novels, he was writing sea fictions like *The Red-Rover* where maritime empire, rather than frontier settlement, is the dominant theme. The Byronic hero of *The Red-Rover*, Wilder, is actually born on the ocean and acquires the surname "Ark," strained coincidences that locate the American wild, navel of natural rights and national sovereignty, in a place beyond the continent, at sea.

The broad commercial reach of the United States on the world's oceans is repeatedly equated by advocates of commercial empire with the spread of freedom throughout the world. Another author writing in *Hunt's Merchants'*

Magazine about the British Navigation Act that limited colonial shipping to British ports argues confusingly that the Navigation Act "provides, at once, for the extension and the dismemberment of the British empire." [24] The idea here is that mercantilist protections will chafe against the natural imperatives of free trade and inspire a series of colonial revolutions like that of the United States. So, in other words, trying to assure your own country's positive balance of trade really benefits the world. According to this logic, commercial imperialism, pursued by Britain and then, in emulation, by the United States, acts as a catalyst to the creation of democracies. Thus in Cooper's *Red-Rover* England, though much resented by all the U.S. principals, is referred to as the "hive of nations," as if its brand of imperialism necessarily generates independent republics rather than colonies.

In the *locus classicus* of the ideology of Manifest Destiny, the *United States Magazine and Democratic Review*, the visionary Democrat John L. O'Sullivan tempered his enthusiasms for the annexation of Mexican territories with an essentially pacifist endorsement of gradual incorporation through commercial influence. In the very same article where O'Sullivan makes his famous statement about the United States' "manifest destiny to overspread the continent," he regrets a certain "mismanagement" of the Texas question. [25] O'Sullivan demurs that "we have laid ourselves open to a great deal of denunciation hard to repel, and impossible to silence," and while he does not offer an alternate method of annexation here, a few months later, in an article baldly titled "Territorial Aggrandizement," he sings the praises of commercial influence. "A monthly line of merchant vessels from New York to Mexico, would do more than a wilderness of Solons to shape and direct the public sentiment of the Mexican people. Thus gradually would they be introduced to some of the conveniences of our institutions." [26] At the height of U.S. land hunger in 1845, O'Sullivan suggests something akin to contemporary notions of a peaceful "McDonaldsization" of the globe. Give them conveniences, and they will belong to us. Melville, who sporadically allied himself with O'Sullivan's boosterish Young America movement, satirized exactly this sort of soft imperialism when he wrote as "The Advocate" in *Moby-Dick* about what he called the "imperial business" of whaling. "It was the whaleman who first broke through the jealous policy of the Spanish crown . . . and, if space permitted, it might be distinctly shown how from those whalemen at last eventuated the liberation of Peru, Chili [sic], and

Bolivia from the yoke of Old Spain, and the establishment of the eternal democracy in those parts."[27]

The political economist Albert O. Hirschman has explored historical equations of market capitalism with freedom that predate the nineteenth-century United States' jingoistic commercial rhetoric. Hirschman suggests that when market capitalism began to develop in early modern Europe the "interest" or rationalized avarice inspired by commercial interaction was first imagined as a check to the more violent passions which had influenced political bids for honor in feudal societies. Commerce and early capitalism came to carry connotations of sweetness and light associated with the polite conversation between the sexes that the French called "*le doux commerce*." While Montesquieu warned in *L'Esprit des lois* that commerce both "soft-ens barbarous mores" and "corrupts pure mores,"[28] the potential dangers of commercial intercourse were largely ignored by market popularizers in early modern Europe *and* in the nineteenth-century United States. What Hirschman writes of the happy usage of "commerce" in seventeenth and eighteenth-century European political discourse could easily apply to the belated paeans to commerce which appear in *Hunt's Merchants' Magazine*: "the persistent use of the term *le doux commerce* strikes us as a strange aberra-tion for an age when the slave trade was at its peak and trade in general was still a hazardous, adventurous, and often violent business."[29] In a United States dependent upon an international market for slave-grown cotton, in-vested in a domestic and an illicit international slave trade, and depleting its contiguous western territories of fur-bearing animals, commerce was not self-evidently *doux*. A few writers in *Hunt's* attempt to distance them-selves from the possible moral taint of trade by specifying that the merchant should not be a mere "petty-trafficker" and naming "traffic," rather than commerce, as the bold, seductive, and potentially deceptive muse of the business class. Like commerce, traffic describes exchanges between per-sons, but with the added connotation of the actual physical work of moving goods. We might imagine that merchants did not want to be called "traffick-ers" for many of the same reasons that slave drivers in nineteenth-century Richmond or Lexington renamed themselves "speculators" and "agents." The actual handling of (human) commodities and proximity to consumer desire felt corrupting.

Etymologically speaking, "traffic" reads as commerce embodied: "the transport of merchandise," "the buying and selling of goods," "bargain-ing." The word's secondary definitions in the *Oxford English Dictionary* carry a "sinister or evil connotation," as in "bargaining in something which should not be made the subject of trade."[30] These secondary meanings hint at the slave trade as well as the warlike tactics of all long distance trade in an era when the plundering of Spanish galleons was a state-sanctioned activity, merchant vessels were heavily armed, and smuggling accounted for at least half of England's overseas commerce. The nationalistic emphasis of that body of European economic theory now identified with the term "mercantilism" recommended piracy, and the theft of New World resources like silver, and stiff protections, like prohibitions on the export of national coin. Yet mercantilism, although sponsored by sovereigns and states, was largely practiced by merchants more interested in private gain than national affiliation. The Dutch were England's victorious rivals through the end of the seventeenth century largely because their sailors, merchants, and capital went everywhere, irrespective of national boundaries. They were on Spanish and Portuguese ships learning Asian trade routes, in France pushing for the formation of overseas companies, reaping the bounty of fishing grounds off the coast of Britain. Hugo Grotius's 1609 classic *Mare Liberum*, which argues from a Dutch perspective for the freedom of the high seas to fishermen and merchant seamen of all nations, makes the oceans a symbol of an international market whose openness was also expressed, if perversely, through the rivalrous and warlike traffic of the early moderns.[31]

The relevance of the early modern origins and meanings of "commerce" and "traffic" to the nineteenth-century United States has to do not only with the relative lateness of U.S. entry into international trade networks, but also with the peculiarities of North American continental geography. In contrast to Ishmael's assertion that the oceans are "new" and the West "old" sites of national character formation, more typical histories suggest that the oceans were the first proving grounds on which the United States tested its potential against European rivals that had set out to master the seas centuries before the American Revolution. The United States experimented with versions of mercantilism belatedly, instituting navigation laws as late as 1817 that resembled British laws set in the mid-1600s.[32] But what is more significant for my purposes is that U.S. mercantilism was aggressively applied to contiguous continental territories in the broadly defined West. These vast regions were nearly as unsettled by Europeans and European Americans as were the high seas until massive migrations of European Americans to the Oregon Territory began in the early 1840s. Like the seas, portions of the continental West were perceived by politicians and merchants in the

United States as akin to the historian Richard White's concept of a "middle ground," spaces of traffic that had to be repeatedly traveled and mapped against the counter-claims of rivals, including the French, Spanish, Mexicans, Russians, British, and American Indians.[33]

Despite the set of seductive spatial metaphors that came to complement the ideology of Manifest Destiny, the North American West remained relatively unsettled by United States citizens up through the late 1830s, when a congressman from Pennsylvania could claim, "Sir, I am from the West, if not the 'far, far West.'"[34] This Pennsylvania congressman defined the far, far West as Missouri, Illinois, Ohio, Kentucky, and Tennessee. In 1845, the *Toronto Globe* still identified Missouri as essentially the *farthest* West, with the "far West" in its entirety including Missouri, Iowa, Wisconsin, Michigan, and "along the Mississippi River for a long distance, say to St. Louis."[35] The far, far Western lands, virtually unknown through the 1830s in the centers of financial and political power in the eastern United States, were crisscrossed by travelers, sailors, and traders of many nations, literally sustained and defined as geopolitical spaces by international commerce. In California, a small settler population of roughly five thousand Spanish-speaking colonists developed cultural autonomy from Mexico, but they were dependent upon, and shaped by, the demands of the world market for hides—hides whose production required the labor of California Indians and which could be traded to Yankee captains for luxury items that expressed caste distinctions amongst *Californios*. *Pesetas de cuero*, hide dollars, were the currency that structured the labor relations of this world and that held it together, just as buffalo hides, fur pelts, guns, horses, and captives made up the economic networks which defined the Great Plains in the 1810s, '20s, and '30s, transforming that "lawless interval," as the author Washington Irving called it, into an identifiable regional economy.[36]

But it was not only this *farthest* West that was experienced as a region of international trade and movement, rather than a settled, prenational culture up through the 1840s. The region now known as the old Southwest, comprising territories along the Mississippi River including Louisiana, Arkansas, Alabama, Mississippi, and western Tennessee, was clearly territory of the United States. Yet these lands were fought, traded, and traveled over by a population no less diverse than the peoples of the Pacific and the Great Plains. When the southwestern borderlands were settled by European Americans in the 1820s and '30s, it was not only the sons of Virginia planters who came in search of the most productive cotton lands the country could offer; small- and big-time speculators came from the metropolitan Northeast, German immigrants came, and displaced southeastern Indians were forced to come, trailed by a host of low-life subcontractors, men the federal government paid to move the Indians swiftly and cheaply up the Mississippi. Dubious "land agents" rushed into the newly vacated Indian holdings, hoping to capitalize on white emigrants' greed. Even more significantly, hundreds of thousands of African-American slaves were moved into the Mississippi Valley in this era to man the huge new cotton plantations. The domestic slave trade grew up with the opening of the Mississippi Valley, and a population of slave traders, slave thieves, abolitionists and "defenders of southern property," meaning lynch mobs and militias, grew up along with it. In the 1850s the Alabama humorist Joseph Baldwin would describe the southwestern frontier not as a "lawless interval," as Irving had characterized the Great American Desert, but as a region riven by lawsuits, each marking a land deal or investment in slaves that had gone bad. [37] This is the commercial borderland whose history Mark Twain reduced, in the late nineteenth century, to the simple joke of "selling something that does not belong to you." An even more obscure nineteenth-century meaning of the term "traffic" as "trash" or "rascally people" is applicable to the cultures of the Mississippi Valley, where swindlers and thieves abounded and a special class of human beings, those sick, lame or aging slaves referred to in bills of sale as *scrubs*, could be cruelly thrown away like garbage, worked to death in the service of plantation economies. [38]

Even the apparently retrospectively homogenous world of New England, Boston and its hinterlands, can be recognized as a site of international commerce at mid-century. In the 1830s Boston merchants and seamen dominated the California hide trade to such an extent that *Californios* and Pacific Islanders used "Boston" as a synecdoche for the United States. Yankee merchants converted to Catholicism to become leading citizens of California, leaving their Protestantism and other attributes of New England heritage behind them, a process Richard Henry Dana, Jr., sardonically refers to as "leaving one's conscience at the Horn." [39] In New England itself, the growth of the textile industry along the rivers of Massachusetts and New Hampshire responded to the demands of growing markets that were necessarily both western and international. The textile mills used cotton grown in the Mississippi Valley to manufacture cheap cloth for the expanding population of slaves in the new southwestern states and in the republic of Texas; New England shoe manufactories used hides from California to make shoes that would be sold back, at a 300-percent markup, to *Californios*. Throughout New England, industrialization stimulated by new markets—many of them western—changed the status of property, as mill owners challenged farmers and other private owners for the use of river water and riverside lands. What had been the almost sacred, feudal idea of the private estate was undermined by legislation that treated land as merely another commodity. By the 1830s river water itself, once protected by the common law truism that water should be left to flow as it naturally flows, could be parceled in units and sold to companies intent on damming, redirecting, and polluting it. Henry David Thoreau's first book-length work, *A Week on the Concord and Merrimack Rivers*, responds to this proliferation of definitions of the commodity in his home region; it is less a narrative of two rivers than of two ways of valuing rivers, with the sluggish Concord River suggestive of a feudal, common-law conception of water as a natural force that should be left alone for quiet enjoyment and the dynamic Merrimack exemplifying an instrumentalist, market-driven idea of river water as an element to be manipulated for industrial use. By the 1840s, when Thoreau published this book, a relatively unified, local culture and a rich ecosystem had been rent by economic energies that turned the New England countryside into a space of shifting, adversarial relations.[40] The trafficking of land and water in New England which was inspired and sustained by international commerce gave birth to philosophical and psychological constructs, such as the flexible Emersonian "self," which were more suitable to a commercial culture than to an agrarian one organized around autonomous villages—the traditional, seventeenth-century ideal.[41]

Character at Sea

Ralph Waldo Emerson wrote of character as an indwelling energy, "a natural power, like light and heat" or an "extraordinary and incomputable agent" that is "no more to be withstood than any other natural force."[42] Although apparently resistant to the contingencies of experience—"no change of circumstances can repair a defect of character"—character can be conducted, like light and heat.[43] Its conductors are "new ideas" and those representative men whose new ideas change the species-character of their race. The blend of rocklike essentiality and sensitivity that Emerson attributes to "character" allows him to recognize the individual as the site of the most profound social revolutions. Sacvan Bercovitch has said as much, noting that "Emerson obviated all conflict whatever by defining inward revolt and social revolution in identical terms."[44] For example, in his 1844 "Address on the Emancipation of the West Indies," Emerson imagines that slavery might be abolished through the gradual development of character, without (further) violent agitation.[45] Emerson's experimentation with a flinty individualism that would be ultimately submissive to "great men" or "higher laws" is well known, and I make brief reference to it here only because it exemplifies many attempts in the first decades of the nineteenth century by the United States to fashion a national character that could weather historical contingency *appropriately*, responding to fast-paced technological and social change while keeping purely national interests in sight. For many nineteenth-century writers, the sea above all other sites represented a challenge to character, and insofar as the West touched the Pacific seas and showed itself to be a sociopolitical domain similar to the seas, it too was a region in which national interests might be forgotten. Both West and sea suggest the contingencies generated by a complex international or transnational scene, a scene in which the essential "nature" of the United States could not be trusted to guide individual choice. In the essay "Character" Emerson recognizes threats to character specifically in maritime business. When Emerson considers the merchant "in his parlor," with "the capes of the Southern Ocean his wharves, and the Atlantic Sea his familiar port," he warns that such a man must have great "natural probity" to "put him above tricks" such as the "private interpretation" of contracts.[46] The huge extent of territory suggested by the twin oceans offered too much room to an erratic individualism—what might be dismissed in Concord as the "hobgoblin of little minds" accrued gravity in the global arena of the oceans.

The necessity that the merchant act for global good, as a bringer of happiness, the liberal equivalent of justice, is made clear in numerous exhortations on "mercantile character" that appear in Hunt's *Merchants' Magazine*. "Industry, honesty, and frugality," or, in a word, "temperance," must dominate commercial character particularly because commercial activities are played out on a world stage where local knowledge of character may be impossible to obtain. As an anonymous commentator on "The Legal Protection of Good Faith" acknowledges, "in the operations of a rich and rapid commerce, great confidence must be often reposed in others, without the minute caution necessary to a perfect protection against fraud or unfairness."[47] Another author complains that merchants are not held to the same responsibilities as "citizens," making them, effectively, a class without a nation.[48] The problem of discerning commercial character is intensified by the size of the commercial class, which in the United States is potentially limitless—and here we see an early version of American exceptionalism, the argument that the United States is a virtually classless society. "The commercial class, without attempting a more precise description, may be said to include all those who stand between producer and the consumer, and in any way aid in the circulation and exchanges of mankind," John Sergeant suggests to his audience of clerks in Philadelphia, adding with nervous awe, "What a large class it is!"[49]

How to make such a large class more exclusive is one of the primary problems addressed in Hunt's Merchants' Magazine, where writers on the "commercial class" repeatedly return to the question of whether or not sailors should be included in it.[50] In part this problem reflects an older, early modern economy in which merchants controlled their own shipping and may have begun their careers as sailors. The sanguine author of "Specula-tions on Commerce" remarks: "You see everywhere the evidences of com-merce; the result of the sagacity of our merchants, and of the skill and spirit of our seamen."[51] A clerk's ode to "Bold Traffic," sent to the magazine by the Boston publisher James T. Fields, makes "the seaman" the principal hero of commerce.[52] Like the sailor, the merchant leads "a life of peril. He can scarcely move without danger. . . . He must have courage to explore new regions of commerce. . . ."[53] At the same time, another author cautions that merchants must not be viewed as "petty traffickers," with the connotations of traffic, as opposed to commerce, again including the physical transport of goods. As the most visible bodies involved in the invisible goods com-merce performs for the nation and the world, sailors became the targets of reformers who recognized in them the central contradiction of capital-ism, its paradoxical reliance upon an ethos of self-restraint (the so-called "Protestant work ethic") and consumer desire. Unlike merchants, sailors were not, in Elaine Scarry's words, "relieved of their sentience" by their proprietary relation to capital.[54] They literally hauled capital around the world, risking life and limb; their notorious malnutrition and sexual disease were problems of sentience that revealed the unequal distribution of goods in a supposedly just market society.

Not surprisingly, sailors made merchants, clerks, and other less visible distributors very nervous about the cultural work that commerce actually performed. Reverend John S. Stone, Rector of St. Paul's Episcopal Church, Boston, delivered a sermon in 1839 in which he named sailors as symbolic of the "slave-making," "corrupting," "colonizing" spirit, the passion for having that destroys the potentially civilizing forces of trade. Stone exhorts his congregation to "wipe out the blot of slavery from the earth; to quench the fires of all-devouring intemperance; and to wash clean form their pollutions those hitherto despised and neglected circumnavigators of the world—our seamen!"[55] Stone's "washing" metaphor pictures unclean bodies blocking the idealized—clean, just—circuits of capital. Ironically, sailors, the least likely beneficiaries of commercial enterprise, were made emblems of the moral faults of greed or lust that were euphemistically and affirmatively translated into self-interest when applied to other members of the commercial class. Ralph Waldo Emerson comforted his essentially middle-class audience thus: "those who live to the future must always appear selfish to those who live to the present."[56] But no one could imagine sailors as men of ideas. Of course self-interest, as a concept, has minimal physical density compared to the personified sin of greed.

In the concluding chapter of *Two Years before the Mast*, Richard Henry Dana, Jr., himself a product of Emerson's Boston, declares his fervent hope that his book "will raise the character of sailors, both as individuals and as a class."[57] In fact *Two Years before the Mast* is obsessed with the problem of character, speaking at once to the degraded character of sailors, the "idle, thriftless" character of Mexican *Californios*, the tyrannical character of ship captains, and the decadent character of the Anglo and European "loafers" who choose to live out their lives in California's international beach towns. Ironically, only the Hawaiians or "Kanakas" with whom Dana works as hide curers in San Diego receive from him a clean bill of moral health; they are his noble savages, although, like Melville in *Typee*, Dana confides that these pristine islanders have been "cursed" by "a people calling themselves Christian," inheriting syphilis and bad manners through commercial exchange.[58] It is an undecided question for Dana whether the bad character of men at sea and in western ports is attributable to the naturally degrading qualities of sea trade or the inherently bad nature of the western country that the trade touches. Repeatedly, brutal and unnecessary punishments aboard ship, like flogging, are displaced from Dana's volatile Captain Thompson onto a personified California. "The nature of the country, which caused us to feel that we had nowhere to go for redress, . . . made the captain feel, on the other hand, that he must depend entirely on his own resources." "I thought of our situation, living under a tyranny; of the character of the country we were in." "The government of the country is an arbitrary democracy; having no common law, and no judiciary."[59] Dana's attribution of lawlessness to

California and *Californios* makes an implicit plea for U.S. settlement and colonization, although he is well aware that this geopolitical outcome is not yet "manifest" when he writes. In lieu of more extensive U.S. colonization, self-culture becomes Dana's primary means of yoking both sea and West to his Bostonian sense of social justice.

One of the richest peculiarities of *Two Years before the Mast* is that, while it was written by Dana when he was at Harvard Law School planning a career in maritime law, the book argues that life at sea is impervious to juridical norms. *Two Years before the Mast* declares the law useless in the domains that most interest Dana, the ocean and California. "In the first place, I have no fancies about equality aboard ship," Dana asserts in his conclusion [60]— a conclusion that notably contradicts Herman Melville's strong advocacy for the democratization of "discretionary" U.S. naval codes in *White-Jacket,* where Melville conceives the law of the sea as a reflection of the laws of the nation that sponsors a given ship. [61] Dana continues, making an anxious defense of flogging, "It will not answer to say that [the captain] shall never do this and that thing, because it does not seem always necessary and advisable that it should be done." [62] The sea is a medium that is too contingent, too radically historical, to admit of law, given that law must be based on precedent and moral imperative. The improvisatory lynch law that Dana witnesses among Yankee trappers in California, whom he congratulates for hanging a Mexican, might be equally appropriate to the sea. Both California, at least as long as it is not U.S. territory, and the ocean resist moral absolutes and the legal reform that such absolutes would recommend. Dana's only recourse, if he is to prescribe improvement, is a return to self-help and the "internal" resource of character. "Certainly the only means which can create any important change for the better, is the gradual one of raising the intellectual and moral character of the sailor, so that as an individual, and as one of a class, he may, in the first instance, command the respect of his officers, and if any difficulty should happen, may upon the stand carry weight." [63] A similar waffling between advocacy for sailors' rights and refusal to endorse legal restrictions on officers mars Dana's first published work, an 1839 article for *American Jurist* entitled "Cruelty to Seamen." In this article, Dana uses the case of the murder of Henry Burr, a ship's cook, by his captain and mate—and the officers' grisly tattooing of the dead body— to argue for the enforcement of an 1835 statute protecting sailors from the abuses of officers. But in "Cruelty to Seamen," as in *Two Years before the Mast,* Dana stops short of specifying which sorts of abuses by officers should never be permissable.[64] While it could be argued that Dana's moral and legal relativism reflects the sociopolitical "fluidity" of life at sea, what I want to point to, again, is that this fluidity is really a hyper-historicity, a condition in which changes of material circumstance and social status happen more rapidly and fatally than in other places. For Dana, the sea is finally *too real* to support such an idealized mechanism as law.

For that matter, the sea proves too real to sustain Dana's appeal to character. Dana's self-culture argument, which reflects a larger movement among both the transcendentalist counterculture and the merchants of Boston to deflect class conflict onto the deliberately problematized and transcendent "individual," does not hold up well at sea. Sea narratives raise the possibility that the soul which never "touches its objects," as Emerson lamented of "the individual" in the essay "Experience," may be little more than a flag of convenience, a series of poses that represent the impossibility of commitment. The immateriality of a character that is "like light and heat" can, in a realm of undeniable contingency, be interpreted as flimsiness, again, the "convenient" self. The political economic problem of the flag of convenience or use of foreign flags to conduct illegal business on the world's oceans was well known to Richard Henry Dana, Jr., and his contemporaries—because of smuggling in the Pacific, which Dana recognizes as the result of Yankee and European resentment of Mexican import duties, and because of the widespread use of the U.S. flag by international slave traders. As W. E. B. DuBois discussed in *The Suppression of the African Slave-Trade*, smugglers who illegally carried slaves from Africa used the U.S. flag as a cover for their business because until 1862 the United States refused to sign international treaties allowing foreign ships the right of search.[65] Although the moral and political issue of the flag of convenience is most prevalent in melodramas like Cooper's *The Red-Rover*, where the Rover's "locker of flags" corresponds to an equally large locker of costumes that allow him to appear as men of several nations, classes, and ages, even Dana entertains the possibility that character is unstable, most wisely interpreted as performance. As is now well known, after Dana returned to Boston and began his career in maritime law, he repeatedly "returned" to the younger, more fluid self of his days as a Pacific sailor; on his frequent business trips, he would adopt the clothing and persona of a rough sailor in order to explore the urban *demi-monde*, entering brothels and low dives.[66] In *Two Years before the Mast*, the phrase "leaving one's conscience at the Horn," used by Yankees who convert to Catholicism and marry *Californios*, is a joke to

Dana, but it is a joke that suggests that California might not merely alter one's character but that this western country also induces one to re-imagine character as a cloak that can be changed at will. U.S. character loses its transcendental bearings when exposed to spaces that should be subject to international law, like the oceans and California. For Yankees like Dana, California appeared as an extended, international port in the 1830s. Unlike the nation, which could be conceived in terms of an idealized, transcendent *geist*, international sites of contention and negotiation do not give rise to transcendent signifieds. We might consider it a curious footnote that Richard Henry Dana, Jr., struggled throughout his life to create a working definition of international law, drafting but never completing a treatise on the subject that began with a review of Hugo Grotius's classic *Mare Liberum*, which asserts rather grandly if unhelpfully that the oceans defy governance by any single state.[67]

The shifting ground of international domains like the sea or much of the Far West prior to the U.S.-Mexican War affected not only U.S. conceptions of an idealized national character, but also U.S. conceptions of race. What Patricia Limerick has said of the West—that it "raised questions for which racists had no set answers. . . . Western diversity forced racists to think—an unaccustomed activity"—could also be said of the sea and has been stressed by many recent historians.[68] Far from being realms of "black" and "white," as Edgar Allan Poe satirically defines his gothic seascape in *The Narrative of Arthur Gordon Pym*, U.S. ships, including merchant ships, whalers, and even naval vessels, as Melville attests in *White-Jacket*, had international, multi-ethnic crews. Moreover, maritime commerce had early given rise to proto-ideologies of race that suggested that this concept was much more fragile and subject to historical circumstance than essentialist arguments from the mid-nineteenth century United States suggest—particularly those theories of polygenesis or separate creations coming from the U.S. South in the wake of the radicalization of the abolitionist movement in the 1830s. As Roxann Wheeler has shown, British conceptions of race born out of early modern commerce with Africa recognized race as a surface characteristic that could mutate through exposure to different climates or "more civilized" peoples. More specifically, up through the eighteenth century many Britons imagined that manners, conveyed through the activities of maritime trade, had the power to alter race, which was conceived as a set of behaviors and changeable physical attributes summed up in the quasi-racial term "complexion."[69]

We hear a great deal about complexion in U.S. sea narrative, where Richard Henry Dana, Jr., returns to Boston with a "face burnt black as an Indian's," where in White-Jacket Melville's fellow sailors aboard the Neversink have "the same dark brown complexion . . . like smoked hams," and where Cooper's romantic Wilder in The Red-Rover is said to have a "dusky complexion," indicating his nativity at sea.[70] While these instances of white brownness could be categorized as the sort of "playing Indian" that often serves to naturalize Euro-American presence in the Americas, the fact that sea narratives depict "brown" whites in a realm that no one can really settle puts brownness and whiteness on a more level comparative plane. The heft of whiteness in White-Jacket, where whiteness is literalized as a heavy coat that cannot be taken off or painted black, a coat that does not protect the wearer and might even drown him, is obviously significant. Melville's recollection of witnessing a "mulatto" sailor whipped on the Neversink and thinking to himself, "Thank God I am white!" then "yet I had seen whites also scourged . . . all my shipmates were liable to that," makes clear that on board this ship blackness and whiteness are no longer usable concepts.[71] (This in contrast to Dana's outrage at the flogging of his fellow sailors aboard the Pilgrim, a rage which stems directly from the Captain's assertion that he will "make a negro" out of a white man,[72] as if both "negro" and "white man" are substantive, inalterable statuses.)

Like his philosophical play with his own white "jacket" or complexion, Melville's comparative analysis of "cannibals" and "Christians" in the Marquesas Islands of Typee undermines both the idealized norm and its antithesis. In Typee, precisely the qualities that historians suggest inspired Europeans to designate non-Europeans as "cannibals"—a resistance to Christianity and a resistance to commerce with Europeans—make the isolated Typees seem "gentlemanly cannibals," representative of a more natural and forthright political economy. In Typee, Melville's very specific targeting of the term "cannibal," which he removes from current ideology by re-historicizing it as a perceived anti-commercial orientation, offers a telling gloss on the multiple reappearances of cannibalism in the later novel Moby-Dick.

Live Meat

The word "cannibal" is as ubiquitous in Moby-Dick as Moby-Dick is in the whaling grounds of the great Pacific. "Cannibal" is, in a sense, the book's shibboleth, the password that grants us entrance into its manners, customs, and broadest structures of feeling. Many critics have commented upon the archaism and apparent savagery of the *Pequod*, "a cannibal of a craft" leaving from the outmoded port of Nantucket, captained by the fatally-named Ahab, a man who on his better days refers to himself quaintly as "cannibal old me." Ishmael's self-declaration that he is a "savage" indebted only to "the King of Cannibals" isn't quite as convincing; perhaps this is his bow toward his beloved bedmate Queequeg, a bona fide cannibal, or perhaps this is his bid to enter himself into the society of a ship that he seems destined to fall out of, alone. [73] But the ubiquitous cannibalism in *Moby-Dick* does not belong only to exceptional characters like Queequeg, Ishmael, or Ahab, nor does it only signify the primitive or "feudal" antipathy to the logic of exchange that Wai-chee Dimock characterizes as Ahabian political economy. [74] Ahab's famous dialogue with Starbuck about how many "barrels" his vengeance might bring onto the Nantucket market is perhaps less indicative of what Melville recognized as a significant contradiction within whaling (hunt or commerce? vengeance or profit?) than the strained analysis of two oddball, intellectual characters intent upon finding binary opposition where none exists. In the poem "John Marr and Other Sailors," "merchant sailors" and "huntsman-whalers" are unproblematically the same persons. [75]

Cannibalism, the *summa* of vengeance, need not cancel the circulation of capital, nor the production of capital, that is the business of the *Pequod* and of the many other whalers at large on the western seas. Cannibalism and capitalism are, in *Moby-Dick*, rather happily complementary. Melville's rhetoric of cannibalism restores passionate social intercourse and conspicuous bodies to "the whaling business," reinventing the fundamental social substance that, as Marx suggests, typically "crystallizes" out of the process of production as the fetishized commodity. [76] The rhetoric of cannibalism distracts us from the abstractions of capitalism, making "whaling," and the larger category of "business," seem creative, if gruesome, expressions of human and animal nature. Tzvetan Todorov has written of cannibalism as, like other supposedly "savage" attributes, such as the absence of writing and money, a condition suggestive of an inability to "fully recognize the other as at once like oneself and different." [77] With cannibalism, as in the practice of exchange without money that Marx dismissed as "philistine," there is no mediation, no theoretical third person, or third term, which calls attention to the difference in equivalence. More literally, a cannibal will eat you because you are his enemy and virtually another species, or he will eat you because you are always already his flesh and bone. Or both. The raw, unmediated quality of a cannibalistic economy is what Melville seems really to see as whaling's special gift to the commercial imagination. The gaping "hunger" of the ocean, personified bluntly as a "pale ravener of horrible meat" in Melville's poem "The Maldive Shark," confers a terrible, glamorous sensuousness upon extractive industry.[78] This "commercial epic," as Michael T. Gilmore has called Moby-Dick,[79] finds places of comfort, veritable pastoral retreats, in animal fat, smeer, butter, Leyden cheese, whale steak, and sundry forms of living and dying meat.

The ordinary officers aboard the Pequod, Stubb and Flask, are the ship's most consistent cannibals, and this is important because these men—unlike Ahab, Ishmael, or even Starbuck—could easily be on any whale ship at any moment in time, so they suggest a larger analysis of whaling rather than the peculiar psychodynamics of the Pequod's "extraordinary voyage." While Starbuck is often labeled as the ship's homo economicus—though Dimock aptly recognizes his interest in exchange as a moral argument against the violence incited by Ahab's logic of repetition—it is really Stubb, not Starbuck, who acts as the classical economist's presumed "rational man." Stubb's notorious risk-taking confirms, rather than cancels, his "rationality" in an economic sense. Under the fantastic pressures of the extraordinary voyage, Stubb continues to be driven by hard-nosed interest: it is he who separates the French ship Bouton de Rose from its blasted whales in order to obtain their valuable ambergris, it is he who eats a fat steak while the crew turns in their hammocks, disturbed by the "sharp slapping" of sharks' tails around the same carcass that is Stubb's pleasurable dinner. It is Stubb, not Starbuck, who greedily anticipates a cup of coffee from the captain of the Jungfrau, whose ship's oil can, from afar, looks to him like the vessel of his favorite beverage. Had the marketers of our contemporary coffee emporium read Moby-Dick more closely, and against the commonplace assumption that Starbuck is the ship's spokesman for profit, we might be drinking "Stubb's" coffee rather than Starbucks coffee in the local mall. Stubb is the naked entrepreneurial capitalist—risk-taking, visionary (hence his ability to discern ambergris in the stench of rotting flesh), with the appetites and insights of a master consumer.

The chapter "Stubb's Supper" is Melville's Rabelaisian tribute to cannibal-capitalism, including his most graphic comparisons of the business of whaling to butchering and bloody combat. In fact the three terms "whaling," "butchering," and "battle" are collapsed on several occasions throughout Moby-Dick, such that the honor often attached to the constellation "battle," "duty," "patriotism," takes on a primitive heft, revealing honor itself as an almost embodied, physically realized prize. As the harpooner Daggoo obligingly cuts Stubb's dinner from the whale's small, Ishmael begins a reverie about the scenes of carnage characteristic of combat at sea. "Though amid the smoking horror and diabolism of the sea-fight, sharks will be seen longingly gazing up to the ship's decks, like hungry dogs round a table where red meat is being carved, ready to bolt down every killed man that is tossed to them; and though, while valiant butchers over the deck-table are thus cannibally carving each other's live meat with carving-knives all gilded and tasseled, the sharks, also, with their jewel-hilted mouths, are quarrelsomely carving away under the table at the dead meat."[80] Though we might pause to consider the almost oxymoronic phrase "valiant butchers"—in contrast to earlier avowals by Ishmael that whalers should not be considered butchers but rather soldiers, who are also not butchers—the "shocking sharkish business" of the narrative drives us rapidly toward further stomach-turning speculation. Ishmael launches into a description of sharks "systematically trotting alongside" slave ships in the mid-Atlantic, awaiting a sample of the human cargo that is periodically thrown overboard. Commerce is reduced to war, which is, in turn, reduced to butchery—each act acquiring more physical density than the last and ending with the fundamental image of "the jaw." By the time we reach the end of Ishmael's almost epic simile, we don't really need the Pequod's pragmatic cook, Fleece, to tell us that Stubb is "more of a shark than Massa Shark himself."[81] But Fleece's remark neatly underlines a particular objective correlative—"shark shows man"—that appears not only in this gruesome chapter but throughout Moby-Dick. Finally it is to "the sharks" that Ahab descends on the third day of the chase.[82]

Buell convincingly argues that Melville intends a leveling of conventional mammal hierarchies by giving us "whalemen bestialized by the hunt" in comparison to the adaptive and retaliatory strategies of "intelligent" whales.[83] In Moby-Dick the bestialization of men has more causal stimuli than the whale hunt per se—or at least Melville opens the whale hunt as a category to include other forms of early capitalist enterprise. The universalization of cannibalism in Moby-Dick proves that whaling is finally not quite as unique a business as Ishmael intends it to be. Sounding strikingly like a contemporary animal rights activist, Melville laments that most human business boils down to the murder and ingestion of live meat. "Go to the meat market of a Saturday night and see the crowds of live bipeds staring up at the long rows of dead quadrupeds. Does not that sight take a tooth out of the cannibal's jaw? Cannibals? Who is not a cannibal?" [84] Besides performing a transvaluation of humans with other animals and suggesting that "meat is murder," Ishmael's reverie on the meat market performs an act of anti-alienation. Again, we are being reassured that business, the marketplace, etc., is invariably about bodies and the fundamental hungers of bodies. Moreover, Melville's grotesque depictions of living and dying meat inspire in the reader a bodily act, a revulsion that functions as an unwitting pledge that the animal and human bodies depicted *are* bodies, rather than mere spectral commodity values. In a world where the property-form keeps multiplying to denature even "heads" and "the hills of Boston," Ishmael suggests that we are never very far from the primal scene. In *Moby-Dick*, carnage is comforting.

Melville's dissemination of the symbolic "jaw" throughout the novel owes some debt to the sensational memoir of Owen Chase, the first mate of a whaler named the *Essex* that in 1820 was "stove" by a maddened sperm whale in the Pacific cruising grounds. Chase drifted for nearly three months with a crew of six in a flimsy whaleboat; his narrative records the crew's cannibalization of one of their members, Isaac Cole, in such detail that it could almost be described as a recipe book for the treatment and preservation of human flesh. [85] Images of gorging on Cole's heart and drying strips of his arms and legs in the sun make Edgar Allan Poe's self-consciously shocking cannibal scene in *Arthur Gordon Pym* seem tame. Melville acknowledged that he was deeply affected by the Chase narrative, although his most extensive marginal notes on the manuscript are ironic: "All the sufferings of these miserable men of the *Essex* might . . . have been avoided, had they, immediately after leaving the wreck, steered straight for Tahiti, from which they were not very distant at the time . . . . But they dreaded cannibals." [86] The implication is clear: cannibalism is always where you are. The reconstitution of human sentience as capital that appears separate from or even inimical to us, alienation—in a phenomenological or the Marxian sense—is a concept Melville resists. Even the minimally dense oil that is finally "tried out" of the whale must be understood in this novel not as a ghostly, circulating capital, but as so much human blood ("not a gallon you burn, but at least one drop of man's blood was spilled for it"). [87] Animal oils are also reconstituted as "butter" and "Texel and Leyden cheese" in the spurious ship's manifest Ishmael studies in order to speculate on how the heavy consumption of "smeer" affects the character of Dutch and English crews. Ishmael concludes that animal fat makes us happy. Finally, Captain Ahab's project of reconstituting a particular, "monstrous" whale out of the commodity he has been shipped to produce is *not*, in this novel, an extraordinary instance of the sentimentalization of capital.

In fact, I would argue that the sentimentalization of capital is the larger project of *Moby-Dick*, where circulation is always, if sometimes too strenuously, naturalized as the circulation of bodies, their organic gasses and fluids—oil, blood, sperm, gastric juices and those organic chemicals resultant from putrefaction which transform whale carcasses into grotesque "animal balloons." When I speak of "sentimentalization" here I am referring to the process of returning sentience to that which might otherwise by considered unfeeling and incapable of inspiring identification in readers;[88] of course this process has been central to the sentimental novel, although I think *Moby-Dick* is less interested in the sympathy and political corollaries of sympathy that typify sentimental "cultural work" than in enacting nostalgia for breathing capital, like whales, whose presence or use has not yet been obscured by arbitrary signs. Count how many times the word "unctuous" appears in *Moby-Dick* and you get a sense of the book's obsession with returning sensuousness and presence to an imperial business in the global commons that, as Casarino remarks, was increasingly arduous to visualize the more multiple and interconnected it became. The onomatopoetic "unctuous" forces us to feel and even mouth the whale oil. The passionate Captain Ahab may not be necessary to capitalism itself, as it was developing circa 1850, but he is necessary to a valorization of capitalism as a fundamentally human, fleshly pursuit.

Ahab's "to hell with business,"[89] to quote C. L. R. James, makes him an unlikely hero of business, a man who cares passionately about the product. Ahabian madness translated through Ishmalian rhetoric transforms American whaling into something other than a profit-driven business and makes room for a broader romanticization of industry. In an 1839 article for the *Knickerbocker* that influenced Melville, the sailor-author J. N. Reynolds described the killing of a famous white whale called "Mocha Dick" off the coast of Chile in a manner that similarly leads to a celebration of the naturalness of U.S. commercial enterprise. Tellingly, Reynolds used the hunt of an extraordinary whale to make clear that in the whaling business—and by implication, in all U.S. industry—the laborer acts freely, according to his personal desire rather than structural necessity. Whaling dissipates the specter of alienated labor and the loss of personal forms of control to a spectral, circulating capital. Reynolds says of the whalers' business: "These characteristics [of whaling] are not the growth of forced exertion; they are incompatible with it. They are the natural result of the ardor of a free people; of a spirit of fearless independence, generated by free institutions. Under such institutions alone, can the human mind attain its fullest expansion, in the various departments of science, and the multiform pursuits of busy life."[90]

The symbolic hunt that is *Moby-Dick*'s central plot has been borrowed from *Davy Crockett's Almanacs* and other written and oral western legends of great white hunters and recalcitrant bears—in fact, Captain Ahab is described once in the novel as "a Missouri bear," as if he really is a western species who has found (temporary) refuge at sea from his inevitable extinction.[91] Whereas Davy Crockett kills hundreds of bears in his 1834 *Autobiography* and squeezes the life-force out of legendary bears in stories like "Sunrise in My Pocket" from the popular *Almanacs*, the crew of the *Pequod* both perpetually conquer their prey and perpetually lose it. The images Melville culls from the antebellum westerns available to him fatten a representational space that has already gotten ahead of the ideas and symbols associated with the landed West, including the hunt and its implicit idea of ingesting the other in order to assume the other's place in western nature. No one in *Moby-Dick* can be assured of where they will end up or who will be ingested by whom.

Again, *Moby-Dick* is a premature postwestern, pointing the way toward what the western was destined to become much later in its artistic career. The West of the Pacific cruising grounds is both West and sea, and what the sea gives to the West here is critical distance, the ability to push the concept of place beyond models of personal property and territorial statehood that are rooted in ideas of land. In *Moby-Dick*, as in contemporary westerns like Cormac McCarthy's *Blood Meridian* (1985) and Border Trilogy, there is no frontier line in which the transformation of savagery into civilization can be seen, or where wilderness turns into the settler-nation; savagery and civilization, wilderness and nation, figure as one in the same. The almost gratuitous, gross-out violence of portions of *Moby-Dick* suggest avant-garde meditations upon violence as both a political and aesthetic tool in late-twentieth-century westerns like McCarthy's or the director Sam Peckinpah's classic *The Wild Bunch* (1969).[92] But if Melville is artistically precocious insofar as he forces us to watch, and to keep watching, whale murder, death, and putrefaction, his representational boldness betrays a kind of nostalgia that is also familiar to the late-twentieth-century western. Just as McCarthy's *Cities of the Plain* (1998) evokes nuclear holocaust to focus, finally, upon the intimate violence (the knife battle) of two plasterboard western enemies, the Cowboy and the Pimp, *Moby-Dick's* gore substitutes for a full elaboration of its complex background environment—extractive industry on the world's oceans. *Moby-Dick* teaches that even in postwestern, postnational space, we are still human because we die and kill, love and hate, like animals; if character has become a flag of convenience, Ishmael testifies that at least bodies touch and tear at each other, and we can expect this to continue for a good long time.

The eternity Romantic writers like Byron typically associate with water figures in *Moby-Dick* as "the universal cannibalism of the sea; all whose creatures prey upon each other, carrying on eternal war since the world began."[93] But, again, I see this as sentimental reassurance. Eternal war implies eternal sentience and the eternal reiteration of "the animal," and, metonymically, "the human" as natural categories. The sea shares with the West that it denatures and critiques a similar promise of presence. Curiously, nineteenth-century writers who addressed the rivers of the West found less assurance in the possibilities of water. Perhaps, as Melville suggests, rivers are experienced as troubling scenes because they enforce a knowledge of just how close the green breast of the land, with all of its connotations of stability, virtue, and self-sufficiency, lies to the dynamic (meat) market of the open ocean. In *Moby-Dick*, Melville writes of the Erie Canal much as he, and other writers, would contemplate the great Mississippi: "the probationary life of the Grand Canal furnishes the sole transition between quietly reaping the Christian corn-field, and recklessly ploughing the waters of the most barbaric seas."[94] The probationary, purgatorial life to be lived between the geopolitical spaces of cornfield and barbaric sea came to be seen as the precise and uncomfortable position of U.S./Americanness in literatures of the old Southwest.

III. RIVER

THE CULTURE OF WATER

The Valley of the Mississippi is a portion of our country which is now arresting the attention not only of our own inhabitants, but also those of foreign lands. Such are its admirable facilities for trade, owing to its numerous navigable rivers,—such as the variety and fertility of its soil,—the number and excellence of its productions,—the genial nature of its climate,—the rapidity with which its population is increasing,—and the influence which it is undoubtedly about to wield in giving direction to the destiny of this nation,—as to render the West an object of the deepest interest to every American patriot. Nor can the Christian be inattentive to the inceptive character and forming manners of a part of the country whose influence will soon be felt to be favourable, or disastrous, to an extent corresponding to its mighty energies. . . .

ROBERT BAIRD, View of the Valley of the Mississippi, or the Emigrant's and Traveller's Guide to the West (1834)

The Mississippi River drew settlers to its fertile banks, but it, the water itself, could not be settled. The river was a fluid and unpredictable road into, and out of, the continental United States. These obvious facts produced more subtle anxieties, as the Mississippi became the West's central market road, a key corridor for not only western produce but also the domestic slave trade. The Mississippi personified nature's bounty and the volatility of domestic and international markets, heady gains and potentially devastating losses, including losses of character and even sentience; it complicated the agrarian moralism of Manifest Destiny without fully canceling the nationalist enthusiasms that the river's fertile valley had inspired. The charisma of the Mississippi River, really the charisma of the marketplace itself, infected its surrounding territories. No matter how vigorously mapped or patrolled by local property owners, the entire river valley remained, at least imaginatively, a landscape of risk.

As slave values soared in response to rising demand for cotton in the 1830s and again in the 1850s, the domestic slave trade which was conducted on the Mississippi reminded slave owners that their slaves' value depended upon their mobility, an attribute which also could be used against owners if it were acknowledged that, in the abolitionist Theodore Dwight Weld's terms, slaves were "property with will."[1] When Jefferson Davis lobbied for the Fugitive Slave Act of 1850 as a Senator from Mississippi, he claimed that the value of riverside properties was compromised because of the easy access to slaves that the river afforded thieves and abolitionists, who were also called "slave-thieves." Davis argued: "Those like myself, who live on the great highway of the West,—the Mississippi River—are most exposed [and] have a present and increasing interest in this matter."[2] Although incidents of slave escape from the Mississippi Valley, especially the southwestern border states of Mississippi, Louisiana, and Alabama, were in reality quite low, slave owners imagined that the river beckoned slaves with the promises of riverboat thieves and abolitionists who would steal them only to resell or exploit them elsewhere. The river imaged, for speculators in slaves as well as owners of riverside farmlands, the social death of bankruptcy if not a metaphorical slavery to the commodities that constituted wealth. The historian Walter Johnson has shown through his analysis of white Southerners "daydreaming about slaves" in their diaries and personal correspondence the intimate dependency of slave owners upon not just slave labor but also upon the idea that slaves were commodities, accouterments or augmentations of white selfhood.[3]

Like slave property, Mississippi Valley real estate played a crucial role in the development of identities both within and beyond the region. The land booms of Kentucky and Tennessee in the 1790s were followed by early nineteenth-century booms in Mississippi, Louisiana, Alabama, and Arkansas. The Mississippi River threatened the value of farmland as much—in reality, more—than it threatened local slave values. The southwestern humorist Thomas Bangs Thorpe, writing for *Harper's New Monthly Magazine* in 1855, warned investors away from riverside properties, as "untold acres of rich land, forming the banks, annually cave into the stream. . . ."[4] In Herman Melville's metaphysical critique of the market culture of the Mississippi, *The Confidence-Man* (1857), a Missouri plantation owner named Pitch attributes his distrust of Emersonian nature to the loss of a riverside farm— "ten thousand dollars' worth of alluvion, thrown broad off upon the waters."[5] In *Adventures of Huckleberry Finn*, published in 1885 but set in the 1840s, Mark Twain represents the uncertainty of value in this volatile riverine environment in his depiction of Bricksville, a destitute town on the Mississippi "that has to be always moving back, and back, and back, because the river's always gnawing at it."[6] This same town hosts the torture of street pigs and dogs and the casual murder of a drunk, Boggs, by a merchant, Sherburn, which results in the formation of a lynch mob. The sudden and irrevocable destruction perpetrated by the river upon this town create a social climate in which equilibrium is sought through reciprocal acts of annihilation. The assumption made by the denizens of Twain's Bricksville that growth contains within it the possible cancellation of presence is an assumption taught by the river. This same assumption fueled the anxious speculative economy of the Mississippi Valley, where the parasitical nature of white freedom, in Toni Morrison's phrase,[7] was evidenced in both the spectacle of slave traffic and in scenes of receding properties. Both the destructive and creative energies of the market were visible in the river, which was literally a marketplace carrying all varieties of domestic and international cargo, slaves, displaced American Indians, European immigrants, gambling parlors and even a nascent show business on the gaudy western steamboats. Not surprisingly, the Mississippi River produced a knowing, troubled literature that offered a powerful critique of domestic and international capitalism. This literature, which is primarily a literature of humor and crime, has come to be known as the literature of the old Southwest.

In the decades before the Civil War the old Southwest engendered, in its various chroniclers—humorists, crime writers, dime novelists, abolitionists, anti-abolitionists—narratives that imaged a variety of alternatives to and exaggerations of the claims of Manifest Destiny. The improbable worlds generated by the southwestern imagination were mutually exclusive but not necessarily oppositional. In the 1830s through the 1850s, the Mississippi Valley produced imaginary nations within nations, fantastic empires, and mutant semi-national confederations. Literature and political rhetoric disseminated images of the river pirate John Murrell's regional confederacy of slave thieves, John Brown's fluid abolitionist state, and the pan-African empire of the proto-black nationalist Martin Delany, which was really a racial negative of Manifest Destiny's turn toward the Caribbean and Latin America. The same broad region that produced what the South Carolina novelist and Young American William Gilmore Simms recognized as "native speech," the same region that played a fundamental role in the development of a uniquely national crime literature and a unique form of retributive justice—the region of lynching, laughing, and the excessive, popular body, was also the region where the nation was imagined to mutate into other nations, or indeed into an entity altogether hostile to the nation-form. After all, the old Southwest could have been Aaron Burr's Spanish-American empire, a prospect reiterated to the reading public by Harper and Brothers' 1836 release of Matthew L. Davis's *Memoirs of Aaron Burr*. The paradox of the Mississippi Valley involves its historical associations with a sentimentalized U.S. "folk" culture and its unavoidable ties to the domestic slave traffic that constituted the nation's most unsettling and perhaps most lucrative antebellum market.

Ernest Hemingway's famous assertion that American literature begins with Mark Twain's *Adventures of Huckleberry Finn* circumscribes the smaller but equally explosive claim that the United States' national-popular culture begins with an accurate recording of the southwestern voice. Recent debates amongst literary scholars about whether Huckleberry Finn's speech is "black" or "white" suggest that Hemingway's assumption really remains credible. Only if we believe that Huck Finn's speech is in fact the nation's speech can it matter whether Twain mimicked the vernacular of a poor white child named Tom Blankenship or that of a witty black child, "Sociable Jimmy," whom he met in a hotel in Paris, Illinois. [8] Ironically, the compound "southwestern" which William Dean Howells used to describe Twain's unique literary voice performs similar cultural work to the more current revisionist reading of Huckleberry Finn's speech as possibly "black." Both claims suggest a powerful desire to recognize Twain's literary realism as a "cord of national unity," to use the phrase that Frederick Jackson Turner recognized as the essential character of the North American frontier.

The desirability of labeling Twain a "Southwesterner," as Howells did, indicates the assumption that Twain's "Lincolnian" achievement, in Howells's words, involved recasting the U.S. South as the (supposedly) less politically dissonant and racially wounded U.S. West. Those who imagined the West as free land and free soil, the solution to the United States' slavery problem and the answer to its continuing race problem, recognize Twain as performing an ingenious sleight of hand by relocating national meaning away from the fallout of the Civil War. Yet Twain's Far West was not the Turnerian frontier, a "line of most rapid and effective Americanization" that healed sectional and racial conflict. For Twain western emigrants were not pioneers who banded together in settled communities of interest; they were competitive businessmen, and the market was their sacred, if unstable, ground. The Mississippi River was Twain's ultimate West because it was water and not land that could ever be settled. It was the site of the commercial traffic that Twain felt was making up the world, for better and for worse. In the antebellum domestic slave trade that was rigorously conducted on and along the river, Twain recognized the same fundamental national plot enacted by claim jumpers and charlatan mining companies in California and Nevada. This fundamental national plot involved selling something that does not rightly belong to you. It was a plot at once western, national, and international. Ultimately, for Twain "our" American pleasure is equal to international piracy and slaving, brutal misappropriations of property. If Twain indeed made the South *western*, he also made the West *southern*, and this total equation of South and West points to his profound critique of the conditions of a white mobility and Manifest Destiny that he also lived and even praised.

In 1838 the *London and Westminster Review* welcomed the birth of "original sounds" from the United States, alluding to a distinctive American vernacular and hailing an "American literature [that] has become national and original." "Naturally enough," the *Review* continued, "this portion of [U.S. literature] is that which in all countries is always most national and original—because made more than any other by the collective mind of the nation—the humorous."[1] The *Review's* celebration of the United States' "original sounds" would be echoed in 1844 by William Gilmore Simms, the South's foremost novelist and an energetic contributor to the Young America cultural movement supported by John O'Sullivan's *Democratic Review*. Writing for the *Southern Quarterly Review*, one of O'Sullivan's regional competitors, Simms recognized the germ of a truly national literature in "the buoyant force and animation" of the United States' humorous speech, a speech which emanated, crucially, from a specific region: "You will find it stretching downwards . . . from the great back-bone, the central ridge of the country, following the course of its waters along the slopes of western and south-western valleys."[2] Simms located the germ of national imagination in the borderlands of what is now called the old Southwest, a shifting region encompassing the states and territories on both sides of the Mississippi River and the even older border territory of Georgia.

As W. J. Cash suggested in the 1940s, the South has been the United States' first and last frontier. Cash's use of the word "frontier" is different than Frederick Jackson Turner's and suggests how southern history might be used to correct the cant of Manifest Destiny that still affects representations of the West. By referring to the South as a frontier, Cash essentially meant that it was a region where national meanings have been continually fractured and re-imagined.[3] For Cash, the southern border suggests a line of de-Americanization, the inversion of the Turnerian frontier. In the 1930s literary critics Constance Rourke and Bernard DeVoto more predictably imagined the old Southwest, which DeVoto called "Mark Twain's America," as the site of a regenerative regional primitivism.[4] It took remarkable foresight and a healthy dose of southern chauvinism for William Gilmore Simms to make equally complex claims about the old Southwest in 1844. Simms boldly named Augustus Baldwin Longstreet's *Georgia Scenes*, a book of regional sketches first published in Augusta in 1835, as the only successful literary humor that the United States had produced. Longstreet was "rare, racy, articulate, native," Simms raved.[5] His emphasis was on the final word, "native." Elsewhere in his review Simms asserts that the people of the southwestern river valleys are "in truth, a native people, children of the soil and sun," free of the "rigidity, the solemnity, the staid forms" that paralyze eastern cities.[6] Simms, a South Carolinian with ties to Mississippi through his father, with whom he traveled and temporarily lived in that border state, found in the southwestern territories the "folk" that German Romantics claimed as the bedrock of the nation. Young Americans reprinted theories of the Volk in their ambitious periodicals. There is symmetry in Simms's vision of the Mississippi Valley, which Andrew Jackson likened to the nation's alimentary canal,[7] as the origin of national sounds. Of course the idea that the West's foremost commercial waterway could also be the birthplace of U.S. popular culture was paradoxical.

No less an ultranationalist than his northern Democratic counterparts, William Gilmore Simms challenged them to acknowledge that their own favorite sons—like the New York writer Cornelius Matthews, whose work he is unfavorably reviewing when he turns to celebrate Longstreet and southwestern speech—might be crippled by their proximity to the means of literary production. "Our publishing press is established in places having intimate intercourse with Europe. New York, Boston, and Philadelphia, from which cities all our literature emanates, is more or less under the immediate control and direction of the European mind. In the same degree are they denuded of originality; and we must look elsewhere, to regions free, if possible, from this paralyzing influence, for whatever nationality our literature is destined to possess."[8] The New York–based *Democratic Review*'s sullen reply to Simms's argument reveals how the cosmopolitanism of New York City actually affected metropolitan imagination. In "American Humor," a direct retort to Simms, the *Review* dismisses Longstreet, claiming that they cannot find a copy of his book, which is unlikely given that *Georgia Scenes* was reissued by Harper and Brothers of New York in 1840. The *Review* then defends admittedly derivative humorists like Washington Irving and Cornelius Matthews on the basis of the value of the English humor they imitate. Finally, the *Review* offers a curious substitute for Simms's "native" wit in the advertisements to be found in the back of political sheets and even religious journals. "These advertisements occupy an original field of American humor; a rich territory; the realm of quacks and virtuosos and auctioneers. The land of patent medicines and candies, and all sorts of curious wants."[9] The

146

geographical metaphors used here to describe advertisements, the veritable poems of an a-national commerce, as "rich territory," "lands" metaphorically equivalent to the great West, are easily trumped by Simms's panorama of the sloping river valleys to the west of the Appalachians. Yet both the New York reviewer and Simms predicted the future of national humor. The huckster's wild exaggerations of value and the "native" accents of the Southwest would powerfully come together in the Mississippi River fictions of Mark Twain.

Among the Young Americans, it was only Simms who suggested that humor be recognized as the popular basis for national culture, which is interesting given that the literary Young Americans were all fighting to establish a national-popular culture, in Antonio Gramsci's terms, meaning a culture that has been reformed to apparent legitimacy by going to the people, "raising" the popular into political rhetorics and more elite literary forms.[10] Now it is commonplace to recognize humor as the most local and "popular" of literary genres. This assumption was easily made in the folkloric revivals of the 1880s and 1930s, but apparently it was less obvious in the earnest decades prior to the Civil War. Even Simms's analysis of the significance of popular humor is wildly contradictory. In the same review where he praises southwestern language for its "buoyant force and animation . . . its copious fund of expression . . . the audacity of its illustration, its very hyperbole" he lambastes newspaper humor for approximately the same features: "dashing effrontery, bold blackguardism, or a fun that is deplorably silly. . . . Our wit consists in odd analogies, strained metaphor, hyperbole beyond grasp, and absurdity. . . ."[11] Humor, it seems, made Young America nervous. Certainly it could work both for and against the project of hegemony. The release provided by political jokes might serve the interests of the state, as the freedom to act out can inspire consent. On the other hand, tendentious jokes, as Freud warns, often assume specific targets, listeners whom the joke will wound or unmask before other listeners who become party to the aggression.[12] Jokes are divisive. In the United States in the 1830s and 1840s, some of the most tendentious literary humor emanated from the territories around the Mississippi River, whose writers were more compelled by cultural divisions than by the sentimental unities implied in phrases such as "native speech." The humor that emanated from the southwestern territories adjacent to the Mississippi reveals the river's deep linkages to metropolitan character.

Southwestern Humor and Interregional Commerce

The most significant southwestern humor was written by Whigs who were frustrated with the Democracy inaugurated by Andrew Jackson and carried forth as a cultural program by the Young Americans. While the grim *American Whig Review* answered John O'Sullivan's call for the annexation of Texas with a lament that "the foul spirit of anarchy and disorganization" infected the Democrats,[13] the scurrilous New York–based sporting newspaper, the *Spirit of the Times*, handed Democrats compelling caricatures with southwestern accents. Many of the southern merchants, planters, and newspapermen who wrote for the *Spirit* raged, in their private lives or in their own local newspapers, at Andrew Jackson's high tariff legislation, at the expansion of the credit economy, at the new competitiveness of political life as state constitutional reforms of the 1820s and 1830s began to abolish property qualifications for voting and holding office. Kenneth Lynn's classic political reading of southwestern humor suggests that the *Spirit of the Times* became a vessel for an exacerbated southern conservatism.[14] But the politics of southern Whigs could not appear openly in the *Spirit of the Times*. The newspaper claimed bipartisanship, and southwestern political energies were translated into a revolutionary dialect humor.

The *Spirit of the Times; A Chronicle of the Turf, Field Sports, Literature, and the Stage*, was founded in 1831 by William Trotter Porter, a prominent Whig who developed his regard for the kingly sport of horseracing in his native Vermont. Porter initially imagined his paper as a sporting paper devoted to the "turf and chase" and mindful of the primary form of urban entertainment, theater. Sporting news had to be sent to the paper by correspondents in the field, gentlemen and amateur journalists. In the 1830s Porter made several trips to the Mississippi Valley to gather such correspondents, cultivating a backcountry aristocracy who coveted leisure sport as a marker of status.[15] Porter identified with this southern form of self-fashioning and carried it to New York City at a time (the 1830s) when the recently constructed Erie Canal had made New York the nation's most vital commercial port. Lynn has argued convincingly that the *Spirit of the Times* established interregional ties amongst the mercantile classes of the Northeast and monied lawyers, politicians, and planters in the South. The southwestern correspondents who wrote to the *Spirit* intended, in part, to convince Northerners of the threat of yokel parvenus who were newly empowered by Democratic politics. Star writers like Johnson Jones Hooper contributed political satires to the paper that painted Jacksonians as clownish anarchists. Lynn suggests how southwesterners hoped to influence New York City's view of the South, yet of course the *Spirit of the Times* was not narrowly subordinated to an obscure, regional imagination. Naturally, interregional intelligence flowed both ways. The nation's most prominent metropolis shared with the Mississippi valley an anxious fascination with the vicissitudes of commercial culture.

The *Spirit of the Times*'s chief editor and publisher, Porter, attempted to limit his intended readership and contain the meanings of his journal to "the refinements, the luxuries, and the enjoyments of society."[16] He discouraged the mingling of classes that might take place accidentally on the streets of New York City, for example, by raising the yearly subscription price of the *Spirit of the Times* from three dollars to five dollars to the impossibly expensive ten dollars. The most costly journals in the 1830s sold for three dollars per year, and Porter would eventually be forced to sell out to another publisher because of his gross misreading of his public.[17] In the South, money was scarce, land was losing value, cotton prices were lower than slave prices, and big-time horse racing had come to a virtual standstill. Porter ignored these signs, although he was forced to print a more varied selection of items because sporting news was so thin. It was the Panic of 1837 that accidentally created a publication venue for southwestern correspondents who had more to report to the nation than outcomes at local racetracks. Johnson Jones Hooper and Thomas Bangs Thorpe blossomed in the *Spirit* during the depression that followed the Panic. The diminution of sporting news and public interest in rural leisure made the *Spirit of the Times* a more realistic, if less purposeful, response to the desires and ambitions of an interregional commercial class.

One of the deep topics of the *Spirit of the Times* in the late 1830s and 1840s is the proximity of poverty and wealth. Of course this is also a crucial theme in popular "mysteries of the city" novels from the same period by sensationalist authors like George Lippard and the French novelist Eugène Sue. When the southwestern correspondent visited the metropolis, he offered New York City a happily defamiliarized version of the problem of holding one's course between a wealth and poverty that were both excessively visible in urban spaces. In an item from 25 January 1840 called "Major Boots in Gotham," the southwesterner, "Boots," describes his consternation at the manner in which class distinctions are played out on city sidewalks. The west side of the walk is reserved for the "proud and kingly," Boots notes, while the east side hosts "the poor and industrious."[18] Boots's advice to "my southern friends" in New York is to walk wherever the sun is shining, advice that converts the touchy problem of being middle-class into a gentler regional preference. A New York correspondent writing to the Spirit in November 1839 suggests another middle course by implying that fulfillment inheres in a mere proximity to wealth. Specifically, this writer defines pleasure as sitting next to a wealthy diner at the old Globe Hotel in New York City and "snuffing" the rich man's dinner. "In the art of living, we are making advances in this country, despite the hard times. Once in an age we treat ourselves to a chop at the Globe, and amuse ourselves while enjoying a frugal dinner with reading a bill of fare, from which an emperor might select a repast. . . . Or, mayhap, some rich citizen near us furnishes the [indulgence] of a more material snuff, by carving away at the next table upon some savory viand."[19] This item was published in the Spirit in the same year that William T. Porter raised the paper's price to ten dollars, a depression year in which the middle course seemed desirable, if virtually unattainable, to the paper's correspondents.

The humor of the Spirit of the Times is neatly calibrated to the shocking shifts of value which can be generated by volatile international markets. A front-page report from Boston on 6 October 1838 neatly summarizes "all the local news" of the day as huge commercial failure: "All the local news may be put into a nutshell without cramming. The aggregate of the late losses of Boston Underwriters upon ships, Argosy, Sardis, and Kentucky, is two hundred and seventy thousand dollars. This comes rather hard, but fortunately, the amount is pretty equally divided among the various companies."[20] The same Boston correspondent who delivers this bomb begins his letter to the editor with a chipper report of "Theatre Doings" in Boston, elaborating on the origins of a farce at Boston's National Theater called "The Striped Pig." The author explains the history of "The Striped Pig" as an ingenious Yankee speculation; a man intent on selling liquor at a local militia muster evaded the license law by pretending to exhibit a striped pig on the muster grounds. For six and a quarter cents, customers paid to enter a tent where a painted farm pig and a "treat of spirituous liquor" awaited them. The selectmen who organized the muster praised the clever man for educating his townsfolk in natural history. "Every mouth teams with striped pig, not literally, but liquorally," the Boston correspondent concludes, yoking the metaphorical reach of his own verbal humor to the Yankee's illegal risk.[21] The Yankee's small triumph, memorialized in theatrical farce, plays counterpoint to the huge losses that greeted speculators all over the United States after the Panic of 1837.

In the same years that nurtured the southwestern humorists, the *Spirit of the Times* is awash with images of financial failure in northeastern cities and a compensatory, fatalistic urban humor that counters the absurd proximity of failure and success. The point of this humor is to make the incongruous culture of the city risible, if not actually pleasurable. On 3 November 1838 the *Spirit* prints an item that almost seems to be a mocking and premature epitaph of John Jacob Astor on its front page: "John Jacob Astor of New York, is said to be worth the trifle of twenty-five millions of dollars—more than twice the sum left by Stephen Girard. This, at six percent, would produce one million five hundred thousand dollars a year—one hundred twenty-five thousand a month; four thousand and one hundred and seventy-three dollars an hour—two dollars and eighty-seven and a half cents a minute—and nearly fifty cents a second! He will be rich by and bye." [22] This item is immediately followed by another that bears no rational relation to it; the second item celebrates sailors' malapropisms, their "travesties" of the names of merchant ships: "The disposition of sailors to *travesty* names of vessels, was amusingly exhibited to us, this morning. We met two seamen in the street, and as we passed them, one said, 'Well, Bill, so you are going out in the Fast-sailor' (Pharsalia). 'No,' replied the other, 'I've shipped in the Palm-iler.' (Palmyra)." [23] While lower-class ignorance is certainly one target of this last joke, the joke also reduces the cultural pretensions of merchant capitalists back to the lowest common denominators of trade: rapid movement and "palm oil" or money. The paper's juxtaposition of sailors' conversation which is tellingly overheard in the street with a crazy calculus of John Astor's fortune down to the "two dollar and eighty-seven cent" minute again positions it on a middle ground between deep capital and the fringe agents of the commercial class, sailors. The *Spirit of the Times's* idealized middle position is also the place of the comic straight man who observes incongruities and excesses, who structures humorous situations without actually delivering a comic performance.

The *Spirit of the Times's* devotion to the New York theater, indicated by the "Theatre Doings" always listed on its front page, further suggests the paper's assumption of an audience that was metropolitan in spirit if not in reality. In antebellum New York City the theater not only offered the primary form of paid entertainment but it also offered a space where various forms of illicit commerce, namely prostitution, were tolerated. Here was a perfect venue for the observation of the mixing of "kingly" and "poor" that "Boots" and other correspondents to the *Spirit* found humorous and befuddling. It is interesting to contrast the three primary spaces of leisure that the *Spirit of the Times* chronicled from its inception in 1831 until it folded in 1856: the theater, the racetrack, and the hunting ground. The paper's hunting and racing news glories in a lack of consequence, in the practitioners' leisure to amuse themselves as they like and the financial comfort that makes deep betting a sport rather than a business. Hunters, spectators at the races, and theatergoers shared the luxury of spending, watching and waiting, but hunting and racing imply a less ephemeral play and a far more restricted company than might be found in the theaters of New York. Hunting and racing were country pleasures meant to take place on private grounds. Presumably Porter imagined the South as the location of landed gentry comparable to the landed classes of Britain; New York would be his London. Porter originally announced his periodical as a stateside version of the leading British sporting journal, *Bell's Life in London.*[24] He reprinted British sporting news, humorous sketches and theater tattle in the *Spirit* and seems to have hoped to cultivate a leisure class in the United States that would be responsive to British models. But several of the southwestern writers who became Porter's correspondents and friends wrote about the country bordering the Mississippi River as if it were New York City, a public space of commerce and visible incongruity where sailors and millionaires might know each other or at least brush shoulders in the street.

One of the first dialect letters submitted to the *Spirit of the Times* from a southwestern correspondent describes the cosmopolitan character of steamboats on the Mississippi River and the bizarre "theatre doings" of Louisville, Kentucky. The writer, Charles Fenton Mercer Noland, submits his letter as Pete Whetstone, a traveler from Arkansas:

> Well, the William French came puffing by—so I shoulders my wallet and walks onto her—... What a heap of people! Some high foluting and some low foluting, just a sprinklin' of all sorts, from quality and bad-quality, to commonality, rubbish, and trash. ...
> I got up to Louisville. Maybe it ain't a big place—why Little Rock wouldn't be missed out of it. Well, I went to the theatre, and it was right chock full; they played what they said was the Rival Pages. Sich a play! Oh, Lordy!—two women dressed in men's clothes—(I reckon that is what's called wearing the britches!)—and one great big overgrown fellow playing the King. Why Jim Cole looks more like a King than that fellow did. Somebody called him the *Ge-rof,*

but he looked to me like a hard-baked loaf of bread, that had got cold, because nobody had teeth sharp enough to bite the crust.[25]

Many of the best southwestern humorists, like Noland, saw something like the culture of the port city in the Mississippi Valley. Here was a space that boisterously hosted "all sorts," some "high foluting" and some "low foluting." Thomas Bangs Thorpe's now famous hunting story, "The Big Bear of Arkansas," begins on a Mississippi steamboat that appears as a place like a city street where one accidentally overhears distinctive stories and accents and then attempts to reframe them for a home audience. Although I will discuss individual southwestern humorists in more detail elsewhere, my point here is merely to underline the similarities, rather than the differences, among southwestern and metropolitan humorists who wrote for the Spirit of the Times. Southwestern humorists were "funny" to New Yorkers not only because they spoke with "funny" accents, but because they and their region shared metropolitan concerns.

In the Spirit of the Times southwestern humor replicated many of the concerns of the commercial city and even some of its typical scenes, such as the theater, the circus, and the crowded "street" or river-space. The primary difference offered by southwestern humorists was that the voice that structured their comic scenes was not the unmarked voice of the middle-class consumer, the Boston theatergoer or the frugal New York diner happy to sit next to wealth. The epistolary form of many reports to the Spirit encouraged southwestern writers to experiment with a regional dialect, and while some continued to divide their correspondence between the patrician voices of upper-class narrators and the dialect of yokel characters, the rural voice dominated in the best southwestern pieces by Noland, Thorpe, and Hooper. For these writers the voice of the culture critic came to speak in the accents of the lower-class buffoon. Pretentious overreaching and bold speculation and the absurd proximities of poverty and wealth, of failure and success, were observed and performed by the same characters. This blending of critic and buffoon in southwestern humor changed the position of the comic observer. Instead of dwelling next to wealth and observing social extremities from a comfortable middle distance, southwestern comedy dwelt next to poverty.[26] Southwestern humor could give little ground to a detached, emergent professionalism and a disinterested, literary voice. In brief, it could barely afford a (representational) middle class. The lack of any comfort zone in southwestern humor between poverty and wealth, failure and success, makes this humor particularly edgy, and, oddly, particularly urban. Perhaps this metropolitan edge should be expected from a region in which the incongruities present in the metropolis were even more marked, where the difference between "bust" and "boom" might be the difference between slave and master.

Southwestern Violence and Literary Nationalism

The booms and busts of the U.S. economy in the 1830s inspired a desire for a literary realism that might be the intellectual equivalent of the hard currency which the nation lacked. In 1836, Ralph Waldo Emerson imagined the new nation sloughing off "old words . . . perverted to stand for things which are not; a paper currency . . . when there is no bullion in the vaults."[27] As language was called upon to return to that half-empiricist construct Emerson called "the world," money, in the 1830s, had become farther removed from it. The southwestern humorist Johnson Jones Hooper referred to 1836 as the "year of grace—and excessive bank issues."[28] Hooper's mock campaign biography of the Andrew Jackson–doppelganger Simon Suggs, which was initially serialized in the Spirit of the Times, offers a cynical, vernacular response to this perilous inflation of value. The opening of American Indian lands to speculators and the importation of large numbers of slaves into the Mississippi Valley made the booms and busts of the 1830s particularly dramatic in that region. The abolitionist writer William Goodell recalled 1836 as the year of "the great Negro speculation," implying that both northeastern and foreign money was channeled into African-American "stock" whose value was on the rise in the newly settled states of Mississippi and Arkansas.[29] As the value of land, cotton, and other commodities fell in the aftermath of the Panic of 1837, only slave prices steadily climbed, especially in the recently "opened" Indian lands around the Mississippi River.

The consistently high value of slaves in the Mississippi Valley helped to inaugurate a crime literature that might be described as, like southwestern humor, national but not nationalist in its aims. I refer to what were essentially crime narratives written by immediatist abolitionists, those associated with William Lloyd Garrison's American Anti-Slavery Society who recognized the racist presumptions of the American Colonization Movement.[30] Immediatist abolitionists were early advocates of secession, and they produced graphic witness testimonies to the public and private crimes of U.S. slavery to make their point. One of the most famous examples of this sort of testimonial is Theodore Dwight Weld's compilation of first-hand accounts from throughout the slave-owning territories, *American Slavery As It Is* (1839). The sampling technique used by Weld and other abolitionist authors argues, implicitly, that the evil of slavery is legion, unlocalized. Most of these narratives move across a variety of locations and are not focused on the southwestern border, even though many of them, including *Uncle Tom's Cabin*, recognize the Mississippi River as a corridor of the slave trade and the southwestern plantation as the slavocracy's moral *nadir*.

In 1837, the murder of a Mississippi Valley abolitionist augmented the image of misrule and anti-abolitionist violence infecting the region. The abolitionist editor Elijah Lovejoy was shot by a mob of "upstanding" citizens as he attempted to defend his press in the riverside town of Alton, Illinois. Lovejoy had recently fled threats in Saint Louis, believing Alton to be a quieter and more respectable town. Lovejoy enters literary history through Edward Beecher's *Narrative of the Riots at Alton* (1838), a hastily penned recollection of the lynching which was advertised as an offering to a national public beyond "merely transient or local excitements," in the words of its original publisher.[31] Beecher's *Narrative* must have been a disappointment to readers who saw in his publisher's assurance a glint of sensationalism, because it is essentially jeremiad. It also certainly is not crafted for a national audience, as it recommends disunion or a cleansing war with the South. In the Mississippi Valley and, by extension, in the greater South, Beecher sees a localized disease: "In one portion of the body politic soundness is gone, the laws have given way, the tremendous reign of anarchy has begun, and our only hope for their final restoration to their wonted majesty and power is in the restorative energies of that portion of the body politic which remains yet uncorrupted."[32] As historian Leonard Richards has shown, the years 1833 to 1838 mark the height of mob activity in the antebellum United States, but "the reign of anarchy," in Beecher's terms, was national, not explicitly southern or southwestern. Moreover, the range of potential targets included abolitionists, Catholics, Mormons, prostitutes, and gamblers.[33]

It remains an open question whether the rise in all types of mob activity in this era can be attributed to anti-abolitionist panic, as some contemporary writers believed. Certainly a variety of people might have been anxious that abolitionist victory could change and perhaps destroy the national economy. As James M. McPherson has noted, emancipation, when it came, effected the "confiscation of about three billion dollars worth of property . . . the principal form of property in one-third of the country."[34] Crime literature generated by conditions in the old southwest ties the moral problem of slavery to the national and even international fears of economic vulnerability that are also present in southwestern humor.

Abraham Lincoln's famous discussion of the post-Revolutionary generation's "increasing disregard for law" in his 1838 "Address before the Young Men's Lyceum of Springfield, Illinois," takes as its touchstones for jeremiadic outrage three instances of mob violence in towns along the Mississippi River. Like Beecher, Lincoln indicates that the Mississippi Valley in particular is a seat of an anarchic violence that threatens national consolidation. Lincoln begins his speech with a localized catalogue: the brutal lynching of a free black man, William McNeal, in Saint Louis; in Vicksburg the murder of gamblers purportedly tied to the slave-stealing ring of a river pirate named John Murrell; and, in Alton, the murder of Elijah Lovejoy.[35] All three instances of mob activity are, of course, symptomatic of the larger social crime of chattel slavery. More specifically, these riots suggest slave owners' fears of losing slave property to the cosmopolitan currents of the river. The Mississippi, emblem of the United States' burgeoning market culture and also a prime conductor of the domestic slave trade, generated regional rhetorics of economic nihilism that would resurface in the modernist and proto-modernist literature that came out of the South in the late nineteenth and twentieth centuries.

Figurations of River Culture

Although no single figure can summon the rich context of the antebellum Southwest, the Mississippi River slave thief John Murrell offers a useful point of entry into the southwestern imagination because his story, a fiction grown from relatively small history, includes speculation, slavery, humor, and crime—all of the elements by which southwestern writers came to identify their region and, by implication, the volatile national project. The Murrell narrative has been retold, with different emphases, throughout the nineteenth and twentieth centuries. Some of the formal elements of the original narrative, which circulated in 1835, have remained intact, particularly the original narrative's treatment of temporality.

The troubled relationship between moral imagination and narrative temporality is at the foreground of one of the most contemporary treatments of John Murrell, Eudora Welty's short story "A Still Moment," which was first published in the 1943 collection The Wide Net and Other Stories. For Welty, John Murrell is a composite, a storyteller-murderer who displaces "the lived present" with a cyclical and necessarily artificial narrative time. Here Mur-

rell's repetition of the same long tale serves as the metaphorical complement to actual murders.

> Murrell riding along with his victim-to-be, Murrell riding, was Mur-
> rell talking. He told away at his long tales, with always a distance
> and a long length of time flowing through them, and all centered
> about a silent man. In each the silent man would have done a piece
> of evil, a robbery or a murder, in a place of long ago, and it was all
> made for the revelation in the end that the silent man was Murrell
> himself, and the long story had happened yesterday, and the place
> here—the Natchez Trace. It would only take one dawning look for
> the victim to see that all of this was another story and he himself
> had listened his way into it, and that he too was about to recede in
> time (to where the dread was forgotten) for some listener and to
> live for a listener in the long ago. Destroy the present!—that must
> have been the first thing that was whispered in Murrell's heart—the
> living moment and the man that lives in it must die before you can
> go on.[36]

There can be no doubt that Welty's "Murrell" is deeper than the Murrell of
the 1835 legend. He is the character who most approximates the author's
perspective, the first to recognize and to speak from the dead center of
artifice, the still moment of the story's title which, once glimpsed, scatters
and repels the two other travelers Welty has set on the Natchez Trace—
Lorenzo Dow, itinerant preacher and inventor of the camp meeting, and
the painter-naturalist John James Audubon. Welty is loose with historical
associations. She mistakenly names Murrell "James." She also dissociates
Murrell from the crimes of the 1830s for which he became famous, placing
him in an earlier era of criminality on the Trace, a notorious hotbed of
highway robbery in the 1810s and early 1820s.

Misplaced and misnamed, Eudora Welty's Murrell still bears a formal
resemblance to the Murrell of antebellum legend. What Welty describes as
Murrell's repetitive "story that kills" structurally approximates the crime
narrative that made the original John Murrell famous in the 1830s. That
crime narrative recounted Murrell's repetitive acts of illegal slave trading,
which included the theft, disguise, sale, relocation, disguise and resale—in
other words, the continual circulation—of black Americans. Once Murrell's
slaves became recognizable as individuals and no longer amenable to disguise or available for resale, the story ended; Murrell killed them, their time
had run up against the motive force of the cycle. Welty writes of Murrell's

attempt to supplant mortal finitude: "Destroy the present!— . . . The living moment and the man that lives in it must die before you can go on." In the original Murrell narrative, the living moment was extinguished in two ways, only one of which involved repetition. There were social deaths—of humans repeatedly disguised and resold or re-commodified, as slaves; this process appeared to make many persons (or *slave* semi-persons) from one. Murrell's illegal slave trading suggests a kind of inflation that is also present in Welty's iterative "tale." Then there were the actual murders Murrell committed, of those slaves who could not be remade, those who had become unmistakably and fatally themselves. These, like the murders in Welty's short story, happened only once.

In the original Murrell legend there were also, always, more victims stepping into Murrell's ruse because what he offered them was the essential promise of liberal democracy: self-ownership. Murrell, the criminal, vowed to help his victims to own themselves. Sometimes his victims were not slaves, but white travelers from Kentucky or South Carolina, perhaps second sons hoping to find their fortunes in the recently opened territories; these men were also vulnerable to false friendship. Murrell would simply rob and kill them. According to the legend, victim after victim was seduced only to "recede in time (to where the dread was forgotten)"—in Welty's phrase. For a black American or a marginal white traveling in the Mississippi Valley in the 1830s, how close was freedom to death? This is Welty's almost Hegelian question. The central problem of "A Still Moment" becomes the likeness of any human design to murder. In contrast, the original Murrell narrative includes the thick social problems of class and race, and in its rant against *slave thieves* this antebellum fiction delivers a surprising, no doubt unintentional exposé of slave-trading and the marketplace that supported it. The original Murrell narrative can be read as evidence of the United States' shared, anxious shame, and also as indicative of the relative innocence of the Southwest in the 1830s, the relative looseness of its pro-slavery ideology at the time that the rhetoric of immediatist abolitionism was also immature. I recognize the Murrell narrative as a significant antebellum literary artifact not only because it openly addresses slavery—a censored topic in Congress as well as in polite literature. Even rarer is the fact that this narrative addresses U.S. slavery from the perspective of a propertyless Southerner.

In 1835, the first pamphlet biography of John Murrell appeared. This 1835 version of the *Life of Murel* detailed Murrell's purported crimes as the leader of a "Mystic Clan" of slave thieves who operated in the southwestern borderlands and used the Mississippi River and its tributaries as corridors for criminal movement. The pamphlet's purported author was a southwestern gentleman named "Augustus Q. Walton," but it is probable that this was a pseudonym used by Virgil Stewart, a clerk in the local Choctaw Purchase who claimed to have infiltrated Murrell's ranks. By 1836, the biography, which initially had been published and distributed in the counties nearest to Murrell's hometown in western Tennessee, had reached New York City, where it was partially rewritten by a professional hack to include associations of Murrell's illegal slave trade with the abolitionists who had launched an inflammatory "mail campaign" against the South in 1835, the very year that the first Murrell narrative appeared. If people living along the Mississippi River were not entirely aware of the abolitionist threat in 1835, New York publishers were willing to exploit it. In 1838 and 1840, respectively, William Gilmore Simms wrote two "border romances" treating the Murrell legend, Richard Hurdis and Border Beagles. Significantly, both of Simms's novels dissociate Murrell from the deeper controversies associated with slavery. By the early 1840s, Murrell was again offered to the national public in the widely circulated National Police Gazette, where he was referred to, broadly, as a "speculator." This common economic activity, as I will explain in more detail, had a multitude of criminal associations. In 1847, a dime-novel version of the Life of Murel, compiled by H. R. Howard, was published in New York by Harper and Brothers. The foremost historian of the Murrell legend, James Lal Penick, Jr., argues that Murrell diminished in popularity shortly after the Howard edition and was virtually forgotten after the Civil War. For Penick, Murrell is not a viable bandit because, unlike Jesse James or Robin Hood, he does not represent socioeconomic redistribution. As Penick suggests, Murrell is self-interested.[37] In other words, he is liberal democracy's criminal image of itself, which made him particularly compelling to later cultural critics like Mark Twain.

I argue that John Murrell did not disappear after the Civil War and thereby prove the irrelevance of the antebellum Southwest's anxious imagination. Eudora Welty, for one, reinvented Murrell, although, again, shorn of the social mechanisms that gave him his mythic status. Mark Twain reinvented Murrell several times, and when he did so he was also reinventing his childhood; he kept the rich contexts that produced the criminal legend essentially intact. Twain directly quotes what appears to be an early (circa 1830s) version of the Life of Murel in his 1883 travel memoir, Life on the Mississippi. He parodies the myth of Murrell's inter-regional conspiracy in the unpublished novella *Tom Sawyer's Conspiracy*.[38] In the biographical essay "A Scrap of Curious History" (1894), Twain describes a secretive group of abolitionists who challenged the town of Hannibal in his boyhood using the same name that was given to Murrell's confederacy, the "Mystic Clan." Twain reworked portions of the Murrell narrative into *The Adventures of Tom Sawyer* (1876) and *Adventures of Huckleberry Finn* (1885). Certainly Murrell cannot be described as a transcendent key to Twain's work. Yet I think Twain's reiterations of the Murrell narrative are indicative of the centrality of the slave thief in the imaginative repertoire of the antebellum Southwest, which is the setting that Twain more than any other literary figure made central to U.S. popular culture.

In *Life on the Mississippi*, Twain calls John Murrell a "wholesale rascal" in comparison to Jesse James, whom he demotes to the status of "retail rascal."[39] Twain made this ironic comparison at the height of Jesse James's notoriety. In 1883, Twain visited the Mississippi Valley shortly after Jesse James had been murdered by one of his own henchmen, and in *Life on the Mississippi*, a partial memoir of this journey, he recalls seeing dime biographies of James hawked and eagerly consumed on the steamboats. The economic nature of Twain's joke, that the undoubtedly famous James is "retail," the nearly forgotten Murrell, "wholesale," implies that the very nature of slave property allowed for a larger scale of economic paranoia, and a larger fear of crime, than would be imaginable after Emancipation. As chattel and persons, "property with *will*," slaves were always potentially complicit in thieves' designs. Moreover, the relative anonymity forced upon slaves by the operations of the legal slave trade erased slaves' individual characteristics and facilitated fraud. The ex-slave William Wells Brown, in his *Autobiography* and his 1853 novel *Clotel* most poignantly exposes the domestic slave trade as it was practiced along the Mississippi River. Brown served as a slave "groom" for a white river trader and assisted in disguising aging slaves by blacking their hair, pulling white whiskers from their faces, and forcing them to assume playful roles in the slave pens of Rodney, Natchez, and New Orleans.[40] The brutality of the slave trade consisted, in part, in its forced masking of black individuals. Even pro-slavery apologists like the Southern lawyer David Hundley imagined that the legal domestic slave trade, because of its tendency to fraud, might destabilize local and national economies.[41]

Both Mark Twain and the various authors of the *Life of Murel* link the domestic slave trade to white hucksterism and charlatanry and more generally to the increasingly destabilized and "mobile" idea of economic value which characterized the Jacksonian period. Southwestern literatures of crime and humor share an anxiety inspired by the apparent fungibility of black bodies and the unlikely but horrifying prospect that this fungibility, like the taint of race itself, might spread to the white population. The projective desire or consumer confidence that Herman Melville interrogates in The Confidence-Man suggests white mobility and its most radical extension, the displacement of racial and social selves in a whirl of exchange reminiscent of what Karl Marx would describe in Capital as a "philistine utopia." Marx's bourgeois ou-topos, where "all commodities can simultaneously be imprinted with the stamp of direct exchangeability, in the same way that it might be imagined that all Catholics can be popes,"[42] is the imaginary-geographical equivalent of Melville's confidence man. This confidence man, who ultimately assumes the second, significant name "the cosmopolitan," is literally a man made out of consumer desire, a man who is black, white, invalid, sound—all things to all people. Melville's fictional confidence man circulates through the booming Mississippi Valley with the generic anonymity of money in much the same way that speculators, slave traders, thieves, abolitionists, and the hybrid climbers David Hundley called "Southern Yankees" circulate throughout popular fictions treating the Mississippi Valley.

Shame, Economic Apocalypse, and the Very Small History of John Murrell
In the summer of 1835, a peculiar panic broke out in Madison County, Mississippi, a panic incited and sustained by the first pamphlet biography of John Murrell. In the long summer of 1835, Madison County came to believe that it was the seat of a slave rebellion Murrell had allegedly plotted with a vast band of conspirators throughout the Mississippi Valley. While anxieties rose in Mississippi, the actual John Murrell began serving a ten-year sentence in a Tennessee prison.[43] Murrell had been convicted in 1834 on two counts of slave stealing. No charges of a region-wide conspiracy to incite slaves to rebel had been made during Murrell's trial. John Murrell, whoever he really was, receded, and in his place the legendary Murrell grew, through rumors inspired by the locally published criminal biography, Augustus Q. Walton's Life of Murel. Although most Tennesseans who had known Murrell shunned the narrative, Mississippi papers disseminated rumors of the slave thief and his plan to overthrow the southern economy.

By the end of 1835, a hastily assembled Committee of Safety at Livingston, Mississippi, would condemn some twenty men, both slaves and whites, to death by hanging on the evidence of several forced confessions which seemed to corroborate the wild charges delineated in the *Life of Murel*. It is really not surprising, in retrospect, that the *Life of Murel* attracted the citizens of Livingston, citizens who seem, like the citizens of other slave-owning communities who have entered the historical record through acts of mob violence, preoccupied with preempting and even staging the end of their lives. The year was 1835, again, the year hundreds of thousands of pieces of abolitionist mail arrived in the South—a year singled out for the most incidents of mob violence in the period of antebellum history (1833–38) that is itself most marked by mob and vigilante activity.[44] The organization of space and the disproportionate number of slaves to white property-holders in and around Livingston nurtured an end-focused culture whose daily fed paranoia provoked sudden, violent mobilization. "The county is settled principally in large plantations," reported the Livingston Committee of Safety, which published a defense of its ad-hoc trials of supposed conspirators, "being at least fifty Negroes to one white man in the neighborhood of Livingston and Beattie's Bluff . . . no organized militia in the county; what would the ordinary array of arms avail, opposed to the stealthy marauder in the night . . . ?"[45] The movements of the slaveholding citizens at Livingston were conceived, by those same citizens, as counter-movements, intended to cancel the inevitable if undetectable, stealth movements of slaves and their white inspirators. As I've noted, it is only in the second version of the *Murel* narrative, freshened by a New York writer, that the white "inspirators" of slaves are tied to organized abolitionism. In this second version, Murrell counsels with "an English lecturer on slavery" meant to suggest George Thompson, who had toured the United States in 1835.[46]

With the addition of not only abolitionists, but English abolitionists, the *Murel* narrative fits more clearly into the genre of anti-abolitionist fiction, with its frequent and trumped-up post-colonial rants against the British—who are depicted as, once again, out to confiscate American properties—and its implicit faith (again reflecting the recent context of the American Revolution) in the power of print to mobilize rebellion. Immediatist abolitionists initially planned to win their moral victory through mass mailings to the South, until Postmaster General Amos Kendall, an anxious Jackson acolyte, declared the interstate transport of abolitionist mail an "international" crime.[47] Only four years before the publication of the *Murel* narrative, the Nat Turner rebellion had shaken the remote tidewater county of Southampton, Virginia, and in retrospect that rebellion was linked to

the secret distribution of black abolitionist David Walker's brilliant 1829
*Appeal to the Coloured Citizens of the World, but in particular, and very expressly,
to those of the United States of America.* Walker's pamphlet apparently entered
through the port of Charleston, carried by free black sailors and sympathetic
whites; supposedly it, or news of it, traveled with black riverboatmen into
the southern hinterlands. [48] In the 1820s, the revolutionary propaganda of
the Charleston free black Denmark Vesey supposedly spread into the South
Carolina backcountry in similar fashion. The Vesey conspiracy, which has
never been completely authenticated, led the South Carolina legislature to
pass the infamous Seamen Acts, which confined free black sailors to prison
while their vessels were in port. [49] It was hoped that stopping abolitionist intelligence at the "mouths" or ports of the continental United States
would inhibit the broad leakage of such intelligence into the extensive river
systems which distinguished the geography of the South. The western district of Tennessee where John Murrell made his home was a riverine environment, promising wealth and threatening destruction because it was
watered by rivers flowing westward into the great highway of the Mississippi. [50]

Despite its seemingly perfect fit into the genres of anti-abolitionist literature and anti-abolitionist theatrical panic, the *Murel* narrative is unique
because, as I have suggested, its pro-slavery ideology is loose and revealing,
its anti-abolitionist rant literally injected into its second edition to correct
the relative innocence (and here I do not equate innocence with virtue) of
the original narrative. Revealingly, the *Life of Murel* depicts the catastrophic
movements built into slave-owning culture, namely slave insurrections and
their violent cancellations, as symptomatic of the unique economic value
of slave property, a value tied to mobility. Only four pages of the original *Murel* narrative actually treat John Murrell's alleged "insurrectionist"
scheme. Murrell relates this scheme to Virgil Stewart, the pro-slavery narra-
tor and, again, probable author of the original *Life of Murel*. Stewart, who was
the primary witness for the prosecution in the actual trial of John Murrell,
told a story of his ingenious "spying" during the trial that, conspicuously,
did not include the discovery of a region-wide plot to raise the slave population against the South. Stewart made these larger allegations for the first
time in print. [51]

While the hint of a massive slave rebellion may have been responsible for
the *Life of Murel*'s immediate consumption in Mississippi's recently settled
counties, this rebellion exists within the biography as only a small proleptic

gesture. In the narrative Murrell interrupts Stewart's queries about the supposed rebellion to deliver a lengthy life history whose plot depends upon the violent, completed movements of his illegal slave trade. Although Murrell's trading methods are condemned by his interlocutor, Stewart, Stewart avers that Murrell's tactics "could not be brought under the penal code." Supposedly Murrell's familiarity with the law made his crimes virtually unpunishable. John Murrell's methods as a slave trader differ from the trading activity of slave dealers operating within the law in two ways: he captures the slaves he puts up for sale, and he defers none of the profit he makes to the slaves' prior owners. Although these crimes provide an immediate excuse for slave owners' rage and for the publication of the Murel biography, they do not deflate the paradox that a decidedly pro-slavery pamphlet should assume the circulation of slave property as its central spectacle of horror.

As the Southern political economist Edmund Ruffin asserted in an 1859 article for DeBow's Review, "slaves, being moveable, will be rated in price, not by their profits in their actual location, but according to their profits in any other region to which they can be easily transferred. . . ."[52] The mobility of slaves stabilized slave value across regional markets, making slaves a more likely speculative risk than land, whose value depended upon fluctuations of local climate (including the level of the Mississippi, which flooded twelve times between 1820 and 1840) and internal improvements which were often slow in coming. The University of Virginia Professor of Moral Philosophy George Tucker presented one of many arguments for gradual emancipation in the 1850s, when he suggested that slave value would increase until the supply of slaves and the products of slave labor outweighed demand.[53] But certainly this prospect was not imaginable when Tucker wrote during the cotton boom of the 1850s, nor during the earlier cotton boom of the 1830s when the Life of Murel was originally published. As Lydia Maria Child accurately predicted in An Appeal in Favor of That Class of Americans Called Africans (1836), the opening of new western territories like Missouri and Texas created demand for slaves even when the price of cotton was low.[54] Slave value was intimately linked to the territorial annexation that came to be understood as U.S. Manifest Destiny. The rising value of slaves in the 1820s and 1830s, as the center of cash crop farming shifted to the border states of Alabama, Mississippi, Louisiana, and Arkansas, opened a new economic niche to planters in the Upper South, who found that their slaveholdings, often unnecessarily large, could be readily converted into cash. Now slaves were more clearly linked to short-term capital gains and slavehold-ers might profitably consider speculating in slaves, buying them for future resale rather than for use.

In the *Life of Murel*, John Murrell counts on the high value of slaves in the 1830s and the greed of investors to carry off his transactions, which re-semble the transactions of legal slave traders in every detail save beginning and end. Like legal slave traders, Murrell has to disguise his slaves to ensure their marketability; moreover, he recognizes that his profits from slaves will increase the farther he moves them from centers of supply (which in his case were the riverside properties from which he steals) to less accessible regions of demand. As Penick notes, the extreme dependency of farmers in the rural Southwest upon transient slave dealers made the Murrell narrative particu-larly credible. In the 1836 edition of the *Life of Murel*, Murrell shows off his talents as a slave thief to Virgil Stewart, proving to Stewart how easily his clan's tactics blend into the normal functioning of the trade. Murrell boasts of his younger brother's theft of a slave named Sam, whom he stole from a planter named Eason in Alabama, holding Sam until Eason advertised him as a runaway, and then reselling Sam to a Thomas Hudnold of Madi-son County, Mississippi, and then stealing Sam again from Hudnold for future resale.[55] Murrell and his fellow thieves wait until a slave is advertised as a runaway to resell him because then they can use the original owner's advertisement for the runaway as protection. When Murrell travels with a stolen slave, he carries the advertisement and, if questioned, pretends to be on his way to return the slave to his original master. Literary historian John Seelye has noted that in *Adventures of Huckleberry Finn*, Mark Twain borrows this particular ruse of Murrell's and attributes it to the Duke and King, who create a false advertisement for Jim while they travel with him down the Mississippi.[56] For Murrell, returning unfortunate slaves to market again and again effectively makes them disappear as anything but a pure value, an index of exchange. In effect, Murrell speeds up the normative process of speculation to such a degree that the slave seems to disappear, bodily, and his value as property shows itself not in holdings but in flashes, surfacing each time resale occurs.

When Murrell kidnaps a slave, he lures him with the prospect of self-ownership. Murrell delivers his pitch only to male slaves, as if the promise of self-ownership might seem in fact too incredible if proposed to a black woman. Stewart recounts Murrell's sales pitch to an unhappy slave named Clitto: "If I steal you, and carry you off, and sell you four or five times, and give you half the money, and then leave you in a free state, will you go?" Clitto agrees. [57] But as the speculative series concludes, black self-ownership has become the equivalent of not having a body. There is an economic logic here: as a capitalist or new owner of himself the slave has been removed from the hyper-embodied labor sector. But this logic takes a cruel turn because, as Murrell well understands, the social convention of race insures that the black body will always be marked. In attempting to achieve freedom, Murrell's slaves become only too remarkable. When a particular slave Murrell handles begins to be widely recognized, the thief must make good on his sleight of hand and cause that slave to disappear: Sam, who is a favorite with Murrell's brother, ends up in the territory of Texas. A more typical case, according to the *Murel* narrative, is that of an unnamed man whom Murrell sells three times in the counties bordering the Arkansas River and then murders in a riverside swamp. Murrell recounts the incident to Stewart, speaking of himself in the third person: "He [Murrell] sold that negro for two thousand dollars, and then put him forever out of the reach of all pursuers . . . his carcass has fed many a tortoise and catfish before this time, and the frogs have sung this many a long day to the silent repose of his skeleton . . ." [58] Mark Twain's quotation of the Murrell narrative in *Life on the Mississippi* ends with precisely these lines, the highly literalized image of a cruel disembodiment effected by the slave market intruding, as it were, into the pastoral space of the river and its "singing" frogs.

As an increasing number of property owners in Kentucky, Virginia, Maryland and the Carolinas sold their slaves southwest, the necessity for the domestic transportation of slaves became more acute and the intrusion of the market—the relation of slave value to slave mobility—became more conspicuous. Historian Michael Tadman estimates that two hundred thousand slaves moved from the Upper to the Lower South in every decade from 1820 to 1860; 70 percent of this slave movement, Tadman argues, can be attributed to the activity of the domestic trade. [59] The rise of the domestic slave trade in the South pushed to front and center a relatively new category of person whose sole purpose was to facilitate the movement and transference of slaves from centers of supply to centers of demand. This new type of person, the domestic slave trader, was not as blatantly piratical as his predecessors in the international trade: he was, above all, a businessman, and in a symbolic sense he represented only the absolute consistency of the slave system in the United States. It is this same consistency that, I think,

John Murrell represents as he, like the slave driver or agent within the law, traffics in slaves.

In David Hundley's 1860 typology, *Social Relations in Our Southern States*, the slave trader joins the ranks of other essentially middle-class figures, including "village storekeepers," "country merchants," and "speculators," to constitute a new class Hundley calls "Southern Yankees." Hundley argues that the Southern Yankee is "swallowed up completely in selfishness" and even "detestable" when a slave trader. Paradoxically, the Southern Yankee is also "in most cases a useful citizen [and] has contributed no little to the unprecedented prosperity of the slave states."[60] This hybrid figure, whose species name indicates his national rather than regional orientation, is essentially representative of the commercial class. But the Southern Yankee's wealth has been reconnected, by Hundley, to the shameful source that many Northern businessmen who also depended upon slave values could easily enough disregard. Southern Yankees, slave traders and slave thieves personify a white economic mobility deeply imbricated in slave value which, as movements of slaves became more conspicuous, began to threaten and shame slaveholding whites.

Because slaveholders' moralistic justification of slavery depended upon an economic understanding of the slave as an integral part of a household economy, as in the Aristotelian *oikos*, the heightened visibility of slave trading marks a moral crisis as well as a crisis of value.[61] Abolitionists recognized this, and through the sampling techniques they used to construct their master narratives, drawing "testimony" from Southern newspapers, they suggest that Southerners, too, were affected by the sight of slave coffles making their inevitable forced marches toward market towns. It was on the road to and from the slave market that the disjunction between the mimetic smiling and dancing slave and the erased slave person appears to have been most visible to slaveholders. On the road to market the same mobility which stabilized slave values from place to place could be seen as the very quality which denied to the slave the social embeddedness and localization which made, for instance, white personhood. The Kentucky Presbyterian Synod, consisting perhaps of some of the same persons who invested in the "great Negro speculation" of 1836, lamented that "there is not a village or road that does not behold the sad procession of manacled outcasts. . . ."[62] Lydia Maria Child's 1836 *Appeal* includes the Reverend James H. Dickey's recollection of the disconcerting pageantry of a slave coffle he witnessed on the road between Paris and Lexington, Kentucky, in 1822.

A chain perhaps forty feet long, the size of a fifth horse-chain, was stretched between the two-ranks, to which short chains were joined which connected the handcuffs. Behind them were, I suppose, about thirty women, in double rank, the couples tied hand in hand. A solemn sadness sat on every countenance, and the dismal silence of this march of despair was interrupted only by the sound of two violins; yes, as if to add insult to injury, the foremost couple were furnished with a violin apiece; the second couple were ornamented with cockades; while near the center waved a republican flag, carried by a hand literally in chains.[63]

Reverend Dickey's memory of the oxymoronic juxtaposition of manacled hand to republican flag no doubt appealed to Child because she was particularly offended by the visibility of slave coffles in the seat of republicanism, the nation's capital. Such scenes, Child lamented, "furnish materials for the most pungent satire to other nations."[64]

Lydia Maria Child's concern about white exposure, the necessary precondition of a national shame, to some extent obliterates the black bodies marching toward separation and abuse in the markets of Washington DC or Richmond. Saidiya Hartman has offered a groundbreaking critique of abolitionist representations of the grotesque pageants of slavery like the coffle march described above. Such representations, Hartman suggests, enact "a movement from repulsion to romance," where, as in this instance, "despite the initial revulsion that the coffle induced, the melancholy spectacle remains at an emotional and contemplative distance, and musings about Negro character displace the hideous with the entertaining."[65] Although the assimilative nature of empathy may be apparent in Child's *Appeal*, I think it worthwhile to grasp for some shadow of her political intent, as ephemeral as that might be, in the critique of the slave trade that opens her narrative. This critique offers a self-conscious historical corrective, a re-suturing of slavery and its horrors to the mercantile capitalism that ushered the United States and other American republics into a troubled modernity.

The choices Child makes about which "scenes of subjection" to include in her narrative history suggest that she was at least dimly aware that the utility of black bodies to American whites had to do with blacks' commodity status in what was both a psychological and actual white market. She incorporates the question of "why I have said so much about the slave-trade" into her narrative, and her pointed answer is that slavery is primarily traffic among whites, a projective self-augmentation enacted through the exchange of blacks. "Every man who buys a slave promotes this traffic," Child argues, "every man who owns a slave directly countenances it; every man who allows that slavery is a lamentable *necessity*, contributes his share. . . ."[66] By invoking the market for slaves, which is in effect a national and international white populace, Child points to the amorality of economically rational action and the amorality of modernity itself. She sharpens her critique by altering the temporality of slavery, making it a series of transactions, presently and continuously enacted, as opposed to the stable past-imperfect evoked by the minstrel shows of the 1840s and later genres of plantation pastoral as well as neoclassical plantation architecture. In her 1838 *Letters to Catherine E. Beecher*, Angelina Grimké even more pointedly explores the temporality of slave-holding, dismantling the paternalistic connotations of the verb "to hold" in the process. Grimké writes: "The only difference I can see between the original man-stealer, who caught the African in his native country, and the American slaveholder, is, that the former committed *one* act of robbery, while the other perpetrates the same crime *continually*. Slave-holding is the perpetrating of acts, all of the same kind, in a *series*, the first of which is technically called man-stealing."[67] Abolitionists and slaveholders batted the accusation of "man-stealing" back and forth amongst themselves, but for both groups the horror of the crime seemed related to its ongoing, serial nature—its lack of stasis or conclusion. The epithet "man-stealer" reflects a common insecurity among abolitionists and anti-abolitionists about the safety of personhood as a spatial and temporal category. Slave trading, stealing, even the wider mobility of a commercial culture threatened traditional meanings of "the human."

Political economists writing in the United States in the 1830s, such as Henry Vethake, George Tucker, and Francis Wayland, typically separate ideas of "wealth," a limited substance which can be used, from ideas of "value," an effect of exchange.[68] This recognition that value need not correspond to utility, or the aestheticization of value, as it were, indirectly approves the growing credit economy that, as the French traveler and engineer Michel Chevalier noted in 1835, gave birth to a nation of speculators who ironically reviled "the speculator" in the abstract and the banking system that made speculation possible.[69] As is well known, the meaning of value encountered a series of crises in the antebellum period, with Andrew Jackson's dismantling of the Second Bank of the United States and debates over the issuance of paper money and specie shortages in the foreground of the public mind. Jackson's own speculations in Tennessee land built for him an unstable fortune that, like all speculative real estate, was plagued by tax liens, title disputes, and competing American Indian claims. As Michael Rogin has argued, Jackson's personal experience of the southwestern land boom led to his monomaniacal drive to legitimate land titles by removing American Indians from their homelands in order to purify white settlers' and speculators' claims.

In Virgil Stewart's *Life of Murel*, John Murrell gives his slave thefts and re-sales the broad name "speculations." The *National Police Gazette* seized upon this euphemism—a euphemism Hundley claimed was used by many slave traders to soften their distasteful work—when it published a series of articles on Murrell in the 1840s. The *Gazette* went so far as to expand the term "speculator" even further, defining "speculator" as "the common term for a professional depredator in the Western country, at the time of which we write."[70] Yet of course speculation—in slaves, and livestock, and land—was a very common means of achieving capital gains for very average citizens. The alliance of speculation with robbery and depredation points again to the ironic distrust of the average U.S. citizen, many of whom were speculators themselves, for the various forms of credit or representational currencies in the period. John Murrell's story racializes this larger problem of knowing and having value, which makes the *Life of Murel* a more radical response to the expansion of the credit economy than any other southwestern fiction of its period.

Imaginary Fiscal Conservatism

The famous Davy Crockett narratives offer a more familiar response to the bank wars, specie shortages, unstable markets, and anxiety that plagued the emergent middle class in the 1830s and 1840s. As a Tennessee congressman, Crockett left the Democrats to craft a generous and unpopular Tennessee land bill, a move that both identified him with a nascent, national working class and made him a darling of Whigs who enjoyed the image of a "frontiersmen" rejecting his veritable kinsman, Andrew Jackson. For historian Caroll Smith-Rosenberg, Crockett represents a wishful return to personal forms of control and embodiment; however, Crockett's environment, which is essentially the same western district of Tennessee that was home to Andrew Jackson and to John Murrell, has no stable boundaries. In Smith-Rosenberg's apt phrase, "only rivers, free flowing, unpredictable, and occasionally uncontrollable, intersected this world."[71] In the 1834 *Narrative of the Life of David Crockett* that Crockett either co-wrote or dictated to Kentucky Congressman Thomas Chilton, bear and the woods suggest an empirically determinable value while rivers are associated with the anticipatory if not specious future values of speculation. Crockett's entrepreneurial efforts, including investment in a grist and powder mill and running lumber to New Orleans, receive harsh rebukes from local rivers. A seasonal flood destroys the mills and Crockett loses control of his lumber boats in the Mississippi, literally and metaphorically "skinning" himself in the process.

Even in Crockett's 1834 *Narrative*, which is realistic compared to the fictional Texas diaries and the humorous *Crockett Almanacs*, Davy Crockett's means of self-augmentation are limited to tall or exaggerated body counts from hunting season. As Crockett denigrates his schemes to establish viable businesses, he boasts improbably, although not impossibly, of killing "one hundred and five bears . . . in less than one year."[72] The pseudo-empiricism of this boast suggests that nature is the appropriate source of value. This fiscal-imaginary conservatism and the sublimated wish for a return to forms of economic personal control are only confirmed in the masturbatory images Smith-Rosenberg finds in Crockett's bear hunts. Even the successful gamble that constitutes the original frame of the Crockett narratives, Crockett's bid for a seat in Congress, is won by the stolid truths of the natural body, by Crockett's refusal to betray his political innocence by giving campaign speeches. Crockett's credibility is founded in a refusal of rhetoric. As Arnold Krupat has noted, the Crockett autobiography was published in the same year as the first Indian autobiography, J. B. Patterson's 1834 *The Autobiography of Black Hawk*.[73] Both "as told to" narratives propose "native speech" as an implicit antidote to the nation's fantastic economy. Replete with orthographic peculiarities invented by their ghost-writers, the Crockett and Black Hawk biographies use the appearance of "Indian" and "western" semiliterate dialect as a foil for the false representations of political insiders, including land speculators, career politicians and self-righteous parvenus.

Border Cosmopolitanism
In comparison to the Crockett narratives, the fictions of the southwestern humorists whom William Gilmore Simms eagerly identified with the nation's nascent popular culture offer a liberal and even cosmopolitan response to Jacksonian political economy. Augustus Baldwin Longstreet's "The Horse-Swap," first published in the *Milledgeville Southern Recorder* in 1833, introduces trade as a necessary and violent southwestern sport. On a court day in an apparently sleepy Georgia village, a horse trader calling

himself the Yellow Blossom from Jasper, "jist a *leetle* of the best man, at a horse swap, that ever trod shoe-leather," trumps up the value of his ugly but smart little horse.[74] Another man—not a villager but yet another stranger in town for court day—takes up the Blossom's banner and presents his own horse for trade. As bystanders gather around the men and begin to "taunt" them to make a deal, it becomes clear that dishonor sticks to whoever proves unwilling to risk. Economic risk, a necessary factor in the expansion of border communities, is upheld by a group of people who are all, tellingly, strangers to each other. This is not a village of locals but of chancers, people extending themselves, dangerously, into somewhere else. If the competence anthropologist Ulf Hannerz associates with cosmopolitanism is not present in Longstreet's rural Georgia, what Hannerz calls the cosmopolitan orientation, the willingness to engage with strangers, is present.[75] Neither the Yellow Blossom nor the other stranger wants to be "backed out." They exchange three dollars and a promise not to seek legal redress only to discover that one horse has a massive saddle sore and the other is deaf and blind. A "loud and general laugh" issues from the bystanders who urged the trade, and the story dissolves.

From a sectional perspective, the joke of "The Horse-Swap" is that the kind of economic adventure which expresses the Jacksonian ethos operates, in the South, only through damaged goods. Yet Longstreet, writing in the early 1830s, imagines himself a regional historian writing to fellow Southerners. Only years later, when the popularity of *Uncle Tom's Cabin* roused feverish indignation in the South, would George Washington Harris exaggerate regional poverty to the extent that it became a veiled threat in his *Sut Lovingood Tales*.[76] In contrast, Longstreet's "Horse-Swap" resembles the English village humor William T. Porter reprinted alongside southwestern sketches in the *Spirit of the Times*, including a satirical piece entitled "Horse-Dealing Extraordinaire" excerpted from a London paper. Longstreet was a devotee of *The Spectator* and a master of Addisonian style, so it is unsurprising that he approached life in the old Southwest from an almost eighteenth-century, trans-Atlantic perspective. His Georgia village is a micro-marketplace, even though its residents betray the distinctively "native" accent that captivated William Gilmore Simms.

This border cosmopolitanism is elaborated in Johnson Jones Hooper's *Adventures of Captain Simon Suggs*, an imitation campaign biography of the Jacksonian "Suggs" which was published in book form in 1845 after most of its vignettes had already appeared in the *Spirit of the Times*. In the *Adventures*,

Hooper foregrounds the relevance of the lower Mississippi Valley to Jacksonian market society. The satirical Suggs neatly encapsulates a mood of bitter defeat among Whigs after the second wave of Jacksonian government was secured with the 1844 victory of the Tennessee Democrat James K. Polk over Henry Clay. [77] Always ready to make "a grand demonstration against some bank," bribe a legislator, or "speculate without money," Suggs undoes institutional structures and replaces them with his avaricious energy, which, almost accidentally, approximates personal charm. Hooper's qualification of Suggs's famous motto, "It is good to be shifty in new country" only extends the scope of its amorality; the author specifies that Suggs only "means that it is right and proper that one should live as merrily and as comfortably as possible at the expense of others." [78]

Where Augustus Baldwin Longstreet presented rural trading as in some sense moral because for both parties it is deep play, Hooper recognizes Suggs's bets as risk free and therefore incapable of heroic framing. Suggs begins his adult career by cheating his father out of the family horse by means of a card trick. The religious leanings of the elder Suggs, who is a "hard Baptist," allow him to imagine that the card trick, which appears to him as a small miracle, must be evidence of predestination. "To be sure— all fixed aforehand," he mutters—to which Simon replies with a fulsome laugh. [79] In this confusion of Providence and petty crime lies the key to Hooper's America, where Manifest Destiny is "manifest" because it has been rigged by savvy yokels like Simon, Andrew Jackson and James Polk, the veritable author of the U.S.-Mexican War. Simon Suggs's speculating without money, a "seeming incongruity," as Hooper admits, depends for its success upon a deeper series of rigged tricks, the worthless treaties that the federal government made with Alabama's Creek (Muscogee) nations. These treaties falsely promised state protection of individual Creek homesteads to those who resisted the long trek across the Mississippi to Indian Territory. In reality, Creeks who remained in Alabama were set upon by lawyers, speculators, and settlers with the full knowledge and even approval of the state; the federal government looked the other way.

Reflecting a Whiggish distaste for Jackson's handling of Indian Removal, if not for Removal itself, Hooper asks the reader: "Have those in whose minds speculation and capital are inseparably connected ever heard of a process by which lands were sold, deeds executed, and all that sort of thing completely arranged, and all without once troubling the owner of the soil for an opinion even, in regard to the matter?" [80] Suggs's speculations in

Indian lands are safe because they merely trace the arcs of already institutionalized theft. Yet Suggs, like David Crockett, who was the only Tennessee congressman to vote against Indian Removal, never personally takes advantage of an American Indian. Rather, he makes his sport by playing on the greed of fellow white speculators, conning them into paying him *not* to bid on desirable Indian lands. Without land or any other form of capital, Suggs manages to augment his fortunes and play up the value of local real estate simply by injecting an excess of competitive energy into the already chaotic scenes around southwestern land offices. In effect, Simon Suggs greases the real estate market by counterfeiting demand.

All types of real and metaphorical counterfeit figure largely in southwestern humor, pointing, again, to the fact that the deep topic of this humor is the crisis of value that plagued the Jacksonian period. Significantly, the southwestern humorists rarely mention slaves, upholding the general ban on that topic in the national press. When these humorists do represent slaves, they are not personalized within a domestic or plantation setting; in fact, they are often linked to counterfeiting, which is an association I find compelling. Simon Suggs's most sustained reference to the fact of slavery in the Southwest occurs in his concluding "autographic letter" to Hooper, where he tells of his involvement with a local wildcat bank, essentially a ring of counterfeiters. The counterfeiters use Suggs to circulate their unsound money by staging slave sales where the fake money will theatrically change hands before crowds of onlookers. The fate of the slaves is wholly irrelevant in this story; Suggs simply buys them with the counterfeit money and resells them for "a thousen dollars . . . in stait money."[81] The point of the story is Suggs's limitless capacity for turning bad credit into cash, or, more broadly, the mysterious interdependence of good and bad monies. Here black Americans are purely instrumental, suggesting, if anything, that "slaves" are a more reliable currency than either the unsound issues of trading companies or the apparently safe monies of state banks.

Writing during the second cotton boom of the 1850s and after *Uncle Tom's Cabin* had opened the topic of slavery to national debate, Joseph G. Baldwin treats the metaphorical counterfeiting or passing off of unsound slaves as a major topic in his 1853 *The Flush Times of Alabama and Mississippi*. For Baldwin, African Americans themselves figure as a form of false currency, a problem that of course is central in the *Life of Murel*. David Hundley argued that the "greatest wickedness" of that type of Southern Yankee known as the slave trader was not his "cruelty to the African," but rather his propensity for passing off "vicious" and "diseased" slaves as "honest and healthy." Hundley apostrophizes: "Ah, Messrs. stock-brokers of Wall Street, for ingenious lying you should take lessons from the southern Negro trader!"[82] In Joseph Baldwin's short story, "The Bar of the South-West," disputed slave property becomes an epicenter of widespread fraud. "Negroes were brought into the country in large numbers and sold mostly on credit, and bills of exchange taken for the price; the negroes in many cases were unsound—some as to which there was no title; some falsely pretended to be unsound, and various questions as to the liability of the parties on the warranties and the bills, furnished an important addition to the litigation. . . ."[83] For Baldwin, "flush times" imply the multiplication of lawsuits, following on the heels of slave sales as well as sales of mismanaged Indian lands. Ghost commodities pursue the white protagonists of southwestern humor as vengeful reminders of the brutal displacements of American Indians and African Americans that made possible the rapid settlement of the southwestern border.

Curiously, what historians have learned of the life of Virgil Stewart, John Murrell's original biographer, places him squarely within this region of anxious laughter and spectral commodities. Before publishing the *Life of Murel*, Virgil Stewart had moved to the recently opened Choctaw Purchase, operated a still, and attempted to set up as a speculator in Indian lands. Stewart "clerked" for an Indian trader named Matthew Clanton, who in the heat of the Murrell debacle accused Stewart of stealing items from his store. Stewart's byzantine, nonsensical retort to Clanton, which appears in the appendices to the *Life of Murel*, reveals that the young man's business tactics were remarkably similar to those he ascribed to John Murrell. Citing the generally "rough" and casual nature of business management in the Southwest, Stewart explains (writing of himself in the third person with a feigned disinterest that is also reminiscent of the fictive "Murrell"): "Mr. Stewart is not acquainted with the rules and customs of clerks, neither did he consider himself Clanton's clerk; he considered himself his agent, and attended to all his business as an agent. Mr. Stewart could see no difference in paying for an article, and using it himself, and selling it to another man; and there is no difference with an honest man." What Clanton called clerking Stewart called acting as an "agent." What Clanton called stealing Stewart called "barter." Ironically, it seems that Virgil Stewart was a dark brother to Simon Suggs, the same sort of protean con man whom he represented John Murrell to be.[84] It was Stewart, not Murrell—who died shortly after being released from jail in 1846, who occupied that disruptive middle place between gentleman and slave, the place of the trader, the clerk, the lawyer, the charlatan, and the Southern Yankee.

During the trial of the real John Murrell, Virgil Stewart was accused by Murrell of being a counterfeiter; Stewart's brother Taney in fact already had been convicted of this crime. The flurry of character defamations directed at Virgil Stewart around the publication of the *Life of Murel* prove that the threat of this kind of propertyless white person to Southern slaveholders was as significant, if not more significant, than the threat of rebellious slaves and abolitionists. In the appendices to the *Life of Murel*, Stewart replied to challenges to his honesty by including the names of some of the most respectable citizens in John Murrell's hometown in his roster of Murrell's alleged clan. Many of those who were named had been the first to question Stewart's veracity when he testified at John Murrell's trial. Stewart was so obsessed about clearing his own name that, in 1836, he undertook a public journey through Mississippi and Tennessee, attempting to gather positive character references from persons who probably had little knowledge of him beyond the claims of his incendiary pamphlet.

When William Gilmore Simms treated Virgil Stewart's story in his second novel to address the Murrell conspiracy, the 1840 *Border Beagles*, he seems to have divided Stewart's character into two oppositional figures, a worthy young lawyer named Harry Vernon and a dishonest bank clerk named William Maitland. Tellingly, Vernon pursues Maitland throughout the novel. For Simms, Vernon and Maitland are good and evil versions of the emergent business class, democratic men who rely on "ready adroitness" and "the gift of gab" rather than, in Simms's phrase, "money and the aid of powerful friends."[85] The primary threat of the southwestern border was, Simms suggests, that here a lack of familial and community associations left democratic energy unchecked by the social visibility that, elsewhere, directed it toward the productive work of nation-building. In *Border Beagles*, Simms introduces the acronym "G.T.T.," meaning "gone to Texas" as Mississippi argot for the phenomenon of young men escaping to the United States' contiguous foreign territory, Texas, after making illegal fortunes in the southwestern states. The permeability of the old border of Texas fostered a duplicitous national character.

Oddly, William Gilmore Simms himself proved to be one of Virgil Stewart's most powerful friends, perversely identifying with the young man's cause. Although there is no indication that Simms helped Stewart clear his name in the 1830s, Simms defends Stewart in the 1855 prefaces to both

Richard Hurdis and *Border Beagles*, remarking that "nobody, at all familiar with the region and period of [Stewart's] story, can possibly entertain a question of its history. . . . I knew Stuart [sic], the captor of Murrell, personally; and had several conferences with him."[86] Significantly, Simms's defense of Virgil Stewart is also a retort to critics of *Richard Hurdis* ("it was objected . . . that it was of too gloomy and savage a character") and of his own worthiness as an author. In the same preface quoted above, Simms betrays one possible root of his sympathy for Stewart's position when he urges aspiring authors to maintain anonymity in print and a dual identity in society. Knowing friends, Simms avers, might stifle an author's growth by demanding consistency between private and authorial personae: "They never separate *you* from your writings. Their personal and local associations perpetually start up to baffle the free influence of your works upon their thoughts and hearts; and they weigh your opinions, or your imaginations, or your designs and inventions, with a continual reference to *yourself*. . . ."[87] It seems that Simms links the unmasking of Virgil Stewart to disrespect for authorial professionalism and an unnecessary stifling of democratic "imaginations . . . designs . . . inventions." There is Emersonian irreverence here, the desire to write whim on the lintel post and leave family and neighbors behind that gives "Self-Reliance" its anarchic edge. Although Simms's juxtaposition of a defense of creative license with a defense of Virgil Stewart's legitimacy as an author may seem inappropriate, it nicely raises the issue of whether Stewart *was* put on trial for the social crime of authoring a controversial book.

Self-interested as it was, Virgil Stewart's *Life of Murel* intended to effect a redistribution of social goods. The slave-owning classes of white southwestern society were targeted and Virgil Stewart, unpropertied climber, attained a temporary prominence. The propagation of the Murrell narrative was a type of speculation without capital that, at least for a short time, paid off. Ironically and inadvertently, a pro-slavery, amateur writer forced a region-wide investigation into the fragile and corrupt foundations of liberal selfhood in the United States. Through his spectacular ruse, Virgil Stewart contributed to the perception of authorship as, like speculating and slave trading, an occupation full of meaning and danger to the national project.

Coda: The Business of Abolition and Other American Destinies
Like speculators, traders, and authors, abolitionists presented a threat not only to Southern, but also national, properties. Anti-abolitionist writers

identified abolitionists as both traders and, more accurately, authors. According to the anti-abolitionist novelist J. W. Page, who wrote one of many fictional replies to Harriet Beecher Stowe, abolitionism was actually an adjunct to the slave-trading business. In Page's *Uncle Robin in His Cabin and Tom without One in Boston*, one Yankee character avers that, "they [the abolitionists] entice them off, and we [Northern traders] grab them flying." [88] Southerners strained to incorporate the domestic slave trade into the wider economic imperialism they recognized, rightly enough, as Northern; as a blatant example of market capitalism in practice, the domestic slave trade "should be" Yankee. If abolitionists were not actually in cahoots with Northern slave dealers, as Page implied, then perhaps abolitionists were drumming up money for Northern landlords who would exploit escaped slaves by making them pay excessive rents. As in the work of Southern political economist George Fitzhugh, here northeastern capitalism receives an almost socialist critique from the slave South. Mary H. Eastman's 1852 novel *Aunt Phillis' Cabin* portrays abolitionists as greedy innkeepers seducing slaves away from their masters only to make them pay dearly for freedom. One of Eastman's characters argues, true to her Yankee frugality: "I don't calculate to give runaway niggers their supper, and night's lodging and breakfast for twenty-five cents. I ain't so green as that." [89] The 1861 "autobiography" *The Disclosures and Confessions of Franklin A. Wilmot, the Slave Thief and Negro Runner*, characterizes the Underground Railroad as what it was euphemistically and ironically named by its practitioners, "the railroad business." Wilmot, who is most certainly a fictional character—perhaps a fabulous version of Pennsylvania congressman David Wilmot, author of the polemical Wilmot Proviso, "confesses" that he joined the Underground Railroad for mercenary reasons. The apparently humanitarian network is really a means of "relieving these sycophantic and blind sympathizers [Northerners] of their surplus funds; and the only way we can do it is to actually run the slaves off to Canada . . ." [90] As in the fictions of the Southwestern humorists, slaves, here, are wholly instrumental, and their freedom is not conceived as a social good; in fact, their freedom is irrelevant. The key problem in the *Wilmot* narrative is competition between Southern and Northern whites, with a trick of sectional reversal placing the Northerners in the unaccustomed role of yokels and dupes.

The *Wilmot* pseudo-autobiography traces the adventures of Franklin Wilmot as he steals various slaves from towns along the Mississippi River and runs them, for Northern money, to Canada. This later narrative suggests what the *Murel* narrative might have been had its author or authors been more keenly aware of the pointedness of abolitionist rhetoric. The flurry of anti-abolitionist propaganda that followed the publication of *Uncle Tom's Cabin* proves the South's full awakening to the fact that it must, first and foremost, fight its battle in print. The anti-*Tom* novels were meant to establish the "reciprocity," in Agnes Heller's terms, which is normally built into the social structure of shame—"shame" implies being visible to others who are also visible to you. [91] Even more than the abolitionist mail campaigns of the mid-1830s, *Uncle Tom* proved the cultural significance of authorship, and its record sales and eager reception was the final note in a broader recognition, among Southerners, that abolitionism was, at the least, a viable communications business.

It is not surprising that pro-slavery Southerners interpreted abolitionism as a mechanism of the North's imperialistic market society. But the degree to which abolitionists themselves used the language of business to describe abolitionist practice is peculiar. Perhaps abolitionists' economic rhetoric indicates the confiscation of billions of dollars of Southern "property" that would be the final result of anti-slavery agitation. Yet the use of the rhetoric of business by even radical abolitionists like John Brown and proto–Black Nationalists like Martin Delany also indicates a strange complementarity between abolitionist thought and the values of the marketplace. Perhaps it was simply impossible for these genuinely revolutionary thinkers to conceive of a possible world wholly outside of the ethos of liberalism.

In an oft-quoted letter to Thomas Wentworth Higginson, John Brown describes his involvement in "the railroad business," or the Underground Railroad, and the irony of this well-known euphemism is sharpened by the fact that in the letter Brown is soliciting funds. Brown writes to Higginson in reply to a letter in which Higginson has declared his own poverty and denied Brown money. The venture Brown describes in this letter is his now famous "Virginia plan": "Rail road business on a *somewhat extended* scale; is the identical object for which I am trying to get means. I have been connected with that business *as commonly conducted* from my boyhood: & never let an opportunity slip. I have been operating to some purpose *the past season;* but now I have a measure on foot that I feel *sure* would awaken in you something more than a *common interest*. . . ." [92] Brown's careful, ironic wording suggests the necessarily secretive nature of his plans as well as a genuine effort to present himself as an experienced ("from boyhood"), productive ("never let an opportunity slip"), and innovative entrepreneur. The italicized or underlined phrases, original to Brown, give the letter the urgent quality of a spoken pitch. Those who had known Brown through his various incarnations as a tanner, surveyor, and wool merchant were less likely to invest in his abolitionist campaigns in Kansas and Virginia, which resembled, at least in their manic enthusiasm, the various speculations that had already resulted in one humiliating bankruptcy. As a friend averred, Brown was a good man, but "no trader."[93]

When Brown was visiting Europe in 1851, trying to sell wool that he had failed to unload in the United States—a business trip Brown's biographer Stephen B. Oates describes as a "fiasco"—Brown conceived of the elaborate system of mountain warfare that formed the broad context of his attack on the arsenal at Harper's Ferry.[94] Richard Realf, a follower of Brown's, recalled Brown's description, at a secret convention in 1858 in Chatham, Ontario, of how the London Exhibition led to his major epiphany. "He made a journey to England in 1851, in which year he took to the International Exhibition in London samples of wool from Ohio, during which period he made a tour upon the European continent, inspecting all fortifications, and especially all earthwork forts. . . ."[95] The earthwork forts gave Brown ideas for the construction of guerrilla strongholds in the Appalachian Mountains. A radical conception of abolitionist revolt sprang from a trip, made for the purpose of selling wool, to the symbolic center of nineteenth-century world capitalism, London's "Crystal Palace" Exhibition. According to Realf, Brown's most ambitious venture would begin at the Virginia arsenal and lead him west toward the Mississippi Valley, "making the line of mountains which cuts diagonally through Maryland and Virginia down through the Southern States into Tennessee and Alabama, the base of his operations."[96] This swath of mountains would also form the territory of a provisional "state," augmenting its population with slaves stolen or escaped from "the plantations on the plains lying on each side."[97] Brown assured listeners at Chatham that in his shifting state, which he had, in an earlier version of the plan, named the "Subterranean Pass Way," he would instruct blacks "in all the business of life," including "the useful and mechanical arts."[98] How and where this provisional state would end was not entirely clear, though Kansas was a possible terminus. Potentially Brown's state might move, like the passageway it was originally imagined to be, ever westward.

To be sure, the "Provisional Constitution" Brown crafted for his imagined state included significant deviations from the United States' current political ideology. Brown's Constitution mandated common property and guaranteed the civil rights of "the Oppressed People, who, by a recent decision of the Supreme Court [the Dred Scott case] are declared to have no rights which the white man is bound to respect; together with all other people degraded by the laws thereof."[99] Yet a much disputed article of Brown's Constitution, which Brown himself insisted on preserving, urged that the Provisional Constitution itself "shall not be construed so as in any way to encourage the overthrow of any State Government [nor the] dissolution of the Union."[100] Brown reasonably imagined himself a counterrevolutionary, taking back the United States from the pro-slavery conspiracy that had already perverted its aims. Significantly, Brown's radicalism did not require self-exile or emigration, possibilities that Martin Delany entertained. Although Brown projected a modified communism, his artisanal state would be funded, at least initially, by capital he had tirelessly solicited from a group of New England philanthropists who called themselves "the Secret Six."

Although John Brown's history is not really set in the Mississippi Valley, his "state" was originally set to move toward the slave populations in Alabama and Tennessee and terminate in Kansas. Given the vague, fluid nature of its territory, it could incorporate almost anything. The most surprising aspect of John Brown's improbable world in the Southern mountains is this fluid territory, which was imaginatively mapped by the requirements of asymmetric war. The utility of mountains as passage ways for fugitive slaves had apparently been suggested to Brown by Harriet Tubman, whom he met in 1858, and when Brown conceived of an appropriate territory for his nation-within-the-nation, he focused on environmental features which seemed to defy all usages associated with property value. Inadvertently, this kind of thinking resulted in an approximation of what contemporary environmentalist writers like the poet-activist Gary Snyder have called "bioregionalism," an identification of a people or provisional nation with a specific ecosystem. Of course neither Brown nor the other conductors of the Underground Railroad were thinking about ecosystems, an anachronistic concept, but they did create a way of seeing the landscape that effectively decommodified it without reverting to the subjective romanticism or pastoralism that frames other nineteenth-century U.S. environmental discourse. Henry David Thoreau's literary retreat to Fair-Haven Hill after spending a night in a Concord prison protesting slavery and the U.S.-Mexican War is only the most famous example of how the rhetorical and visual conventions of landscape depiction seemed to empty political commitment in the antebellum United States.

In the British abolitionist Richard J. Hinton's comprehensive 1894 history, *John Brown and His Men*, Hinton includes a list of Underground Railroad routes that he remembers from his own past as an abolitionist guerrilla and colleague of John Brown. The routes are remarkably distant from the economic and aesthetic values of mainstream U.S. culture. Hinton recalls that "one [route] was that of the coast south of the Potomac, whose almost continuous line of swamps from the vicinity of Norfolk, Va., to the northern border of Florida offered refuge for many who could not escape and became 'marooned'. . . ." Another "rugged, lonely, but comparatively safe route to freedom" was the "great Appalachian range and its abutting mountains"; this was the preferred route of Harriet Tubman and, later, of John Brown himself. To the west, there were the "limestone caves" of northern Georgia, east Tennessee, and northern Alabama. Finally, the "valley of the Mississippi was the most westerly channel, until Kansas opened a bolder way of escape. . . ." [101] Notably, the Mississippi Valley, which conceived of itself as particularly vulnerable to abolitionist "thieves," is low on Hinton's list of escape routes. His "railroad" typically runs along routes that would not be considered suitable market roads, and again, the natural features he remarks are those (such as swamps and caves) that would repulse speculators. The landscape values of artists and writers of the period fall by the wayside, too, as the happy utility of swamps and caves challenges the tired, eighteenth-century aesthetic categories, "the sublime" and "the picturesque," which dominated early nineteenth-century environmental perception and turned North American nature into a hackneyed symbolbook. As Thomas Cole intones in one of his many primers of landscape appreciation, the 1841 "Lecture on American Scenery," mountains are "sublime," lakes are "tranquil," waterfalls suggest change within stasis, and trees, "variety." [102] In contrast, to the Underground Railroad conductor even the rugged Appalachians, potentially sublime, appear "comparatively safe." Abolitionist landscapes offer an entirely unique perspective on the geography of the United States.

In Martin Delany's serial novel *Blake; or the Huts of America* (1860–61), the impenetrable woods of Arkansas and Georgia and the famous Dismal Swamp, stretching from Nat Turner's home county of Southampton, Virginia through coastal North Carolina, seem, initially, to be the sort of alternative, abolitionist landscapes that Richard J. Hinton describes. But Delany proves true to the cynical proclamation that opens his novel, "in our country commercial interests have taken precedence of all others,"[103] by incorporating even the Dismal Swamp into a capitalist world-system. Demystifying the infamous Swamp—or defining it by yet another layer of mystification, Delany insists that "the revenue is obtained for keeping up an organized existence in this much-dreaded morass"[104] by the renewal of what are essentially conjuring "licenses" that expire every seven years. The High Conjurers who represent a pocket of Afrocentric power in the Tidewater Country are also "ambassadors" and imperial capitalists, "regularly sent out to create new conjurers, lay charms, take off spells" and, it is assumed, create demand. Through the protagonist Henry Blake, Delany defines freedom itself as an "arithmetic," using a heavy rhetoric of economic value: "Whatever liberty is *worth* to the whites, it is *worth* to the blacks; therefore, whatever it *cost* the whites to obtain it, the blacks would be willing and ready to *pay* . . ."[105] (emphasis mine). Given this rhetoric of freedom, it is not surprising that Delany's free territories are, essentially, markets.

Henry Blake's whirlwind tour of the South utilizes the region's extensive river systems, beginning with the Mississippi River, to reverse the dispersion of black Americans effected by the domestic and international slave trade. "Swiftly as the current of the fleeting Mississippi was time passing by, and many states lay in expanse before him, all of which, by the admonishing impulses of dearest relations, he was compelled to pass over as a messenger of light and destruction."[106] As Eric Sundquist and other critics have noted, Blake's anti-slavery vision describes a black Manifest Destiny:[107] "Beyond the [Red] river lie his hopes, the broad plains of Louisiana with a hundred thousand bondsmen seeming anxiously to await him."[108] Making the Mississippi River and its tributaries corridors of black "intelligence"— the key instrument in Blake's insurrectionist scheme—Delany reclaims the market road that commodified African Americans and speaks directly to white fears about the openness or permeability of the riverine South. The haunting threat that ends the only extant, unfinished edition of *Blake*, "Woe be unto those devils of whites, I say!" includes the idea that white safety is compromised by black money and its fatal corollary, white greed. Blake cautions other slaves that "they must have money, if they want to get free," adding that "it is your certain passport through the white gap, as I term it."[109] The "white gap" is self-interest, and this is coterminous with U.S. "patriotism," according to Blake.[110] Blake proves this equation by repeatedly paying off ferryboatmen who transport his band of fugitives across crucial rivers (the Red, the Mississippi, the Ohio) leading to the free black settlements of Canada. Money alone buys the larger social mobility signified by these rivers, which are not *patriae* or fatherlands, but, again, market roads that extend beyond racial and national affiliation. The oft-represented landscapes of the Red River and the Mississippi—home to Davy Crockett, Andrew Jackson, John Murrell, and Harriet Beecher Stowe's Simon Legree, among others—are, Delany suggests, the *essential* U.S. landscapes. And these landscapes necessarily lead away from their own centers toward international waters. In *Blake*, an "Africanized" Cuba is Delany's ultimate geopolitical prize.

Blake's travels to Canada and then to the Caribbean and Cuba only trace the imperialist ambitions of white America—but by merely tracing these imperial designs Delany shows how easily they might be detached from any certain racial destiny. A fear of black nationhood and even empire had been inspired in American whites by the Haitian revolution of the 1790s and remained a prime motivator for U.S. imperial designs on Central America and the Caribbean. Recent scholarship has recognized Delany's prescient call for a black or racially mixed Cuba in *Blake* and in an 1849 article for the abolitionist newspaper he co-edited with Frederick Douglass, *The North Star*. In the *North Star* article, titled "The Redemption of Cuba," Delany calls upon the "colored" population of Cuba—Blacks as well as Asians and Yucatan Indians who have been brought to the island as slaves—to join in the spirit of 1848. Citing the revolutionary mantra "liberté, égalité, fraternité," Delany issues a powerful imperative: "Let the colored races look well to their own interests—let them act for themselves."[111] Later, in the 1852 *Condition, Elevation, Emigration, and Destiny of the Colored People of the United States, Politically Considered*, Delany imagines black American settlement throughout the Caribbean, Central America, and West Africa that might result in an alternate cotton economy, a black world-system which would extinguish the imperialist designs of Southern whites. It is certainly important to note the remarkable prescience of this "global" Black Nationalism, which foreshadows Marcus Garvey's attempts to create a black shipping empire.[112] Yet it is important to remember, I think, that Delany's strong rhetorical response to Southern expansionists in *Blake* begins from *within* the continental United States, with what is effectively a denationalization of the Mississippi River.

As I've noted, this corruption of the nation's central corridor of trade was exactly what many whites in the United States feared, as they feared the potential openness created by trade itself. When Southern imperialists touted the "annexation" of Cuba in *DeBow's Review*, they cited the necessity of Caribbean empire as a means of protecting the Mississippi corridor. "Let Cuba be Africanized [as Delany urged], and then with another San Domingo blocking the mouth of the Mississippi, all we can do by internal improvements will help us little. Our seas will be divested of ships, and those white-winged birds of commerce will fly to other oceans, unfurl their pinions, and droop upon our waters." [113] Here the fear expressed involves the stoppage of economic movement. Another writer for *DeBow's* worried that France or England would take Cuba and use it to "police the seas," thereby (implicitly) ending the illegal importation of captured Africans from Cuba into Texas which was, as late as the 1850s, still augmenting the slave population of the Gulf States. [114] While these arguments ostensibly support the continuance of a fluid and relatively unchecked international commerce, they also betray a fear that commerce might move in the wrong direction, spreading the "mongrelization" that many Southerners saw as the central cultural trait of the Cubans up through the "mouth" of New Orleans. One Southern apologist noted that the prospect of granting citizenship to Cubans was "wild and dangerous"—meaning, essentially, that they were too foreign, too "colored" to become U.S. citizens without, in this writer's phrase, "any previous training." [115] Imperial expansion to the South, *DeBow's* acknowledged, was in fact defensive. "The safety of the South is to be found only in the extension of its peculiar institutions, and the security of the Union in the safety of the South—towards the equator." [116] Although the United States' imperial desires could be naturalized in metaphors suggestive of Emerson's ever-expanding circles, in reality the imperial project was burdensome and potentially never-ending, as were the fears of racial and national amalgamation that drove it.

As Martin Delany recognized, the Mississippi River was ever vulnerable to ethnic infection from below. Delany saw the Mississippi Valley as potentially the site of competing nationalisms and competing racial economies. Delany's was a metaphorical imaging of the business of the Underground Railroad that recognized this alternate market road as the scaffolding of a "colored" capitalist world system. Ultimately, Delany's vision was both revolutionary and shockingly American; it is perhaps not surprising that, in later life, Delany would be identified as somewhat of a conservative, criticizing Wendell Philips's call for a black vice-president and allying himself, loosely, with the "redeemer" Democrats that rose in the post-Reconstruction South. [117] In reality, there was no *one* Henry Blake to transform antebellum southern rivers into corridors of black intelligence and money, just as there was no larger-than-life John Murrell to subvert the profits and social meaning of white traffic in slaves. But the market-rivers opened niches to smaller figures, like John Kagi, a lieutenant under John Brown who marked out a chain of counties extending through Alabama and Mississippi to participate in the fluid semi-nationalist "state" Brown had, again, initially named "the Subterranean Pass Way." Then there was Alexander Milton Ross, a Canadian abolitionist who traveled from New Orleans to Vicksburg, "circulating a knowledge of Canada, and the best means of reaching that country. . . ."[118] Ross and his associates in the railroad business sent intelligence North, telling allies to look out for "packages of hardware" when slave men had escaped, or "dry goods" when slave women were traveling.

The federal government's ambitious, socio-geographic mapping of the Mississippi River as part free, part slave (the Mississippi would be, as it ran between Missouri and Illinois, slave territory from the Missouri bank to the river's "central thread") paradoxically assisted in performing economic and ontological reversals. Judge Roger Taney would establish in the 1857 Dred Scott decision that the transformations effected upon slave bodies in transit between free and slave territories were not binding. But the uncertain status of Scott's daughter Eliza, who was born on the Mississippi River aboard the steamboat *Gypsey*, helped make the constitutionality of the Missouri Compromise a factor in the Scott case. If Eliza had been born when the boat was north of the state line of Missouri, as that line extended into the Mississippi River, she would have been a citizen of Illinois or Wisconsin and "free," even if her mother and father could be established as slaves by the court.[119] The uncertain boundaries drawn through watery spaces generated unpredictable legal and philosophical quandaries.

Although the Mississippi River was not a primary Underground Railroad route, numerous lawsuits brought by slave owners against steamboat operators, particularly in Missouri and Kentucky, attest to slaves' use of riverboats as a means to freedom. Boatmen who unwittingly carried fugitive slaves were charged with destroying property and expected to compensate owners in full. So the "white gap," as Martin Delany called it, was not necessarily open to easy bribes; white self-interest was already circumscribed by federal law, which oversaw interstate commerce. Yet some escaping slaves made it through, and the legal cases that record these instances typically involve slaves impersonating other blacks, using, apparently, borrowed free papers, licenses, or permissions. In the 1846 Missouri case of *Eaton v.*

Vaughan, a Captain Eaton of the steamboat *Wapello* was fined nine hundred dollars for taking Vaughan's slave Charles to Saint Louis, even though Eaton followed the standard procedure of asking for Charles's free papers and even had Charles "examined" twice. Eaton protested that Charles simply appeared to be the man whom he was impersonating, Pompey Spence, "a free negro to whom the license to reside in this State had been granted." [120] Although slave permissions and free black licenses were intended to limit the kinds of exchange possible in a growing domestic slave market, this proliferation of paper also made possible a counter-economy of blacks working to pass each other off to the North. These African Americans, like Charles and Pompey Spence, may not even have been involved in the abolitionist "railroad business." The economy their story suggests is one of affect and mutual obligation.

When Jefferson Davis worried about the potentially corrupting openness of the Mississippi River, and, by extension, the marketplace, he probably envisioned the "railroad business," and he may have even imagined some version of the "colored" empire threatened by Martin Delany, Haiti, and the specter of a mongrel Cuba. But, most probably, Davis did not envision the slave Charles and his friend Pompey Spence, or at least the sort of movement these figures represent. I feel an obligation to point to the possibility of Charles and Pompey Spence in the actual world, even though they too may be only semi-actual, for who knows if "Pompey Spence" was an acquaintance, a friend, or a mere forgery. Charles and Pompey Spence and their story of sacrificial exchange fall out of the closed circuit of commercial rhetorics I have analyzed in this chapter.

Both affirmative and critical narratives that treat the Mississippi River and the old Southwest as the antebellum nation's central market, and therefore an image of the nation itself as porous, avaricious, and cosmopolitan, *more than a nation*, miss a key thread of human behavior in their imaginative excess. I refer to the exchanges of human substance or self, the antebellum "sympathy" among people of color, among whites, and even between blacks and whites that Caleb Crain has recently characterized as "a principle higher and more appealing than nationality, an ideal to which America as a nation aspired—the disinterested fraternity of men." [121] Although Crain's work admirably makes this "provocation of sympathy, without any tethering of it" readable in U.S. letters, his project is so interesting precisely because the provocation of sympathy tends to be overwritten—and rendered virtually unreadable—in most nineteenth-century American literature. "Sympathy" comes to us almost exclusively through the unsatisfying sentimental gestures of domestic fiction or the neo-Platonic generalizations of transcendentalists. It was the doubly unreadable economy of inter-racial sympathy that Mark Twain attempted to capture in the friendship of Huck and Jim, a "realistic" friendship that, as Eric Lott suggests, is continually fractured in the *Adventures of Huckleberry Finn* by the more visible and marketable burlesque sentimentality of the minstrel show. [122] The peculiar cosmopolitanism of southwestern regional imagination insures that trade, not love, is the substance and soul of a "folk" who continued to imagine itself most compellingly, even after the Civil War, as a nation of slaves and thieves.

5. MARK TWAIN'S MANIFEST
AND OTHER DESTINIES

Mark Twain's literary reconstruction of the Mississippi Valley has long been celebrated as the invention of an "American" *zeitgeist*, a national-popular voice which imaginatively healed the post-colonial fracture and racial trauma that followed the Civil War. In his memoir *My Mark Twain*, William Dean Howells makes the famous statement that Twain "was the Lincoln of our literature." Howells links Twain's literary unification to his "breadth of parlance," a "coarse" speech which is at once "Southwestern," "Lincolnian," and "Elizabethan."[1] Howells's use of the regional marker southwestern is historically accurate, given that this is how the Mississippi Valley and its dialects were conceived in the 1840s, the era Twain wrote about in his classic river novels. However, Missouri was no longer "the southwest" in the early twentieth century, when Howells was describing Twain. The necessity of continuing to label Twain as a "Southwesterner" indicates an assumption, shared by Howells and by other admirers of Twain, that Twain's Lincolnian achievement involved recasting the southern United States as the North American West. The compound "southwestern" performs revisionary work. Those who imagined (and still imagine) the West as the solution to the United States' slavery problem, the answer to its continuing race problem, and the virtual winner of the Civil War, in political scientist Anne Norton's phrase,[2] recognize Twain as effecting an ingenious sleight of hand.

The story goes something like this: Mark Twain incorporated the discordant meanings of the South into a frontier paradigm similar to Frederick Jackson Turner's idea of the frontier, which included the assertion that the advancing line of western settlement was a "cord of national unity" and the assertion that, at the frontier, very different sorts of people learned to mingle, depend upon each other, and forge a multi-ethnic national character. Turner recognized the Mississippi River as one such frontier, writing that "on the tide of the Father of Waters, North and South met and mingled into a nation. Interstate migration went steadily on—a process of cross-fertilization of ideas and institutions."[3] Couldn't this be the deep and affirmative national meaning carried by Huck Finn, the poor white Missourian who "talks black" and makes the Mississippi River a temporary cord of union between himself and a fugitive slave?[4] Turner was quick to minimize the importance of "the slavery struggle" to its relation to westward expansion, and many critics have recognized Twain as likewise subordinating Southern racial dissonance to the more nebulous promise of the West. After all, when the Civil War broke out Twain ran to Nevada, where he strived to make a lot of money, "if the war doesn't ruin us," as he wrote to his sister Pamela Moffett from the Nevada Territory in 1861.[5] When Twain is read as a westerner and a Turnerian, he is also implicitly read as a belated advocate of Manifest Destiny. The logic here is that imperial conquest of the continent gave the United States the space, quite literally, to begin to sort out its sectional and racial conflicts. If Huck Finn didn't know, in the 1840s, that he could "light out for the [western] territory" adjacent to the Mississippi, could he have allowed himself the realization that Jim was "white inside" as he drifted between slave states toward the nation's most infamous auction blocks?

The Twain-as-Turnerian argument makes sense, and it hasn't been set up here merely as a straw man. Yet this argument fails to take into account a few key facts about Twain. For Twain "pioneers" were not primarily farmers or ranchers, as they were for Frederick Jackson Turner. Turner's praise of the Mississippi aside, for him the "most significant thing about [the frontier] is that it lies at the hither edge of free land." Turner's frontier was "the frontier of *settlement* [which] advanced and carried with it individualism, democracy, and nationalism"[6] (emphasis mine). In contrast, Twain's pioneers were not producers who banded together in settled communities of interest; they were competitive businessmen, and the market, meaning the systematic working out of economic desire, was their sacred if unstable "ground." The Mississippi River proved an ideal setting for Twain precisely because it was water and not land that could ever be settled. It was a site of the commercial traffic that he felt was making up the world, for better and for worse. A version of this argument originates with Philip Fisher, who has eloquently described the speculator as Twain's culture hero, the ideal figure for a new country in which future values must be energetically projected. Fisher writes that "the world in which [Twain] moves is one in which people buy each other's useless worthless shares and all get rich together on faith. They float together in the insubstantial air of a society of massive credit, debt, risk and collapse." This almost casual optimism about the social value of speculative "floating" falters at the conclusion of *Adventures of Huckleberry Finn*, where, as Fisher acknowledges, "Tom Sawyer stages his heartless phony rescue of Jim [and] a speculative reality is evoked and then collapsed, but not without real wounds."[7] The perennial problem posed by the conclusion of *Huckle-*

berry Finn is, essentially, the problem of reconciling Mark Twain's lifelong obsession with the United States' business culture with the cynicism, anti-imperialism and even anti-nationalism that is also present in his work from as early as the 1860s.

The impulse to minimize the brutality of the ending of *Huckleberry Finn*—or simply not to read the last nine chapters, as Ernest Hemingway recommended—is matched by the desire, for many readers, to separate out Twain's later political writings from his earlier work. Yet it was in California and Nevada, where Twain lived from the outbreak of the Civil War until 1867, that he seems first to have noticed modern racism and linked it to the United States' unique brand of empire. Amy Kaplan has offered a suggestive analysis of Twain's *Letters from Hawaii*, originally published in 1866 in the *Sacramento Union*, to argue that "the routes of transnational travel" first enabled Twain's exploration of U.S. race relations.[8] While the still "foreign" territory of Hawaii may have contributed to the opening of Twain's racial memory, I think it crucial to recognize that the intersections of race prejudice and international capital would have been visible to Twain in fluid sites within the apparently domestic territory of the United States. Given the essentially international economies of many western places in the nineteenth century, it is not surprising that Twain linked the regional economies of Nevada, California, and the Mississippi Valley to cosmopolitan and racially inflected commodity-forms like those Africans and African Americans categorized as "chattel" or the Chinese "coolie" labor that played a crucial role in the western construction industry. Troubling connections among world economic systems, local western economies, and the institutionalization of "race" in the United States would be explored, if incompletely, in Twain's classic river novels before blossoming into anti-imperialist political diatribes aimed at King Leopold of Belgium and other late-century offenders abroad.[9]

Twain's excoriating satires on the abuse of Chinese laborers in San Francisco, which could not even be published until he moved to New York in the late 1860s, betray the West not as a solution to southern history but rather as a version of that same history which is more readable because more naked. Short satirical pieces like "Disgraceful Persecution of a Boy," published in New York's *Galaxy* magazine in 1870, point out institutionalized racism against Chinese workers in California using language that recalls, without explicit acknowledgment, the discourse of antebellum apologists for slavery. Echoing the words of Chief Justice Roger Taney in the landmark Dred Scott decision of 1857, Twain laments that in California "a

Chinaman had no rights that any man was bound to respect." To underline this point, he cites in "Disgraceful Persecution" as well as in the longer satire "Goldsmith's Friend Abroad Again" (1870–71) numerous instances of legal protections of white racial privilege that have operated against the Chinese in California, including the short-lived Foreign Miner's Tax of 1851 and the exorbitant "vaccination fees" Chinese immigrants were required to pay upon landing in western ports. In the classic study *Mark Twain Social Critic*, Philip S. Foner implies that Twain essentially discovered the problem of race in the North American West, where he gained critical distance from the African-American slavery that had informed his youth in Missouri.

I want to suggest here that if Twain indeed made the South *western*, he also made the West *southern*. This interpenetration of regional identities has some historical precedent. As Henry Nash Smith noted many years ago, in the pre–Civil War era southerners were likely to recognize the South and West as "a single physiographic region" articulated to international circuits of capital. The extensive river systems of the South and Southwest, many of which emptied into international seas like the Gulf of Mexico, suggested to persons living near these rivers an international context for regional ambitions. Twain's fellow Missourian, the Senator Thomas Hart Benton, argued up through the 1850s that the West would be a coastal republic, articulated to the Pacific Ocean by its rivers and potentially separated from the United States by the Great American Desert; even the potent dream of a transcontinental railroad could not easily shake Benton's faith in the greater possibilities of North American world empires articulated through water. Mark Twain's own career as a Mississippi riverboat pilot began in what might be characterized as a "southern" and internationalist imperial fantasy; he hoped to reach the Amazon basin and begin a lucrative career in the international coca trade. Twain's cultural history brings denaturing international contexts and international commodities, like coca and slaves, into dialogue with the apparently natural emergence of the United States as a continental settler-nation.

For Twain, the Mississippi River is simultaneously the landscape of an antebellum commercial culture whose vibrancy was underwritten by a barbaric slave traffic *and* the landscape of a late-century commercial culture deemed decadent by prominent cultural critics like Brooks Adams and Theodore Roosevelt. In the *Law of Civilization and Decay* (1896), Adams flatly stated that "commerce from the outset seemed antagonistic to the imagination" and predicted that cultures which had reached the commercial stage would remain "inert until supplied with fresh energetic material by the infusion of barbarian blood." [10] Adams idealized the soldier and prescribed the renewal of military, rather than commercial, conquest. Troubled by Frederick Jackson Turner's prediction of the end of the frontier as a stimulant for national consolidation, Adams sought fresh "Indian wars" abroad. Although Theodore Roosevelt found the *Law of Civilization and Decay* unsubtle, he essentially crafted his political persona in accordance with Adams's imperialistic, hyper-masculine ideal. [11]

Mark Twain's classic writings of the 1870s through the 1890s both predict and defy this late-century embrace of conquest abroad, highlighting the emptiness of military honor and the potentially self-annihilating result of territorial wars against the creativity of essentially commercial figures who reopen their small lives to alterity and possibility, figures like Tom Sawyer and Beriah Sellers in *The Gilded Age*. Yet by the end of his life Twain could satirize the Adams-Roosevelt model of U.S. nationalism without fully believing that he had championed superior ideas. Ostensibly a Republican, Twain conceived of Theodore Roosevelt as the worst president the United States had ever had. When he dictated his rambling biography to Albert Bigelow Paine in the first decade of the twentieth century, he slandered the president rather perversely, likening him to Tom Sawyer. [12] Finally, the productive and eminently commercial imagination of Tom Sawyer had gotten mixed up in San Juan Hill, the United States' imperialist designs on Asia, and what Twain deemed Theodore Roosevelt's deceitful pretense of limiting corporate greed. By the 1890s, monopoly capitalism had overshadowed the romance of the scrappy entrepreneur, and "commercialism," even for Twain, was difficult to recognize as a means by which new worlds, and selves, might be happily brought into being. In an unpublished essay from the early twentieth century, Twain complained that "money" had become the handmaiden of the most brutal forms of domination, both at home and abroad; King Leopold's atrocities in the Congo were "cold blooded murders . . . all for *money*. . . . None of his atrocities in Africa has ever had any but the one object—the acquirement of money which did not belong to him." [13] Moreover in the United States democratic ideals were foundering and a "hard, sordid, dishonest, oppressive" culture had grown up, instigated, again, by "money-lust." Apparently innocent speculations like Tom Sawyer's famous fence-painting ruse now seemed to preview an era of global exploitation.

In truth, productive speculators or "world-makers" like Tom Sawyer, Beriah Sellers, and even Huck Finn always had been tied to a systemic imperialism whose global implications were even larger than late-century beach-head moments like the battle of San Juan Hill. Tom Sawyer's fellow travelers were the Duke and Dauphin and Tom Driscoll of *Puddn'head Wilson*, men who were not imaginative frauds or "businessmen," but actual slave traders. While the gentle Huck Finn is not, by design, a slave trader, his embrace of a liberal *freedom from*, or negative freedom, lands him in the company of slave traders who cruelly, although not unexpectedly, sell his best friend. Myra Jehlen has written that "it is impossible in the Mississippi River towns through which Huck and Jim journey to imagine being a hero," and that Jim's freedom is necessarily contradictory to Huck's because it includes communitarian commitment and "something very like a revolution."[14] Freedom for Huck, in turn, is simply freedom from commitment, what Jehlen calls "pathlessness" and what she intends as self-centeredness. The amoral justice of a market that could carry both western produce and enslaved persons is the nature of the river that seems to fit Huck like a second skin. Reading *Adventures of Huckleberry Finn* through Twain's later writings, including his retelling of Huckleberry Finn in the fragmentary *Tom Sawyer's Conspiracy*, denatures the white mobility that Twain also lived and often praised. When put into conversation with each other, both of these "river stories" betray Huck's apparently heroic western travel as an iteration of the same international networks of capital and power that sponsored the slave trade.

By the time Twain began work on the river novella *Tom Sawyer's Conspiracy* in 1897, he wholly identified the United States' commercial culture with what Forrest G. Robinson has called a "culture of bad faith" where normative behavior involves exploiting others and, even more perversely, swindling yourself into believing that such exploitation is normal.[15] Twain originally imagined the plot of *Tom Sawyer's Conspiracy* to pivot around Tom Sawyer's selling of a cork-blackened Huck Finn into slavery and then stealing him out again, for fun.[16] This potential plot—though it was abandoned—suggests the extent to which *Tom Sawyer's Conspiracy* offers a revisionist, even explosive reading of *Adventures of Huckleberry Finn*, where it could be said that Huck has played Tom's "nigger." Certainly not one of the other "Huck and Tom" adventures Twain wrote as sequels to his "boys' novels" attempts the kind of meta-criticism that *Tom Sawyer's Conspiracy* achieves. Perhaps the plot of Tom selling a minstrelized Huck finally offered too cutting a criticism of the earlier novel. In *Tom Sawyer's Conspiracy*, which Twain left unfinished in 1899, Tom does not sell Huck for scandal and laughs.

Instead, Tom himself plays the parts of slave, slave trader, and slave thief. Tom "blacks up" to impersonate a slave so that he can sell himself to a local trader and then scare the villagers of Saint Petersburg by having himself fictitiously run off by "ablitionists." This ruse does provoke terror in the village when Jake Flacker, detective, identifies the faux abolitionists (really Tom and Huck) as "members of Burrell's gang," an allusion to the legendary slave-stealing ring of John Murrell. [17] As Tom and Huck are repeatedly and mistakenly cast as "niggers," abolitionists, and slave thieves, Twain plays with the question of which misidentification is most true. Of course, this question has troubled many readers of the Adventures of Huckleberry Finn. Reading the Adventures of Huckleberry Finn (1885) against Tom Sawyer's Conspiracy (1899) transforms the earlier novel into a deep exploration of the meanings of whiteness and westward emigration, linked if not synonymous ideas in the antebellum period that were sponsored by African Americans caught within those networks of distribution which defined an emerging white middle class.

The Unnatural Pioneer

Huckleberry Finn's venture down the Mississippi River is a kind of speculation, as well as an act of emigration, by which Huck hopes to elude his abusive father and gain ownership of himself. The trip is a calculated risk that places Huck, historically, in the company of the many poor but climbing whites who emigrated to the Mississippi Valley from the 1820s through the 1840s. In a small way, Huck tests the concept of Manifest Destiny, the promise that Providence will look after those who keep moving farther from where they started, toward a yet to be consolidated territory whose apparent openness allowed antebellum boosters like John L. O'Sullivan to speak of the United States' "infinite expandability." As Frederick Jackson Turner would write in his nostalgic revisitation of Manifest Destiny in the 1890s, "America has been another name for opportunity. . . . Movement has been its dominant fact." [18] But in Twain's river fictions the Mississippi River and the culture of the river make plain that nature does not necessarily complement the emigration of white Americans into western lands that do not belong to them, that the generalized (and, for Euro-Americans, "happy") concept of white mobility must be understood in relation to historical contingencies that denature it. The successes of the class of person Huck represents, the poor-to-middling whites who came to farm along the Mississippi or work in its thriving carrying trade, were subject to many unpredictable and essentially foreign limitations, perhaps most fundamentally to the physics of the river itself.

The "June rise" which initiates Huck and Jim's downriver journey represents a belated spring thaw that would have opened the season of navigation on the Mississippi River. Steamboat carriers depended upon a succession of rises, issuing from various tributaries, to provide the five- or six-foot stage necessary for transporting full cargoes.[19] Just on the other side of the seasonal rises that facilitated trade and allowed western farmers access to markets, the flood signaled financial collapse. Historian John W. Monette notes that there were twelve significant Mississippi floods from 1820 to 1840.[20] Floods washed away the wood yards necessary for fueling steamboats, buried boat landings deep in mud, destroyed crops and homes. In *Life on the Mississippi*, Twain represents the Mississippi flood as a moment of transition in which socioeconomic status might shift radically, down or up. Some canny speculators managed to convert unpredictable river levels into capital. "When the river is rising fast, some scoundrel whose plantation is back in the country, and therefore of inferior value, has only to watch his chance, cut a little gutter across the narrow neck of land some dark night, and turn the water into it, and in a wonderfully short time . . . the whole Mississippi has taken possession of that little ditch, and placed the countryman's plantation on its bank, quadrupling its value. . . ."[21]

As a carrier of the booms and busts of the nation's market economy, the Mississippi was described by Andrew Jackson as a domestic alimentary canal that found its mouth through New Orleans. It was the center of the North American West and, it was hoped, proof that the western United States would someday be central to the world. "Every Man of the western Country turns his eyes intuitively upon the mouth of the Mississippi," Jackson noted, "Blocked up, all the fruits of his industry rot upon his hand—open and he carries on a trade with all the nations of the earth."[22] Twain, writing to his friend Ann E. Taylor in 1857 from New Orleans, recognized the city's centrality through the cosmopolitan crowd that gathered at its overstocked markets. Of New Orleans's French market, Sam Clemens wrote: "I thought I had seen all kinds of markets before—but that was a great mistake—this being a place such as I had never dreamed of before. . . . Out on the pavement were groups of Italians, French, Dutch, Irish, Spaniards, Indians, Chinese, Americans, English, and the lord knows how many more different kinds of people."[23] While working temporarily as the Saint Louis correspondent to the *Muscatine Journal* in 1855, Twain delivered a similar encomium to Saint Louis's "brisk" levees and cultural connections to far-flung ports. "A panorama of Australia, China, and the Japanese Expedition, is now on exhibition at Wyman's Hall," he reports, "which far exceeds anything of the kind in beauty, interest, excellence, and truthfulness to nature. . . . One portion of this painting in particular, (and it was all good)—a sun-set scene in China—was enchantingly beautiful: even more so than Muscatine sun-sets in summer." [24] The mere comparison of the sunsets of Muscatine, Iowa, to the sunsets of anywhere, China, performs a startling imaginary geographical linkage between a relatively small western river port and the Pacific Rim. Even ex-slaves took pride in the thriving commerce of the river and the stimulating worlds that accrued around its primary ports. In his memoir, the Saint Louis barber and former slave James Thomas recalled with pride the New Orleans port of the 1830s and 1840s as a rival to New York, handling the transport of "horses, cattle, hogs, mules, corn flower" and, in what appears almost as an afterthought, "occasionally a crowd of blacks." [25] The slave market in New Orleans was the biggest in the country by the 1840s, moving slaves from the Atlantic seaboard and Upper South into the cotton frontiers of Mississippi, Arkansas, and Texas. Meanwhile Caribbean islands like Cuba had become depots for international slave ships whose illegal West African "cargo" might reenter the U.S. through scarcely nationalized western territories like the Republic of Texas.

The nationalistic pride normally inspired by the sight of traffic on the West's greatest market road was problematized by the sight of slave cargoes being moved against their inclination toward the same Southwest that even Henry David Thoreau, in the essay "Walking," would indicate held a magnetic attraction for Euro-American bodies. Whatever one's politics, the transformation of humans into freight imaged the opposite of Providential destiny; it was anti-emigration. In the chapter of Uncle Tom's Cabin titled "La Belle Rivière," Harriet Beecher Stowe depicts genteel southern women attempting to reconcile themselves to the presence of a slave trader, Haley, and his human cargo aboard their Mississippi steamboat. "All [aboard] was full of life," Stowe remarks, "—all but Haley's gang, who were stored, with other freight, on the lower deck." [26] In a famous letter to his friend Mary Speed, a young Abraham Lincoln observed twelve chained slaves traveling down river aboard a Mississippi boat. Considerably agitated by the sight, Lincoln sought comfort for himself in the apparent cheerfulness of the slaves amidst "these distressing circumstances. . . . One whose offense for which he had been sold was an overfondness for his wife, played the fiddle continuously. . . ." [27] By allowing the substitution of the slave's music for his inevitable if undetectable grief, Lincoln aestheticizes this scene, transmuting it into a valediction.

The presence of slaves in river traffic imaged the social death characteristic of all speculative risk, and in *Adventures of Huckleberry Finn* this slave presence disrupts the confirmation of U.S. national ambition normally offered by western travel. When Huck Finn says, "No'm. Killed a nigger," in answer to Sally Phelps's question of whether or not any "person" was hurt when a steamboat that he claims carried him to Arkansas blew a cylinder head, he voices the novel's only specific reference to the slave cargo and slave boatmen who were visible on boats like the ones remarked by Lincoln, James Thomas, and Stowe. As John Seelye has noted, Huck Finn's river is unrealistically empty. [28] Perhaps this is because explicit reference to the "shameful sights to be seen" on the river, in Stowe's phrase, would have utterly destroyed the illusion of pastoral idyll that makes *Huckleberry Finn* such a frustratingly divided book. Other human sacrifices to the greater economy of the Mississippi Valley who might have been visible in river traffic at the time of Huck's travels include Creek (Muscogee) Indians, who were being transported across the river in order to "open" prime Alabama cotton land to white settlers. [29] European immigrants traveling aboard the riverboats made another species of live freight, confined in the often disease-ridden deck quarters which were also home to livestock, slaves, bales of hay and baggage. Cholera, yellow fever, and other deadly diseases thrived in these filthy deck quarters, and sick travelers were sometimes forced to disembark on unpopulated river islands by steamboat captains who hoped to prevent the spread of disease in riverside towns. [30]

If Mark Twain fails to mention outright the less pleasing species of traffic which must have been observable to him from the time of his childhood through his young adulthood as a steamboat pilot on the Mississippi, he nevertheless alludes to the domestic slave trade and its presence on the river in *Adventures of Huckleberry Finn*, in a significant if deeply ironic way. After all, despite Huck's belated efforts and good intentions, Jim travels downriver to be sold in Arkansas, the cotton frontier that stimulated the slave trade, including illegal importation from Africa, by offering a seemingly bottomless source of demand. As many critics have noted, Twain's portrayal of Jim's sale well after the Civil War had cancelled the commodity value of African Americans should have provoked only small anxieties; circa 1885, when *Adventures of Huckleberry Finn* was published, readers knew that Jim would be free, at least eventually. [31] Yet the dramatic irony built into the novel by its historical distance from the slave problem does not free the narrative from a broader nervousness about race.

There are many ways of talking about racial discomfort in the novel, and I would like to suggest that it might be productive to consider the novel's interrogation of U.S. racism by focusing first on its anxious and divergent definitions of whiteness. I approach this topic through the more familiar representational problem of minstrelsy, which Eric Lott has addressed most powerfully and which I will touch upon, too, although in a quite different way. Lott recognizes Huck's great compliment to Jim that Jim is "white inside," a compliment inspired by Jim's refusal to escape when Tom has been shot during the boys' fake raid on the Phelpses' home, as "the crowning statement on the centrality of blackface's contradictions to Twain's imagination." Blackface imagery and practice in Twain's work allows the exercise of the imperial psychological orientation Homi Bhabha calls "ambivalence," where the imperial imagination is haunted by the difference of the colonized even when most readily aware of their humanity. The black who is "white inside" reassures that "they must be versions of 'us,' caught in a cycle of mimicry . . . and yet perennially unable to make the grade." [32]

Twain reasserts the internal whiteness of Jim in the later novella *Tom Sawyer's Conspiracy*, where Huck goes so far as to say that Jim is "the whitest man inside that ever walked." [33] At the same time, the terms "white nigger" and "counterfeit nigger" are ascribed to the Duke, who has been passing himself off as a slave in order to be sold for profit by the King. The same troubled term, "white nigger," is ascribed to Tom, who was also hoping to profit, in gossip, by selling and stealing himself as a slave. Tom recognizes the Duke as another "white nigger" when he sees him sleeping in the cabin of the local slave trader, Bat Bradish. Tom's means of identifying a blackface minstrel are predictable enough: he counsels Huck that you tell a "white nigger" by the palms of his hands ("the inside of a nigger's hands ain't black") and by the way he talks in his sleep ("he hasn't learned to talk nigger in his sleep, yet"). [34] But predictable as Tom's racist epistemology is, it accrues surplus meaning from the larger narrative of *Tom Sawyer's Conspiracy*. Here the "white nigger" is an uncomfortable, imperfect inversion of the "black" who is white inside. White niggers can easily "wash up" to visible social personhood but their transracial play reveals that they have no proper inside, not the individuating map of the palm nor the "nigger talk" that Twain seems to have identified with authenticity, beginning in 1874 with his first narrative written in African-American dialect which is significantly titled "A True Story."

By making one of his central, most beloved characters, Tom Sawyer, into a defamiliarized sign of white racial privilege—a figure both "white" and "nigger" at the same time apparently because he sees his only partially successful performance of blackness as preferable to remaining unexceptionally white—Twain offers a primitive version of what is now known as critical whiteness studies.[35] Naming Tom Sawyer himself as the problematic sign of whiteness, the exemplary "white nigger" of *Tom Sawyer's Conspiracy*, Twain allows us to think about how whiteness works as a sociological and epistemological problem in the earlier river fictions in which Tom appears. Through Tom, Twain breaks "whiteness" away from the constellation "mobility," "property," and "nature," the constellation of Euro-American virtues that had underwritten U.S. Manifest Destiny and conferred a national-racial character upon the North American West that even in the 1840s seemed *mythic*, in the Barthesian sense, de-historicized and apparently inevitable.

In *Tom Sawyer's Conspiracy*, Tom's race is a conspiracy, exceptional in a historically particular, unnatural way that exposes the geopolitical space of the Mississippi River as likewise unnatural, caught up in a proliferation of the commodity-form that threatens to cancel even the most apparently essential human values. Unlike Jim's "blackness," which is filled with a culturally validated whiteness equivalent to personhood, Tom's "whiteness" is empty, "nigger" or non-person—as that abusive term implies. Tom's "white nigger" enactment is nakedly appropriative. Again, he plays "black" to sell himself and create a juicy scandal in Saint Petersburg. Tom's racial play indicates Twain's experimentation with whiteness as an appropriative and empty sign reminiscent of the "eating of the other" that bell hooks has identified with late-twentieth-century white commercial co-optation of black styles and bodies.[36] More significantly, Tom's incorporative whiteness appears as an effect of colonial structures which were still in place in the time Twain writes about, the 1840s. Tom appropriates "nigger" status so that he can actively engage in the domestic and always international slave trade that had shifted the meaning of "nigger" from the relatively neutral *negro* to the pejorative "slave" by the eighteenth century.[37] It is important to recognize that in *Tom Sawyer's Conspiracy*, Tom's peculiar minstrelsy does not include an imitation of the falsely perceived behavioral characteristics of African Americans, in other words an enactment of what we might now recognize as romantic racialism. Rather, Tom's minstrelsy in the novella includes a ham performance of whiteness itself, when whiteness is conceived as the institutionalization of European colonialism through the slave traffic.

The *Adventures of Huckleberry Finn* is a less cynical, anxious novel than the fragmentary *Tom Sawyer's Conspiracy*, but it too interrogates what we might call the white race problem. Floating on a raft that precariously supports his worldly possessions, Huckleberry Finn reenacts the anxieties that the slave traffic inspired in antebellum whites, whose skin privilege depended largely upon their ability to hold property, black property in particular. Howard Horwitz has remarked that white nervousness about the alienability of property, and the implicit slipperiness of liberal selfhood, contributes to Huck and Jim's peculiar interest in "kings." [38] The *Adventures of Huckleberry Finn* is heavy with a fear of white social death, a kind of white non-personhood roughly equivalent to what Twain later identifies as the status of the "white nigger." This status does not apply only to poor whites. Even Huck, with his unclaimed monies in Judge Thatcher's safe and his precariously floating slave charge, is not exactly poor. His position, again, is reminiscent of middling speculators and riverside plantation owners. Mississippi Valley property holders' imperfect grasp on riverside lands and slave properties that seemed eager to defy them made "whiteness" a particularly unstable category on and along the river.

Economic and Racial Drift

Drifting and floating on the raft proves to be a politically ironic movement in *Adventures of Huckleberry Finn*, a parody of Manifest Destiny in which Providential protection is denied to the earnest white boy who initially rejoices in the naturalness of his travel. The river sensually "joggles" Huck and seems to fit him so well he can even "smell" the passage of time in it. "Sometimes moonlight, sometimes storms, and we a floating along, talking, and singing, and laughing," Huck reflects. [39] But of course Huck and Jim's gentle floating makes them targets for theft and easy prey to river pirates like the Duke and King. Even Huck describes floating as a mobility which denies agency when he, in a canoe, and Jim, on the raft, drift past the Ohio River in a thick fog. Jehlen describes this moment as the point in which freedom in the novel is sundered, and Jim's freedom as revolutionary reform loses to Huck's liberal freedom from emplottedness. [40] Certainly the missing of the Ohio nixes Jim's escape. Yet at this same moment in the novel Huck narrates a frightening loss of control, a literalized environmental determinism in which his body recognizes itself as at odds with the nature that once seemed to have been poured into it "like melted wax," to borrow Ralph Waldo Emerson's simile for the interpenetration of self and world. [41] Floating past the Ohio cancels Jim's freedom and complicates Huck's illusion of freedom as he realizes that the weather runs contrary to his intentions and that he is not, at least not wholly, natural. Implicitly, there is a rent in Huck's normativity here, if not in his racial normativity per se. Huck recalls in an anxious past-present tense: "first I know I'll run into a bank or a tow-head or something; I got to set still and float, and yet it's a mighty fidgety business to have to hold your hands still at such a time." [42] The surrender of craft signified by Huck's holding of his hands prompts his further reflection upon how floating does not even feel like moving. It offers a somatic image of the anti-emigration suggested to more analytical minds by the appearance of slave cargoes on the river: "No, you feel like you are laying dead still on the water; and if a little glimpse of a snag slips by, you don't think to yourself how fast you're going, but you catch your breath and think, my! how that snag's tearing along." [43] It is significant that immediately after experiencing this loss of control over his own mobility Huck attempts to reassert mastery over Jim by cruelly pretending to Jim that Jim imagined their separation.

Huck's problem of ownership is not really the problem of a poor child, but rather the problem of any slaveholder—a large and inclusive class—who might desire to imagine his household as an autonomous unit, as in the Aristotelian *oikos*, that is unaffected by market forces. Walter Benn Michaels has made a complementary argument about *Uncle Tom's Cabin*, where he suggests that the real spectacle of horror in that novel is not slavery per se, but the imperfect nature of white mastery over purportedly domestic, patriarchal economies. [44] For Twain, the river is a field of desire in which capital is continually broken up, moved, or transformed. Riverside lands tumble into floodwaters, slaves occasionally stow away on steamboats or disappear at the hands of abolitionists and slave thieves, who for slaveholders were the same people. The movement of the water and the things it carries is unpredictable. Huck identifies the river in the moderate flood stage of "the June rise" in which his journey begins as a theater of floating capital, capital which takes the rather innocent form of unclaimed driftwood and fragmented, unmanned rafts. Even to Huck, his chosen form of movement, drift, signifies a ready vulnerability to appropriation. Moreover, a raft is a thing that he has learned is easy to take. Early in the novel, Huck and Pap gather "part of a log raft—nine logs fast together" to sell as firewood in Hannibal. The occasional canoe floating on the river represents a more speculative venture, insofar as it is difficult to see if a canoe is really un-manned. When Huck first glimpses the canoe that will take him to Jackson's Island, he "just expected there'd be somebody laying down in it, because people often done that to fool folks, and when a chap had pulled a skiff out most to it they'd raise up and laugh at him." [45] Huck himself lies down in the canoe as he drifts past the dock at Hannibal, but it is nighttime and, fortunately, no one attempts to board him. These floating rafts and canoes that are given to Pap and Huck by the river suggest that capital naturally flows where it is most needed, that the river indeed may approximate a distributive justice.

Yet this commercial ideal is repeatedly undermined, as I have suggested. Its most obvious antitheses are the Duke and King, who rig the river system with phony handbills creating false values and unnatural desires. The Duke and King advertise themselves as "tragedians" and Jim as a "fugitive" from Louisiana. Their false paper sets the market flowing in directions Huck could not have anticipated from his childhood experiences waiting for what the spring "rises" might bring. The advertisement the Duke prints up in Bricksville for Jim allows the frauds to hold Jim and sell him as finders; John Murrell used a similar ruse, and Twain's allusion links Huck and Jim, once again, back to the river's most famous slave thief. In *Tom Sawyer's Conspiracy*, the Duke and King again attempt to hold Jim with spurious papers. In this later narrative, Jim is accused of murdering a slave trader and is about to be tried for murder. Informed of this dire situation by Tom and Huck, the frauds imagine that they might still profit from Jim if they can produce a "requisition for Jim from the Governor of Kentucky" claiming that he is already awaiting trial for murder in that state. They will then take Jim and sell him further downriver. "All bogus, you know," the Duke confides in Huck, "but the seals and the paper, which is genuwyne—and on them papers we can go and grab Jim wherever we find him and there ain't anybody can prevent it." [46] Paper is more fluid than water, it seems, and generates a more efficient and predictable, if less just, capital flow. The printer's craft also plays a role in Tom Sawyer's creation of the trumped-up conspiracy that ultimately lands Jim between a public hanging and sale to the deeper South. In *Tom Sawyer's Conspiracy*, Tom prints 150 fake handbills for the "white nigger" that is actually him so that he can pass himself off to the local trader, Bat Bradish.

By the time the handbills establish Tom as a slave, the point is moot. The trader, Bat Bradish, is about to be murdered and Jim is about to be accused.

Jim is the only man in Saint Petersburg with a reasonable motive for killing the trader because Bradish had convinced Miss Watson to sell him "last summer," in the time-space of *Huckleberry Finn*. But, as in *Huckleberry Finn*, here Jim is falsely accused. Bradish actually was killed by another pair of "white niggers," the King and Duke. It turns out that since their encounter with Huck and Jim the frauds have been making money by selling themselves as slaves rather than tragedians. Somehow Bat Bradish got in the way of the scheme after money had changed hands. Tom knows that the Duke killed Bradish because he knows that the Duke is the same "white nigger" he found with Bradish when he was trying to interest the trader in himself. "Ain't it curious?" Tom remarks to Huck on their common cause with the frauds. "They got in ahead of us on our scheme all around: play counterfeit nigger like we was going to do." [47] Other than the query "ain't it curious," Tom and Huck offer scant commentary on why the once oppositional roles of "speculator" and "nigger" seem to have merged. Early in the planning stages of the conspiracy, Tom answers Huck's complaint that no black man will want to participate in their scheme by saying simply, "There's a lack—we've got to supply it." [48] The lack, in part, is that Jim is now legally free and no longer eligible to enact Tom's sadistic plots. Clearly one of the interrogations Twain seems to be making in this novella is what happens to masters—or more broadly what happens to white folks—when there are no longer slaves to entertain them. The simple answer is that they try to become slaves and entertain themselves—that is, minstrelsy. The more complicated problem here is why impersonating a slave requires selling yourself to a trader and then stealing yourself away from him to "make talk." It is as if, one year after the *Adventures of Huckleberry Finn* in the fictional time-space of Twain's oeuvre, the principal characters of that novel are trying, rather desperately, to compensate for the loss of speculative energy that fueled their earlier, more successful plot.

Without an active domestic slave market, and slave commodities circulating within it, the suspense and poignancy of the *Adventures of Huckleberry Finn* would be nil. Even at the end of *Huckleberry Finn*, when Tom Sawyer finally reveals Jim's legal freedom, Jim is effectively deglamorized by being paid forty dollars in wages for his performance as a fugitive slave. Tom's paying of wages to Jim is one of the many dull notes in the novel's anticlimactic, unsatisfactory conclusion. Jim's worth, in every sense of that word, was greater to the novel while he was a slave. His actual monetary worth as a slave ranged from eight hundred dollars, which is what Miss Watson collected on him, to the two- to three hundred dollars that would be paid finders who encountered him on the road. As a slave, Jim is white treasure. Huck recognizes that Jim can't sit up on the raft in the daylight because of the excitement he will provoke in white onlookers: "people could tell he was a nigger a good ways off." The fact that Jim, like a celebrity, cannot be seen in public, enforces privacy and finally friendship between Huck and Jim. [49] Jim's desirability makes Huck, too, potentially famous or infamous. White people can't stop talking to Huck about Jim. "There's two hundred dollars on him," a boy tells Huck after Jim has been sold in Pikesville to Silas Phelps. "It's like pickin' up money out'n the road . . . they ain't no trouble 'bout that speculation, you bet you." Judith Loftus, the woman who sees through Huck's lame disguise as a girl, tells Huck that Jim has been traced to Jackson's Island and then describes Jim as sure money. "Does three hundred dollars lay around every day for people to pick up?" In *Adventures of Huckleberry Finn*, the distinction between "money" and "people" is initially quite clear: "people" is white, "money" black. Once Jim really is free, there can be no compensation to the white world of the Mississippi Valley for the excitement, the glamour, the possibility of undeserved advancement signified by a black body adrift on the river.

As the many abolitionists and, later, politicians who considered compensating slaveholders for the loss of slave capital in the event of emancipation came to acknowledge, there really was no way to account for the tremendous value of slaves to white Americans. Some, like Henry Clay, could name a price; in 1839, Clay estimated on the Senate floor that 1200 million dollars in slave capital would have to be "compensated" if emancipation occurred. [50] Years later, in 1855, Ralph Waldo Emerson suggested that while no price would be high enough, still the nation should try to pay itself back for the loss of its slaves. In Emerson's metaphysical politics, drawing the larger circle was theoretically important, even if the circle never got finished because the arc of desire, as in this case, was simply too large. "If really the matter could come to negotiation and a price were named," Emerson lectured, "I do not think any price founded on an estimate that figures could tell would be quite unmanageable. Every man in the land would give a week's work to dig away this accursed mountain of sorrow once and forever out of the world." [51] Emerson could not have predicted the theatrical compensation staged in *Tom Sawyer's Conspiracy*, where it becomes clear that the loss of the slave, or of the particular slave Jim, has to be addressed by a novel performance of whiteness. What the "nigger" had been to the "white" was an idea of value detached from labor, a natural resource and treasure, white gold. The gold and silver rushes of the Far West that were Twain's first successful fictional topic figure as merely a pallid afterthought to the international slave rush. It was the trans-Atlantic slave trade that first allowed the West to imagine itself as the future center of the world.

At the end of *Tom Sawyer's Conspiracy*, which is not quite a conclusion because the text is fragmentary, Tom Sawyer states before a judge that Jim is not guilty of murder. Then Tom recounts, in his typically stylish cant, the essential plot of his conspiracy. When the fragment simply stops, it has become clear that Tom has both saved Jim from the gallows and rendered him obsolete. What Tom reveals is what the reader already knows: everyone really acting in this plot is white. Jim's testimony in court is cursorily summarized and irrelevant. Jim's voice is reduced in *Tom Sawyer's Conspiracy* to an evasive "mumbling."[52] The minstrel behaviors that vaguely represent Jim throughout the novella are so exaggerated as to be grotesque. Twain either really doesn't care about Jim anymore by the time he writes *Tom Sawyer's Conspiracy*, or he is elaborately acting out a disowning of this once carefully-rendered character as a masochistic self-reproach. Curiously, Twain would have us believe that Tom Sawyer created the conspiracy that is the primary plot of the novella in response to a request from Jim, as if it were really Jim, not Tom, who authors the genealogy of whiteness that Tom and Huck perform. Supposedly Jim inspired the "white nigger" plot indirectly, by rejecting two prior plots that Tom had dreamed up. The first plot was called "civil war"; the second, "revolution." To be nice to Jim, Tom abandoned these alternatives, showing a generosity that Huck lavishly praises without questioning why a former slave who is living in a slave state might tell a white boy that he does not want "civil war" or "revolution." Perhaps even the reader is not meant to ask these questions.

At any rate, Twain distracts us with Huck's almost shocking statement near the beginning of the novella that Tom Sawyer has "countermanded the Civil War." This indeed would be Tom Sawyer's greatest evasion. For achieving it, Huck thinks Tom ought to be compared to "Harriet Beacher Stow and all them other second-handers [who] gets all the credit for starting that war and you never hear Tom Sawyer mentioned in the histories ransack them as you will, and yet he was the first one that thought of it."[53] What a premise: Tom Sawyer should be famous for not bringing the slavery struggle to a head, while Stowe has been credited with injecting it, irrevocably, into the United States' popular culture. It is impossible not to wonder what, if anything, Twain meant by playing with the idea that Tom Sawyer might be the anti-Stowe, the figure who depopularizes an earnest, if limited, antebellum dialogue about freedom and supplants that dialogue with a racial mystery by which no one profits and a black man, again, is locked up. Was this pale anti-Stowism what Twain, when affected by what he called his "deep melancholy" in the later years of his career, conceived of as Tom Sawyer's contribution, or even as his own contribution, to the national imaginary after the Civil War?

In "Chapters from My Autobiography," which Twain published in the *North American Review*, Twain begins his self-description with a genealogy in which his ancestors figure as "pirates" and "slavers," the sorts of characters that Tom Sawyer modeled in play. "Back of the Virginia Clemenses," Twain recounts, "is a dim procession of ancestors stretching back to Noah's time. According to tradition, some of them were pirates and slavers in Elizabeth's time. But this is no discredit to them, for so were Drake and Hawkins and the others. It was a respectable trade, then, and monarchs were partners in it. In my time I have had desires to be a pirate myself. The reader—if he will look deep down in his secret heart, will find—but never mind what he will find there; I am not writing his Autobiography, but mine." [54] The associational reach of Twain's *Autobiography* suggests that he actually was writing "the reader's" *Autobiography*, too, or at least an ethnobiography of European America. His leap from Biblical progenitors to pirates and slave traders neatly encapsulates the nineteenth-century United States' compromised version of modernity, where eschatological idealism competed with a brutal, international history to tell the story of the world from here. Twain confides that he prefers to recognize himself in the pirate, who is implicitly synonymous with the slaver; piracy and slaving is where "our" American pleasure lies.

This glib, unsettling, Tom Sawyerish message reasserts itself in the last installment of the *Autobiography* that Twain published before he died, which ends with a silly anecdote, the sort of shtick that Michael J. Kiskis has noted found its way back into Twain's *Autobiography* from his earlier work on the stage. [55] Twain tells a story about how, when he was in desperate need of three dollars rent money in the late 1860s, he stole a dog from the celebrated "Indian fighter" Nelson A. Miles for three dollars, sold it to a stranger, then reclaimed the dog for Miles (refunding the stranger's money), and returned the dog to Miles for a finder's fee of three dollars. "I went away with a good conscience, because I had acted honorably; I never could have used the three that·I sold the dog for, because it was not rightly my own, but the three I got for restoring him to his rightful owner was righteously and properly mine, because I had earned it. . . . My principles have remained to this day what they were then."[56] This is a strange note on which to end an autobiography, inasmuch as it can be seen as an ending given that it was the last installment of the memoir to be overseen by Twain himself.

What is odd, I think, is how generalized this "bit," this selling what does not belong to you, became in Twain's writings, both fictional and autobiographical. Several scholars have argued that for Twain writing was equivalent to selling what is not yours. Twain accused almost all of his former publishers of misusing copyright and profiting by his imagination, which he was quite certain did not belong to them. Then there are the memoirs and fictions where ex-slaves (Jim, Roxy in Puddn'head Wilson) are sold by men who do not own them, or white boys sell themselves as something other than what they are, or claim jumpers profit from mines not rightfully theirs. Finally there are the figures of international imperialist intrigue, those who bought and sold countries, like the Philippines, that never really belonged to them. It is significant that Nelson A. Miles, who had been instrumental in military offensives against the Sioux in the late 1870s and who had helped to "capture" Geronimo, figures in Twain's apparently absurdist bit about selling the dog. The bare plot of this joke is fundamental to U.S. national emergence. Twain recognizes that the romantic pirate of child's play, the Indian fighter and the historical "slaver" are one. For Twain, piracy, land theft, slaving, "selling what does not belong to you," offers not just a precondition of modernity, but a precondition of comic imagination and, implicitly, of knowledge. In his autobiographical history, the Enlightenment comes to Europe, ironically, out of piracy and slavery; piracy and slavery produces the Americas; finally piracy, in its multiple forms, annexes the American West.

The West Was Another Country, A Lot Like the United States

On 26 April 1861, just two weeks after Confederate forces had fired on Fort Sumter, Samuel Clemens wrote his elder brother Orion a short but strangely urgent letter. "I am on the wing for Hannibal, to collect money due me," Clemens begins. "I shall return to St. Louis to-morrow. Orion bring down 'Armageddon' with you if you have it. If not, buy it." [57] Twain planned to meet his mother, brother, and sister in Saint Louis and at this early moment in the Civil War he probably was already considering a proposal from

Orion to leave for the Nevada Territory, where Orion had been appointed territorial secretary by Abraham Lincoln only a month earlier. Clearly Twain was thinking about *Armageddon*, the book, if not the actual end of his vibrant and profitable world as a Mississippi river pilot. This book that he asked his brother to bring or even buy had been published in the 1840s by a Nashville preacher, Samuel D. Baldwin, who prophesied that Armageddon would come about between 1860 and 1875 and that it would take place in the Mississippi Valley. It would involve a battle between the United States, Russia, and other European forces; afterward, a millennium of peace would ensue. Twain never again comments upon the book in his letters. If Orion brought it to him, and if he read it, perhaps it at least confirmed his belief that the Mississippi held a central place in international and Biblical history.

By the summer of 1861 that particular center of the world, the Mississippi, was lost to Twain, and with it a certain confidence that imagination and speculation could be linked to justice and craft. The tone of Twain's letters from before the outbreak of the war is quite distinct from the tone of those that follow it. Twain's letters from the time of his piloting days brim with an unselfconscious, non-ironic faith in energy, skill, and the cosmopolitan sociability that the commercial culture of the great western river promised. In 1858 Twain, who had just become an apprentice river pilot after spending five years struggling as a journeyman printer and hack journalist, could casually write to Orion that "I cannot correspond with a paper, because when one is learning the river, he is not allowed to do or think about anything else."[58] Twain's next sentences curtly dismiss the Tennessee lands that were a burdensome family inheritance which haunted the Clemens family for decades with what Twain sarcastically called the specter of "prospective wealth." From his newfound security as a pilot, Clemens cautions his brother: "I am glad to see you in such high spirits about the land, and I hope [you] will remain so, if you never get any richer. I seldom venture to think about our landed wealth, for 'hope deferred maketh the heart sick.'"[59]

As Twain would suggest many years later, in "Old Times on the Mississippi," river piloting forced realism upon him, forced an engagement with "eluding and ungraspable objects" which were defined by something, or someone, other than himself. "It was plain that I had got to learn the shape of the river in all the different ways that could be thought of,—upside down, wrong end first, inside out, fore-and-aft, and 'thort-ships,'—and then know what to do on gray nights when it had n't any shape at all."[60] The keen observational skills and "prodigious memory" required by this craft become the tools of a literary realism that Twain describes as akin to doctoring. He disingenuously laments his loss of the mooning sentimentality of the poet. The precise kinds of movements Twain learned as a river pilot, "trimming" other boats in port and gently "scraping" the river bottom, probably improved his writing, as did the exposure that he claims the steamboats offered to a wide variety of dialects and styles of storytelling. What piloting offered was an integration of skill, and the engagement of the empirical that skill implies, with imagination, the tall talk of fellow travelers as well as the financial adventures which were particularly available to men who worked on the river.

In 1860, Twain, now a well-established pilot, admitted in a letter to Orion that he was "deep in another egg purchase," speculating in the New Orleans poultry and egg market to such a degree that he was having a hard time sending a portion of his wages back to his mother and brother, both of whom required his support.[61] Still, pilots' wages were high and the fluctuations of the New Orleans market posed no great threat to Sam Clemens, who told his brother that he took a "stern joy" in flashing an occasional hundred-dollar bill at members of the Western Boatman's Benevolent Association. In December 1860 Twain became a Mason, an initiated member of the business class. He was a key distributor and beneficiary of the river's market culture; whether egg prices rose or fell, his belief in "energy," which he seems to have understood in a primarily economic context, remained secure. "What is government without energy?" Sam wrote Orion, who was in financial straits and petitioning him for money. "And what is a man without energy? Nothing—nothing at all. What is the grandest thing in Paradise Lost—the Arch-Fiend's terrible energy! What is the greatest feature of Napoleon's character? His unconquerable energy! Sum all the gifts man is endowed with, and we give our greatest share of admiration to his energy. And to-day, if I were a heathen, I would rear a statue to Energy, and fall down and worship it!"[62] Twain's letter concludes, somewhat chidingly, "I want a man to— I want you to—take up a line of action, and follow it out, in spite of the very devil." One year later Twain found himself trailing his brother to Nevada Territory for fear of being forced by the government to pilot a Union gunboat. Perhaps he should have heeded the New Orleans medium, Madame Caprell, who had once warned him that "l'ouvrage de l'anneé est détruit dans un jour,—which means," explained the patronizing Sam to his less worldly brother, "the work of a year is destroyed in a day."[63]

The Civil War destroyed Sam Clemens's faith that the commercial imagination could make a beautiful and benevolent world, but it did not supplant
his faith in "energy" with a belief in the righteousness of the war itself.
The war merely made Twain ironic and bitter about the kind of world he
had loved, and he found much more of that world in the Far West, which
figures in his letters as a carnival mirror of the once booming Mississippi
Valley. It is believed that in May 1861 Sam Clemens left New Orleans on the
Nebraska, which was the last steamboat to be allowed through the Union
blockade at Memphis and into the Upper Mississippi. Clemens then hid
in the Saint Louis home of his sister Pamela Moffett for several weeks. On
18 July 1861 Orion and Sam left the United States for Nevada, which had
only recently and quickly been named federal territory so that its mineral
resources might be used for the Union cause. The Clemens brothers fought
over the design of the territorial seal, which Sam thought should feature a
buzzard, a reference not only to the omnipresence of that bird in the territory but also to the carcass-picking greed Sam saw all around him. The
staid Orion dissented. Sam wrote to his mother that Orion "got one [a seal]
put through the Legislature with star-spangled banners and quartz mills
and things in it. . . . It is all right, perhaps—but I know there are more
buzzards than quartz-mills in Nevada Territory. I understand it though—
he wanted the glory of discovering and inventing and designing the coat-
of-arms of this great Territory—savvy?—with a lot of barbarous latin about
'Volens and Potens'—(able and willing, you know), which would have done
just as well for my buzzard as it does for his quartz-mills." [64] While Orion
literally erected the monument to Energy that Sam had once imagined, Sam
sneered from the sidelines.

Twain's letters from Nevada and California indicate that the Far West for
him was not a solution to the Civil War, but rather a wound that the war
made, a rent in national confidence that proved that money was necessarily
dirty and invention, cruelty. It is in Nevada and California that Twain seems
to discover himself, too, as a charlatan, a discovery which contributed to the
self-deflating humor of his stage performances and autobiographical writings, but which in the letters is poignant. Twain's first letters from Nevada
to his mother and sister attempt to resituate the center of the world in "this
country," the western territory which Twain carefully distinguishes from
"the United States." But the effort at re-centering always reads as ironic and
also as a plea, for interest if not money. To Pamela, Twain writes in 1861
that "Orion and I have confidence enough in this country to think that if

the war will let us alone we can make Mr. Moffett [Pamela's husband] rich without ever costing him a cent of money or a particle of trouble. We shall lay plenty of claims for him, but if they never pay him anything, they will never cost him anything."[65] As Twain's mineral and lumber claims repeatedly fail to pay off, his references to his brother-in-law, "Mr. Moffett," become more insinuating. Yet when Pamela apparently expresses a desire that she and her husband move to the territory, Twain chides: " . . . Just keep your shirt on, Pamela. . . . Don't you know that undemonstrated human calculations won't do to bet on? . . . Don't you know that I have never held in my hands a gold or silver bar that belonged to me?" [66] Twain's letters to Orion include repeated requests for cash, curses at the new country and at the very ground ("it's the d——dest country for disappointments the world ever saw," "our infernal rock"), and the overriding caution: "don't let my opinion of this place get abroad." [67] While the Mississippi River, protean as it was, really could be worked, the desert West gave Twain little to prove himself on, little by which to develop craft. Recognizing that he had, in fact, nothing of his own to sell, Twain fell back upon his "opinion," a style of tall talking that his experience in the Far West had given a bitter edge.

By the time Twain accepted a position as a journalist at Nevada's *Virginia City Territorial Enterprise* in late 1862, he was casually equating his writing with robbery, blackmail, and sadism. "I take an absorbing delight in the stock market," he wrote to his mother and sister in February 1863. "I love to watch the prices go up. My time will come after a while, and then I'll rob somebody. I pick up a foot or two occasionally for lying about somebody's mine. I shall sell out one of these days, when I catch a susceptible emigrant."[68] The hyperbolic irony here suggests Twain's humor in *Roughing It*, where culpability has become irrelevant in a world in which values literally have no ground, and where the ground itself is continually shifting due to the environmental effects of extractive industries like logging and quartz mining. Despite Twain's apparent intention to offer a realistic alternative to dime-novel fantasy, *Roughing It* essentially stages the end of western nature and its replacement by a knowingly anti-referential style of writing about the West. The famous scene in *Roughing It* that recounts how Twain accidentally started a forest fire on his logging claims at Lake Tahoe serves as both western nature's epitaph and an excuse for Twain's virtuosic writing, his crafted description of flames "trailing their crimson spirals away among remote ramparts and ridges and gorges, till as far as the eye could reach the lofty mountain-fronts were webbed as it were with a tangled network of red lava streams."[69]

In later works like "A Double-Barreled Detective Story" (1902), the bulk of which is set in Nevada, Twain dismisses rhapsodic treatments of western nature as con artistry, but that equation is not as self-consciously present in Roughing It as it is in Twain's letters from California and Nevada. "If I don't know how to levy black-mail on the mining companies,—who does, I should like to know?" Twain rants in another letter to his mother, knowing that his dishonesty as a western journalist is already trumped by the functional dishonesty of the companies, which paid off reporters for favorable descriptions of their mines.[70] Twain saw that the value of western mineral deposits, and more broadly the value of western nature, was obscured by multiple representational gestures intended to draw investors and settlers. But in a sense Twain's despised performance as a western journalist served the same function that he had played in his beloved role as a Mississippi river pilot; he was simply making the circulation of economic desire easier. As a western journalist, Twain was a "carrier" again.

Yet without the river, without nature, without craft other than talk, Twain developed a comic imagination that was willfully disruptive and potentially annihilating. His first significant works of fiction are practical jokes, bits of theatrical cruelty that he apparently recognized as a means of enacting reform. The short piece known as "Petrified Man" or "A Washoe Joke," in which Twain falsely reports the discovery of a remarkable stone man by a "Justice Sewell or Sowell of Humboldt County," was intended as retribution for the Nevada Judge G. T. Sewall's failure to honor a business agreement with Orion. "Every day, I send [Sewall] some California paper containing it," Twain wrote to his sister-in-law, Mollie, "moreover, I am getting things so arranged that he will soon begin to receive letters from all parts of the country, purporting to come from scientific men, asking for further information concerning the wonderful stone man. If I had plenty of time, I'd worry the life out of the poor cuss."[71] Twain applied this sort of literary sadism to a more interesting cause in 1864, when he printed an article in the Virginia City Territorial Enterprise alleging that money raised at the "Sanitary Fancy Dress Ball" by the ladies of Carson City for the relief of Union soldiers "had been diverted from its legitimate course, and was to be sent to aid a Miscegenation Society somewhere in the East."[72] The "miscegenation society" hoax, which Twain later claimed he had given to his editor for publication when he was drunk, earned him a challenge to a duel and ultimately drove him from Nevada.

What is interesting about this second hoax is that it very effectively exposed the racism of the ladies of Carson City, who had, in fact, entertained the notion of diverting the funds from the ball away from the Saint Louis Fair because some portion of the proceeds of the Fair were earmarked for the Freedmen's Society. As one of "the ladies' " many defenders charged in the *Territorial Enterprise*: "one thing *was decided* [by the ladies], that [the funds] should go to the aid of the sick and wounded soldiers, who are fighting the battles of our country, and *for no other purpose*." [73] It seems likely that Twain was responding to local women's fear of fiscal contamination by the Freedman's Society when he trumped up the "miscegenation society" hoax. Whether intentionally anti-racist or no, the hoax makes Carson City, Nevada, the first staging ground for Mark Twain's disruption of American racial manners. Twain exposed a racial timocracy in the desert West that suggests the transported southern tidewater culture that he would satirize in his Missouri fictions. Ultimately, his critique of Carson City through the mechanism of journalistic hoax was Tom Sawyerish, in that it was a theatrical and cruel lesson that simultaneously betrayed the ladies' racial phobia and reinstated "miscegenation" as a legitimate object of concern. Tom Sawyer's escapades with Jim at the end of *Adventures of Huckleberry Finn* have a similar double effect, transforming Jim into an abject and romantically maternal "slave" while more critically exposing the Phelpses' dependence upon black property to maintain their skin privilege. Twain's brilliant exposures of the perils and wounds of whiteness rarely image a time or a place where whiteness is not conceived as the center of critical interest and the dominant, appropriative norm. The Far West, at least, was not *that* other country.

Life after Death, or the Real Manifest Destiny

Just one year before his death, Mark Twain published a short story that projected a powerful corrective to frontier ideology and its complementary claims to the cultural and racial centrality of European Americans. Twain's "Extract from Captain Stormfield's Visit to Heaven," which he began in 1868 but did not publish until 1909, offers an ethnography of Heaven by two participant-observers, the blustery Captain Stormfield, a Mississippi steamboat pilot, and Sandy McWilliams, his almost Socratic friend. Both narrators are dead, and the world they inhabit is the realization of Manifest

Destiny or simply "destiny." It is the district of Heaven that represents the geographical proportions and diverse populations of the United States.

Far from being "the land which has no history," as Frederick Jackson Turner once referred to North America, or "the line of most rapid and effective Americanization," as Turner called the frontier, Twain's Heaven is a large empire where the history of empire, as it were, coexists in the same time-space with the imperial claims of the turn-of-the-century United States. Where Roberto Maria Dainotto has complained that regionalism has been a rhetorical form which obscures the erasures performed by Western European and U.S. imperialism, allowing "place" to arise as a sentimental substitute for history, Twain makes the domain of Heaven large enough to contain the multiple histories of colonization and imperial influence that inform modernity. "Extract from Captain Stormfield's Visit to Heaven" has been labeled one of Twain's premier science fiction stories in part because of his assertion that the technological sophistication of Heaven's architects allows for the indefinite physical expansion of North American space. Heaven must necessarily contain multitudes, so its territory is "shaped" like familiar nation-states, yet large enough, again, to hold all time. This paradoxical "infinite space" of the nation figures as a wry literalization of John L. O'Sullivan's assertion, in one of his many arguments for U.S. Manifest Destiny from the 1840s, that "the representative system as practically enjoyed in this country, will admit of an indefinite expansion of territory."[74] Sandy explains Heaven's geography in more commonplace terms: "All [is] the same shape as they are down there, and all graded to the relative size, only each State and realm and island is a good many million times bigger here than it is below."[75] Twain blows up the geography of the United States not simply for fun or bombast, but in order to make sufficient room for the colonized populations who are cursorily excised in the turn-of-the-century imperialist or "frontier" rhetorics that implicitly compete with his "Heaven."

In Mark Twain's Heaven, every national and ethnic category has been broken down into its constituent parts, dominant ideologies lift, and the "country" that results reads to Stormfield, who embodies early twentieth-century U.S. progressivism, as a muddying of racial color and a babble of untranslatable languages. Stormfield complains, "I notice that I hardly ever see a white angel; where I run across one white angel, I strike as many copper-colored ones—people that can't speak English. How is that?"[76] What looks unnatural to Stormfield is actually the demystification of the idea of an American "composite nationality," in Frederick Jackson Turner's phrase. Heaven proves that the future, for every mortal being, bears out neither the assimilative ideology of the melting pot nor the "transnational" cultural pluralism that would be promised by early twentieth-century pragmatists like Randolph Bourne. Twain rewrites Providential destiny as a dystopic multiculturalism portending the "identity politics" that characterized the United States in the 1980s and 1990s and resulted in segregationist backlash, most dramatically in California's anti-immigration legislation, Proposition 187, and Proposition 209, the initiative that sought to end affirmative action policy in California's state agencies. In essence, Mark Twain foresees the future of Manifest Destiny as U.S. post-modernity, a situation on the North American continent in which competing nations and diasporic nationalisms vie for recognition in the wake of the exposure of European American or "white" hegemony.

California, the "Golden State" of the West, is singled out for special attention in the "Extract from Captain Stormfield's Visit to Heaven." Sandy, who has been dead and in Heaven longer than Stormfield, explains to him that of all places in U.S.-Heaven, California is the worst for whites. "You see what the Jersey district of heaven is, for whites; well, the California district is a thousand times worse. It swarms with a mean kind of leather-headed mud-colored angels—and your nearest white neighbors is likely to be a million miles away." [77] Of course the California district of Heaven is predominately non-white because it is populated by waves of prior occupants, including Native Californians and Mexican *Californios*. Turning California-Heaven into a "majority minority" culture, Twain unwittingly predicts the actual demographics of the state in the twenty-first century, and he also returns the right of first occupancy to peoples who were systematically killed, removed, or assimilated throughout the United States' westward advance. Sandy explains, "You see, America was occupied a billion years and more, by Injuns and Aztecs, and that sort of folks, before a white man ever set foot in it. During the first three hundred years after Columbus's discovery, there wasn't ever more than one good lecture audience of white people, all put together, in America—I mean the whole thing, British Possessions and all." [78]

Twain's debunking of the European discovery narrative, which of course obscures the continent's first occupants, is not unique, suggesting a handful of anti-frontierist writings from the era of the last Sioux battles and the legal as well as symbolic end of American Indian sovereignty in the late nineteenth century. But Twain diverges from reformist projects like Helen Hunt Jackson's record of "our nation's . . . cruelties and perjuries" against Native Americans in *A Century of Dishonor* (1880) by exploring instead the psychological effects of white minoritization in an inevitable future state, where the racial tables have turned.[79] Musing about California, Sandy continues, *"What a man mostly misses, in heaven, is company."* [80] Whiteness figures here as "loneliness" and "homelessness," as existential rather than imperative or Providential mobility. "I have shot along, a whole week on a stretch," Sandy admits, "and gone millions and millions of miles, through perfect swarms of angels, without ever seeing a single white one, or hearing a word I could understand."[81] Sandy and Stormfield are quite literally traveling, looking for the "company" and reassurance of whiteness most of the time. Heaven's sophisticated transportation technology, the wishing carpet, allows instantaneous emigration to whatever destination one wishes to visit. But this technology, itself predictive of the instantaneous global public promised by current technologies like the internet, ultimately merely confirms that Heaven is the location of what Freud called the *unheimlich* or unhomelike, the familiar within the strange.

Sandy once wished to be in England, imagining that he could find more "whiteness" there than in the Americas. "But it is not so very much better than this end of the heavenly domain," he reports. "As long as you run across Englishmen born this side of three hundred years ago, you are all right; but the minute you get back to Elizabeth's time the language begins to fog up. . . . Back of those men's [Langland and Chaucer's] time the English are just simply foreigners, nothing more, nothing less; they talk Danish, German, Norman French . . . ; back of them, they talk Latin, and ancient British, Irish, and Gaelic; and then back of these come billions and billions of pure savages. . . ."[82] Not only does Heaven refute European-American claims to continental inheritance and the inevitable absorption of "doomed" First Nations, but it also deconstructs whiteness as a transcendent, "essential" racial category by simply and bluntly historicizing it. In Heaven's England, Sandy lives the past and present of Anglo identity as linguistic dissonance and, again, dystopic multiculturalism. In sum, Twain uses the diachronic dimension of his Heaven to divorce national territories from ideological fictions that posited a monoracial future against multiracial, conflictual pasts. "Extract From Captain Stormfield's Visit to Heaven" offers a prescient alternative to Frederick Jackson Turner's "The Significance of the Frontier in American History" as well as Theodore Roosevelt's more harshly assimilationist prescriptions for twentieth-century "Americanism."

If Heaven is the "other destiny" that advocates of Manifest Destiny could not foresee in the decades prior to the Civil War, and that late-century apologists for manifest destiny refused to see, then it is a destiny that necessarily disrupts Euro-American happiness. Happiness, to a certain extent, depends upon the fulfillment of expectations, and in Heaven white America's expectations are flatly denied. The denial of expectations and reorientation of happiness is concomitant with the de-centering of whiteness in this postmortem and, in a sense, post-human empire. Heaven plays with human expectations of happiness by allowing the dead to try them out, in other words by initially granting any "unharmful" vision of bliss. For Stormfield, heavenly bliss involves becoming an angel, sporting the full "uniform"—wings, palm branch, halo, harp, and a cloud to sit on—and singing with Heaven's multitudes. Heaven grants him that, but the experience disappoints, largely, again, because he must share his particular bliss with people quite different from himself. "I tautened up my harp-strings and struck in. Well, Peters, you can't imagine anything like the row we made. It was grand to listen to, and made a body thrill all over, but there was considerable many tunes going on at once, and that was a drawback in the harmony, you understand; and then there was a lot of Injun tribes, and they kept up such another war-whooping that they kind of took the tuck out of the music."[83] Stormfield finally exits his cloud. The difference present everywhere in Heaven, which is significantly present most prominently as difference in sound or speech, makes settlement in any one place undesirable, at least for discontented cosmopolitans like Stormfield. For Stormfield and Sandy, frequent, searching travel is the dominant lifestyle of the postmortem United States.

Heaven's resiliently international "national" culture fosters a cosmopolitanism that verges on solipsism, insofar as real engagement with people who are "other" in time or place never occurs. This lack of engagement is signified by Stormfield and Sandy's continual complaints that they cannot understand the languages of other peoples in Heaven. With all eternity on their hands and goals easily met by wishing, one wonders why these complainers don't simply become polyglots. It is difficult to discern if Twain intends to criticize his protagonists for their apparent self-segregation. Taken in the context of Twain's earlier western writings, Stormfield and Sandy might be said to choose not segregation but sanity—because the mixing of "foreign" tongues figures in Twain's Roughing It (1872) as descent into anti-referentiality and alienation.

In Roughing It Twain portrays the Far West as a linguistically diverse region, like Heaven, but one in which "all the peoples of the earth" have opened themselves to each other's speech and produced a uniquely hybrid slang. "Slang was the language of Nevada. Such phrases as 'You bet!' 'Oh, no, I reckon not!' 'No Irish need apply,' and a hundred others, became so common as to fall from the lips of a speaker unconsciously—and very often when they did not touch the subject under discussion and consequently failed to mean anything."[84] The lesson here is that the end of referentiality will come when too many vernaculars meet and mingle with each other, "as each adventurer had brought the slang of his nation and his locality with him."[85] The Far West proves to be a place where the superimposition of distinct local or national "slangs" signals the superimposition of distinct local or national places. The loss of linguistic referentiality in Nevada reflects an equally profound loss of the geopolitical coordinates that make a coherent world.

Nevada is, effectively, a "nowhere" place; more literally, it is a world grown too large too quickly. It is not surprising that the apparently absurdist repetitions that define it, like the frequently uttered phrase "No Irish need apply," reflect a desire to hold onto ethnic or class statuses that once, in another country, conferred a sense of social position upon speakers. Ethnic pejoratives like "Micks" and "Greasers" indiscriminately roll off the tongues of Twain's Nevada prospectors, and when "No Irish need apply" begins to circulate so wildly that it even follows the "Amen" at a miner's funeral, Twain comments on how this phrase has acquired a purely phatic value: "it was probably nothing more than a humble tribute to the memory of a friend [the dead man] that was gone; for . . . it was 'his word.' "[86] In the miners' instantly urban culture, "No Irish need apply" functions as a content-free interjection, as much a dead letter as the dead miner who has been identified with it, as "his word."[87] Words may never touch their referents in this polyglot West because the regional lexicon balloons with constant influxes of foreign words and phrases, creating a vocabulary so rich that it defies any individual's capacity for effective use. To avoid the challenges of linguistic hybridization typical of the miners' West, residents of Mark Twain's Heaven attempt to theoretically suburbanize language, allotting distinct languages to geographic neighborhoods that are bordered, if interpenetrating. But again the inclusion of all historical time in any given place in Twain's Heaven destroys any effort to maintain stable "zones" of linguistic and cultural identity.

The virtual mobile home of the mother tongue, which in Heaven has been disconnected from any particular locale, seems to come closest to Captain Stormfield and Sandy's definition of happiness. This unusual image of bliss, as a kind of peripatetic or perhaps diasporic language, wreaks as much havoc on traditional notions of place and property as the trailer parks, truck stops, motels, Indian reservations, riverboat casinos, and environmentalist biospheres of the New American West. A wise old resident of Heaven named Sam Bartlett, "who had been dead a long time," enlightens Stormfield that "happiness" has always been a mobile affect rather than a settled property, suggesting that it cannot be owned in perpetuity but is continually renewed through encounters with stimuli—in this story, often "foreign" languages—that bring displeasure: "happiness ain't a thing in itself—it's only a contrast with something that ain't pleasant."[88] The simple revision of happiness away from the notion of a place that can be occupied and settled disconnects happiness from the Jeffersonian equation of happiness with cultivated and settled land, an idea that, of course, underlines the United States' foundational ideologies. The equation of happiness with property surfaces in the *Declaration of Independence*, where John Locke's "life, liberty, and the pursuit of property" from the *Second Treatise on Government* has been revised to Thomas Jefferson's "life, liberty, and the pursuit of happiness." In the United States, happiness is property, if under erasure; it is assumed that happiness is equivalent to the solid ground beneath your feet, the land you love, the land that can be worked, fenced, and built upon to create a better future. This is the charisma of the North American West, with its fabled "land lotsa land"; this is why the West has been perpetually confused with a generalized national happiness. Both these notions of westernness and national happiness are displaced in Mark Twain's early twentieth-century Heaven, which is supposedly everyone's future. Twain's Heaven is the ultimate de-territorialized space of national imagining and corrective to claims of Manifest Destiny. It is the anti-image of a single, culturally unified, continental nation calling itself simply "America."

EPILOGUE

While Mark Twain envisioned destiny as dystopic multiculturalism, it is significant that he still called this condition of extreme social discomfort "Heaven" and gave it the shape of the United States of America. The "Extract from Captain Stormfield's Visit to Heaven" is not exactly a condemnation of the American experiment, as that experiment had been imagined from the perspective of the United States. There have been far more oppositional and creative revisions of "America" than Twain's, including, to name only a few, the important geopolitical re-centering of *nuestra América* that has been offered by Latino/a intellectuals and activists, the utopian experiments of American Associationists, and the bids for sovereignty or statehood made throughout the nineteenth century by Native Americans, Métis, radical abolitionists, Mormons, and free Blacks. Twain's point about Heaven is not really oppositional, because he allows the emergence of his settler-nation as a continental and world power to be confused with bliss; yet he makes clear that in the United States national happiness is founded upon the deaths of "billions" of non-white "angels," and so national happiness involves a continual, searching process, acute loneliness, and difficult self-reckonings. In short, this American bliss is an uneasy, sometimes unlocatable home—and the places that most resist its realization, or the places that most resist Euro-American homecoming, are western territories like California, where history keeps coming back to the present through non-white resident populations. The North American West has never offered easy solutions, and I hope to have shown that even those writers who used the West as a symbol to give flesh to nationalist ambitions sometimes stumbled upon its unique populations and unique environments, or the unique U.S. imperial mechanisms that were practiced to subdue them— all regional particularities that proved correctives to the will to abstraction which complements a settler-nation's will to power.

In recent years, the West has given us solutions to the effects of U.S. history only in the form of poignant questions, like Rodney King's famous "Can't we all get along?" during the 1992 Los Angeles riots. This book does not intend to posit solutions, nor to make excuses. Yet, like Twain, I am willing to entertain the possibility that the troubled present which has resulted from the violent history of U.S. expansion and settlement might be something other than Hell, if we consider that happiness might be achieved through a difficult reckoning with history. This book does not, itself, perform such a reckoning so much as it looks at nineteenth-century U.S. writers struggling with the national history they were making up, and U.S. writers finding unexpected counter-narratives in the very places they wanted to see as blank templates on which their nation could inscribe its exceptional future. None of the writers considered here, with the somewhat compromised exceptions of John Brown and Martin Delany, came up with radical answers to the inconsistencies, doubts, and cruelties they discovered in the political and rhetorical strategies of national emergence which are now summed up in the phrase "Manifest Destiny." Many of these writers were, in fact, architects of these inconsistencies, doubts, and the cruelties that resulted from images intended to mobilize territorial occupation. But few of them managed to achieve the obliteration of the local, or the collapse of western places into the static time of ideology, that Manifest Destiny has come to stand for. While this may not be cause for celebration, I do think it cause for a modest hope that we will continue to hear the interruptions of material history through the resilient localism that carries it.

Notes

Introduction

1. Thomas Bangs Thorpe, "Remembrances of the Mississippi," *Harper's New Monthly Magazine* 12 (Dec. 1855): 34.

2. Thanks to John Stauffer for the observation that Thorpe may refer to the Mississippi as a corridor for pro-and anti-slavery guerrillas entering "bleeding Kansas."

3. By "republican virtue" I mean essentially Jeffersonian and post-Jeffersonian articulations of European agrarian philosophy which suggested that civic virtue depends upon property ownership and the maintenance of domestic, patriarchal economies. The American yeoman is supposedly the ideal citizen of the republic, most fitted to participate in the franchise, because his independence as owner and cultivator of his own property makes him "disinterested" and thus capable of making decisions on moral grounds. As Jefferson would assert, "The small land holders . . . are the most precious part of the state." Henry Nash Smith quotes Jefferson and elaborates his version of "republican virtue" as "the freehold concept" in *Virgin Land: The American West as Symbol and Myth* (1950; Cambridge and London: Harvard University Press, 1978) 126–128.

4. Smith refers to two conceptions of U.S. empire, the mercantilist/maritime and the agrarian, early in *Virgin Land* (12). Later he will dismiss mercantile and maritime theories of nationalism as "literary" or "half-literary" (178) and "southern" (154).

5. Wai-chee Dimock helpfully elaborates upon the collapse of time into space that enables the ideology of Manifest Destiny: "The familiar strategy for antebellum expansionists was to invoke some version of 'Providence,' whose plans for the future happened to coincide exactly with America's territorial ambitions. American expansion in space and providential design in time turned out to be one in the same. . . . This manifest destiny had no spatial limits, for as another expansionist enthusiastically put it, America was 'bordered on the West by the day of Judgment.' " Wai-chee Dimock, *Empire for Liberty: Melville and the Poetics of Individualism* (Princeton NJ and London: Princeton University Press, 1989) 133. See also Albert Katz Weinberg, *Manifest Destiny: A Study of Nationalist Expansion in American History* (New York: AMS Press, 1979).

6. John L. O'Sullivan, "Annexation," *United States Magazine and Democratic Review* 17 (July 1845): 5.

7. Herman Melville, *Moby-Dick; or, The Whale* (hereafter cited as MD), ed. Harri-

223

son Hayford and Hershel Parker (1851; New York and London: W. W. Norton and Company, 1967) 334.

8. My repeated use of the term "international" is meant to be jarring, in order to emphasize the fact that the North American West was for a long time not the domestic space that advocates of Manifest Destiny projected, but rather a region occupied by various Native American nations as well as European and U.S. colonists.

9. Daniel Drake, *Discourse on the History, Character, and Prospects of the West* (1834; Gainesville FL: Scholars' Facsimiles and Reprints, 1955). As Perry Miller notes in the introduction to this volume, Drake plays an interesting, and typical, double game: he recognizes internal commerce in the West as a social good but fears the corrupting influence of the foreign—even while recognizing that the West's internal commerce necessarily includes an influx of European emigrants and products.

10. I refer to the groundbreaking work in what has come to be known, since the late 1980s, as the "New Western History," by historians Richard White, Patricia Nelson Limerick, Donald Worster, and William Cronon; also the groundbreaking work in the study of cultures of U.S. imperialism associated most immediately with Amy Kaplan, Donald Pease, and John Carlos Rowe.

11. I am thinking here of the relatively recent contributions of Shelley Streeby, James F. Brooks, and Curtis Márez to our understanding of the U.S.-Mexican border. Although Streeby's work shares some of the goals of the Kaplan-Pease "imperial studies" project, it also adds a valuable regional dimension to that work, which tends to elide local sites of contention with a more contemporary understanding of "the international," as Anne Goldman has noted. See Shelley Streeby, *American Sensations: Class, Empire, and the Production of Popular Culture* (Berkeley and London: University of California Press, 2002); James F. Brooks, *Captives and Cousins: Slavery, Kinship, and Community in the Southwestern Borderlands* (Chapel Hill: University of North Carolina Press, 2002); Curtis Márez, "Signifying Spain, Becoming Comanche, Making Mexicans: Indian Captivity and the History of Chicano/a Popular Performance," *American Quarterly* 53 (June 2001): 267–307; and Anne Goldman's New Regionalist critique of Kaplan in *Continental Divides: Revisioning American Literature* (New York: Palgrave, 2000). New Regionalist or New Western Studies that share some of the same assumptions and theoretical interests as Border Studies, including work by Goldman, Krista Comer, and Neil Campbell, have also significantly informed this work.

12. Vizenor productively opposes manifest manners, whose concern is "the

simulations of dominance and absence of the other," to what he conceives as the "trickster hermeneutics" of "postindian survivance." Clearly Vizenor's focus is a contemporary postindian/postwestern United States, but his insights into the "melancholia of dominance" that marks early rhetorics of Manifest Destiny has been quite useful for this study. See Gerald Vizenor, *Manifest Manners: Postindian Warriors of Survivance* (Hanover N H and London: Wesleyan University Press, 1994).

13. Foucault introduces "heterotopia," a concept he ultimately abandoned, twice—in the preface to *The Order of Things: An Archaeology of the Human Sciences* (New York: Vintage Books, 1970) and in the 1967 lecture "Of Other Spaces." I am quoting from a translation of the latter. See Michel Foucault, "Of Other Spaces," trans. Jay Miskowiec, *Diacritics* 16 (Spring 1986): 24. The terms "spatial praxis" or spatial practice can be traced to Henri Lefebvre, who defines spatial practice as essentially the production of hegemony or "the reproduction of social relations" in his classic *The Production of Space*, trans. Donald Nicholson-Smith (1974; Oxford, UK and Cambridge MA: Blackwell, 1995) 33, 50.

14. Richard White, *The Middle Ground: Indians, Empires, and Republics in the Great Lakes Region, 1650–1815* (New York and Cambridge: Cambridge University Press, 1991) x, xi.

15. Patricia Nelson Limerick, *The Legacy of Conquest: The Unbroken Past of the American West* (New York and London: W. W. Norton and Company, 1987) 71.

16. Stegner sets the ground rules for authentic westernness in his classic essay, "History, Myth, and the Western Writer," *The Sound of Mountain Water* (1946; New York: Penguin, 1969) 187. Nathaniel Lewis does a wonderful job of re-imagining the parameters of nineteenth-century western writing in *Unsettling the Literary West: Authenticity and Authorship* (Lincoln and London: University of Nebraska Press, 2003) especially 19–47.

17. I refer to Barthes's well-known assertions that myth "does away with dialectics," generating a world "which is without contradictions because it is without depth, a world wide open and wallowing in the evident" in Roland Barthes, *Mythologies* (1957; London: Paladin, 1973) 143.

18. Comer writes of the role that landscape has played in western literatures: "Landscape is not only one of the most telling features of western regionalism, it is also the most analytically slippery—what I call the 'wild card' of western discourse. Herein is landscape's usefulness to cultural critics: it is one of the most defended, but also the most vulnerable and revealing, signs in western studies. Though landscape would appear to be a stable entity or category, tied to something 'really there' like earthly topography, it

is deployed all the time, in many different political guises, to make all kinds of extratopographic meanings." Krista Comer, *Landscapes of the New West: Gender and Geography in Contemporary Women's Writing* (Chapel Hill: University of North Carolina Press, 1999) 11, 15.

19. I am thinking here not so much of the classic *Lay of the Land* as of its sequel, which extensively treats the writings of women pioneers. See Annette Kolodny, *The Land Before Her: Fantasy and Experience of the American Frontiers, 1630–1860* (Chapel Hill: University of North Carolina Press, 1984).

20. Virginia Scharff's recent study of how women's mobility defined the North American West from the early nineteenth century and into the twentieth suggests that there is an important unpublished history of mobile and commercially-oriented western women. As Scharff aptly remarks, "we have to take seriously people we too often dismiss as 'draftees in the male enterprise' of nation-building, to see the ways in which the West, as a distinctive place and political process, has waxed and waned and survived as a force in history." Virginia Scharff, *Twenty Thousand Roads: Women, Movement, and Time* (Berkeley: University of California Press, 2003) 4.

21. Raymond Williams, *Marxism and Literature* (Oxford and New York: New York University Press, 1977) 112.

22. Immanuel Wallerstein, "The Rise and Future Demise of the World Capitalist System: Concepts for Comparative Analysis," *The Essential Wallerstein* (New York: The New Press, 2000) 71–106.

23. Twain, qtd. in Philip S. Foner, *Mark Twain Social Critic* (New York: International Publishers, 1958) 284.

24. John L. O'Sullivan, "Territorial Aggrandizement," *United States Magazine and Democratic Review* 17 (Oct. 1845): 244, 246.

25. O'Sullivan, "Annexation" 9.

26. Edward L. Widmer helpfully traces the vicissitudes of O'Sullivan's thought in *Young America: The Flowering of Democracy in New York City* (Oxford: Oxford University Press, 1999).

27. Michael Hardt and Antonio Negri, preface, *Empire* (Cambridge MA and London: Harvard University Press, 2000) xii.

28. Kaplan writes: "[Hardt and Negri] regard Theodore Roosevelt as pursuing an old-style European imperialism, and Woodrow Wilson with his League of Nations as foreshadowing the emergence of today's postmodern regime, in which the sovereignty of the nation dissolves in the borderless world of Empire. I would argue that these two tendencies are not as distinct as Hardt and Negri contend, but that both are at work in varied configurations throughout the history of U.S. imperialism. The American Empire has long

followed a double impetus to construct boundaries and to break down those borders through the desire for unfettered expansion." See Amy Kaplan, introduction, *The Anarchy of Empire in the Making of U.S. Culture* (Cambridge MA and London: Harvard University Press, 2002) 1–22.

29. Although I detect a stronger sense of "the locale" than Anne Goldman finds in much of the work that has been done on the United States as an imperial nation, I respect Goldman's project "to readmit [the locale] to history, to insist that it assume a particular face, in order to correct American Studies' diffuse, too expansive focus on the intersections of 'nation' and 'empire.'" (*Continental Divides* 11). Goldman's *Continental Divides* is one of the very few works in the New Regionalism or New Western Studies that focuses on nineteenth-century literature and political discourse, and so her book offers interesting insights into how the postmodern theories that tend to inform the New Regionalists do or do not apply to earlier cultural formations.

30. Doreen Massey and Pat Jess, eds., *A Place in the World? Places, Cultures, and Globalization* (New York and Oxford: Oxford University Press, 1995) 58–59.

31. For Twain's own account of his projected South American adventure, see Mark Twain, *Mark Twain's Letters* (hereafter cited as MTL), Vol. 1: 1853–1866, ed. Edgar Marquess Branch, Michael B. Frank, and Kenneth M. Sanderson (Berkeley: University of California Press, 1988) 68.

32. Forrest G. Robinson's classic reading of Twain's river novels is particularly germane to this work. See Forrest G. Robinson, *In Bad Faith: The Dynamics of Deception in Mark Twain's America* (Cambridge MA: Harvard University Press, 1986).

33. Calhoun's assertion appears in Henry Nash Smith, *Virgin Land* 148.

34. Michael Kiskis has suggested that Twain came back to the oral performances and cultures of his youth in his later, autobiographical writings. See Michael J. Kiskis, "Coming Back to Humor: The Comic Voice in Mark Twain's Autobiography," *Mark Twain's Humor: Critical Essays*, ed. David E. E. Sloane (New York: Garland, 1993) 545.

35. See J. G. A. Pocock, *Virtue, Commerce, and Society* (Cambridge: Cambridge University Press, 1985).

36. James T. Fields, "Mercantile Literature," *Hunt's Merchants' Magazine* 1 (Dec. 1839): 538.

37. I use the phrase "invisible goods" here in part as a play on the idea of the natural distributive justice attributed to the market mechanism by its popularizers in the early modern era. I also use the phrase to refer to beliefs that commerce promoted "manners," and "civility," evident in the writings of Montesquieu, Hume, and others. Albert O. Hirschman has written

perhaps the most compelling monograph on the rhetoric of early modern capitalism, *The Passions and the Interests: Political Arguments for Capitalism before Its Triumph* (Princeton NJ: Princeton University Press, 1977). A more recent elaboration of commercial rhetoric and its relation to emergent theories of race appears in Roxann Wheeler, *The Complexion of Race: Categories of Difference in Eighteenth-Century British Culture* (Philadelphia: University of Pennsylvania Press, 2000).

38. Hundley's peculiar, accusatory and celebratory account of "Southern-Yankees," a class including merchants and slave traders, appears in David Hundley, *Social Relations in Our Southern States* (New York: Henry B. Price, 1860).

39. One of the best readings of the Whig influence in southwestern humor through Twain remains Kenneth S. Lynn, *Mark Twain and Southwestern Humor* (Boston: Little, Brown, and Company, 1959).

40. This literature will be reviewed in depth in chapter 3.

41. Stephen Greenblatt, *Marvelous Possessions: The Wonder of the New World* (Chicago: University of Chicago Press, 1991) 17–22.

42. Writing specifically of the work of Emerson in the symbolic formation of U.S. nationalism, Bercovitch contends that "far from pressing the conflict between individual and society, Emerson obviated all conflict by defining inward revolt and social revolution in identical terms, through the bipolar unities of the symbol of America." See Sacvan Bercovitch, *The American Jeremiad* (Madison: University of Wisconsin Press, 1978) 184.

Inventing the American Desert

1. John Wesley Powell, *Report on the Lands of the Arid Region of the United States*, ed. Wallace Stegner (1878; Cambridge: The Belknap Press of Harvard University Press, 1962).

2. Stegner's association of arid western landscapes with the "fragility of goodness," in cultural geographer Yi-Fu Tuan's phrase, runs throughout his work, from the essay "History, Myth, and the Western Writer," through his brilliant history of John Wesley Powell and his late-life essays. See particularly Wallace Stegner, *Beyond the Hundredth Meridian: John Wesley Powell and the Second Opening of the American West* (Boston: Houghton Mifflin, 1954). Krista Comer offers an excellent analysis of Stegner's self-positioning as a regional intellectual in *Landscapes of the New West* 38–49.

3. Henry Nash Smith identifies prophecies of a perpetual "desert" in the midcontinent up through the 1850s, notably in commercial and southern journals such as *Hunt's*, *DeBow's*, and the *Southern Quarterly Review*.

4. Josiah Gregg, *The Commerce of the Prairies*, ed. Milo Milton Quaife (1844; Lincoln: University of Nebraska Press) 325.

5. Washington Irving, *Astoria*, ed. Richard Dilworth Rust (1836; Boston: Twayne Publishers, 1976) 152. Subsequent citations of *Astoria* refer to this edition, unless otherwise noted.

6. Washington Irving, *The Adventures of Captain Bonneville* (hereafter cited as *Bonneville*), ed. Robert A. Rees and Alan Sandy (1837; Boston: Twayne Publishers, 1977) 269.

7. For more details on the Narcissa Whitman story, see Narcissa Whitman, *The Coming of the White Women, 1836*, as told in the journal of Narcissa Prentiss Whitman, comp. T. C. Elliot (Portland OR: Oregon Historical Society, 1937).

8. Antelyes notes the correspondence of this slogan ("54° 40′or fight") with the 1836 publication of *Astoria* in *Tales of Adventurous Enterprise* (New York: Columbia University Press, 1990) 159.

9. John L. Allen, "The Garden-Desert Continuum: Competing Views of the Great Plains in the Nineteenth-Century," *Great Plains Quarterly* 5 (Fall 1985): 207–20. Allen remarks that the Plains had been promoted as a potentially rich agricultural region by some boosters even since the era of the Louisiana Purchase. However, they were always conceived of as less potentially productive than the valleys of the Northwest, and official geographies, typically printed in the Northeast, labeled them as a "desert" region through the most intense period of Western emigration in the 1840s.

10. John Widtsoe, who served on the Special Advisors Committee for the Bureau of Reclamation in the mid-to-late 1920s, qtd. in Donald Worster, *Rivers of Empire: Water, Aridity, and the growth of the American West* (New York and Oxford: Oxford University Press, 1985) 188.

11. John Brown's interest in making Kansas the terminus of a radical abolitionist state is discussed in chapter four. The Black freedmen's dream of a "Kansas Exodus" at the height of Reconstruction-era violence in the South is discussed in Robert G. Athearn, *In Search of Canaan: Black Migration to Kansas, 1879–1880* (Lawrence: University of Kansas Press, 1978). Among treatments of the Mormon West, I have found the works of Wallace Stegner and Terry Tempest Williams particularly evocative.

12. For example, Timothy Egan, "Pastoral Poverty; The Seeds of Decline," *The New York Times* 8 Dec. 2002, late ed.: sec.4: 1+; "Dry High Plains are Blowing Away Again," *The New York Times* 3 May 2002, late ed.: A1+; and "As Others Abandon the Plains, Indians and Bison Come Back," *The New York Times* 27 May 2001, late ed.: sec.1: 1+.

1. American Desert, Empire Anxiety, Historical Romance

1. Nathaniel Hawthorne, preface, *The House of the Seven Gables*, ed. Seymour L. Gross (New York and London: W. W. Norton, 1967) 3.

2. Hawthorne, *House of the Seven Gables* 2.

3. I'm borrowing heavily from the language used by Brook Thomas and by Walter Benn Michaels in their discussions of American historical romance and, in particular, the "theories" of this genre present in Hawthorne's various prefaces. Thomas has written of the Romance, as Hawthorne defines it, as an essentially subversive genre as opposed to the realist novel: "[In the United States] the middle-class has convinced itself that its world and its beliefs are the products of nature, not history, and has given this particular ideology universality. If, as Hawthorne claims, the novel presents the probable at the expense of the possible, a middle-class audience might easily mistake the probable as the only possible. This reification of the probable would rob art of one of its most vital functions: to offer alternative visions of the world we live in." Brook Thomas, *"The House of the Seven Gables: Reading the Romance of America,"* PMLA 97 (Mar. 1982): 195–211. In contrast, Michaels recognizes Hawthorne's preference for the romance as anxiety about "the violently revolutionary power of mimesis, the representing form of a market society inimical to the social stability, the individualism, and the rights of property that Hawthorne meant the romance to defend." Michaels quips that the American Romance is "the text of clear and unobstructed title," asserting an unassailable property right in its subjects and claims. Walter Benn Michaels, *The Gold Standard and the Logic of Naturalism* (Berkeley: University of California, 1989) 88, 89.

4. Terence Martin, "The Romance," *The Columbia History of the American Novel,* ed. Emory Elliott (New York: Columbia University Press, 1991) 73.

5. Richard Slotkin uses the apt term "fake-lore" to describe Irving's legendary histories. Slotkin's discussion of what he calls the "backwash of a closing frontier"—the anxious narratives of national degeneration that came about in the wake of the popularization of the Great American Desert myth—is relevant to this analysis and essentially begins in the same place, although Slotkin sees the Great American Desert as a blip in the representational history of the West and I see it as indicative of a larger trend of transnational, commercial theories of nation-building opposed to Manifest Destiny. See Richard Slotkin, *The Fatal Environment: The Myth of the Frontier in the Age of Industrialization, 1800–1890* (New York: Atheneum, 1985).

6. In "Literature of Exploration and Empire," Eric Sundquist offers the most complete and admirable treatment of early western exploration literature by U.S. writers to date. Moreover, his treatment of diverse early western narrative genres in terms of their coincidence with U.S./American eschatological idealism is elegant and understandable—given historical outcomes. But I

think Sundquist's rather eager return to idealism obscures the multiplicity of antebellum U.S./western rhetorics. See Eric J. Sundquist, "The Literature of Expansion and Race," *The Cambridge History of American Literature*, vol. 2, Sacvan Bercovitch, gen. ed. (Cambridge: Cambridge University Press, 1995) 129.

7. Gregg, *Commerce of the Prairies* 326.

8. James Fenimore Cooper, *The Prairie, A Tale* (1827; New York: The New American Library, 1964) 22.

9. In *The Fatal Environment*, Slotkin suggests that in the United States "the hunter myth speaks to the love-hate response of Americans to the processes of social and economic development. . . . The hunter speaks for the values of a 'natural' and 'unfettered' pre-capitalist Eden. Yet he facilitates the spread of progress and civilization, and himself embodies the go-getter values, the willful and dominant temperament, the pragmatic turn of mind, and the belief in racial superiority that characterized nineteenth-century bourgeois culture" (65).

10. Cooper, *Prairie* 33.

11. James P. Ronda discusses Jefferson's "attachment to the fertile lands beyond the Missouri" in *Revealing America: Image and Imagination in the Exploration of North America* (Lexington MA: D. C. Heath and Company, 1996) 210.

12. James Fenimore Cooper, preface, *The Oak Openings; or, The Bee-Hunter* (1848; New York: W. A. Townsend and Company, 1860) viii.

13. Annie Heloise Abel, *The History of Events Resulting in Indian Consolidation West of the Mississippi: From the Annual Report of the American Historical Association of the Year 1906* (Washington DC: n.p., 1908) 242–244.

14. Bernard DeVoto, *The Course of Empire* (Boston: Houghton Mifflin Company, 1952) 402–03. DeVoto quotes Jefferson: "Whether we remain in one confederacy or form into Atlantic and Mississippi confederacies, I believe not very important to the happiness of either part . . . and did I now foresee a separation at some future day, yet I should feel the duty and the desire to promote the western interests as zealously as the eastern."

15. Jefferson, qtd. in Irving, *Astoria* 23.

16. Thomas Hart Benton, *Selections of editorial articles from the St. Louis Enquirer* (1844; New Haven: Research Publications, Inc., 1975), microfilm, 43–44.

17. Cooper, *Prairie* 9.

18. From James Franklin Beard, introduction, James Fenimore Cooper, *Letters and Journals*, ed. James Franklin Beard, 6 vols. (Cambridge: The Belknap Press of Harvard University Press, 1960–68) xxviii. *The American Democrat* and Tocqueville's book were only hypothetical rivals in the sense that Cooper

apparently abandoned the hope of making *The American Democrat* a public school text before finishing it. Henry Reeve's translation of *De la Démocratie en Amerique*, with an introduction by John C. Spencer, was adopted and used for many years in the New York system.

19. Cooper to Samuel F. B. Morse, Belgium, 31 July 1832, in Beard, *Letters and Journals* 2:290.

20. William Cullen Bryant, review of *The Prairie*, *The United States Review and Literary Gazette* 1–2 (July 1827): 306.

21. William Cullen Bryant, "The Prairies," in *The Poetical Works of William Cullen Bryant*, ed. Parke Godwin, 2 vols. (1883; New York: Russell and Russell, 1967) 1:228–232.

22. Bryant, review of *The Prairie* 307.

23. Daniel Drake, *Discourse* 55.

24. Robert Baird, *View of the Valley of the Mississippi, or the Emigrant's and Traveller's Guide to the West* (Philadelphia: H. S. Tanner, 1834) 260.

25. Bryant, review of *The Prairie* 307.

26. James Fenimore Cooper, *The Pioneers* (1823; New York: Penguin Books, 1988) 4.

27. Cooper, qtd. in Orm Overland, *The Making and Meaning of an American Classic: James Fenimore Cooper's The Prairie* (New York: Humanities Press, 1973) 137. Overland's exhaustive reading includes a thoughtful discussion of the (generally poor) critical reception of *The Prairie*.

28. Cooper actually pushes the date of Boone's settlement of the upper Missouri up to 1804 to bring it closer to the time of his setting.

29. Sundquist, "Literature of Expansion and Race" 145.

30. Meriwether Lewis, qtd. in Ronda, *Revealing America* 214.

31. See Bernard DeVoto's discussion of the expedition's relevance to the continuing search for a Northwest Passage, via the continent's river systems, to the Pacific in his introduction to *The Journals of Lewis and Clark*, ed. Bernard DeVoto (Boston: Houghton Mifflin, 1997) xxv–xxvi.

32. Ray Allen Billington notes that the most important party of trappers to follow in the wake of Lewis and Clark was that of Manuel Lisa, who took forty-two trappers to the mouth of the Big Horn River to establish Fort Manuel. Lisa returned to St. Louis in the summer of 1808 with the knowledge that only large companies could trade successfully in the Northern Rockies—due to the hostility of Indians to small groups and the time-consuming nature of the journey into the heart of the fur country. Under Lisa's guidance the Missouri Fur Company, including Lisa, William Clark, Auguste and Pierre Chouteau, Major Andrew Henry, and Pierre Menard, was formed

in 1809—this was the company that dominated the trade in the Northern Rockies for the next half-dozen years. See Ray Allen Billington, *Westward Expansion: A History of the American Frontier* (New York: MacMillan, 1974) 379.

33. James T. Hall, "Letters from the West. No. XIV," *The Port Folio* 20 (Mar. 1825): 215.

34. Cooper, *Prairie* 63.

35. Timothy Flint, *Biographical Memoir of Daniel Boone*, ed. James K. Folsom (1833; New Haven: College and University Publishers, 1967) 52.

36. Overland, *Making and Meaning of an American Classic* 67. Both Overland and E. Soteris Muszynska-Wallace name the Long chronicle and the journals of Lewis and Clark as Cooper's most important sources on the regions beyond the Missouri River. See E. Soteris Muszynska-Wallace, "The Sources of *The Prairie*," *American Literature* 21 (May 1949): 191–200.

37. Edwin James, comp., *Account of an Expedition from Pittsburgh to the Rocky Mountains. Performed in the Years 1819, 1820. By order of Hon. J.C. Calhoun, Secretary of War, under the command of Maj. S. H. Long, of the U.S. Top Engineers. Compiled from the notes of Major Long, Mr. T. Say, and other gentlemen of the Party.* Reprinted as volumes 14, 15, 16, and 17 of *Early Western Travels: 1748–1846*, ed. Reuben Gold Thwaites (Cleveland: The Arthur H. Clark Company, 1905) 31, 91–92. Citations hereafter refer to this edition. The original edition of the *Account* was published by Carey and Lea in Philadelphia in 1823; the Thwaites edition is drawn largely from a second edition of the manuscripts published, also in 1823, by Long, Hurst, Rees, Orme, and Brown of London. Thwaites notes that Edwin James's *Account* is the only narrative of the Long Expedition, but that James not only had access to the notes of his associates while compiling the text but also personal assistance from Long and Dr. Thomas Say, the expedition's ethnologist.

38. Calhoun, qtd. in James, *Account* 14:38.

39. For more on the Transcontinental (Adams-Onís) Treaty, see David J. Weber, *The Mexican Frontier 1821–1846* (Albuquerque: University of New Mexico Press, 1982) 12.

40. James F. Brooks discusses the Pawnee tribes' ultimate centrality "in the great captive exchange complex that operated throughout the continent, stretching from the Southwest Borderlands northward to the Great Lakes and beyond" (*Captives and Cousins* 14).

41. Edward Everett, "Long's Expedition," *North American Review* 16 (April 1823): 269.

42. Thwaites's evaluation of the expedition's performance appears in his preface to his edition of *Account* (14:21–24).

43. Everett, "Long's Expedition" 268.
44. The art historian Kenneth Haltman has found that the field sketches from the Long expedition by Titian Ramsay Peale, II, one of the expedition's artists and one of Charles Wilson Peale's many sons, are filled with visual images that similarly express the Long party's dismay. Apparently Peale's private images reveal the "patently little power in the landscape" enjoyed by the scientist-explorers, while his finished sketches were altered to assert "quiet statements of accessibility"—as in the accessibility of the forbidding "desert" West. See Kenneth Haltman, "Private Impressions and Public Views: Titian Ramsay Peale's Sketchbooks from the Long Expedition, 1819–1820," *Yale University Art Gallery Bulletin* (Spring 1989): 38–53. Thanks to Alex Nemerov for this reference.
45. James, *Account* 16:136.
46. Gregg, *Commerce of the Prairies* 88, 50, 48.
47. Stephen H. Long, "A General Description of the Country Traversed by the Exploring Expedition. Being the copy of a report of Major Long to the Hon. J.C. Calhoun, Secretary of War. Dated Philadelphia, Jan. 20. 1821," in James, *Account* 17:148.
48. Abel, *History of Events Resulting in Indian Consolidation* 245–46.
49. Paxson discusses the proposed national road and the implications of the Santa Fe Trail for the Indian policy of the Monroe presidency in Frederic L. Paxson, *History of the American Frontier 1763–1893* (Boston and New York: Houghton Mifflin, 1924) 327.
50. Reginald Horsman, *Race and Manifest Destiny: The Origins of American Racial Anglo-Saxonism* (Cambridge: Harvard University Press, 1981) 204.
51. Vine Deloria, Jr., has offered one of the most complete treatments of the manner in which American Indians figure in the U.S. Constitution. Of the ways in which the constitutional liminality of Native peoples served U.S. interests, Deloria writes, "It could not be argued with any degree of credibility that Indian lands and tribes remained 'foreign,' because their geographical location was obviously within the boundaries of the country. Because of their location, then, and solely because of this geographical dimension,— even though politically and legally tribal nations remained foreign to the United States—Indians became, in the eyes of many people, a domestic concern. Consequently, in 1871 Congress prohibited the future recognition of any Indian tribe as a political entity with which the United States could make treaties." Vine Deloria, Jr., and David E. Wilkins, *Tribes, Treaties, and Constitutional Tribulations* (Austin: University of Texas Press, 1999) 28.
52. Garrick Bailey and Roberta Glenn Bailey, "Indian Territory," in Frederick E.

Hoxie, ed., *Encyclopedia of North American Indians* (Boston: Houghton Mifflin, 1996).

53. *Annals of Congress*, 18th Cong., 2nd sess., 641.

54. *Annals of Congress*, 18th Cong., 2nd sess., 642.

55. William Cooper, *A Guide in the Wilderness; or, The history of the first settlement in the western counties of New York, with useful instructions to future settlers, in a series of letters addressed by Judge Cooper, of Cooperstown, to William Sampson, barrister, of New York* (1808; Dublin: Gilbert & Hodges, 1810) 19.

56. *Annals of Congress*, 18th Cong., 2nd sess., 643.

57. Elias Boudinot, *Cherokee Editor: The Writings of Elias Boudinot*, ed. Theda Perdue (Knoxville: University of Tennessee Press, 1983) 142.

58. *Annals of Congress*, 18th Cong., 2nd sess., 640.

59. *Annals of Congress*, 18th Cong., 2nd sess., 640.

60. Lewis Cass, "Removal of the Indians," *North American Review* 30 (Jan. 1830): 109.

61. Andrew Jackson, Second Annual Message, 6 Dec. 1830, *The State of the Union Messages of the Presidents, 1790–1966*, 3 vols. (New York: Chelsea House, 1967) 1:334.

62. James Fenimore Cooper, *Notions of the Americans* (hereafter cited as *Notions*), vol. 2 (1828; New York: Frederick Ungar Publishing Company, 1963) 286.

63. Colin G. Calloway, *Our Hearts Fell to the Ground: Plains Indian Views of How the West Was Lost* (Boston: Bedford Books, 1996) 31–36.

64. "I Breathe Death," Kiowa legend in Calloway, *Our Hearts Fell to the Ground* 51–55.

65. Cooper, *Notions* 2:287.

66. James Barbour, "Bill for the Preservation and Civilization of the Indian Tribes," *American State Papers, Indian Affairs* (Washington DC: Gales and Seaton, 1832–) 2:646–649.

67. Cass, "Removal of the Indians" 70.

68. Cass, "Removal of the Indians" 77.

69. Zebulon Pike, *The Expeditions of Zebulon Montgomery Pike*, ed. Elliott Coues, vol. 2 (Minneapolis MN: Ross & Haines, 1965).

70. *Annals of Congress*, 18th Cong., 2nd sess., 642.

71. This context is offered by Theda Perdue in her preface to Boudinot, *Cherokee Editor*.

72. William Christie Macleod, *The American Indian Frontier* (New York: Alfred A. Knopf, 1928) 464. Macleod attributes this phase of "the Georgia crisis" to the state of Georgia's argument with the federal government over whether or not the state legislature should recognize the Cherokee nation's newly

remodeled government, which had a constitution and three branches like that of the United States. When Georgia refused to recognize the Cherokee government and declared Cherokee lands to be the public domain of the state, the state was prepared to use military force (in spite of or against the federal government) to make the Cherokee comply.

73. Annie Abel remarks that some historians have viewed Calhoun's support of the Indian Territory idea (he marked territories west of the state of Missouri and, to the north, west of Lake Michigan as potential Indian lands) as a strategy for preventing more free states from developing in the new West (*History of Events Resulting in Indian Consolidation* 343).

74. Cooper, *Notions* 2:342–43.

75. Cooper, qtd. in Overland, *Making and Meaning of an American Classic* 52. Overland comments upon how *The Prairie* enacts the return of wayward settlers from the Far West to the more developed borderlands at the edges of the Mississippi.

76. Slotkin writes: "Cooper always treats the Frontier as belonging to a time and condition of life that have passed or are passing away. . . . The reason for this belief appears clearly in *The Prairie*, which represents the Great Plains region as a vast and intractable desert, in which even so hard a lot as the Bush clan will be unable to make a settlement. This view was held not only be Easterners like Cooper, but by Westerners committed to a general policy of expansion into new territories" (*Fatal Environment* 106).

77. Cooper, *Prairie* 9.

78. Cooper, *Prairie* 196.

79. Cooper, *Prairie* 78.

80. Shepard Krech, *The Ecological Indian: Myth and History* (New York: W. W. Norton and Company, 1999). Krech usefully demystifies romantic associations of Native Americans with a pristine nature, but a more nuanced discussion of the clash of Native American and British-European concepts of property can be found in William Cronon, *Changes in the Land*.

81. *Black Hawk's Autobiography*, ed. J. B. Patterson (1834; reprint, Roger L. Nichols, ed., Ames: Iowa State University Press, 1999). Black Hawk comments upon ownership on p. 51 of this edition: "My reason teaches me that land cannot be sold. The Great Spirit gave it to his children to live upon, and cultivate as far as is necessary for their subsistence; and so long as they occupy and cultivate it, they have the right to the soil—but if they voluntarily leave it, then any other people have a right to settle upon it. Nothing can be sold but such things as can be carried away."

82. Cooper, *Prairie* 11.

83. Limerick, *Legacy* 71.

84. Cooper, *Prairie* 130.

85. Cooper, *Prairie* 31.

86. Cooper, *Prairie* 33.

87. This brief discussion of horse trading and raiding is drawn from Patricia Albers, "Symbiosis, Merger, and War: Contrasting Forms of Intertribal Relationship among Historic Plains Indians," *The Political Economy of North American Indians*, ed. John H. Moore (Norman: University of Oklahoma Press, 1993) 94–132, Anthony McGinnis, *Counting Coup and Cutting Horses: Intertribal Warfare on the Northern Plains: 1738–1889* (Evergreen CO: Cordillera Press, 1990), and Andrew C. Isenberg, *The Destruction of the Bison* (Cambridge: Cambridge University Press, 2000).

88. See Roy Harvey Pearce, "The Significances of the Captivity Narrative," *American Literature* 19 (1947): 1–20.

89. Christopher Castiglia, *Bound and Determined: Captivity, Culture-Crossing, and White Womanhood from Mary Rowlandson to Patty Hearst* (Chicago: University of Chicago Press, 1996) 7. James F. Brooks offers the most comprehensive and analytically nuanced cultural history of Native American–Euro-American–Mexican captive networks on the southwestern plains in *Captives and Cousins*.

90. Cooper, *Prairie* 95.

91. Here I recall Mark Twain's famous satirical notation of Cooper's insistence on referring to his women characters by the sterile "females" in Mark Twain, "Fenimore Cooper's Literary Offenses," *Selected Shorter Writings of Mark Twain*, ed. Walter Blair (Boston: Houghton Mifflin, 1962) 230.

92. Cooper, *Prairie* 99.

93. Gregg, *Commerce of the Prairies* 36–37.

94. Susan Shelby Magoffin, *Down the Santa Fe Trail and into Mexico: The Diary of Susan Shelby Magoffin, 1846–1847*, ed. Stella M. Drumm (1926; New Haven CT: Yale University Press, 1962) 72.

95. Castiglia, *Bound and Determined* 8, 38.

96. Nuanced discussions of inter-ethnic and international trading in captive women can be found in Curtis Márez, "Signifying Spain," and James F. Brooks, *Captives and Cousins*.

97. Sarah Ann Horn, *A Narrative of the Captivity of Mrs. Horn, and Her Two Children, with Mrs. Harris, by the Camanche [sic] Indians*, included in Carl Coke Rister, ed., *Comanche Bondage: Beale's Settlement and Sarah Ann Horn's Narrative* (Glendale, California: The Arthur H. Clark Company, 1955) 184.

98. Horn, *Narrative of the Captivity of Mrs. Horn* 178.

99. Roberto Fernández Retamar, "Against the Black Legend," *Caliban and Other*

Essays, trans. Edward Baker (Minneapolis: University of Minnesota Press, 1989) 60.

100. Cooper, *Prairie* 163.

101. Cooper, *Prairie* 390.

102. James Ohio Pattie, *The Personal Narrative of James O. Pattie*, ed. Timothy Flint (1833; Ann Arbor: University Microfilms, Inc., 1966) 47.

103. Pattie, *Personal Narrative* 38, 88.

104. Streeby writes that "because these romances focus on empire-building and international warfare rather than intranational consolidation, and because the possibility of incorporating Mexico through annexation raises fears of race mixing, the conclusions of these novels project a variety of possible outcomes" (*American Sensations* 99–100).

105. Pattie, *Personal Narrative* 102, 123.

106. Pattie, *Personal Narrative* 157. Richard Batman's commentary on this scene appears in Batman, *American Ecclesiastes: The Stories of James Pattie* (New York: Harcourt Brace Jovanovich, 1984) 19.

107. Pattie, *Personal Narrative* 138.

108. Limerick, *Legacy* 230.

109. Pike, *Expeditions* 2:415.

110. Pike, *Expeditions* 2:419.

111. Pattie, *Personal Narrative* 253.

112. The Pattie narrative receives this praise in Constantine Rafinesque, "Abrégé des Voyages de Pattie, Willard, et Wyeth," *Bulletin de la Societé de Géographie* 3 (Mar. 1835): 181–201.

2. Desert and World

1. Rafinesque, "Abrégé des Voyages" 181–82.

2. *U.S. Statutes at Large* 4 (1834): 729.

3. My reading of a range of U.S. trading narratives as presciently post-national is informed, in part, by several recent cultural histories of the southwestern "borderlands." Both James F. Brooks and Curtis Márez have recognized legal and extralegal commerce among American Indians, Mexicans, and U.S. citizens as constitutive of cultural performances that do not match modern national or minoritized "ethnic" identities, even though the historical exchanges Brooks and Márez analyze do seem to generate post-modern theories—and experiences—of nationality and/or ethnicity as hybridity or hinge. See James F. Brooks, "Served Well by Plunder: La Gran Ladronería and Producers of History Astride the Río Grande," *American Quarterly* 52 (Mar. 2000): 23–57; and Curtis Márez, "Signifying Spain." I am grateful for each scholar's insights into the imaginatively, narratively gener-

ative *and* traumatic conflict between state-sponsored capitalist development and subversive local economies in the U.S. borderlands.

This work is also indebted to world systems theory and to those New Western Historians whose work has taken a "global turn," particularly Richard White, beginning with the groundbreaking *Roots of Dependency: Subsistence, Environment, and Social Change Among the Choctaw, Pawnees, and Navajos* (Lincoln: University of Nebraska Press, 1983); also White, *The Middle Ground*.

4. Michel de Certeau, *The Practice of Everyday Life*, trans. Steven Rendall (Berkeley: University of California Press), especially "Part III: Spatial Practices."

5. Zenas Leonard, *Narrative of the Adventures of Zenas Leonard* (1839; Ann Arbor: University Microfilms, 1966) 11.

6. Leonard, *Narrative* 50.

7. Irving to Pierre M. Irving, New York, Sept. 1834, *Letters*, vol. 2, ed. Ralph M. Aderman, Herbert Kleinfield, and Jenifer S. Banks (Boston: Twayne, 1979) 798–99.

8. Antelyes notes the correspondence of this slogan "54°40'or fight" with the 1836 publication of *Astoria* (*Tales of Adventurous Enterprise* 159).

9. Jeffrey Rubin-Dorsky and Adam Sweeting both present rich portraits of Irving as a man of his time, emblematic of the anxieties and concerns of the decades following the War of 1812. Rubin-Dorsky in particular treats Irving's relation to place—his atypical (for a U.S. writer) disinterest in American space, his anticipatory rhetorical production of the sense of homelessness and boundlessness experienced by his audience, the post-heroic generation, whose anxieties about the loss of the nation as home stemmed from feelings of inadequacy vis-à-vis the previous generation, the Founding Fathers. See Rubin-Dorsky, *Adrift in the Old World: The Psychological Pilgrimage of Washington Irving* (Chicago: University of Chicago Press, 1988) and Adam Sweeting, *Reading Houses and Building Books: Andrew Jackson Downing and the Architecture of Popular American Literature, 1835–1855* (Hanover NH: University Press of New England, 1996).

10. Irving, qtd. in Pierre M. Irving, *The Life and Letters of Washington Irving*, vol. 3 (New York: G. P. Putnam, 1862) 56–57.

11. Hone, qtd. in Stanley T. Williams, *The Life of Washington Irving*, vol. 2 (New York: Oxford University Press, 1935) 82.

12. Edward Everett, review of *A Tour on the Prairies*, *North American Review* 41 (July 1835): 28.

13. On September 30, 1832, Irving wrote in his journal: "after breakfast set off with Portales on horseback ahead of the rest—to look for Prairie hens—Mr Latrobe precedes us on foot— / scale a hill—limestone rock & stones full of

shells and miniature basalt like giant causeway—boundless view of silent Prairies—distant hill like Paté de Strasbourg." Washington Irving, *Journals and Notebooks*, vol. 5, ed. Sue Fields Ross (Boston: Twayne Publishers, 1986) 78.

14. Washington Irving, *A Tour of the Prairies* (1835; Norman: University of Oklahoma Press, 1956) 64.

15. On December 18, 1832, Irving wrote to his brother Peter: "The offer was too tempting to be resisted: I should have the opportunity of seeing the remnants of those great Indian tribes, which are now about to disappear as independent nations, or to be amalgamated under some new form of government. I should see those fine countries of the 'far west,' while still in a state of pristine wildness, and behold herds of buffaloes scouring their native prairies, before they are driven beyond the reach of the civilized tourist." Irving to Peter Irving, Washington City, 18 Dec. 1832, *Letters* 2:733.

16. Irving, *Journals* 91, 133.

17. Gerald Vizenor wryly comments on Lewis and Clark's need "to be seen" by Indians in *Manifest Manners* 2–3.

18. Washington Irving, *Astoria* 152.

19. Lucy Maddox, *Removals: Nineteenth-Century American Literature and the Politics of Indian Affairs* (New York: Oxford University Press, 1991).

20. Henry Schoolcraft wrote, in the *Literary World*, that Irving had accepted $5,000 to take up the Astoria project. Antelyes concludes that this figure was inaccurate; Irving allowed Astor to pay his nephew Pierre Irving, his research assistant on this project, $3,000. Twenty-five shares of Green Bay land, valued at approximately $4,000, remained in Astor's name but produced $2,100 in interest for Irving (*Tales of Adventurous Enterprise* 151–52).

Always eager to criticize Irving, Cooper relished the faint air of scandal that hovered about the Irving-Astor relationship. He wrote to Mrs. Cooper on Astor's death, in 1848, of the news that Irving was to be Astor's executor: "What an instinct that man has for gold! He is to be Astor's biographer! Columbus and John Jacob Astor. I dare say Irving will make the last the greatest man." See James Fenimore Cooper to Mrs. Cooper, "Globe," 1 Apr. 1848, *Letters and Journals* 5:328.

21. Williams, *Life of Washington Irving* 2:86. Any reading of Irving's Western histories has to contend with Peter Antelyes's remarkably thorough and insightful analyses. I have learned much about Irving from Antelyes's discussion of Irving's special relation to the "tale of adventurous enterprise," which Antelyes defines, approximately, as a narrative genre that promotes the ideals of the marketplace but also provides examples of how market-

place values might run to excess, the goal of this kind of narrative being the harnessing of "self-interest" to the communal interest of American expansionism. I tend to agree with Antelyes's readings of *Tour on the Prairies* and *The Adventures of Captain Bonneville*, but I find his analysis of *Astoria* limited. Antelyes writes that "*Astoria* does not question the identification of economic expansion with the American mission, nor does it locate the dangers of that mission in commercialism itself. Instead it presents the enterprise as the proper course of American history, and finds the threat to that course in external factors, such as foreign influences, savage 'others,' incompetent insiders, and an inhospitable environment." (*Tales of Adventurous Enterprise* 149) I disagree primarily with Antelyes's (to my mind) hopeful demarcation of an "inside" and "outside" in the narrative and in Astor's commercial venture; I see Irving struggling, and really failing, to locate the venture in such terms—it cannot be other than hybridized, "contaminated" or perhaps energized by other nations and environments. Antelyes's reluctance to take this into account shows up most readily in his dismissal of Irving's suggestion, based in a letter from Thomas Jefferson to Astor that is reprinted in *Astoria*, that the West may grow up to be a "sister" republic other than the United States (*Tales of Adventurous Enterprise* 182).

22. Everett Emerson, review of *Astoria*, *North American Review* 44 (Jan. 1837): 202.
23. Emerson, review of *Astoria* 235.
24. Emerson, review of *Astoria* 234.
25. Washington Irving, "Empire of the West," in *Miscellaneous Writings: 1803–1859*, vol. 2, ed. Wayne R. Kime (1840; Boston: Twayne Publishers, 1981) 135–37.
26. John Carlos Rowe, *Literary Culture and U.S. Imperialism: From the Revolution to World War II* (New York: Oxford University Press, 2000). Rowe's savvy remarks about the immateriality of many of the United States' efforts to expand its spheres of influence are invaluable.
27. Emerson, review of *Astoria* 212.
28. Irving, *Astoria* 4.
29. Pierre M. Irving, *Life and Letters of Washington Irving* 3:46.
30. For biographical details see Pierre M. Irving, *Life and Letters of Washington Irving*; Philip McFarland, *Sojourners* (New York: Atheneum, 1979); and Williams, *Life of Washington Irving*. On some level Irving may have been fascinated by the international interval that preceded a manifest destiny that he could not fully imagine in the 1830s, although he had predicted it some fifteen years before. In the nostalgic "Traits of Indian Character," published in the *Sketch-Book*, Irving recognized the destruction of the Massachusetts

Indians in the colonial era as predictive of an assured continental destiny
("In a little while, and they [all Native Americans] will go the way that their
brethren have gone before.") The project of "throw[ing] a degree of melan-
choly lustre" on the "remnant" Indians may have seemed less relevant to
Irving when he approached the West as the scene of intense, ongoing com-
mercial activity rather than a receding wilderness. Washington Irving, *The
Sketch Book of Geoffrey Crayon, Gent.*, ed. Haskell Springer (1819–20; Boston,
Twayne Publishers, 1978) 233, 231.

31. Letter from Louis de Bonneville to Washington Irving, qtd. in the appendix
to Washington Irving, *Astoria*, ed. Edgeley W. Todd (1836; Norman: University of Oklahoma Press, 1964), 521.

32. Albert-Alexandre Pourtalès, *On the Western Tour with Washington Irving*, ed.
George F. Spaulding, trans. Seymour Feiler (Norman: University of Oklahoma Press, 1968) 62.

33. Mark Twain, *Letters from Hawaii*, ed. A. Grove Day (1866; Honolulu: University of Hawaii Press, 1966) 274.

34. Brooks Adams, "The Spanish War and the Equilibrium of the World," *Forum*
25 (Aug. 1898): 641–51. Adams is also quoted in Walter LeFeber, *The New
Empire: An Interpretation of American Expansion 1860–1898* (1963; Ithaca NY:
Cornell University Press, 1998) 83.

35. I am referring to the effect that Renato Rosaldo has so aptly named "imperialist nostalgia" in his *Culture and Truth: The Remaking of Social Analysis* (Boston:
Beacon Press, 1989).

36. Timothy Egan, "As Others Abandon the Plains" 1+.

37. George Catlin, *Letters and Notes on the Manners, Customs, and Conditions of North
American Indians*, vol. 1 (1844; New York: Dover, 1973) 262.

38. Catlin, *Letters and Notes* 259–60.

39. Pocock, *Virtue, Commerce, and Society*. Although Pocock has been criticized
for the elegance and perhaps reductiveness of his models, I still find his
definitions useful heuristics.

40. Catlin, *Letters and Notes* 263.

41. Irving, *Bonneville* 269.

42. Irving, *Bonneville* 269.

43. Irving, *Journals* 97.

44. Robert J. C. Young, *Colonial Desire: Hybridity in Theory, Culture, and Race* (London and New York: Routledge, 1995). I would also like to acknowledge the
necessary influence of Homi Bhabha on any and all discussions of "hybridity" as cultural performance.

45. Amy Kaplan, "Left Alone with America," *Cultures of United States Imperialism*,

ed. Amy Kaplan and Donald Pease (Durham NC: Duke University Press, 1993) 12.

46. Leonard, Narrative 71.

47. For the relative weakness of the U.S. state in regard to expansion see Richard White, It's Your Misfortune and None of My Own: A New History of the American West (Norman: University of Oklahoma Press, 1991); Immanuel Wallerstein, "The Rise and Future Demise of the World Capitalist System"; and Catlin, Letters and Notes 263. John O'Sullivan's advocacy for the Confederacy can be seen in three tracts he wrote from London urging formal reconciliation with the South, including Union, Disunion, and Reunion: A Letter to General Franklin Pierce, Ex-President of the United States (London: R. Bentley, 1862), perhaps the darkest of the three. Edward L. Widmer offers useful insights into this phase of O'Sullivan's degeneration as a political thinker in Young America 206–07.

48. Irving, Astoria 81.

49. Irving, Astoria 84.

50. Irving, Astoria 80.

51. Irving, Astoria 30.

52. Irving, Astoria 49.

53. For a concise history of the American and Pacific Fur Companies, see John Denis Haeger, John Jacob Astor: Business and Finance in the Early Republic (Detroit MI: Wayne State University Press, 1991).

54. Alexis de Tocqueville, Democracy in America, ed. Phillips Bradley, trans. Francis Bowen (1862; reprint, with an introduction by Alan Ryan, New York and Toronto: Alfred A. Knopf, 1972) 386–87.

55. For more on Josiah Nott's theories of racial amalgamation, see Horsman, Race and Manifest Destiny, particularly 130–131. See also Josiah Nott, MD, "Two Lectures on the Connection Between the Biblical and Physical History of Man," Louisiana University, 1848 (Wyles Collection, University of California, Santa Barbara).

56. Hirschman, The Passions and the Interests especially 50–75.

57. Amartya Sen's parody of this theory of capitalism neatly summarizes the thinking of Bonneville and like-minded traders: "you are being chased by murderous bigots who passionately dislike something about you. . . . As they zero in on you, you throw some money around you as you flee, and each of them gets down to the serious business of collecting the notes. . . ." Amartya Sen, foreword to Hirschman, The Passions and the Interests x. See, again, Bonneville's letter to Irving in Todd, ed., Astoria 520–21. James Beckwourth, The Life and Adventures of James P. Beckwourth as told to Thomas D. Bonner (1854; Lincoln and London: University of Nebraska Press, 1981) 365.

58. Edwin James, *Account of an Expedition from Pittsburgh to the Rocky Mountains* (1823; Ann Arbor: University Microfilms, Inc., 1966) 245.

59. U.S. *Statutes* 2 (1802): 139–46, and 4 (1834): 729–35.

60. Henry Leavitt Ellsworth, *Washington Irving on the Plains and Prairies; or, A Narative Tour of the Southwest in the Year 1832*, ed. Stanley T. Williams and Barbara D. Simison (New York: American Press, 1937) 14–16.

61. Pourtales, 43.

62. Ellsworth, 125.

63. Beckwourth, *Life and Adventures* 120–21.

64. Edgar Allan Poe, *The Journal of Julius Rodman*, in Edgar Allan Poe, *The Imaginary Voyages*, ed. Burton R. Pollin (Boston: Twayne Publishers, 1981) 564. The *Journal* was originally published in *Burton's Gentleman's Magazine*, January to June 1840.

65. Francis Parkman, *The Oregon Trail*, ed. David Levin (1849; New York: Penguin, 1985) 178.

66. Beckwourth, *Life and Adventures* 433.

67. For one of many accounts of Beckwourth's (albeit reluctant) role as Chivington's guide in the massacre of the Southern Cheyenne at Sand Creek see Dee Brown, *Bury My Heart at Wounded Knee: An Indian History of the American West* (New York: Henry Holt and Company, 1970) 87–94. Brown assumes that Beckwourth did guide Chivington to Black Kettle. In his comprehensive *The Contested Plains*, Elliott West offers a counter-narrative in which Beckwourth does not play a primary role. See Elliott West, *The Contested Plains: Indians, Goldseekers, and the Rush to Colorado* (Lawrence: University of Kansas Press, 1998). The question of whether Beckwourth simply was as self-interested as most traders in Indian country or whether he has been scapegoated remains, as far as I know, still open.

68. Irving, *Journals* 162.

69. Lewis Cass, "Policy and Practice of the United States and Great Britain in Their Treatment of Indians," *North American Review* 24 (April 1827) 404. See also W. J. Rorabaugh, *The Alcoholic Republic* (New York: Oxford University Press, 1979) and William E. Unrau, *White Man's Wicked Water: The Alcohol Trade in Indian Country, 1802–1892* (Lawrence: University of Kansas, 1996).

70. Walter Whitman, *Franklin Evans, or The Inebriate, A Tale of the Times* (1842; New Haven CT: College and University Press, 1967) 45. David Reynolds, *Beneath the American Renaissance: The Subversive Imagination in the Age of Emerson and Melville* (Cambridge: Harvard University Press, 1988).

71. Randolph Marcy, U. S. A. "Border Reminiscences," *Harper's New Monthly Magazine* 39 (Oct. 1869): 649.

72. Cass, "Policy and Practice" 405.

73. Little Turtle qtd. in Unrau, *White Man's Wicked Water* 17. Nichols, ed., *Black Hawk's Autobiography* 35. Beckwourth, *Life and Adventures* 533.

74. Mark Doolittle, "Temperance a Source of National Wealth: A Prize Essay," *American Quarterly Temperance Magazine* 2 (Feb. 1834): 43.

75. Horace Mann, *Remarks upon the Comparative Profits of Grocers and Retailers, as Derived from Temperate and Intemperate Customers* (Boston: n.p., 1834) 12.

76. Nichols, ed., *Black Hawk's Autobiography* 17; Astor, qtd. in Unrau, *White Man's Wicked Water* 28; Beckwourth, *Life and Adventures* 365.

77. Sallie Wagner, *Wide Ruins: Memories from a Navajo Trading Post* (Albuquerque: University of New Mexico Press, 1997).

78. Magoffin, *Down the Santa Fe Trail* 76, 131–32. The asterisk represents an illegible word in Magoffin's diary.

79. Scharff wisely suggests that what Magoffin chooses to record has to do both with the "myriad claims of womanhood" in her era and the relatively undefined nature of this Far West. "In Magoffin's time, the West was not a 'trans-Mississippi' entity. It was still a series of encounters ranging from the episodic—bloody or indifferent or curious—to the long-standing—antipathetic or necessary or loving—taking place in widely dispersed, tenuously linked locales" (*Twenty Thousand Roads* 37).

80. Magoffin, *Down the Santa Fe Trail* 154.

81. Magoffin, *Down the Santa Fe Trail* 259.

82. Rowe, *Literary Culture and U.S. Imperialism* 8–9.

83. "Oakford's," *Godey's Lady's Book* 43 (Dec. 1851): 332. http://www.accessible .com/accessible/text/godeysii/00000026/00002657.htm. "Lois Ambler," *Harper's Weekly* 1 Feb. 1868: 74, http://app.harpweek.com. "Tom Brown at Harvard," *Harper's Weekly*, 25 Mar. 1871: 267, http://app.harpweek.com.

84. "Faster, Over the Sparkling Snow," *Harper's Weekly*, 25 Jan. 1873: 78, http://app.harpweek.com.

85. Edgeley W. Todd's edition of *Astoria* includes a note on all of the background reading Irving did to prepare for *Astoria* (xlvii).

86. James, *Account* 16:280–81.

87. James, *Account* 15:96–97.

88. Sharitarish, "We Are Not Starving Yet," 1822; printed in Calloway, *Our Hearts Fell to the Ground* 59.

89. See James, *Account* 14:317–18 and Irving, *Astoria* 112.

90. Orm Overland comments on Lewis and Clark's judgments of Indian nations based on their relative involvement in trade with whites (*Making and Meaning of an American Classic* 56).

91. Patricia Albers discusses the mid-18th century formation of a stable class of Native American middlemen in "Intertribal Relationship among Historic Plains Indians" 102–03.

92. "Winter on the Plains," *Harper's New Monthly Magazine* 39 (Oct. 1869): 22–34.

93. Irving, *Astoria* 70.

94. Alan Leander McGregor offers an excellent analysis of Irving's use of the language and symbols of feudal culture to valorize the Astorian venture. Specifically, McGregor discusses Astor in relation to the genre of "mercantile biography" created by magazines in the 1830s and 1840s like *Hunt's Merchants' Magazine*. Mercantile biographies attempted to dissociate businessmen like Astor from what was considered the dirty or immoral practice of business; "religious language and feudal honorifics" cast the everyday businessman in the anachronistic role of Renaissance warrior-prince. See McGregor, "Lords of the Ascendant: Mercantile Biography and Irving's *Astoria*," *Canadian Review of American Studies* 21 (Summer 1990): 15–30.

95. Irving, *Astoria* 311.

96. Irving, *Astoria* 266.

97. Irving, *Bonneville* 130.

98. Irving, *Bonneville* 26, 241.

99. Irving, *Bonneville* 28.

100. Irving too readily characterizes American Indians as the least scrupulous and most volatile traders on the Plains. Antelyes has noted that Irving's Indians serve as antitypes to his visionary merchants, Astor and Bonneville, in a representational sleight-of-hand which conveniently locates the most violent energies of the market in the wilderness itself (*Tales of Adventurous Enterprise* 104–05). Slotkin has made similar arguments about the displacement of anxieties about market culture onto the wilderness.

101. See Marcel Mauss, *The Gift: The Form and Reason for Exchange in Archaic Societies*, trans. W. D. Halls (New York and London: W. W. Norton and Company, 1990). See also Marshall Sahlins, *Stone Age Economics* (Chicago: Aldine & Atherton, 1972) and Pierre Bourdieu, *Outline of a Theory of Practice*, trans. Richard Nice (Cambridge: Cambridge University Press, 1977) 171.

102. Irving, *Astoria* 111.

103. Irving, *Astoria* 355.

104. Irving, *Astoria* 11.

105. Irving, *Astoria* 13.

106. Irving, *Astoria* 13.

107. On February 3, 1846, Irving wrote to his nephew Pierre: "I have been closely occupied, during the greater part of my sojourn in England, in studying the

Oregon question, and in preparing an article for publication, in the hope of placing our rights and our conduct in a proper light before the British public. I have not finished the article to my satisfaction, and circumstances have concurred to make it very doubtful whether I shall give it to the press.

"A close and conscientious study of the case has convinced me of the superiority of our title to the whole of the territory, and of the fairness of the offers we have made for the sake of peace, and in consideration of the interests which have grown up in the country during the long period of joint occupancy. British diplomatists have greatly erred in not closing with our proposition of the 49th parallel, with some additional items of accommodation. They should never have published so pertinaciously for the three additional degrees on the Pacific and the north bank of the Columbia. This was merely to protect the interests of Hudson's Bay Company; but they might have been protected by some other arrangement involving no point of pride. The full possession of the Columbia River is a matter of importance in our eyes, as being one of the great outlets of our empire." Washington Irving to Pierre M. Irving, London, 3 Feb. 1846, *Letters* 4:10–11.

3. The Postwestern Space of the Sea

1. Melville, MD 333.
2. Melville, MD 334.
3. Melville, MD 280, 169, 330, 145.
4. Cesare Casarino, *Modernity at Sea: Melville, Marx, Conrad in Crisis* (Minneapolis and London: University of Minnesota, 2002) 6. Casarino remarks, "while the world of the sea remains to this day an important part of the global political economy, the sea narrative was not able to maintain its centrality in culture during the twentieth century. As the ship turned into a space-ship, many of the functions that formerly were the prerogative and domain of the sea narrative were inherited and metamorphosed by science fiction." It could be said that sea narratives have gained new interest in recent years, however; the ocean has offered a trying ground for the new literature of extreme sports or (to coin an awkward phrase) extreme industry, as in Sebastian Junger's *The Perfect Storm: A True Story of Men against the Sea* (New York: W. W. Norton and Company, 1997). Moreover, the terrorist attacks on the World Trade Center of 9/11 have turned attention to the ocean's suitedness to transnational terrorist and smuggling networks, creating a new kind of "sea story," as in William Langewiesche's "Anarchy at Sea," *The Atlantic Monthly* (September 2003) 50–81.
5. Melville, MD 13.

6. Henry David Thoreau, "Walking," *Thoreau: Collected Essays and Poems*, ed. Elizabeth Hall Witherell (New York: Library of America, 2001) 234.

7. Melville, *MD* 12.

8. Melville, *MD* 13.

9. Melville, *MD* 384.

10. Herman Melville, *John Marr and Other Poems*, ed. Henry Chapin (Princeton NJ: Princeton University Press, 1922) 38, 81–82. Haskell Springer and Douglas Robillard suggest that the sea stands for a nostalgically "full" past in *John Marr*. See *America and the Sea: A Literary History*, ed. Haskell Springer (Athens: University of Georgia Press, 1995) 141–42.

11. In his helpful study of the nineteenth and twentieth-century development of "icons of endangerment" to represent the global commons of the oceans, Lawrence Buell notes that the question of whether sperm whales were an endangered species was a point of dispute in Melville's day—and that at least in *Moby-Dick* Melville chooses to dismiss the question. In Buell, *Writing for an Endangered World: Literature, Culture, and Environment in the U.S. and Beyond* (Cambridge and London: The Belknap Press of Harvard University Press, 2001) 210.

12. The character of whaling as a mode of production has been given nuanced treatment by historians, cultural and literary critics. Marcus Rediker suggests that whaling was an artisanal occupation in comparison to merchant sailing because of the archaic share system (as opposed to the wage) used among whalers—a profit-sharing mechanism used in the nineteenth-century maritime world only by whalers, fishermen, and pirates. See Marcus Rediker, *Between the Devil and the Deep Blue Sea: Merchant Seamen, Pirates, and the Anglo-American Maritime World, 1700–1750* (Cambridge: Cambridge University Press, 1987). Casarino characterizes whaling as "at once the most archaic and the most advanced of sea practices" because it was an exception the wage system yet hosted "the most international, multiethnic, . . . multiracial labor force" of any sea trade (*Modernity at Sea* 5). Buell emphasizes the role of whaling in entering the U.S. into the global economy of the nineteenth-century (*Endangered World* 205)—an emphasis that is, interestingly, shared by the business journal *Hunt's Merchants' Magazine*, which in 1840 boasted that the "profits" of whaling "have, perhaps, been greater than those of any other single object of our national enterprise." "The American Whale Fishery," *Hunt's Merchants' Magazine* 3 (Nov. 1840): 46.

13. Paul Gilroy, *The Black Atlantic: Modernity and Double Consciousness* (Cambridge: Harvard University Press, 1993); James Clifford, *Routes: Travel and Translation in the late Twentieth Century* (Cambridge: Harvard University, 1997).

14. Casarino, *Modernity at Sea* 10.

15. For a cogent discussion of James's contribution, via Melville, to the Cold War-era formation of U.S./American Studies, see Donald Pease, "C. L. R. James, *Moby Dick*, and the Emergence of Transnational Americas Studies," *Arizona Quarterly* 56 (Autumn 2000): 93–123; Pease recognizes a predecessor to the new "transnational Americas studies" in C. L. R. James, *Mariners, Renegades, and Castaways: The Story of Herman Melville and the World We Live In* (1953; Hanover NH and London: Dartmouth University Press, 2001).

16. Foucault, "Of Other Spaces" 24. It is the anti-referential quality of heterotopia that particularly interests Casarino, who acknowledges Foucault's declaration of the ship as heterotopia par excellence as the jumping off point for his project. Casarino writes: "Heterotopias come into being as the interference between representational and nonrepresentational practices: this is that onto-epistemological modality of interference that I referred to . . . as immanent interference and that occurs when a practice folds back upon itself and questions both itself and all other practices. It is precisely this movement toward itself occasioned by the presence of a nonrepresentational element that enables heterotopias to question and contest all other spaces" (*Modernity at Sea* 12).

17. John Sergeant, "Mercantile Character," *Hunt's Merchants' Magazine* 3 (July 1840): 11. This article is a reprint of a lecture given at the Mercantile Library Company of Philadelphia and at the Mercantile Library Association of New York City in 1839.

18. Sergeant, "Mercantile Character" 11.

19. Immanuel Wallerstein, "The Rise and Future Demise of the World Capitalist System."

20. Cooper, qtd. in Thomas Philbrick, *James Fenimore Cooper and the Development of American Sea Fiction* (Cambridge: Harvard University Press, 1961) 48.

21. Edward Everett, "Accumulation, Property, Capital, and Credit: An Address, delivered before the Mercantile Library Association, at the Odeon, in Boston, September 13th, 1838," *Hunt's Merchants' Magazine* 1 (1839): 28–29.

22. Cooper, qtd. in Philbrick, *James Fenimore Cooper* 48.

23. These quotations from *Notions* can be found in James Fenimore Cooper, *Notions of the Americans: Picked up by a Travelling Bachelor*, vol. 1 (Philadelphia: Lea and Carey, 1828) 12–16. These passages by Cooper are also quoted in Philbrick, *James Fenimore Cooper* 48. Philbrick makes a strong point of Cooper's personal history in the U.S. Navy and merchant marine and the enduring effect that this maritime work had upon his understanding of national potentiality.

24. "British Navigation Act," *Hunt's Merchants' Magazine* 4 (May 1841): 414.

25. O'Sullivan, "Annexation" 6–7.

26. O'Sullivan, "Territorial Aggrandizement" 244.

27. Melville writes, with tongue barely in cheek, that "Until the whale fishery rounded Cape Horn, no commerce but colonial, scarcely any intercourse but colonial, was carried on between Europe and the long line of the opulent Spanish provinces on the Pacific coast. It was the whalemen who first broke through the jealous policy of the Spanish crown, touching those colonies; and, if space permitted, it might be distinctly shown how from those whalemen at last eventuated the liberation of Peru, Chili [sic], and Bolivia from the yoke of Old Spain, and the establishment of the eternal democracy in those parts." Melville, *MD* 100.

28. Montesquieu, *The Spirit of the Laws*, ed. and trans. Anne M. Cohler, Basia Carolyn Miller, Harold Samuel Stone (Cambridge: Cambridge University Press, 1989) 338.

29. Hirschman, *The Passions and the Interests* 62.

30. "Traffic," *Oxford English Dictionary*, 2nd ed. 1989.

31. *Cambridge Economic History of Europe*, ed. J. H. Clapham et al., vol. 4 (Cambridge: Cambridge University Press, 1941–1989) 191–270. See also Lawrence Juda, *International Law and Ocean Use Management* (London: Routledge, 1996), 8–10.

32. William McFee, *The Law of the Sea* (Philadelphia: J. B. Lippincott, 1950) 146.

33. While I don't wish to suggest that White's meticulous history of Native/ Euro-American encounters in the Great Lakes region (*The Middle Ground*) is reducible to "a concept," White's work does suggest a way of thinking about spaces that have not quite been conquered, where all parties at least temporarily find themselves on a level field of contest.

34. Harmar Denny, *Annals of Congress* 8 May 1830; "Far West," *Oxford English Dictionary*, 2nd ed. 1989.

35. J. Farquharson, "Report of the Windsor and Sturgeon Bay Road Committee," *Toronto Globe*, 14 Oct. 1845.

36. Douglas Monroy, "The Creation and Re-Creation of Californio Society," *California History* 76.2–3 (1997): 173–195; Moore, ed., *Political Economy of North American Indians*; McGinnis, *Counting Coup and Cutting Horses*.

37. Joseph G. Baldwin, *The Flush Times of Alabama and Mississippi: A Series of Sketches* (1853; Baton Rouge: Louisiana State University Press, 1987); Michael Tadman, *Speculators and Slaves: Masters, Traders, and Slaves in the Old South* (Madison: University of Wisconsin Press, 1989); James Lal Penick, Jr., "John A. Murrell: A Legend of the Old Southwest," *Tennessee Historical Quarterly* 48.3

(1989): 174–183; Walter Johnson, *Soul by Soul: Life Inside the Antebellum Slave Market* (Cambridge MA: Harvard University Press, 1999).

38. Michael Tadman discusses "scrubs" in *Speculators and Slaves*. For a riveting account of disposable people in the late twentieth-century global economy, see Kevin Bales, *Disposable People: New Slavery in the Global Economy* (Berkeley: University of California Press, 1999).

39. Brian McGinty, "The Boston Men," *American History Illustrated* 15.1 (1980): 8–11, 40–45; Samuel Eliot Morison, *The Maritime History of Massachusetts, 1783–1860* (1921; Boston: Northeastern University Press, 1979).

40. For a specific linkage of Thoreau's river narrative and the commodification of river water in New England, see Theodore Steinberg, *Nature Incorporated: Industrialization and the Waters of New England* (Cambridge: Cambridge University Press, 1991). An outline of New England's role in instigating the dismantling of common law protections of water also appears in Morton J. Horwitz, *The Transformation of American Law 1780–1860* (Cambridge: Harvard University Press, 1977) 31–62.

41. Christopher Newfield makes an eloquent and convincing argument for the relationship of the nineteenth-century development of Emersonian self-hood to the compromises of modern liberalism and contemporary corporate culture in Christopher Newfield, *The Emerson Effect: Individualism and Submission in America* (Chicago: The University of Chicago Press, 1996).

42. Ralph Waldo Emerson, "Character," in *Essays: First and Second Series* (1844; New York: The Library of America, 1990) 267–68.

43. Emerson, "Character" 269.

44. Bercovitch's now classic reading of the ambiguities of dissent in nineteenth-century U.S. discourse stresses that "America," as a symbol, "wed the ideals of individualism, community, and continuing revolution"—repositioning revolution as the normative state of society, and of the soul, in order to naturalize a non-dialectical, "progressive view of history" (*American Jeremiad* 183).

45. Ralph Waldo Emerson, "An Address . . . on . . . the Emancipation of the Negroes in the British West Indies," *Emerson's Anti-Slavery Writings*, ed. Len Gougeon and Joel Myerson (New Haven CT and London: Yale University Press, 1995) 31.

46. Emerson, "Character" 266–267. Thomas Augst has offered rich historical contexts for the problem of mercantile character in the nineteenth-century U.S. Following Emerson, Augst identifies the popular view among the emergent middle-class that "unlike other forms of capital, [character] retains value regardless of the unpredictable tempests in the economic realm." See

Thomas Augst, "The Business of Reading in Nineteenth-Century America: The New York Mercantile Library," *American Quarterly* 50.2 (1998): 285.

47. "The Legal Protection of Good Faith," *Hunt's Merchants' Magazine* 1 (Sept. 1839): 227.

48. The following discussion appears in an article suggesting that U.S. civil law is too forgiving to merchants, encouraging unwise speculation and fraud: "As our laws between debtor and creditor rather encourage than suppress the impositions and injustice we have spoken of, there is but one other tribunal to which we can look for correcting them. Public opinion must inculcate sound doctrines, and visit with indignation those who offend them. . . . Do not believe there is one sort of honesty, one code of morality, for your business, and another for your ordinary transactions . . . that any thing can be just and honorable in a merchant, that is not so in the man and the citizen . . ." (388). "Lecture on Commercial Integrity," *Hunt's Merchants' Magazine* 1 (November, 1839): 388.

49. Sergeant, "Mercantile Character" 11.

50. Stuart Blumin's discussion of how the emergent middle-class used working-class images and rhetoric to define its own limits is relevant here. See Stuart Blumin, *The Emergence of the Middle-Class: Social Experience in the American City, 1760–1900* (Cambridge: Cambridge University Press, 1989).

51. "Speculations on Commerce," *Hunt's Merchants' Magazine* 3 (Sept. 1840): 237.

52. "Unmask, bold Traffic! Thou art weaving now / Thy golden fancies round the seaman's brow; / Thou hast at will the magic power to guide / His heart from home, and child, and cherished bride." This anonymous clerk's ode to "bold Traffic" is printed in James T. Fields, "Mercantile Literature" 538.

53. "Lecture on Commercial Integrity" 380.

54. Elaine Scarry's almost lyrical reading of Marx's *Capital*, vol. 1 appears in Scarry, *The Body in Pain: The Making and Unmaking of the World* (Oxford: Oxford University Press, 1985) 264.

55. John S. Stone, D.D., "Evils of Commerce: The Annual Sermon, preached at New Haven, on the 19th of June, 1839," *Hunt's Merchants' Magazine* 1 (July 1840): 80.

56. Emerson, "Character" 272.

57. Richard Henry Dana, Jr., *Two Years before the Mast* (1840; New York and London: Penguin, 1981) 482.

58. Dana, *Mast* 322–23.

59. Dana, *Mast* 144, 157, 233.

60. Dana, *Mast* 463.

61. Half-ironically, Melville asserts in White-Jacket: "Certainly the necessities of navies warrant a code for its government more stringent than the law that governs the land; but that code should conform to the spirit of the political institutions of the country that ordains it. It should not convert into slaves some of the citizens of the nation of freemen. Such objections can not be urged against the laws of the Russian Navy (not essentially different from our own), because the laws of that Navy, creating the absolute one-man power in the Captain . . . conform in spirit to the territorial laws of Russia, which is ruled by an autocrat. . . ." Herman Melville, White-Jacket, or, The World in a Man-of-War (1850; New York: Random House, 2002) 144.

62. Dana, Mast 464.

63. Dana, Mast 467.

64. See Richard Henry Dana, Jr., Cruelty to Seamen (1839; Berkeley CA: n.p., 1937).

65. W. E. Burghardt DuBois, The Suppression of the African Slave Trade to the United States of America, 1638–1870 (1896; Baton Rouge: Louisiana State University Press, 1969). DuBois discusses the use of United States' flag as a flag of convenience exhaustively in Chapter IX. For a sea melodrama that takes the United States' role in the illegal international slave trade as its primary topic, see Richard Drake, Revelations of a Slave Smuggler: Being the Autobiography of Captain Richard Drake, An African Trader for Fifty Years—From 1807 to 1857; During Which Period He Was Concerned in the Transportation of Half a Million Blacks from the African Coasts to America (1857; reprint, Northbrook IL: Metro Books, 1972).

66. Robert F. Lucid discusses Dana's covert urban explorations in sailor's garb in Robert F. Lucid, introduction, Richard Henry Dana, Jr., The Journal of Richard Henry Dana, Jr., ed. Robert F. Lucid (Cambridge: The Belknap Press of Harvard University Press, 1968) xxxviii.

67. George Grafton Wilson discusses Dana's unfinished treatise on international law in his introduction to the (eighth) edition of Henry Wheaton's Elements of International Law, which is edited by Dana. Henry Wheaton, Elements of International Law, The literal reproduction of the edition of 1866 by R. Henry Dana, Jr., ed. with notes by George Grafton Wilson. (Oxford: Clarendon Press; London: H. Milford, 1936) 24a. See also James David Hart, The Other Writings of Richard Henry Dana, Jr. (New York: [s.n.], [1940]).

68. Limerick, Legacy 260. Useful discussions of the multiethnic, multiracial character of maritime environments can be found in Marcus Rediker, Devil and the Deep Blue Sea; W. Jeffrey Bolster, Black Jacks: African American Seamen in the Age of Sail (Cambridge MA: Harvard University Press, 1997); and Peter Linebaugh and Marcus Rediker, Sailors, Slaves, Commoners, and the Hidden History of the Revolutionary Atlantic (Boston: Beacon, 2000).

69. Wheeler's analysis of the "residual proto-ideologies" that influenced the emergence of modern racism has been particularly useful to me because she examines the articulation of racial difference within commercial discourse. See Wheeler, *The Complexion of Race*.

70. Dana, *Mast* 459; Melville, *White-Jacket* 44; James Fenimore Cooper, *The Red-Rover, A Tale* (1827; Albany: State University of New York, 1991) 31.

71. Melville, *White-Jacket* 277.

72. " 'I'm no negro slave,' said Sam. 'Then I'll make you one,' said the captain" (Dana, *Mast* 152).

73. Melville, *MD* 67, 444, 232.

74. Dimock's argument moves swiftly between the economic metaphors offered in *Moby-Dick* itself and deconstruction of these metaphors to probe the fundamental logics of the text: "Ahab, of course, has no use for substitution and exchange. His universe is one of mimetic repetition: in trying to dismember his dismemberer, he is trying to be like the whale, to do what the whale has done to him. Vengeance affirms the primacy of temporal continuity, of mimesis in time. Starbuck, with no desire to imitate a 'dumb brute,' rejects not only mimesis but the very idea of 'continuity.' . . . Starbuck cultivates the art of discontinuity, the art of discrete substitution" (*Empire for Liberty* 120).

75. Melville, *John Marr* 16.

76. Marx writes: "Let us now look at the *residue* of the products of labor. There is nothing left of them in each case but the same phantom-like objectivity; they are merely congealed quantities of the same homogenous human labor, i.e. of human labor-power expended without regard to the form of its expenditure. All these things now tell us that human labor-power has been expended to produce them, human labor is accumulated in them. As crystals of this social substance, which is common to them all, they are values—commodity values . . ." Karl Marx, *Capital*, vol. 1, trans. Ben Fowkes (New York: Penguin Books, 1990) 1:128.

77. Tzvetan Todorov, *The Conquest of America: The Question of the Other* (1984; Norman: University of Oklahoma Press, 1999) 157.

78. Melville, *John Marr* 74.

79. Michael T. Gilmore, *American Romanticism and the Marketplace* (Chicago: University of Chicago Press, 1985).

80. Melville, *MD* 249–50.

81. Melville, *MD* 254.

82. Melville, *MD* 463.

83. "The mirror opposition of whalemen (especially Ahab) bestialized by the

hunt versus whale (especially Moby-Dick) maddened by being hunted is culturally avant-garde insofar as it implies a comparative pathology of early capitalist enterprise and of intelligent mammals under pressure of systematic harassment" (Buell, *Endangered World* 214).

84. Melville, MD 255.

85. Owen Chase, *Narrative of the Most Extraordinary and Distressing Shipwreck of the Whale-Ship Essex, of Nantucket; Which Was Attacked by a Large Spermaceti-Whale in the Pacific Ocean* (New York: W. B. Gilley, 1821).

86. Herman Melville, "Manuscript Notes on Owen Chase," reprinted in MD 600.

87. Melville, MD 178.

88. Important studies of sentimentalism and the sentimental novel in the United States are so numerous that naming just a few risks omitting several of equal value. My own understanding of the genre began in the work of Jane Tompkins, Ann Douglas, Philip Fisher, and Shirley Samuels.

89. James, *Mariners* 5.

90. J. N. Reynolds, "Mocha Dick," *The Knickerbocker, New York Monthly Magazine* 13 (May 1839): 92.

91. Dimock brilliantly notes the novel's reiteration of Ahab's resemblance to the "vanishing" Indian. See especially pp. 116–20.

92. Of course studies of violence in the western are many and varied. Susan Kollin offers a useful analysis of various critical positions on the genre's relationship to violence in "Genre and Geographies of Violence: Cormac McCarthy and the Contemporary Western," *Contemporary Literature* 42.3 (Fall 2001): 557–88. See also the classic Philip French, *Westerns: Aspects of a Movie Genre* (New York: Viking, 1973).

93. Melville, MD 235–36.

94. Melville, MD 215.

The Culture of Water

1. Theodore Dwight Weld, *American Slavery as It Is: Testimony of a Thousand Witnesses* (1839; Salem NH: Ayer Company Publishers, 1991) 111. Weld deconstructs the absurd "chattel principle": "The idea of property having a will, and that too in opposition to the will of its owner, and counteracting it, is a stimulant of terrible power to the most relentless human passions."

2. Jefferson Davis, qtd. in Wilbur H. Siebert, *The Underground Railroad: From Slavery to Freedom* (New York: n.p., 1898) 312–13.

3. Johnson, *Soul by Soul*, chapter 3, "Making a World Out of Slaves."

4. Thorpe, "Remembrances of the Mississippi" 27–28.

5. Herman Melville, *The Confidence-Man: His Masquerade* (1857; New York: Penguin, 1990) 131.

6. Mark Twain, *Adventures of Huckleberry Finn* (1884; New York; Penguin, 1985) 155.

7. Toni Morrison, *Playing in the Dark: Whiteness and the Literary Imagination* (Cambridge MA: Harvard University Press, 1992).

8. I am referring here to the controversies surrounding Shelley Fisher-Fishkin's *Was Huck Black? Mark Twain and African American Voices* (New York: Oxford University Press, 1993). This book did a great service to readers of Twain insofar as it made clear the debt Twain owes to African-American storytellers, from "Sociable Jimmy," the wise child he chanced to meet in an Illinois hotel to "Uncle Daniel," a virtuosic storyteller who lived as a slave on the farm of Samuel Clemens's uncle, John Quarles. While no one should question the quality of Fishkin's archival work, her linguistic argument has been problematic for some critics. Could it be surprising to any student of southern dialects that African-American voices inhabit white southern speech? James R. Kincaid's critique of the book in *The New York Times* (23 May 1993) is more cynical and pointed: "[Fishkin] gives little attention to the implications of her own position. She does not much consider this 'blending' of black and white in the vernacular, even whether it is really a blending or, as one of her notes puts it, a 'warring' between the two voices. Finally, while she addresses the blunt charge of white literary tradition 'appropriating' black experience, she does not consider the possibility that her reassuring book may simply make things comfy again, make Huck into a cute little 'darky' like Jimmy, one who can protect us from such things as Toni Morrison's frightening readings of 'the parasitical nature of white freedom' portrayed in the novel, the way in which Huck's growth depends on Jim's 'serviceability' and thus is inextricably tied to 'the term "nigger" ' . . ."

4. The Nation's Mouth

1. H. W., "Slick, Downing, Crockett, Etc.," *London and Westminster Review* (Dec. 1838): 136–45. Reprinted in William Bedford Clark and W. Craig Turner, *Critical Essays on American Humor* (Boston: G. K. Hall and Company, 1984) 19.

2. William Gilmore Simms, "Writings of Cornelius Matthews," *Southern Quarterly Review* 6 (Oct. 1844): 337.

3. Taken as a whole, Cash's *The Mind of the South* does suggest an interesting expansion of Turner's "frontier hypothesis" that actually negates Turner's famous sense of an ending. It seems to me that if the South were considered as, in fact, one of the western border territories in the nineteenth century, the monolithic interpretation of the South as "un-nationalized" and the

West as supremely "national" would be subject to healthy revision. This is essentially the move that Twain makes and to some extent Cash makes it, too, although his stated purpose in *The Mind of the South* is to invoke "the frontier" in order to disassemble another popular historical myth, that a ruling class of aristocratic, "Cavalier" planters utterly dominated a relatively homogenous South before the Civil War. W. J. Cash, *The Mind of the South* (New York: Alfred A. Knopf, 1941).

4. Every discussion of southwestern or U.S. humor owes a considerable debt to the groundbreaking studies of humor that came out in the 1930s, even though the politics that motivate such studies and their anxious search for an "American folk culture" now seem, as I suggest, somewhat predictable or condescending. Nonetheless, the works of Constance Rourke and Bernard DeVoto are elegantly written and rich in historical anecdote. See Constance Rourke, *American Humor: A Study of the National Character* (New York: Harcourt, Brace, and Company, 1931); Bernard DeVoto, *Mark Twain's America* (1932; Lincoln: University of Nebraska Press, 1997).

5. Simms, "Matthews" 337.

6. Simms, "Matthews" 337.

7. "Every Man of the western Country turns his eyes intuitively upon the mouth of the Mississippi. He there beholds the only outlet by which his produce can reach the markets of foreign nations or the Atlantic States: Blocked up, all the fruits of his industry rots upon his hand—open and he carries on a trade with all the nations of the earth." Andrew Jackson, qtd. in Michael Rogin, *Fathers and Children: Andrew Jackson and the Subjugation of the American Indian* (1975; New Brunswick NJ: Transaction Publishers, 1995) 144.

8. Simms, "Matthews" 337.

9. "American Humor," *Democratic Review* (Sept. 1845): 219.

10. I am making a rather loose reference here to Gramsci's well-known but prickly concept of the national-popular, which expresses more a longing for an impossibly "popular" national culture than an assertion that such a culture could exist. See Antonio Gramsci, "Concept of 'National-Popular' " in *Selections from the Cultural Writings*, ed. David Forgacs and Geoffrey Nowell-Smith, trans. William Boelhower (Cambridge: Harvard University Press, 1985) 206. Eric Lott offers a very useful gloss on the concept of "the national-popular" and its troubled semi-realization in U.S. blackface minstrelsy in *Love and Theft: Blackface Minstrelsy and the American Working Class* (New York: Oxford University Press, 1993) 91.

11. Simms, "Matthews" 336.

12. Sigmund Freud, *Jokes and Their Relation to the Unconscious*, ed. and trans. James

Strachey (New York: W. W. Norton and Company, 1960) 118. Freud writes: "Generally speaking, a tendentious joke calls for three people: in addition to the one who makes the joke, there must be a second who is taken as the object of the hostile or sexual aggressiveness, and a third in whom the joke's aim of producing pleasure is fulfilled."

13. "The Position of Parties," *The American Whig Review* (Jan. 1845): 18.

14. Lynn writes: "The Whiggery of the [southwestern] humorists is worth insisting on, for it tells us much about their entire caste of mind, including their comic imagination. In a preeminently political era, political allegiance was as importing a key to American writing as religious belief once had been. . . . To the Whig mind, the quality of violence inherent in Jacksonianism was what made the movement so disturbing . . ." (*Mark Twain and Southwestern Humor* 58). To my mind, Lynn's study of southwestern humor (minus the rather humdrum readings of Twain) has been the most provocative until the brief but brilliant analysis by Neil Schmitz, "Forms of Regional Humor," *Columbia Literary History of the United States*, gen. ed. Emory Elliott (New York: Columbia University Press, 1988) 306–23.

15. All details of Porter's biography here come from what is still the most complete history of Porter's tenure with *The Spirit of the Times*: Norris W. Yates, *William T. Porter and the Spirit of the Times: A Study of the Big Bear School of Humor* (Baton Rouge: Louisiana State University Press, 1957).

16. Porter, qtd. in Yates, *William T. Porter and the Spirit of the Times* 15.

17. Yates, *William T. Porter and the Spirit of the Times* 31–32.

18. "Major Boots in Gotham," *The Spirit of the Times* 9 (25 Jan. 1840): 560.

19. "Note on the Globe Hotel," *The Spirit of the Times* 9 (16 Nov. 1839): 433.

20. "Sayings and Doings in Boston," *The Spirit of the Times* 8 (6 Oct. 1838): 265.

21. "Sayings and Doings in Boston" 265.

22. "John Jacob Astor of New York," *The Spirit of the Times* 8 (3 Nov. 1838): 297.

23. "The Disposition of Sailors to Travesty, " *The Spirit of the Times* 8 (3 Nov. 1838): 297.

24. Yates, *William T. Porter and the Spirit of the Times* 3.

25. N. of Arkansas [Charles Fenton Mercer Noland], "Pete Whetstone on His Travels: Steamboat Robert Fulton, mighty close to Old Virginny, April 20, 1839," *The Spirit of the Times* 8 (4 May 1839): 102.

26. Lynn comments upon how the humorists who wrote for the *Spirit* were themselves anxiously balancing on the edge of aristocratic pretension: "The southwestern humorists who wrote for the *Spirit* were, most of them, newspapermen and lawyers trying to get on in the world, men allied with, but not of, the planter class. But as Porter puffed them up in his editorial in-

troductions to their work, they were all men of learning and culture, scions
of ancient families, inheritors of vast wealth" (*Mark Twain and Southwestern
Humor* 75).

27. Ralph Waldo Emerson, *Nature* in *The Norton Anthology of American Literature*,
gen. ed. Nina Baym, fifth ed., vol. 1 (1836; New York: W. W. Norton and
Company, 1998) 1082.

28. Johnson Jones Hooper, *Adventures of Captain Simon Suggs, Late of the Tallapoosa
Volunteers; together with "Taking the Census" and Other Alabama Sketches* (1845;
Tuscaloosa: The University of Alabama Press, 1993) 82.

29. William Goodell, *The American Slave Code* (1853; New York: Arno Press, 1969)
61. The year 1836 has been described by several southern commentators of
the period as the year when slavedrivers and traders most conspicuously
multiplied, banks extended loans to eager buyers, and even the Trustees
of the General Assembly of the Presbyterian Church invested upwards of
ninety thousand dollars in southwestern banks financing the slave trade.
The banks became so identified with the domestic slave trade that, according to ex-slave James Thomas, both slave and free African Americans declared themselves Jacksonian Democrats. But ironically Jackson's policies
resulted in the expansion of the credit economy and, with it, the domestic
slave trade. See Goodell, *American Slave Code* 48; and James Thomas, *From
Tennessee Slave to St. Louis Entrepreneur: The Autobiography of James Thomas*, ed.
Loren Schweninger (Columbia MO: University of Missouri Press, 1984) 69.

30. For a classic discussion of immediatist and gradualist abolitionism in the
United States and Britain see David Brion Davis, *The Problem of Slavery in
Western Culture* (Oxford: Oxford University Press, 1988).

31. "Advertisement" in Edward Beecher, *Narrative of Riots at Alton* (1838; reprint,
New York: E. P. Dutton and Company, 1965) xxxi.

32. Beecher, *Riots at Alton* 5.

33. Leonard L. Richards, *"Gentlemen of Property and Standing": Anti-Abolition Mobs
in Jacksonian America* (New York: Oxford University Press, 1970) 10.

34. James M. McPherson, *Abraham Lincoln and the Second American Revolution* (New
York: Oxford University Press, 1991) 17.

35. Abraham Lincoln, "The Perpetuation of Our Political Institutions: Address
Before the Young Men's Lyceum of Springfield, Illinois, January 27, 1838,"
Abraham Lincoln: His Speeches and Writings, ed. Roy P. Basler (New York: World
Publishing Company, 1969) 78–80.

36. Eudora Welty, "A Still Moment," *The Collected Stories of Eudora Welty* (New
York: Harcourt, 1980) 192.

37. "Murrell always acted from personal motives, displaying none of the innate

nobility of the folk hero. All true outlaw heroes must become the symbolic champion of an oppressed or submerged people." James Lal Penick, Jr., *The Great Western Land Pirate: John A. Murrell in Legend and History* (Columbia: University of Missouri Press, 1981) 53. Much of the corrective history that I refer to here comes from Penick's careful recrafting of the Murrell biography.

38. Twain began writing this unfinished short novel in 1897. For a brief discussion of the novel's history and contents, see R. Kent Rasmussen, *Mark Twain A–Z: The Essential Reference to His Life and Writings* (New York: Oxford University Press, 1995) 474–75.

39. Mark Twain, *Life on the Mississippi* (1883; New York: Penguin, 1980) 178.

40. William Wells Brown, *The Narrative of the Life of William Wells Brown* in William Loren Katz, ed., *Five Slave Narratives: A Compendium* (1847; New York: Arno Press, 1968) 13–110.

41. Hundley, *Social Relations*. Hundley suggests that "for ingenious lying" the "Negro trader" beats out the New York stockbroker and names slave traders as the most despicable of an emergent Southern business class he calls "Southern Yankees" (142).

42. Marx describes "philistine utopia" as the ideal end-state of Proudhon's bourgeois socialism. Karl Marx, *Capital* 1:161 n. 26.

43. Penick, "John A. Murrell" 174. Penick offers a useful reading of Murrell's historical biography against the fictive biography that was generated by Virgil Stewart, Murrell's primary accuser in the trial and the probable author of the first pamphlet edition of the criminal biography, the *Life of Murel*. The spelling of Murrell's name as "Murrell," which I employ throughout when referring to the historical Murrell, is verified by Penick as the spelling that most frequently appears in court records in which Murrell figures.

44. Richards, *"Gentlemen of Property"* 12. Penick also alludes to the coincidence of the abolitionist mail campaign of 1835 and the publication of the Murrell "conspiracy" (*Great Western Land Pirate* 3).

45. H. R. Howard, ed., *The History of Virgil A. Stewart, and his Adventure Capturing and Exposing the "Great Western Land Pirate" and His Gang in Connection with the Evidence: also of the Trials, Confessions, and Execution of Five Professional Gamblers by the Citizens of Vicksburg, on the 6th of July 1835* (New York: Harper and Brothers, 1838) 233. Howard's republication of the Murrell biography by Augustus Q. Walton, pseud., includes an expanded version of the earlier criminal biography in addition to documentation of the events at Livingston and a similar vigilante offensive against gamblers at Vicksburg.

46. For the "addition" of George Thompson to the Murrell narrative, see Penick, *Great Western Land Pirate* 166–67.

47. Richard R. John, *Spreading the News: The American Postal System from Franklin to Morse* (Cambridge: Harvard University Press, 1995) 271.

48. See Sean Wilentz, "Introduction: The Mysteries of David Walker," in David Walker, *David Walker's Appeal, in Four Articles, Together with a Preamble to the Coloured Citizens of the World, but in particular, and Very Expressly, to those of The United States of America* (1829; New York: Hill and Wang, 1995).

49. A summary of the Vesey legend is offered in Randall M. Miller and John David Smith, eds., *Dictionary of Afro-American Slavery* (Westport CT: Praeger, 1997) 775.

50. Penick writes: "The western district of Tennessee [in which Murrell lived] is one of three discrete geographical sections of that state. It is watered by rivers that flow directly westward into the Mississippi" (*Great Western Land Pirate* 32).

51. Penick suggests that "Stewart made no mention of these things [the insurrectionist scheme] in the course of the trial, and may not have thought of them yet" (*Great Western Land Pirate* 88).

52. Ruffin qtd. in Gavin Wright, *The Political Economy of the Cotton South* (New York: W. W. Norton and Company, 1978) 117. Wright's emphasis on the commodity dimension of slave property strongly influences this analysis. For a more local analysis of how slaveowners functioned as speculators as well as householders, see Edward W. Phifer, "Slavery in Microcosm: Burke County, North Carolina," *Journal of Southern History* 28 (May 1962): 137–165.

53. George Tucker, *Political Economy for the People* (Philadelphia: n.p., 1859).

54. Lydia Maria Child, *An Appeal in Favor of That Class of Americans Called Africans* (1836; New York: Arno Press and The New York Times, 1968) 121.

55. Hudnold contributes a signed statement to H. R. Howard's revised *Life of Murel* in which he states that "a negro man . . . was stolen from William Eason . . . and sold to me . . . and restolen from me within a few nights thereafter . . . whom I have never heard of since. . . ." (26).

56. John Seelye, introduction, *Adventures of Huckleberry Finn* xxii.

57. Walton, *Life of Murel* 39.

58. Walton, *Life of Murel* 34.

59. Tadman, *Speculators and Slaves* 5, 31. Tadman's data contrasts sharply with the suggestion of Fogel and Engerman that most slave migration reflected the migration of entire plantations. See Robert William Fogel and Stanley L. Engerman, *Time on the Cross: The Economics of Negro Slavery* (Boston: Little, Brown, 1974) 78–79.

60. Hundley, *Social Relations* 156.

61. Walter Benn Michaels's discussion of the horrifying spectacle of "slaves

without masters" in *Uncle Tom's Cabin* is relevant here. Michaels refers to Stowe's implication that what is most wrong with slavery is the incomplete nature of mastery, given that paternalistic masters like George Shelby are in fact mastered by impersonal market relations that undermined the supposed stability of the patriarchal household (*Gold Standard* 103–04).

62. Goodell, *American Slave Code* 53.

63. Child, *Appeal* 33.

64. Child, *Appeal* 36.

65. Hartman, *Scenes of Subjection* 33.

66. Child, *Appeal* 37.

67. Angelina Grimké, *Letters to Catherine E. Beecher in Reply to an Essay on Slavery and Abolitionism Addressed to A. E. Grimké* (Boston: Isaac Knapp, 1838) 4–5.

68. For an overview of antebellum ideas of economic value, see Brian Harding, "Transatlantic Views of Speculation and Value, 1820–1860," *Historical Research* [Great Britain] 66 (1993): 209–221. See also Henry C. Carey, *Principles of Political Economy* (Philadelphia: n.p., 1837–40); Henry Vethake, *The Principles of Political Economy* (Philadelphia: n.p., 1838); and Francis Wayland, *The Elements of Political Economy* (New York, 1837).

69. Michel Chevalier, *Society, Manners, and Politics in the United States: being a series of letters on North America*, trans. from the third Paris edition (Boston: n.p., 1839).

70. *National Police Gazette* 24 Oct. 1846.

71. Caroll Smith-Rosenberg, *Disorderly Conduct: Visions of Gender in Victorian America* (New York: Oxford University Press, 1985) 96.

72. David Crockett [Thomas Chilton], *A Narrative of the Life of David Crockett of the State of Tennessee* (1834; Knoxville: University of Tennessee Press, 1973) 194.

73. Arnold Krupat, *For Those Who Come After: A Study of Native American Autobiography* (Berkeley: University of California Press, 1985), chapter 2.

74. Augustus Baldwin Longstreet, *Georgia Scenes Completed*, ed. David Rachels (1835; Athens: The University of Georgia Press, 1998) 14.

75. See Ulf Hannerz, "Cosmopolitanism and Localism in World Culture," in Mike Featherstone, ed. *Global Culture: Nationalism, Globalization, and Modernity* (London: Sage, 1990) 239.

76. Neil Schmitz offers a brilliant reading of Harris in his "Forms of Regional Humor," where he asserts that "Harris . . . brings the Southwestern tale to its end. The Southern rage, the Southern cruelty, that Longstreet had contained in *Georgia Scenes* is here set off in a series of demolitions" ("Forms of Regional Humor" 321). Schmitz's brief overview remains one of the most useful readings of the cultural work of southwestern humor.

77. For a useful publication history of Hooper's *Adventures of Captain Simon Suggs* see Johanna Nicol Shields, introduction, Johnson Jones Hooper, *The Adventures of Captain Simon Suggs* (1845; Tuscaloosa: University of Alabama Press, 1993).

78. Hooper, *Adventures of Captain Simon Suggs* 12.

79. Hooper, *Adventures of Captain Simon Suggs* 29.

80. Hooper, *Adventures of Captain Simon Suggs* 35.

81. Hooper, *Adventures of Captain Simon Suggs* 143.

82. Hundley, *Social Relations* 142.

83. Baldwin, *Flush Times* 237.

84. Penick describes Virgil Stewart's life prior to Murrell's trial: "Stewart moved to Yalobusha County in Mississippi's Choctaw Purchase, a region recently opened to settlement. There he set up a 'little provision store' and perhaps a still on the banks of the Yalobusha River" (*Great Western Land Pirate* 35). Apparently Matthew Clanton accused Stewart of stealing corn, with which he may have planned to manufacture whiskey.

85. William Gilmore Simms, *Border Beagles: A Tale of Mississippi* (1840; New York: A. C. Armstrong and Son, 1882) 26, 67.

86. William Gilmore Simms, "Advertisement," *Richard Hurdis* (1855; Fayetteville: University of Arkansas Press, 1995) xxviii.

87. Simms, "Advertisement" xxvi.

88. Page qtd. in Tadman, *Speculators and Slaves* 181.

89. Mary H. Eastman, *Aunt Phillis' Cabin, or Southern Life as It Is* (1852; Upper Saddle River NJ: 1968) 59.

90. Franklin A. Wilmot [pseud.], *Disclosures and Confessions of Franklin A. Wilmot, The Slave Thief and Negro Runner, with an Account of the Under-ground Railroad!* (Philadelphia: Barclay and Company, 1860) 14.

91. Agnes Heller, *The Power of Shame: A Rational Perspective* (London: Routledge and Kegan Paul, 1985) 9.

92. John Brown to Thomas Higginson, Feb. 12, 1858, qtd. in Stephen B. Oates, *To Purge This Land with Blood: A Biography of John Brown* (New York: Harper and Row, 1970) 227.

93. Oates, *To Purge This Land with Blood* 57.

94. Oates, *To Purge This Land with Blood* 70.

95. Realf, qtd. in Richard J. Hinton, *John Brown and His Men, With Some Account of the Roads They Traveled to Reach Harper's Ferry* (1894; New York: Funk and Wagnalls, 1968) 182.

96. Hinton, *John Brown and His Men* 183.

97. Hinton, *John Brown and His Men* 183.

98. Hinton, *John Brown and His Men* 183.

99. Hinton, *John Brown and His Men* 619.

100. Hinton, *John Brown and His Men* 633.

101. Hinton, *John Brown and His Men* 172–173.

102. Thomas Cole, "Lecture on American Scenery," *The Collected Essays and Prose Sketches* (1841; Saint Paul MN: John Colet Press, 1977) 197–212.

103. Martin R. Delany, *Blake or the Huts of America* (1860–1861; Boston: Beacon, 1970) 4.

104. Delany, *Blake* 114.

105. Delany, *Blake* 192.

106. Delany, *Blake* 101.

107. Sundquist brilliantly links Delany with U.S. revolutionary rhetorics and their appropriation by Southern expansionists with designs on the Caribbean. See Eric J. Sundquist, "Slavery, Revolution, and the American Renaissance," in Walter Benn Michaels and Donald E. Pease, eds., *The American Renaissance Reconsidered* (Baltimore MD: The Johns Hopkins University Press, 1985) 1–33; and Eric Sundquist, *To Wake the Nations: Race in the Making of American Literature* (Cambridge MA: The Belknap Press of Harvard University Press, 1993).

108. Delany, *Blake* 69.

109. Delany, *Blake* 43.

110. Jeffory A. Clymer offers a very useful reading of Delany's metaphor of the passport for traversing the "White Gap," focusing not only on money or self-interest, but the figure of the passport itself. Clymer writes, "In 1856, shortly before Delany finished working on his novel, Congress for the first time asserted that the federal government held the exclusive right to issue passports and that they should be given only to American citizens. . . . Because the modern passport is a marker of citizenship, Delany's reference to passports metonymically, and subversively, represents the transformation of the fleeing slaves from embodied legal property into personhood. But because the passport vouches not just for a particular individual identity, but an identity as a specifically marked subject, Delany's passage also ironically highlights America's historical linkage of citizenship and whiteness." Jeffory A. Clymer, "Martin Delany's *Blake* and the Transnational Politics of Property," *American Literary History* 15 (Winter 2003): 720.

111. Martin R. Delany, "The Redemption of Cuba," *The North Star* 20 (July 1849) 2.

112. Robert S. Levine has assembled a helpful sampling of Delany's writings that shows the broad spectrum of his geopolitical interests. *Martin R. Delany: A*

Documentary Reader, ed. Robert S. Levine (Chapel Hill: University of North Carolina Press, 2003).

113. J. S. Thrasher, "Cuba and the United States," DeBow's Review 17 (Nov. 1854) 43–49.

114. W. J. Sykes, "Cuba, and the United States," DeBow's Review 14 (Jan. 1853): 63.

115. Sykes, "Cuba, and the United States" 65.

116. S. R. Walker, "Cuba and the South," DeBow's Review 17 (Oct. 1854) 524.

117. A useful introduction to the Delany biography is offered in Floyd J. Miller, "Introduction," in Delany, Blake xi–xxix.

118. Alexander Milton Ross, Narrative of Alexander Milton Ross in The Underground Railroad, ed. Charles L. Blockson (New York: Prentice Hall, 1987) 38–39.

119. Cited in Helen Tunnicliff Catterall, ed., with additions by James J. Hayden, Judicial Cases concerning American Slavery and the Negro, vol. 5 (New York: Octagon, 1968) 121–22.

120. Eaton v. Vaughan, 9 Mo. 743, Jan. 1846. Cited in Catterall, Judicial Cases 5:167.

121. Caleb Crain, American Sympathy: Men, Friendship, and Literature in the New Nation (New Haven: Yale University Press, 2001) 2.

122. Lott argues: "Blackface minstrelsy indeed underwrote one of the nineteenth century's most powerful antiracist novels—a tribute to the political fractures of minstrelsy and Huckleberry Finn both. This is no simple matter of minstrel show 'trappings' or 'residues' in Twain's novel (as we often hurry to say), an issue of unfortunate, merely historical formal qualities in the portrayal of Jim disrupting Twain's liberal thematic intentions. The text is shot through with blackface thinking. Written as well as situated in the minstrel show's boom years . . . Huckleberry Finn relies on comic dialogues between Huck and Jim (much of the humor at Jim's expense), many and various novelty acts (the king and the duke's scams, the circus, etc.), and riotous burlesques of social and cultural manners . . . The whole book may thus conform to a tripartite minstrel show structure of comic dialogues, olio, and Southern burlesque." Eric Lott, "Mr. Clemens and Jim Crow: Twain, Race, and Blackface," The Cambridge Companion to Mark Twain, ed. Forrest G. Robinson (Cambridge, UK: Cambridge University Press, 1995) 133.

5. Mark Twain's Manifest and Other Destinies

1. William Dean Howells, My Mark Twain: Reminiscences and Criticisms, ed. Marilyn Austin Baldwin (1910; Baton Rouge: Louisiana State University Press, 1967) 84, 5.

2. Norton delivers one of the most eloquent, and vehement, post-Turnerian statements about the late "rise" of the West from the ruins of North-South

sectionalism. "If we are to see in North and South (as they saw in themselves) thesis and antithesis in apocalyptic struggle, then it is not surprising to see the culturally synthetic West rise with Hegelian inevitability out of their collision. . . . One might say that Westerners, and the West, won [the Civil War]." Anne Norton, *Alternative Americas: A Reading of Antebellum Political Culture* (Chicago: University of Chicago Press, 1986) 203. Philip Fisher neatly encapsulates a version of Turner's argument for the subordination of the "slavery struggle" to the frontier when he notes that Twain "had, by means of his flight [from the Missouri Volunteers] decided that his was to be the generation that lived in the shadow of the gold rush rather than that of the Civil War." Philip J. Fisher, "Mark Twain," in the *Columbia Literary History of the United States*, ed. Emory Elliott (New York: Columbia University Press, 1988) 627.

3. Frederick Jackson Turner, *History, Frontier, and Section: Three Essays by Frederick Jackson Turner* (1893; Albuquerque: University of New Mexico Press, 1993) 81.

4. Again, the complementarity of Frederick Jackson Turner's notion of a culturally "synthetic" West with Shelley Fisher Fishkin's argument for a racially synthetic "voice" in *Adventures of Huckleberry Finn* has not been mentioned in the varied responses to Fishkin's controversial *Was Huck Black?*

5. Samuel Clemens to Pamela A. Moffett and Jane Lampton Clemens, 25 Oct. 1861, Carson City, Nev. Terr. MTL 1:130.

6. Turner, *History, Frontier, and Section* 60, 86.

7. Fisher, "Mark Twain" 629, 630.

8. Kaplan brings an important dimension to Twain criticism by emphasizing that "Twain's career, writing, and reception as a national author were shaped by a third realm beyond national boundaries: the routes of transnational travel, enabling and enabled by the changing borders of imperial expansion." I simply don't think that it is necessary to leave the continent of North America to find this "third realm." My interest in defamiliarizing the continental claims of the nineteenth-century United States requires a rereading of the continent, particularly the West, as never quite as clearly "domestic" as it appears in nineteenth-century expansionist and later "frontier" rhetorics. See Amy Kaplan, "The Imperial Routes of Mark Twain," *Anarchy of Empire* 51.

9. Philip S. Foner traces Twain's anti-imperialism to the late 1860s, citing his 1868 article on the Burlingame Treaty for the *New York Tribune*, "The Treaty with China. Its Provisions Explained." In this article, Twain "condemned the foreign 'concessions' wrested from China" and called for the abolition

of "communities in which white foreigners conducted themselves on Chinese soil as if they owned the area" (*Mark Twain Social Critic* 258).Twain's satires of U.S. exploitation of Chinese immigrants, "Disgraceful Persecution of a Boy," and "Goldsmith's Friend Abroad Again" were published in the *Galaxy* magazine in 1870–71. According to R. Kent Rasmussen, Twain deliberately waited to publish his opinions on U.S. treatment of the Chinese until he left the *San Francisco Call*, where he had been hired as a full-time reporter in 1864 (*Mark Twain A–Z* 178).

10. Brooks Adams, *The Law of Civilization and Decay: An Essay on History* (1896; New York: Alfred A. Knopf, 1951) 58, 61.

11. Roosevelt recognized Adams's nostalgia for a militaristic, feudal-patriarchal economy as simplistic, primarily because this nostalgia neatly excised the realities of slavery and peonage. In his review of the *Law of Civilization and Decay*, Roosevelt wrote: "The fact that modern society rested upon the slave, is of such transcendent importance as to forbid any exact comparison between the two, save by way of contrast." Theodore Roosevelt, "Law of Civilization and Decay," in *American Ideals and Other Essays, Social and Political*, vol. 2 (New York: Charles Scribner's Sons, 1906) 183.

12. Twain's choicest rantings about Roosevelt were excised from Paine's biography and reprinted by Bernard DeVoto in Mark Twain, *Mark Twain in Eruption: Hitherto Unpublished Pages about Men and Events*, ed. Bernard DeVoto (1922; New York: Grosset & Dunlap, 1940). The creation of future values that Twain once associated with economic speculation and the telling of "tall tales" has become quite dangerous in Twain's version of Roosevelt's America, as Twain juxtaposes Roosevelt's self-generated accounts of his "bear hunts" to his warmongering off the coast of Japan.

13. Foner, *Mark Twain Social Critic* 304. Foner suggests that this statement comes from Twain's "Defense of General Funston," published in 1902 in the *North American Review*—but it does not. Most likely it is in one of the several "miscellaneous" and unpublished anti-imperialist writings that make up Foner's extensive archive.

14. Myra Jehlen, "Banned in Concord: Adventures of Huckleberry Finn and Classic American Literature," *The Cambridge Companion to Mark Twain*, ed. Forrest G. Robinson (Cambridge: Cambridge University Press, 1995) 109, 110, 99. Jehlen writes, in full: "It is also impossible in the Mississippi River towns through which Huck and Jim journey to imagine being a hero. This in turn makes Sherburn a cold-blooded killer and Huck a saint (and Tom a fool). Let me repeat that as a saint, however, Huck is no more bent on social reform, no more optimistic about it, than is Sherburn. That is, his radical

liberalism, not unlike Emerson's, is also conservative. He never reacts to social inequities by imagining them reformed; they appear to him as natural, ineluctable parts of a system as fixed as the system of nature" (109–10).

15. Robinson's reading of the effect of Tom Sawyer's "speculations" in Saint Petersburg is in some sense a negative image of Fisher's; both equate the formation of community with willful self-deception, but they value such willful self-deception quite differently. For Robinson, Tom Sawyer provides the "give" in a rigidly conventional town, articulating in an almost purgative sense the hypocrisy that sustains local mores. So although Tom figures as virtual embodiment of the will to deceive, he is also, as in Fisher's reading, crucial to community self-recognition. See Robinson, *In Bad Faith*.

16. Walter Blair traces Twain's development of the plot of "Tom Sawyer's Conspiracy" through a series of notebook entries, beginning in 1896. "A notebook entry of 1896 shows Mark Twain hitting upon the idea of relating these [story fragments] to a plot which Huck would describe: 'Have Huck tell how one white brother shaved his head, put on a wool wig and was blackened and sold as a negro. Escaped that night, washed himself, and helped hunt *for himself* under pay.' A year later the author thought of using Huck himself as 'the white brother': 'Tom sells Huck for a slave.' Some pages later in the notebook containing this entry, among items headed 'For New Huck Finn,' he writes 'Huck,' crosses it out, replaces it with 'Tom' and concludes the sentence: 'is disguised as a negro and sold in Ark for $10, then he and Huck help hunt for him after the disguise is removed.' " Walter Blair, "Introduction to Tom Sawyer's Conspiracy," *Mark Twain's Hannibal, Huck and Tom*, ed. Walter Blair (Berkeley: University of California, 1969) 153.

17. Mark Twain, *Tom Sawyer's Conspiracy* (hereafter cited as TSC) in *Mark Twain's Hannibal, Huck and Tom* 171, 229.

18. Turner, *History, Frontier, and Section* 88.

19. These (and following) general remarks about the importance of river levels come from Louis Hunter's standard history. See Louis C. Hunter, *Steamboats on the Western Rivers* (Cambridge: Harvard University Press, 1949), especially "Techniques of Operation."

20. John W. Monette, "The Mississippi Floods," in *Publications of the Mississippi Historical Society*, Vol. 7, ed. Franklin L. Riley (Oxford MS: Mississippi Historical Society, 1903) 427–78.

21. Twain, *Life on the Mississippi* 119.

22. Andrew Jackson, "Announcement to His Soldiers," 14 Nov. 1812, in Andrew Jackson, *Correspondence of Andrew Jackson*, ed. John Spencer Bassett, vol. 1 (Washington DC: Carnegie Institution of Washington, 1926–1935) 241–42.

23. Samuel Clemens to Ann E. Taylor. 1 June 1857. New Orleans, Louisiana. MTL 1:72.

24. Samuel Clemens to the Muscatine *Tri-Weekly Journal*. 24–26 Feb. 1855. St. Louis MO. MTL 1:50–51.

25. Thomas, *From Tennessee Slave to St. Louis Entrepreneur* 116.

26. Harriet Beecher Stowe, *Uncle Tom's Cabin, or Life among the Lowly* (1852; New York: New American Library, 1981) 199.

27. Abraham Lincoln to Mary Speed, 27 Sept. 1841, in Basler, ed., *Speeches and Writings* 81.

28. Seelye, introduction, *Adventures of Huckleberry Finn* xx.

29. For the larger context of the forced transport of the Creeks across the Mississippi, see Rogin, *Fathers and Children* 144.

30. Louis C. Hunter discusses the routes of immigrants and disease through the Mississippi Valley in Hunter, *Steamboats* 419–41.

31. Examples of earlier criticism that points to the dramatic irony that affects both the narrative and reception of *Adventures of Huckleberry Finn* include Laurence B. Holland, "A 'Raft of Trouble': Word and Deed in Huckleberry Finn," *Glyph* 5 (1979): 69–87; and James M. Cox, *Mark Twain: The Fate of Humor* (Princeton: Princeton University Press, 1966). Cox in particular argues that Twain reinvents the southerner without cost, giving Huck the task of freeing a slave in the slave South once Emancipation has rendered that act clearly laudable and unnecessary (169–72).

32. Lott, "Mr. Clemens and Jim Crow" 140, 149.

33. Twain, TSC 214.

34. Twain, TSC 204.

35. A good summation of the current (at least pre-9/11) state of "critical whiteness studies" appears in *The Making and Unmaking of Whiteness*, ed. Birgit Brander Rasmussen, Eric Klinenberg, Irene J. Nexica, and Matt Wray (Durham NC: Duke University Press, 2001). The work of David Roediger has been central in defining this field, from both black and white perspectives. See, for example, David Roediger, ed. *Black on White: Black Writers on What It Means to Be White* (New York: Schocken Books, 1998). See also Theodore W. Allen's comprehensive *The Invention of the White Race: The Origin of Racial Oppression in Anglo-America*, 2 vols. (London and New York: Verso, 1997).

36. hooks's influential analyses both critique the romantic racialism that comes into play in white constructs of "blackness," and, to some extent, reinscribe a romantic "blackness" by equating a somewhat abstract "black body" with authentic pain and, again, a somewhat insufficiently historicized "white-

269

ness" with *anhedonia* or the inability to feel pleasure. bell hooks, *Black Looks: Race and Representation* (Boston: South End Press, 1992).

37. David L. Smith offers a useful gloss on Twain's use of the pejorative term "nigger" in *Adventures of Huckleberry Finn*. "Most obviously, Twain uses 'nigger' throughout the book as a synonym for 'slave.' There is ample evidence from other sources that this corresponds to one usage common during the antebellum period. We first encounter it in reference to 'Miss Watson's big nigger, named Jim' (chap. 2). This usage, like the term 'nigger stealer,' clearly designates the 'nigger' as an item of property: a commodity, a slave. This passage also provides the only apparent textual justification for the common critical practice of labeling Jim 'Nigger Jim,' as if 'nigger' were a part of his proper name. This loathsome habit goes back at least as far as Albert Bigelow Paine's biography of Twain (1912). In any case, 'nigger' in this sense connotes an inferior, even subhuman, creature who is properly owned by and subservient to Euro-Americans." David L. Smith, "Huck, Jim, and American Racial Discourse," *Satire or Evasion? Black Perspectives on 'Huckleberry Finn,'* ed. James S. Leonard, Thomas A. Tenney, and Thadious M. Davis (Durham NC: Duke University Press, 1992) 105.

38. Howard Horwitz has noted Twain's complex anxieties about the alienability of property, anxieties Horwitz explores most thoroughly in *Life on the Mississippi* but that he also recognizes in Huck and Jim's envy of the absolute sovereignty of kings. Horwitz's nuanced analysis of Twain's response to the Lockean construction of self through property has added depth to my own reading of Huck's inability to control his "floating" through the river market. Horwitz neatly summarizes the paradox of Lockean or, more broadly, of liberal conceptions of selfhood: "Ideally, one is the inalienable master of oneself, and thus of one's labor and material property; but if identity is available only in terms of material property, which be definition is exchangeable, self and self-mastery are redefined— . . . revealed to be contingent— in every transaction." Howard Horwitz, *By the Law of Nature: Form and Value in Nineteenth-Century America* (New York: Oxford University Press, 1991) 87–114.

39. Mark Twain, *Adventures of Huckleberry Finn*, ed. Walter Blair and Victor Fischer ([hereafter cited as AHF] 1885; Berkeley: University of California Press, Mark Twain Library, 1985) 270.

40. Jehlen, "Banned in Concord" 103.

41. "I—this thought which is called I—is the mold into which the world is poured like melted wax. The mold is invisible, but the world betrays the shape of the mold. You call it the power of circumstance, but it is the power of me." Ralph Waldo Emerson, "The Transcendentalist," *Selections from*

Ralph Waldo Emerson, ed. Stephen E. Whicher (Boston: Houghton Mifflin, 1957) 195.

42. Twain, AHF 100.

43. Twain, AHF 100.

44. In short, Michaels finds that for Stowe the transfer of slaves due to a master's death or indebtedness reveals the "horror" of the market relation at the heart of an apparently paternalistic and personal economy (*Gold Standard* 103–04).

45. Twain, AHF 38.

46. Twain, TSC 224.

47. Twain, TSC 211.

48. Twain, TSC 174.

49. Philip J. Fisher discusses the inability of both Huck and Jim to appear in public as Twain's means of creating an experimental privacy apart from the "new public world" of the early twentieth century, when the marketing of public images made the construction of a private self a secondary, rather than primary, project in the cultivation of personality. See Philip Fisher, *Still the New World* (Cambridge MA: Harvard University Press, 1999) 140. I would simply suggest that Huck, unlike Jim, *can* appear in public, although his range of disguises is limited by his visible (or audible) origins in white poverty; the limited range of Huck's credible disguises makes it harder for him to perform a safe, unassailable public role, as Tom Sawyer can.

50. Clay qtd. in Goodell, *American Slave Code* 34–35.

51. Ralph Waldo Emerson, "Lecture on Slavery," *Emerson's Antislavery Writings*, ed. Len Gougeon and Joel Myerson (New Haven: Yale University Press, 1995) 106.

52. Twain writes, in Huck's voice, that Jim "went on a mumbling to himself, the way a nigger does, and saying he wouldn't give shucks for a conspiracy that was made up out of just any kinds of odds and ends that come handy and hadn't anything lawful about it. But Tom didn't let on to hear; and it's the best way, to let a nigger or a child go on and grumble itself out, then it's satisfied" (TSC 171). Here Twain, or Huck, is mocking Jim's literalism in regard to the definitions of "conspiracy," "insurrection," "revolution," and "civil war."

53. Twain, TSC 167.

54. Mark Twain, *Chapters from My Autobiography*, ed. Shelley Fisher Fishkin (1906; Oxford: Oxford University Press, 1996) 322–23.

55. Kiskis writes that "as Twain relocated himself in autobiography, he became increasingly interested in the process of the story. He was excited by the

series of autobiographical dictations (at least through 1906 and 1907) because of the emphasis on talk. Twain claimed that talk was at the heart of
true autobiography and the reason for his enjoyment. . . . In effect, Mark
Twain found himself facing his own beginnings as a storyteller: talk was
the primary currency of his youth as he sat and listened to tales around slave
kitchens, of his piloting days as he sat in wheelhouses, of his adulthood as
he and Jim Gillis retold the story of the jumping frog as he stood night after
night on the lecture platform" ("Coming Back to Humor" 545).

56. Twain, *Chapters* 490–94.

57. Samuel Clemens to Orion Clemens. 26 Apr. 1861. *Hannibal City* en route
from St. Louis to Hannibal, MO. MTL 1:120.

58. Samuel Clemens to Orion and Mary E. (Mollie) Clemens. 9 Mar. 1858. St.
Louis, MO. MTL 1:77.

59. Twain, MTL 1:77.

60. Mark Twain, "Old Times on the Mississippi," *Selected Shorter Writings of Mark
Twain*, ed. Walter Blair, (1875; Boston: Houghton Mifflin, 1962) 86, 87.

61. Samuel Clemens to Orion Clemens and Family. 21 Nov. 1860. St. Louis, MO.
MTL 1:103.

62. Samuel Clemens to Orion Clemens. 27 June 1860. City of Memphis en route
from Memphis, TN to St. Louis, MO. MTL 1:96–97.

63. Samuel Clemens to Orion and Mary E. (Mollie) Clemens. 6 Feb. 1861. Cairo,
Ill. MTL 1:112.

64. Samuel Clemens to Jane Lampton Clemens. 20 Mar. 1862. Carson City, Nev.
Terr. MTL 1:176.

65. Samuel Clemens to Pamela A. Moffett and Jane Lampton Clemens. 25 October 1861. Carson City, Nev. Terr. MTL 1:130.

66. Samuel Clemens to Jane Lampton Clemens and Pamela A. Moffett. 8 and 9
Feb. 1862. Carson City, Nev. Terr. MTL 1:156–57.

67. These scattered quotations come from two letters by Twain to his brother
and male friends, although nearly every letter to Orion from the spring of
1862 is filled with curses, pleas, and regrets. Samuel Clemens writes to
Orion that his hopes are high for a claim called the "W. W.," then adding
"—but then it's the d——dest country for disappointments the world ever
saw . . . by the new law I can get a perpetual title to our ground very easily, and I mean to do it and leave the country for a year, if we don't strike
something soon." In Samuel Clemens to Orion Clemens. 22 June 1862. Aurora, CA/Nev. Terr. MTL 1:221. Samuel Clemens cautions friend Billy Clagett
"Don't let my opinion of this place get abroad" in a postscript to a letter
detailing recent disappointments in Aurora. "Keep this entirely to yourself,

you know," Clemens continues, fearing that his bad opinion will further deflate the claims: "Clayton will assist us by experimenting with our infernal rock at half-price until we get some that will pay. We haven't taken out any yet that will even do to experiment with." Samuel Clemens to William H. Clagett. 18 Apr. 1862. Aurora, CA/Nev. Terr. MTL 1:192–93.

68. Samuel Clemens to Jane Lampton Clemens and Pamela A. Moffett. 16 Feb. 1863. Virginia City, Nev. Terr. MTL 1:245.

69. Mark Twain, *Roughing It* ([hereafter cited as RI] 1872; New York: Penguin, 1981) 194.

70. Samuel Clemens to Jane Lampton Clemens and Pamela A. Moffett. 18? May 1863. San Francisco, CA. MTL 1:253.

71. Samuel Clemens to Orion and Mary E. (Molly) Clemens. 21 Oct. 1862. Virginia City, Nev. Terr. MTL 1:242.

72. Editors' Note. MTL 1:289.

73. Editors' Note. MTL 1:289.

74. O'Sullivan, "Territorial Aggrandizement" 244.

75. Mark Twain, "Extract from Captain Stormfield's Visit to Heaven," *Mark Twain's Short Stories*, ed. Justin Kaplan (New York: New American Library, 1985) 656.

76. Twain, "Extract" 656.

77. Twain, "Extract" 658.

78. Twain, "Extract" 656.

79. See Helen Hunt Jackson, *A Century of Dishonor: A Sketch of the United States Government's Dealings with Some of the Indian Tribes* (1880; Minneapolis MN: Ross & Haines, 1964) 31. Jackson's reformism is oddly divided between outrage at the displacement of American Indian nations whom she recognizes as retaining "rights of first occupancy" to their lands and capitulation to the paternalistic argument that American Indians, while rightful "occupants," should not be regarded as capable of sovereignty.

80. Twain, "Extract" 658.

81. Twain, "Extract" 656.

82. Twain, "Extract" 658.

83. Twain, "Extract" 638.

84. Twain, RI 337.

85. Twain, RI 337.

86. Twain, RI 344.

87. Gavin Jones offers a different, and compelling, reading of one of the passages from *Roughing It* that I address here, wherein a miner named Scotty Briggs discusses the funeral of his friend Buck Fanshaw with a priggish

preacher from the East. It is Briggs who interjects the phrase "No Irish need apply" at the end of the preacher's sermon for his dead friend. Jones writes: "The clichéd, dull propriety of the 'aristocratic' language of the East is confronted by a western vernacular that has become so democratically representative of individuality that it no longer really means anything: Buck Fanshaw's favorite phrase, 'No Irish need apply,' originally expressing hatred of Irish-Catholics, is inevitably taken out of context by Scotty Briggs when he uses it at the end of Fanshaw's funeral. . . . The very comedy of the passage originates in the fact that Briggs replaces the parson's dead metaphors with ones so alive with idiosyncratic meaning that they are virtually unintelligible." See Gavin Jones, *Strange Talk: The Politics of Dialect Literature in Gilded Age America* (Berkeley: University of California Press, 1999) 60.
88. Twain, "Extract" 640.

INDEX

abolitionists, 18, 122, 141; black nationalism and, 184–85; British, 162–63; John Murrell and, 157–59, 161–70, 176; Lydia Maria Child's writings on, 11, 164, 168–69; and nineteenth-century literature, 11–15, 157–59, 177–88; and the Provisional Constitution of John Brown, 180–81; religion and, 164, 167–68; secession advocated by, 154–55; and the Underground Railroad, 179–84. *See also* slavery

Adams, Brooks, 84, 192

Adams, John Quincy, 42, 45, 50

Adventures of Captain Bonneville, 26, 28, 79, 85, 94

Adventures of Captain Simon Suggs, 172–74

Adventures of Huckleberry Finn, 11, 140, 142, 160, 165, 188, 194, 265n122, 271n49; ending of, 191; Huck's downriver journey in, 195–96; as a parody of Manifest Destiny, 201–3; racial issues examined in, 204–5, 214, 270n37; slave trafficking depicted in, 197–99

The Adventures of Tom Sawyer, 160

Alabama, 119, 140, 164, 186

Allen, John L., 229n9

American Anti-Slavery Society, 154

The American Democrat, 36, 55

American Quarterly Temperance Magazine, 96

American Whig Party, 13–14

Antelyes, Peter, 81, 240–41n21

An Appeal in Favor of That Class of Americans Called Africans, 164, 167–68

Arkansas, 119, 140, 164, 182, 198

Astor, John Jacob, 34–35, 74–75, 81–83, 97, 99, 104, 151

Astoria, 16, 25, 28, 79, 94, 246n94; commercial success of, 83; critical reviews of, 81–82, 240–41n21; lawless interval described in, 80–83; racial issues in, 87–90; trading culture portrayed in, 74–77, 83, 102–6

Audubon, John James, 157

Aunt Phillis' Cabin, 178

Austen, Jane, 38

Austin, Mary, 23, 28, 98

Baird, Robert, 37, 139

Bakhtin, Mikhail, 38, 79

Baldwin, Joseph, 120, 174–75

Baldwin, Samuel D., 209

Barbour, James, 50–51

Barthes, Roland, 36, 225n17

Bartlett, Sam, 220

Batman, Richard, 67

Beckwourth, James, 17, 92–94, 96, 106

Beecher, Edward, 155

Benton, Thomas Hart, 35, 97, 192

Bercovitch, Sacvan, 121–22

Biographical Memoir of Daniel Boone, 41

Black Hawk's Autobiography, 96–97, 171, 236n81

Black Legend, 64–65, 67

black nationalism, 184–85

Blair, Walter, 268n16

Blake; or the Huts of America, 182–84

Blood Meridian, 134

Bonner, Thomas D., 92

Boone, Daniel, 33, 41, 65, 110

Border Beagles, 159, 176–77

border cosmopolitanism, 171–77

Bosch, Hieronymus, 44

153; imperialism, 10–11; nineteenth-century authors' writings about, 10–12; oceans and commerce of, 114–21; Panic of 1837, 150, 154; perceived natural boundaries of, 35; power in the nineteenth century, 8–9, 105, 114–15, 118–19; regional economies of, 119–21; slavery in, 11–12, 13–15, 18, 117–18; tourism in, 75–79, 83, 92; trade laws regarding Native Americans, 91; war with Mexico, 78, 83, 97–99, 109, 127, 181; war romances of Mexico and, 59–69

United States Magazine and Democratic Review, 3, 7, 8, 12, 116, 145

United States Review and Literary Gazette, 36

van Dyke, John C., 23
Vethake, Henry, 169
Virginia, 166, 182
Virginia City Territorial Enterprise, 212
Virgin Land, 2
Vizenor, Gerald, 4, 224–25n12

Wagner, Sallie, 97
Wallerstein, Immanuel, 8
Walton, Augustus Q., 159

Wayland, Francis, 169
A Week on the Concord and Merrimack Rivers, 121
Weld, Theodore Dwight, 139
Welty, Eudora, 156–60
Western Monthly Review, 65
Wheeler, Roxanne, 127
White, Richard, 5, 87, 119
White-Jacket, 127, 128
Whitman, Narcissa, 26, 62
The Wide Net and Other Stories, 156
Wide Ruins, 97
The Wild Bunch, 134
Williams, Raymond, 8
Williams, Stanley T., 81
Wilmot, David, 178–79
Wilson, Woodrow, 226n28
Wisconsin, 119
Wister, Owen, 45
women in the West, 7, 28, 97–99, 226n20, 245n79
Worster, Donald, 23
Wyoming, 39

Yanktonai Sioux Indians, 49
Young, Brigham, 3
Young, Robert, 86
Young Americans, 147, 148

In the POSTWESTERN HORIZONS series

True West:
Authenticity and the American West
Edited by William R. Handley and Nathaniel Lewis

Manifest and Other Destinies:
Territorial Fictions of the Nineteenth-Century United States
By Stephanie LeMenager

Unsettling the Literary West:
Authenticity and Authorship
By Nathaniel Lewis

María Amparo Ruiz de Burton:
Critical and Pedagogical Perspectives
Edited by Amelia María de la Luz Montes
and Anne Elizabeth Goldman